RESILIENT LEADERSHIP

Bob Duggan & Jim Moyer

Resilient Leadership

All rights reserved
Copyright © 2009 by Bob Duggan & Jim Moyer

Interior Book Design and Layout by
www.integrativeink.com

No part of this publication may be reproduced, stored in a retrieval system, or transmitted in any form or by any means electronic, mechanical, photocopying, recording, or otherwise, without the written permission of the author or publisher.

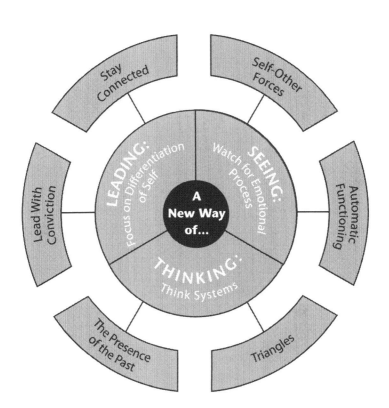

Contents

ACKNOWLEDGEMENTS .... *vii*

INTRODUCTION .... *ix*

SETTING AND MAJOR CHARACTERS .... *xiii*

A NEW WAY OF <u>SEEING</u> **1**

    CHAPTER 1: WATCH FOR EMOTIONAL PROCESS 1

    CHAPTER 2: SELF-OTHER FORCES 45

    CHAPTER 3: AUTOMATIC FUNCTIONING 79

A NEW WAY OF <u>THINKING</u> **117**

    CHAPTER 4: THINK SYSTEMS 117

    CHAPTER 5: TRIANGLES 141

    CHAPTER 6: THE PRESENCE OF THE PAST 175

A NEW WAY OF <u>LEADING</u> **225**

    CHAPTER 7: FOCUS ON DIFFERENTIATION OF SELF 225

    CHAPTER 8: LEAD WITH CONVICTION 259

    CHAPTER 9: STAY CONNECTED 301

APPENDIX *363*

SUGGESTED READINGS *409*

ENDNOTES *413*

Acknowledgements

My earliest memory of the thrill of authorship is a recollection of my mother patiently helping me with a school writing project, affirming my effort, but also showing me how to craft language in even better ways. From there, the list is long of teachers who continued to support my efforts to find words that could share in some measure with others what I knew to be true.

In a particular way, I owe a deep debt to Ed Friedman, whose creative mind and masterful use of words enthralled me with the possibilities of a new way of seeing, thinking and leading. I am privileged to say that I studied under such an unconventional master. My co-author, Jim Moyer, has been a patient and wise mentor to me for many years, from the days when I first discovered how much I had to learn about leadership. To many others—unnamed, but of whose inspiration, correction and affirmation I am keenly mindful—I wish to acknowledge the debt of gratitude that I surely owe. Thank you, one and all.

Bob Duggan

It took just the right content, timing and colleague to provide the impetus for me to co-author this book. The insightful and essential work of Ed Friedman and Bob Duggan provided the content. The time to write the book arrived unexpectedly as I found a summer with time on my hands. And Bob has been a source of professional stimulation, inspiration and enjoyment in my family's life for over 20 years.

As a young man, I was attracted to new techniques related to management and leadership. I eventually came to realize the difference between information and knowledge about leadership. Now I am coming to understanding the difference between knowledge about leading and leadership itself. The words SEE –THINK- LEAD point me toward that new understanding as I recognize that conscious awareness is the bridge between thinking and leading.

I am especially thankful to my wife Carlyn for her encouragement during the months of effort to write and publish this book. I am also thankful to my son Aaron and his wife Lauren for their assistance in publishing the book and my son Adam and his partner Jennifer for their support and encouragement.

Jim Moyer

INTRODUCTION

This book tells the story of Mike Sampson, who learns how to be a better leader, father and husband after being introduced to **Resilient Leadership** by an executive coach, Jacob Wolfe. The story is fictional, but the situations draw on real-life experiences of the authors[1] over many years, working in a variety of organizational contexts. The **Resilient Leadership** model is a practical way of mastering and applying the key insights of Bowen Systems Theory.[2] It shows leaders how to function in healthier, more effective ways within the organizations—the emotional systems—of which they are a part.

Mike Sampson's story is a narrative about significant personal change in a leader at a turning point in his career and in his life. The story describes how Mike grows to become more of a "self," and as a result a more powerful leader. Because of who he becomes and how he learns to be present to those he leads, Mike achieves a level of personal and professional success that previously would have been well beyond his reach.

As Mike's story unfolds, you will see that like any skill or virtue, **Resilient Leadership** is about developing a habit of being, a way of leading that is increasingly more effective as its behaviors are practiced over and over with tireless persistence. You will also see the value of working with a coach/mentor who can guide and support you—in the event that you, too, might wish to embark on a journey of personal growth similar to Mike's. The pages that follow will introduce you to new understandings by sharing what this kind of leadership looks like in various familiar situations. The work of acquiring those skills takes much longer than is required to read this book, to be sure. But this book will open for you a doorway to new ways of seeing and thinking, and with those new perspectives you can practice the skills and develop the competencies that will move you steadily in the direction of being a more resilient leader.

The **Resilient Leadership** model suggests that a leader can navigate the complexities of leadership more expertly if he or she understands something about the "hidden chemistry" of organizational families. Those hidden forces are what the technical jargon of Bowen Theory calls "emotional process,"[3] a term with which you will become very familiar as you follow the saga of Mike Sampson. **Resilient Leadership** encourages a leader to "**watch for emotional process**" because doing so will reveal the unseen, instinctual forces that drive a relationship network of any size, whether it is one's own family or a corporate entity with thousands of employees. Knowing how to **watch for emotional process** will give you the ability to see things that others miss and afford you an invaluable perspective that pays off in unsuspected but significant ways.

The **Resilient Leadership** model emphasizes that the presence of a leader to an emotional system is far more significant than the leader's personality, any management techniques he or she may employ, or how well he or she functions as a role model to be imitated by others. Rather, it is the nature of a leader's presence—his calm assertion of self or her anxious inability to take a stand—that most decisively affects the emotional field of which he or she is a part. The way a leader is present to the organization has an impact on those he or she leads, even when they have no immediate contact with him or her. This is because *how a leader is present is infectious*, and the consequences of that presence spread throughout the organization's emotional system as quickly as a wildfire spreads through dry grass.

This book will offer you a fresh, insightful and innovative understanding of how to exercise leadership in a way that is powerfully transformative. The **Resilient Leadership** model stands apart from much of contemporary literature in the field of leadership. Some of what is suggested here may strike you as counterintuitive, or even an outright contradiction of traditional understandings you hold about what it is that makes a leader more effective. So much the better! If there are fresh, new ideas with which you find yourself wrestling in this book, then you probably understand the model better than one who reads

Introduction

merely looking for the latest set of techniques and quick fixes.

Being a resilient leader is a lifelong task, a goal towards which we must strive constantly, rather than a final destination at which we will someday arrive. The skills required to be a resilient leader operate on a continuum of functioning, from a quite modest level—where one's abilities are in the early stages of development—to the highest level—where we observe those exceptional people we sometimes call "naturally gifted leaders." Those are the rare individuals who embody to extraordinary degree remarkable qualities of leadership to which most of us simply aspire. But the truth is that such "naturally gifted leaders" did not fall from heaven fully skilled, mature, polished and competent in every aspect of leadership. Leadership is not a set of genes we inherit from previous generations; neither is there an ideal personality profile that embodies excellent leadership.

Mike Sampson, as you will see, becomes a masterful leader through a combination of nature and nurture: a set of inherent "gifts" from his family of origin, and a number of life experiences that he brings to a very intentional relationship with an executive coach, Jacob Wolfe, who teaches him how to develop the qualities and skills that can make him a more resilient leader. By showing Mike how he can become more aware of emotional process in himself and in others, Jacob helps him to be present to his organization in more powerful ways.

We invite you to learn about this new way of leading by observing a "case study," by following the story of Mike Sampson. Some readers may also wish to know more about Bowen Systems Theory, on which the **Resilient Leadership** model is based. For those so inclined, the Appendix will provide a more systematic, theoretical overview. However you chose to read this book, you will be introduced to an extremely valuable perspective on how your own leadership can become more effective, whether in your home and family setting, or within the network of professional relationships that comprise the organization in which you work. Should this book motivate you to pursue the journey of leadership growth in a more deliberate manner, we invite you to look for additional resources at the authors' website, www.resilient-leadership.biz.

Setting and Major Characters

Resilient Leadership takes place in Washington, DC, in the early 2000s.

- Mike Sampson – Mike is the Vice President of Operations for Clearview Hotels, Incorporated (CHI). CHI is a lodging company headquartered in Washington, DC, with 500+ hotels in the US.

- Jacob Wolfe – Jacob is a veteran executive coach living in Fairfax, Virginia, who has developed a coaching methodology based on Bowen Systems Theory known as **Resilient Leadership**.

- Vanessa Jackson – Vanessa is the Chief Operating Officer of CHI.

- James McMaster – James is the founder and Chief Executive Officer of CHI.

- Kelly O'Reilly – Kelly is a former finance executive for All British Airways.

- Karla Sampson – Mike's wife, Karla, is a successful real estate salesperson working for Hale Real Estate in Falls Church, Virginia.

- Mike Sampson Senior – Mike Senior is Mike's father and lives in a continuing care retirement community in Front Royal, Virginia.

- Jacelyn Sampson – Jacelyn is Karla and Mike's 23-year-old daughter who lives in Orlando, Florida, with her fiancé, Russ.

- Richard Sampson – Richard is Karla and Mike's 21-year-old son who lives in Jacksonville, Florida, with his fiancée, Lilly.

A New Way of **SEEING**

Chapter 1: Watch for Emotional Process

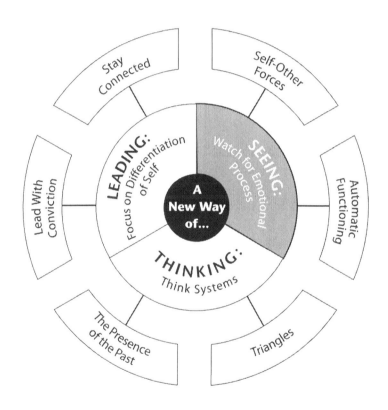

Opening Bell—Wake Up

"What is this?"
"Where is my name?"
"What the hell is going on?"

Mike was not shouting at people standing with him in the long line for the Boston Logan shuttle out of Reagan National, but he was definitely in line and definitely shouting.

Just ahead of him, the mother of twin five-year-olds quickly and efficiently gathered them around her and stepped away from Mike. He saw her move to safety and was embarrassed and irritated at the same time.

Nearby, the security guard also moved in reaction to Mike's outburst – but in a much different way – he began to walk toward Mike.

"Sir, can I help you with something?" the guard asked with a purposeful tone and commanding look. Mike did not hear the voice of the guard but recognized the look…

"Sorry; I'm sorry," Mike said, sensing that he needed to become very quiet very quickly.

With everyone around him finally turning back to what they were doing 30 seconds earlier, Mike took a deep breath.

Mumbling to himself and gripping his cell phone with both hands, he re-read the e-mail with great attention – rereading each sentence one by one.

"At 8:30 this morning, James McMaster and I released information to the media and the investor community about my decision to leave Clearview Hotels, Inc., effective at the end of the fiscal year. There is a copy of the public release attached to this e-mail, but I wanted to communicate with each of you as soon as possible, answer your questions and provide you information so you can address questions that will come up.

"My decision to leave CHI was a difficult choice for me. I have spent most of my professional career here, and I have been blessed with great jobs and a great working environment.

"But circumstances have come up in my family's business that require my fulltime attention. I will share more information about my situation when we next meet.

"James and I have been discussing this transition for the past several weeks, and we both want to assure you that the steps we are now about to take will not impact you in the short run.

"My replacement has not been identified, but an external search has been going on for some time and we are expecting the results of this search soon. You should know that the Board of Directors is also interested in considering internal promotions to the position of COO.

"It is now time to begin managing the transition process as a team, so I am asking you to join me for an afternoon meeting this Friday from 1:00 p.m. to 4:00 p.m. We will meet here in the boardroom. I know that this is short notice, but I am asking you to rearrange your schedule to be with me and James in this meeting on Friday. Please see the attached press release.

"Thanks to all of you for making my years here at Clearview a genuine pleasure, both professionally and personally.

"Vanessa Jackson."

After reading the message three times, two huge frustrations hit Mike with force. He could not open the attachment with the "old" cell phone he was carrying, and his name was not on the addressee list for the memo; it was on the copy list.

His name is not listed as an addressee, but the other three senior vice presidents of operations were addressees of the memo.

He thought to himself again, "There were three addressees on this memo... the senior vice president of the Central Division of Clearview Hotels, Inc., Steve Alba; the senior vice president of the Southeast Division of Clearview Hotels, Inc., Irwin Briggs; and the senior vice president of the West Division of Clearview Hotels, Inc., Akiko Lee.

"They are all there—all three of them—but not me.

"Why am I not an addressee like the other SVPs? Why am I on the copy list along with ten other 'also important' people? Is it a mistake? Am I making something out of nothing? Every person in the HQ building knows there are four SVPs, not three. Am I supposed to be at the meeting on Friday, too?"

Mike once again asked himself, but this time in a quiet, empty and self-absorbed way, "What the hell is going on?"

The DC - Boston shuttle door closed and Mike sank into his center aisle seat wondering if it was wise to have traded in his Acura for a new BMW last week, which would cost him $275 a month over his car allowance. He felt sick to his stomach.

BACK HOME

About the same time Karla Sampson, Mike's wife, was making her way to 220 Lincoln Street, just west of Tysons Corner shopping area. She was excited about showing a beautiful home to a young couple who were coming back for their third and, maybe, final walk-through. Karla loved the real-estate business and, in particular, she loved helping people find a home in which to raise a family. It was well known that she would always go the "extra mile" if a prospective client had kids in tow. Especially among young married couples, Karla had built a clientele and solid referral business in Falls Church, Virginia, after working with Hale Real Estate for the past 17 years.

Just as she pulled into the driveway of the vacant home, her cell phone rang. It was her daughter, Jacelyn, calling from Orlando. At the same time her clients arrived, so she decided to let the call go into voicemail.

After opening hellos, the walk-through began and Karla sensed that they were getting ready to make an offer. After a few minutes Karla stepped outside to give the couple some time to themselves. She dialed *86 to pick up Jacelyn's voicemail.

"Mom, Russ just proposed – just 15 minutes ago! He gave me a beautiful ring and asked me to be his wife! I started to laugh and cry at the same time. Call me right away!"

Jacelyn's voice was filled with excitement and Karla wanted to return the call immediately but knew she would be on the phone for at least an hour. She waited to return the call.

Just then another call rang through. It was Crystal, Mike's executive assistant at work. This call will be short, she thought.

"Hello, Crystal, how are you doing today?"

"Great, Karla. Do you have a moment?"

"Sure I do," replied Karla who knew that Crystal only called if there was something going on that mattered.

Crystal went on quickly, "I just picked up a message from Mike about an important meeting that Vanessa is calling for this Friday afternoon. I have not heard from him—his plane is just arriving in Boston—but I think his plans will be changing for Friday."

"So, it looks like he will be back Thursday night?" said Karla.

"Yes, I think so. If it's all right with you, I want to hold off making arrangements for your surprise weekend in Hilton Head until I hear from him. He still doesn't suspect anything."

"Yes, I think you should wait. What is the meeting about?" Karla asked.

"Not sure, but I think it is a big deal. All of the SVPs are returning to DC and the boardroom has just been booked on the electronic office calendar."

"Thanks, Crystal; call me back when you have more information. I don't expect to hear from Mike until tonight."

The homebuyers opened the door and asked Karla to come back into the living room. They had decided to continue looking at other homes. Karla had misread the situation.

INSIDE CHI HQ

Crystal did not know more, but she suspected more. For the last few weeks she had noticed Vanessa and Mr. McMaster meeting with outside consultants from C.W. Eagan Associates. She had looked them up on the Internet and knew they were high-end headhunters. Recently the meetings had become more frequent and longer.

Then there was the draft memo that Mr. McMaster, Vanessa, the finance guy and the PR guy were working on together. It was a critical document and getting close to being finalized. Something was up. Mike didn't seem to know anything about it.

Vanessa came out of her office and walked to Crystal's desk.

"Have you spoken to Mike today?" Vanessa asked.

"Not yet, his plane is just landing in Boston."

"Okay, when he calls ask him if he got a note from me about Friday. It's about a meeting that I want him to be in at 1:00 p.m. with the other SVPs, but also tell him that I want to see him before that meeting at 11:00 a.m. for a one-on-one meeting."

"Sure, can I tell him what the meeting is about?" Crystal knew Mike would ask.

"Not yet. I am still putting things together." Vanessa smiled and walked back into her office and shut the door.

Crystal immediately called Mike's cell phone.

Full Alert

"Good morning, Mike. How is Boston?"

"It's cold for April and foggy as usual. What's up?"

Mike had slipped into his officious business tone of voice.

"I just got your note about change of plan for Friday. When do you want to come back to DC?"

"I have an open ticket, but I don't want to take any chances of an overbooked 'last call' flight out Thursday night. I have an evening dinner at the Inner Harbor that will end at 8:00 p.m. Get me a flight that leaves Logan at 9:30 p.m. or so. I can fly into Reagan or Dulles."

"No problem. Vanessa just came by my office to ask me to book you into a one-on-one meeting for 11:00 a.m. Friday. I'll send you the confirmation information as soon as I book your flight."

"Did Vanessa mention what the meeting is about?"

"No. She mentioned that she was working on something and just went back into her office."

"Is the meeting just with me?"

"Far as I know. Hold on; let me check the calendar." Crystal quickly pulled up the calendar.

"Nothing is on the calendar; sorry, Mike."

"Thanks, Crystal. I will call you back later today or first thing in the morning."

Mike looked at his appointments.

Starting at lunch, he had back-to-back meetings with general managers, marketing types and an outside developer who wanted to discuss a new hotel project near Harvard Square in Cambridge.

Twenty-seven text messages had arrived during flight. One was from Karla that read: "Call ASAP!" He also saw he had five new voicemails.

Mike quickly dialed her cell line and got voicemail. No message—he didn't want to concern her. He dialed *86 and skipped through several new voicemail messages until he got to hers.

"Mike, I just got a voicemail from Jacelyn. Russ has just proposed this morning. She is excited beyond words. Call me as soon as you can. I love you, Honey."

Just then the cab entered the Boston tunnel. Now out of communication, Mike leaned back, closed his eyes and got even sicker to his stomach.

He thought to himself, "Jacelyn is not ready for marriage. Russell is a kid. Russell is an idiot."

Dim Tunnel

The Sumner and Callahan tunnel system that connects Logan Airport with downtown Boston is a constant topic of discussion between inbound airline travelers and the people who work in downtown Boston. Downtown meetings can take place within 45 minutes of arrival at Logan with the right weather, carry-on luggage, a short queue at the cab line and a clear shot through the tunnel. Mike got three out of four this morning. But the tunnel traffic was a mess.

Mike's level of anxiety was beginning to peak. Too many things were going wrong this morning. Mike began his negative self-talk: "I am going to miss my noon meeting. I hate being late. Being late is a sign of poor planning and it is disrespectful to others. When people make me wait, I almost always write them off.

"Jacelyn is thinking about getting married much too early, and the dumb kid she is living with has no sense of direction. Besides, he is living with our Jacelyn. What a jackass.

"God only knows what is going on at the home office. I may be fired on Friday morning.

"And of course Karla is no help. She's out somewhere having coffee with a bunch of her agent buddies probably talking about wedding dresses."

All Mike could do to get control back was check the messages he had skipped through to hear Karla's. None of them demanded immediate action, so he decided to read and prepare responses to as many of the text messages as he could in preparation to transmit them at the other end of the tunnel. He sent a short text to Crystal, asking her to alert the Boston team that he was running late.

When Mike felt out of control, he was very uncomfortable, and it showed in his thinking, his words, his actions, his demeanor, his attention span. Everyone knew when Mike was uncomfortable because he made them feel uncomfortable, too.

Because Mike is smart, a quick learner and socially adept, his desire to control all that went on around him had been more or less accepted by the leadership team at CHI, with one notable exception: Vanessa. She knew that behind his back he had earned the label of "control freak" and "self-serving" or worse by his peers and team members.

Vanessa also knew that this character trait is career limiting. She had seen it in others who reached a point in their careers and then stopped. So about two months ago, she decided to see if Mike had what it takes to move to the next level. She gave Mike some very direct feedback about his leadership style and asked him to retain the services of an experienced executive coach, one that she knew personally—Jacob Wolfe.

Strangely, Karla placed an article on executive coaching from the Sunday *Post* business section on his nightstand that same week.

As he sat in the tunnel with emergency lights flashing ahead, he wondered, "Why have I not called this guy, Jacob, yet?"

BOSTON FAIRMONT COPLEY PLAZA – 12:45 P.M.

Crystal had called Sally Harrison, the Area VP of operations, and advised her that Mike was running late and would be at the luncheon by 12:45 p.m. Sally quickly adjusted the meeting agenda and delayed the luncheon until Mike walked into the room.

Mike expected that the 20 or so general managers from the local hotels would be in the room. The group was bigger than he expected— about 75 people. There were the faces he knew and a lot of others he didn't.

"Welcome, Mike. We're really glad you could make it today. Tunnel torture again?"

"Yes, the tunnel was in rare form today, but I am really glad to be here," Mike replied with a tense smile.

Mike's first order of business was to ask Sally if she and her team had seen the press release from the home office. She had. He asked to take a look at her copy and quickly scanned it just as lunch was beginning.

While people were finishing their lunches, Mike began making the rounds, saying hello and meeting new people.

Just as the light conversation began to settle back into business, one of the old timers, Jesse Baker, the general manager from Lexington, speaking so all could hear, asked Mike the big question: "Mike, we got a copy of the press release right before you arrived. Can you give us an update on what is going on down there in DC?"

Mike knew this was coming and he was ready to bluff his way through the answer. "The executive team for CHI is preparing for significant growth of business in the coming three to five years. With Vanessa's transition out of CHI, we will need to make some adjustments to the senior team structure. Meetings have been going on for weeks in DC and will be continuing this week. We have a meeting on Friday to continue our discussions. I anticipate that more information will be available in about ten days."

None of what Mike said was false, but none of it clarified anything, either. But, everyone in the room thought he must know more than he was going to talk about, and that was the purpose of his little speech anyway.

Mike continued the meeting with briefings, discussions and a lot of smiles. He took the opportunity to review performance numbers for the division and ended the meeting on a positive note: "All the numbers are up, projections for the remainder of the year are strong, current performance against budget is strong. Life is good."

Hotel Room

Mike usually went out to dinner with a group of his team members, but tonight he excused himself, saying he had a lot of work to catch up on. He went to his room and changed into his jogging sweats, intending to gain some control with a long, slow run.

He tried to reach Karla on her cell phone again, with no answer. This time he left a message, "Honey, call me as soon as you can. Something has come up and I need to talk to you." That would get her attention. He clipped the phone to his waistband and left for his run. Karla didn't call back.

After the run and shower, he got dressed in shorts and t-shirt, ordered a salad from room service and got back to work.

The phone rang and Mike jumped for the phone thinking it was Karla – thank God.

It was Vanessa Jackson.

He strained to sound calm and relaxed. "Hello, Vanessa. How did today go for you?"

"Well, it was very eventful and pretty stressed. Do you have a moment to talk?"

"Sure, how can I be of help?" Mike's heart was pounding so hard that his T-shirt was pulsing.

"Well, I have decided to leave CHI as my message said earlier today. I have done a lot of thinking and praying about my choice. I finally made the decision a short while ago and informed James. He has been very supportive of me; he is a great CEO, and boss and friend."

Vanessa's words were sincere and her voice, usually strong and direct, waffled and drifted just a bit. This hit Mike hard. Vanessa was not just good at the COO position; she was remarkable. She was the one person primarily responsible for the success of CHI over the past seven years.

She continued, "But I am calling to talk about your situation, Mike. We are looking at my replacement from both inside and outside the organization. We have two top-notch candidates from outside the company; one is from here in the US and another from the UK. Both are women.

"The Board has asked James and me to submit candidate names from inside the company, and we have one name on the list so far." Now Vanessa's tone became stern.

"James and I are split on adding your name to the list. He thinks you would be a very strong candidate. I agree that you have many of the key qualities we're looking for, but to tell you the truth, I am not supportive of your candidacy, at least not now."

Mike sat down on the bed so hard a lamp fell off the bed stand. While he mentally groped for a response, Vanessa went on.

"Let me ask you a question; have you started your executive coaching with Jacob yet?"

Mike froze. "It's on my punch list, Vanessa; I'll get in touch with him soon."

"Has he called you yet?"

"Yes."

"Well, a good way to get started is to return his phone calls, don't you think?"

Mike gritted his teeth. "You're right; I'll call him tomorrow."

There was a long pause, after which Vanessa said, "Let's do this. You call Jacob and tell him that you and I are meeting on Friday at 11:00 a.m. and ask him to join us here in my office if he can."

"Will do," Mike said.

Vanessa ended the call with a curt, "Fine. I will see you on Friday. Goodnight, Mike."

Mike disconnected the call, sarcastically mumbling to himself, "Gee, thanks for the call."

He felt like screaming. He needed another run.

More Pressure

Thirty seconds after Vanessa hung up, Jacelyn's call rang into room 226.

"Dad, Dad, has Mom told you the news?" Without waiting for his response, she chattered on excitedly. "I'm engaged! Russ has asked me to marry him! Can you believe it?"

Mike just lost it.

"Why? Why are you engaged?" Mike didn't wait for his daughter's reply, either. "You can't get married right out of college—you are only 23 years old, for God's sake! You and your 'Mr. Right' don't even have steady jobs yet.

"Are you listening to me, Jacelyn?"

Jacelyn wished more than anything that she had not called her dad, that she had not had this conversation, that she had not asked Russ to listen in on an extension. For the first time in her life, Jacelyn hung up on her dad.

Mike threw a shoe at the TV.

About ten minutes later, the phone rang again and Mike knew who was calling and what she was going to say. He considered not answering the phone.

"Hello," Mike said to Karla.

"Mike," Karla said, "I just got off the phone with Jacelyn and I think we need to talk."

Mike was silent.

"Are you out of your mind? Your only daughter is overflowing with joy at being engaged, and you talk down to her as if she were a little child. What's wrong with you, Mike?"

Karla's voice was rising in anger as she spoke. Mike started to mumble a reply, but she cut him off. "I want to talk with you tomorrow, but I have a question before we say good-night."

"Which is …" Mike snapped back.

"How old was I the night you proposed to me?"

Mike did not want to answer. "Twenty-three," he said.

"No, I was twenty-one, and neither one of us thought we were too young to get married. Have a good night, Mike. I will talk to you tomorrow."

Mike just sat on the bed for a few moments. Then he picked up his notepad. Mike frequently made notes to himself, usually in the evening to help him think about what was going on and also prepare for the next few days. He did not do this every night, but found it helpful when he did.

Today
- *Vanessa is quitting—why?—and she is not supporting me as the next COO—why?*
- *Jacelyn is getting married—too damn young and Karla is on her side.*

Issues
- *Get things back under control.*
- *What is coaching with Wolfe about? Maybe it's really outplacement guidance.*
- *Jacelyn is not being responsible—she needs to grow up*

Follow up
- *Stay focused on Boston visit.*
- *Call Jacob Wolfe.*
- *Visit a few target hotels and get things turned around now —push much harder.*

APRIL 2, 6:15 A.M.

It was very early, but Mike could not wait any longer. He dialed Jacob Wolfe's number and left a message about the meeting on Friday.

Mike hung up the phone and darted for the door. He was off to his first hotel visit of the day.

THE HAMMER

Yesterday, Mike had praised the Boston area leaders for their strong performance. But in truth his real visit to the Boston area was to apply pressure on three hotel general managers who were not moving their units in the correct direction.

For years, Mike had kept his own performance scorecard on each of his hotels. This year, one of his oldest units in nearby Newton was at the top of his hit list.

Admittedly, Newton was more than 40 years old and the area where the hotel was built had experienced significant challenges. Once at the center of an emerging commercial district, a thoroughfare now bypassed the 550-room hotel's location dramatically slowing growth in the area. But Mike didn't want excuses; he wanted results.

He met up with Sally and her area controller, Rick, in the lobby at 7:30 a.m. on the dot. Paul Brady, the hotel's general manager, was not there to meet them. They waited. Paul arrived 20 minutes late. It was not a good start for the visit.

Paul walked in and shook everyone's hand while blaming his tardiness on the traffic.

Mike, already irritated, said, "Let's get started."

They walked into the Cambridge Suite right off the lobby. The room temperature was almost freezing. Sally asked Paul to have someone come to the room to adjust the temperature. He walked to the house phone in the room to dial engineering; it did not work. Then he asked a banquet houseman just outside in the hallway to call for an engineer to come to the room.

Sally opened the meeting. "Mike, thanks for visiting with some of our area hotels. We are keeping our eye on the ball at each hotel and Paul has a good plan to continue making progress here at Newton."

She nodded to Paul to get started.

For about ten minutes Paul reviewed the location, market and physical plant challenges his team faced at the Newton property. The list was comprehensive and well documented. Paul began to describe his plan for addressing these issues, but Mike cut him off. "I have four questions for you.

"What are the current trends for these last three months for transient, group and contract business for your competitive set in the area?

"What is your occupancy, RevPar and ADRs, compared to our competitors down the street?

"Who are your three biggest repeat group clients for summertime midweek conferences and meetings?

"What are the three top priorities for customer satisfaction and employee engagement? And, what are you doing about these priorities?"

Paul had no answers for the first two questions.

Sally asked for a break to get the answers with the help of her controller. As the two of them were working to bring up their reports, she silently hoped that Paul would figure out that only he and his team could answer the last two questions.

When the group reassembled, Sally gave respectable answers to the first two questions.

When she had finished, Mike looked expectantly at Paul. He fumbled his way through answers to the second two questions and then asked if he could get additional information to Mike later in the day.

Mike shook his head. He had heard enough; then and there, he made his mind up about Paul.

The remainder of the meeting went quickly. The room got even colder. Mike did not ask any more questions. He was considering how and when to replace Paul.

He thought to himself, "Success is a matter of knowing the facts and taking control of the situation to achieve results. End of story."

The meeting ended at about 11:30 a.m. as the engineer arrived to adjust the room temperature.

Everyone left the meeting fully aware that it did not go well.

The Ride

After a very quick lunch, Mike and Sally rode in one car and Rick drove the second car to the next hotel about 30 minutes away.

During the ride, Mike began a diatribe against Paul, cutting off Sally when she tried to deflect some of his criticism. He concluded his character assassination by shouting: "Figure it out, Sally; it's either you deal with Paul or I will!"

Sally remained silent and was relieved when they pulled up to their second stop.

The second meeting went much better. The general manager, Eric Bloom, was waiting in the lobby. The arrival and greeting were cordial. Mike and Eric had worked together in the past and were good friends. But most importantly, Eric knew what Mike would be asking and he had prepared a concise fact-based briefing. Eric had all the answers.

Mike was pleased and let everyone know that Eric had gotten it right. Sally felt just as uncomfortable with Mike's effusiveness over Eric as she had over his attack of Paul.

"Mike is under a lot of stress—he gets this way whenever he is stressed," she thought to herself.

Sally dropped Mike off at his hotel and made an excuse to get away for the evening. She was exhausted.

Mike knew she was worn out and hoped that she had learned a lesson herself today. Sally was too damn nice and did not know how to motivate people to get up and get moving.

"She will never make it to the next level," he thought as she drove away.

ANXIETY

Back in his room, Mike was no longer able to put Jacelyn and Karla and last night's phone calls out of his mind. He had learned to compartmentalize his thinking during the workday, but now it was time to worry again.

He felt sick to his stomach, really sick.

Mike decided not to run and make up for it by only eating a high protein snack. He clicked on the 7:00 p.m. evening news.

Just then the phone rang. It was Jacob Wolfe.

They chatted for a few moments, and Mike was relieved to discover that Vanessa had not given Jacob any details about the situation. To Mike, that was good because he could start fresh with this guy. More control.

Mike invited Jacob to the Friday meeting and filled him in on the search for Vanessa's successor. "I am sort of a candidate," he concluded.

With a full laugh, Jacob asked, "How does someone become sort of a candidate?"

"Well, some people think I am a viable candidate and some do not," Mike replied.

"And what does Vanessa think?" Jacob asked.

"She does not think I am a candidate," Mike shot back.

Laughing again, Jacob said, "Well that is where you are today, my friend. The question is, where will you be next month?"

Mike thought about that remark for a long moment without answering.

"I'll see you on Friday." Jacob was gone.

NEW PLAN

Mike jumped into the shower after finishing his snack. He began to wonder if he should change his plans and go home a day early. He turned ideas over in his head.

He sat still on the end of the bed and then decided to defer a decision for a few more hours. He keeled over on the bed and went right to sleep.

At 2:30 a.m. he woke up and saw that his message light was on. It was Karla. He had slept right through the phone's loud ringing. The message was short, and it was clear that Karla was still upset over his behavior with Jacelyn.

"Hello, Mike. I was hoping to hear from you today. Call me. Any time before midnight." Mike felt the muscles in his stomach tighten.

He thought about her for a moment. Karla was a caring and loving wife with a core the substance of granite. She was seldom out of sorts, but they had differed for years in their parenting of Jacelyn. It had often been a source of tension in their relationship, with Mike growing more critical the more she was protective of Jacelyn. He knew that this was going to be a major issue, not easily gotten past, and he dreaded the confrontation that he knew was coming.

"I'd better go home and get it over with," he said out loud to himself. He took out his note pad to make some notes.

Today
- *Replace the GM at Newton.*
- *Help Sally toughen up—go back to Boston ASAP.*
- *Sally is not listening to me about Paul.*

Issues
- *Losing control—career, Jacelyn, health.*
- *What is Vanessa's connection to Jacob Wolfe?*
- *I feel really distant from Jacelyn—I hate that feeling—and Karla is still mad as hell at me.*

Follow up
- *Go home early tomorrow morning.*
- *Take time off in the middle of the day to talk with Karla.*
- *Call Karla and Crystal in early a.m.*

BACK TO DC

At 5:00 a.m. on Thursday, Mike called and left messages for Sally and Crystal, letting them know that he was returning to DC because of some pressing issues and that he would return to Boston before the end of the month to finish up his unit rounds.

A half-hour later, he went to the airport and waited to board the first shuttle to DC. He arrived at the home office at 9:15 a.m., and then remembered that Crystal had taken the day off.

Now focused on family matters, he called Karla. He explained that he was back in town and suggested that they meet at home for lunch on the back deck. She agreed, her voice still frosty with anger.

Mike felt tense over what he feared could be an explosive confrontation with Karla. On his way out of the office, he picked up a stack of paper from the overflowing inbox.

On his way home he picked up some ready-made sandwiches, chips and one red rose at the grocery store. He pulled into the garage and paused to pull up the last period operating statements for the company and his region on his cell phone. Nationally, CHI's performance was flat compared to last year. Mike scanned the bottom of the regional pages for total performance numbers. Boston stuck out like a flashing orange sign. Every performance indicator was down – some by more than 20 percent.

Mike felt his chest tighten. Here he was at home in the middle of the day. If the report had posted while he was still in Boston, he surely would not have come home.

He flipped open his cell phone and hit the speed dial for Sally Harrison. The call went into voicemail.

"Sally, this is Mike. Listen, I just got the period end flash report and it looks like your area has tanked. I sure wish we had known about this before the meeting earlier this week. Call me on my cell as soon as you get this message," Mike almost shouted and hung up.

Staring at the flash report on his phone screen, he muttered, "Damn."

As he stepped out of the car in his driveway, Mike realized that he should have stayed in Boston today.

He took several deep breaths to decompress and to compartmentalize.

LUNCH ON THE DECK

Karla had already set out some plates and silverware on the deck. He kissed her as he walked into the kitchen and handed her the rose.

"Hello, Beauty," the expression he used all the time, which she knew he really meant.

They both sat down to begin a difficult conversation.

"Honey, I am sorry for how I spoke to both you and Jacelyn. I know that she is growing up and needs to make her own decisions. But we are still her parents and our job is to prevent her from getting in over her head, too."

Karla just listened.

"We both know that she is too young to get married. For God's sake, we still are giving her money every month to make ends meet. She needs to at least be able to pay her own food bill before she gets married!"

Karla opened the water bottles and poured both of them a glassful.

"I do not approve of the marriage and while I think Russ has a lot on the ball, he sits in front of the TV and plays video games half the time. They are still just kids!"

Mike's phone rang. It was Sally Harrison. Mike gritted his teeth, "I'm going to let that go; Boston can wait."

"What do you think, Honey?" Mike said, hoping that she would be in a conciliatory mood.

Karla gave him an icy smile and said, "I think Jacelyn and Russ are going to get married."

Mike just looked at Karla. "And …and… and…what are you going to do about that?"

Karla said, "Go to the wedding, if she lets us come."

His anger triggered, Mike lost his hard-won control. "So you think this is a good idea. You think Jacelyn is ready to get married. You think that we should just jump up and celebrate the arrival of a new son-in-law. We should just welcome this guy who can play a pinball machine like a musical instrument, but has trouble figuring out how to make his next car payment. That is what you think!"

Karla's voice was controlled, but clearly full of anger at Mike's tirade. She said, "I like Russ; he is a respectful and gracious young man and he loves Jacelyn a great deal."

Mike sat back. As so often happened with Karla in these kinds of situations, it seemed like they were having two different conversations. He was talking about making a living, and she was talking about something else.

"So what do we do now?" Mike said.

Karla shot back, "I think you need to call Jacelyn after you calm down and just talk with her. The conversation you had with her the other night is not finished, and the two of you need to work things out. She's brokenhearted at your response, and you haven't even made the time to get back to her. What is going on in your head?"

Mike realized at that point that he had not only lost control of the situation with Jacelyn, but his relationship with Karla was growing more and more strained. He knew how stubborn she could be when she dug in her heels—especially where Jacelyn was involved. Things were unraveling.

He finished lunch quickly and went to his home office. He had not talked with Karla about his trip to Boston, about Vanessa's imminent departure, about her critique of his leadership effectiveness and the impact on his candidacy for a bigger job, about the meeting tomorrow at 11:00 a.m., or about Jacob Wolfe.

He just decided to cut off from the world for a while.

He went for an early evening jog. He came home and thought about calling Sally Harrison back but did not have the energy. He also thought about calling Jacelyn back and did not know how to start the conversation. Karla was out for the evening at a woman's book club.

He sat in his office and stared out the window. A lot of things were unraveling.

He decided not to make any notes this evening. "What's the use?" he thought.

Vanessa's Office

At 10:45 a.m. Crystal knocked on Mike's office door and said, "Jacob Wolfe has just called from the lobby. Do you want me to go get him?"

"No, I will go down and meet him," Mike replied.

As Mike walked toward Jacob in the small lobby area of CHI, he was surprised to see a man peering expectantly at him from a wheelchair. It had to be Jacob. He was a slender man in his mid-sixties with a big smile and strong handshake. His penetrating gaze was unnerving; Mike wondered if Jacob could be some kind of body language expert or mind reader.

"Hello, Mike, I am glad to meet you," Jacob said in an easy way.

"Welcome to CHI," Mike said in a not-so-easy way. "Can I offer you a cup of coffee or bottle of water?"

"Water will be good," replied Jacob.

Vanessa was waiting at the sixth floor elevator lobby for the two to arrive. When the door opened, she shook Mike's hand and said welcome back from Boston, and then she hugged Jacob.

"Jacob Wolfe, it is just great to see you again." Vanessa lit up when she looked at Jacob. It was clear that she had a deep affection for him.

"Let's go into my office and get started right away."

Vanessa had a spacious but not overstated office. They sat at the table in the middle of the room.

Vanessa began. "First, thank you both for arranging your schedule to be here on short notice." She paused. "Jacob, I am moving on from this position. Do you already know that?"

"Yes, I do, Vanessa. I am excited to know what you will be doing next."

"I will get to that later, but for this meeting, I want to talk to the both of you about some changes we are making as a result of my departure."

Vanessa went on to explain that she and James McMaster are working with the Board of Directors and an executive search firm to find a suitable replacement for the COO job with the goal of having someone in place by September first.

"We have two external candidates and one internal candidate so far." Vanessa stopped and looked at Mike for a moment. "Mike is the senior vice president of operations for the Northeast and doing a great job. Mr. McMaster thinks he is a good, strong fourth candidate for COO. I do not agree.

"Mike knows this." Vanessa paused and looked directly at Mike. "But what you don't know, Mike, is that in my opinion the leadership shortcomings that you have are absolute deal breakers. Unless you address the issues I am going to share with you today, I will prevent you from becoming a candidate for this position." She settled back in her chair and waited for this thought to settle.

Mike felt his face redden, and his breathing grew short and quick.

After a moment, she looked back at Mike. "On the other hand, I believe in your potential, and I know what Jacob is capable of as a leadership coach."

"Here is what I know about you, Mike. You are smart, a quick learner, good on your feet, extremely effective with customers, driven, respected up and down the organization and a bottom line performer year after year.

"However, to accomplish your goals, you over-manage, over-control and overwhelm your people. People do respect you, but they also fear you. You are hotheaded, intensely articulate in heated debate, and so self-confident that others cower in your presence. You are so damn smart in the business that you think you know everything and you almost do know everything. Everything about the business of the business, that is, but you do not know enough about working with the people in the business.

"Mike, here is the key: You have about zero self-awareness. You do not realize that your style of management is destroying careers and hammering the culture of CHI. Soon, either you will have some sort of a meltdown or your team will—maybe both."

There was dead silence in the room.

"Mike, here are two more things you do not know. Ten years ago, I was exactly like you —just not as smart.

"Eight years ago, I met Jacob Wolfe."

Then after a long silence, Vanessa slowly pushed her chair back from the table, stood up, walked out of her office and shut the door.

Jacob Wolfe

Mike was sitting forward, elbows on knees and looking down at the floor. For the first time in a long time he had no idea what to do or say. He could feel Jacob's eyes on him.

He thought, "My wife and daughter are both furious with me. I have just been dressed down by my boss, someone that I look up to as a role model. She has deeply embarrassed me in front of a man I have just met, and she spoke with intense and direct criticism. Now she has left the room."

He wondered, "Is she coming back?"

He wondered, "Is she right about me?"

He looked at Jacob, "Is this the way you start all of your coaching sessions?"

Jacob smiled, "This was not a coaching session."

Mike followed up, "So what was it?"

Jacob quickly responded, "That depends on what you do now." He went on, "Let me ask you a question: What did you hear Vanessa say?"

"She said I am smart in my business sense and a failure in my people sense. She said I am headed for a meltdown."

"What else?"

"She said that she would not endorse me for her replacement," he said, his voice rising in anger. "Over the recommendation of the CEO, I might add!"

"What else?"

"She said that she was just like me ten years ago, and then she met you. That's about all I can remember."

"You know, Mike, I have not spoken to Vanessa in two years. Today is the first time I have seen her in person in four years. And I just spoke to you on the phone for the first time last night. So, I have no idea what the issues are that you are dealing with in your job or in your life. Finally, I don't know what you or Vanessa or I will do next.

"But I absolutely know one thing for sure." Jacob paused for a moment. "Vanessa is pulling out all the stops to give you every opportunity to be the next successful COO. And she wants you to get the position so much she can taste it."

Mike was incredulous, "Are you kidding? That's just nuts! Where did you get that idea from the last 15 minutes?"

"It is not an idea; it's a fact. Here's how I know. I've been in meetings like this more than once in my career. And I know an executive doesn't waste time challenging someone—like Vanessa did you—unless she's pretty sure the person has what it takes to rise to the challenge. Vanessa wouldn't be wasting her time and energy on you unless she felt very strongly that you have what it takes to succeed her."

Mike was stunned and speechless. He was beginning to see the events of this week in a very different light.

Jacob said, "Mike, I am going to take off now. Think about this discussion and give me a call sometime."

Mike jumped up before Jacob could wheel away from the table and asked, "Can we meet tomorrow afternoon?"

"Well, tomorrow is Saturday. Why don't you get some rest over the weekend and give me a call on Monday morning?" Jacob smiled, looked directly into Mike's eyes, shook his hand and navigated his chair through Vanessa's office door.

SVP MEETING

Mike went back to his office and closed the door. Just then his cell phone alarm reminded him about the SVP meeting at 1:00.

He wasn't sure that he was even supposed to go to the meeting. So, he built up the courage to go over to Vanessa's office to ask her. She was not there. He decided to ask her executive assistant, Helen Sharp, if she knew anything about the meeting or the memo. She did, but was surprised to learn that Mike's name wasn't on it.

"Are you kidding? Let me look at the memo." Helen quickly pulled up the memo on her computer. "O my God, Mike, I am so sorry. You are right. The mistake is my fault. Boy, I am glad you checked this out. Vanessa would have gone nuts if you missed the meeting because of my oversight. Of course you are invited to the meeting. Do you want me to issue a correction or something?"

Mike felt relief. "No, it's fine, Helen. By my count you make one mistake about every 24 months, and this is no big deal."

To Mike, it was a huge deal.

At 1:00, the SVP meeting started on time in the boardroom. Vanessa, James McMaster and Dennis Baum, the headhunter from C.W. Eagan & Associates, joined the four SVPs.

James began the meeting by confirming the facts of the memo sent out earlier in the week. He acknowledged Vanessa for her many achievements, her creativity and hard work.

Vanessa spoke of her appreciation for the support she got every day from James, and she acknowledged the accomplishment of each of her team members, one by one. She spoke in detail and at length about Gayle, Mike, Irwin and Steve.

Dennis Baum spoke next. He reported that the executive search for Vanessa's replacement had been ongoing for some time. At the first round of cuts, 11 people met the requirements. Following interviews on the phone and some in-person interviews, the field had now been narrowed to two candidates.

Dennis went on to say that internal candidates were being considered. At that point, everyone but Mike wondered if they themselves were being considered. The thought was so palpable that James interrupted.

"Vanessa and I have discussed the idea of promoting one of the four of you. As we mentioned in the memo circulated earlier this week, the Board has requested that we produce an internal candidate list. Vanessa and I will make an appointment with each of you individually in the next week or so to discuss your interest and our views on your candidacy for the post. In the end, the final selection will be mine to make with the advice and counsel of the Board and Vanessa.

"One more thing," James added, "we foresee no other significant organizational changes before the new COO is selected and placed."

Baum finished the briefing about the external interview process.

Time was provided for questions and answers. Nothing of significance was asked. It was clear that time was needed to let the news sink in. Vanessa ended the meeting at about 2:30 p.m.

COACHING – FIRST CONTACT

A weekend, some sleep, two runs and several long discussions with Karla had made a world of difference for Mike Sampson. On Monday morning he called Jacob at 8:00. To his surprise, Jacob answered the call himself.

"Jacob, this is Mike Sampson. Can we schedule a meeting for later today?"

"Hello, Mike. Sure, we can meet today. Let's meet for an hour and a half. Will 2:00 p.m. at my office work for you?" He gave Mike the address.

"See you then."

COACHING SESSION – A NEW WAY OF SEEING

Mike arrived early and was surprised at Jacob's office location. His office was in an old one-story storefront that was built in the 1970s or earlier. The parking lot was pocked with potholes and several of the dozen or so offices were vacant. All in all, it struck Mike as a bit of a dump.

Somewhat disappointed, Mike exited his car and knocked on Jacob's office door at 2:00. Jacob opened the door.

Jacob smiled from his wheelchair. "Mike, welcome; please come in."

The space was large and plain. There was a six-seat round table in the middle of the room, a computer and printer at one end of the room and a desk and bookcases at the other end. Three walls were solid and covered with erasable white boards and the fourth wall was a floor to ceiling window that looked out onto a beautiful wild flower garden with a lily pond and a statue of Buddha. There were two or three folded up flip charts stacked in one corner and a coat rack loaded with baseball hats in another. Sitting on the table was a small ant farm. The office was very plain, almost shabby.

Jacob watched Mike look the place over and said, still smiling, "How do you like my office?"

Mike said the office was big and comfortable. "Big, comfortable and cheap," Jacob added with a grin.

"I haven't seen an ant farm since I was a kid." Mike laughed, beginning to relax.

"Well, ants are really interesting to study. I learn a lot about people by watching ants," Jacob said. "OK, let's get started. What do you want to talk about?"

Mike was ready. "I am still steamed about the way Vanessa handled the meeting last week. I think she was completely out of line. What do you think?"

Jacob thought for a moment, "Have you told Vanessa how you feel?"

"No."

"Should you...should you talk with her about the way you feel?" Jacob asked.

"Yes, I think I should," Mike replied. "But do you think she was out of line?"

"I really don't know. It was surely a unique meeting. One way to think about what happened is to decide if the purpose of the meeting was achieved. Do you think that Vanessa's purpose was to embarrass you in front of me?" Jacob asked.

"Vanessa is not like that," Mike replied.

"What is the question you want answered? Jacob asked.

"I want to know why Vanessa pulled me in to a room and conducted herself the way she did. I want to know why Vanessa wants me to talk with you. And I want to know if there is a way I can change her mind about supporting me for the job of COO."

"Right; good questions," said Jacob. "You can only get those answers by talking to her, so you should do that. What else do you want to talk about, Mike?"

"Well, what are we going to do here? How long will we be involved in coaching? How often will we meet? How does it all work?"

Jacob explained that their coaching arrangement would work

best if they met every week for a few months to start with and then decide what to do next. Sometimes they would meet in person and sometimes they could just talk on the phone; Mike would determine what would work best.

The coaching discussions would center on topics chosen by Mike. "We work on what you want to work on when you are ready. Our agenda is your agenda," said Jacob. "I do have some ideas about how to help people be more effective leaders, of course, but what we cover depends mostly on your priorities."

Mike's anxieties about working with a coach were quickly subsiding, and his curiosity was being stirred up. "Tell me a little bit more about your approach," he said, focusing very intently on how Jacob was handling himself. "Is coaching a form of therapy, or what?"

Jacob went on, "No, coaching is not therapy. If you want to deal with deep personal issues of that sort, I can—and will—be happy to give you a referral to someone who is qualified to do that kind of work. I work with executives to help them become better leaders. My job is to talk with you to help you SEE things, THINK things and DO things that you most likely would not see, think or do without having our conversations. The outcome, hopefully, is that you will become a much better leader. It is that simple."

"I bet it's not really simple," Mike replied.

"You're right, Mike; it's not simple, not at first. In fact, I often tell my clients that I am introducing them to 'A New Way of SEEING,' 'A "New Way of THINKING,' and 'A New Way of LEADING.'"

As he spoke, Jacob propelled his wheelchair to the white board and wrote the words SEEING, THINKING, LEADING. "It's not simple at the outset, Mike. But like everything else, once you learn and practice using the ideas and tools we will discuss, they can actually become almost second nature."

"Where do we begin?" Mike said.

"At the meeting last week Vanessa spoke about your self-awareness and your need to be more self-aware. The way I heard her comments suggested to me that she feels you engage in activities with inadequate awareness of how your actions and words impact others. Do you recall her remarks the same way?"

"More or less."

"I think you need to talk some more with Vanessa about her

perspective. When you do, get her to be more specific about her self-awareness comment. Ask her to give you some examples, recent examples, of situations where she felt your lack of self-awareness had a negative impact on others or on the outcome of a situation."

Jacob went on, "I am talking about the idea of 'SEEING' situations at a different level of awareness. The higher a manager goes in an organization, the more important perspective is, and that means 'SEEING' situations from points of view other than your natural or default point of view."

Mike was nodding in agreement. "I know exactly what you mean. Some of my managers just don't get it. They don't look at the big picture, and I am constantly trying to point out the need to pay attention to all sorts of things they are missing."

"Exactly, Mike. You know how important it is that a leader has a powerful vision for any organization. Without that capacity for vision, a leader rarely succeeds. No one wants to follow a leader who does not have a vision." Jacob paused to let the thought sink in.

Then he continued, "But to develop the right vision, you've got to pay attention to the right things—you've got to SEE in a new way. I think Vanessa was telling you that you're not seeing some pretty important pieces of the leadership puzzle."

"And do you have an idea of what it is that I'm missing?"

"Not particularly, Mike. But here is one perspective that I think is pretty important to pay attention to: All animals, really all sentient beings, engage in events of life by taking actions that are very heavily influenced by instinctual forces. Most of us are completely oblivious to the role that those forces play in our everyday lives. We just don't see how powerfully they influence us and those around us. Those forces are collectively referred to by the term '**emotional process**.' That's an expression coined by one of my mentors, Murray Bowen, and it's a very important notion to understand."

"I've read some of that stuff about emotional intelligence, is that what you mean?"

"Well, the emotional intelligence material is related, but what Bowen discusses when he talks about **emotional process** is a bit deeper. It includes all of the life forces we share with other living beings. I use the image of the ocean, whose depths and currents we are rarely aware of, but which is always beneath us and always influences us as we sail along on its surface. Despite the fact that we are usually oblivious to those forces, they are powerfully influencing us. But once you recognize their presence and learn about how they operate, you can navigate the seas of life as a much more effective leader. That's why I will be talking a lot to you about SEEING **emotional process** and understanding more deeply how it influences your behavior and that of others."

As Jacob sat forward to continue his explanation, Mike thought to himself that it was sounding like a lot of jargon that he didn't really understand and wasn't sure would be very helpful.

"Here is the point. What can set a truly great leader apart is his ability to become more aware of how often we humans are influenced by **emotional process**, even when we may think we're being very thoughtful and deliberate. If you're interested and motivated, I can help you become more aware of the role that **emotional process** plays in how you operate, not just at CHI, but in all of your relationships. And once you become more self-aware in that way, you will be able to see its effects in other people and in CHI as an organization. That's what I mean by 'A New Way of SEEING.'"

Jacob sat back and went silent.

Mike was struggling to follow, but wasn't sure he really grasped what Jacob was talking about. "I'm not sure I get it, Jacob. I'm open to what you have to say, but, frankly, I'm not sure I follow."

Jacob burst out with a loud laugh. "We're going to get along great, Mike. I like your honesty. Let's take a break."

Jacob knew breaks allowed time for his clients to either catch up on cell phone traffic or more deeply consider the coaching material just covered. Either one was just fine.

Mike went outside for a moment and stood in the April sun. The light prevented him from seeing his cell phone screen, so he stepped into the shade. About ten minutes later he went back inside.

Going Deeper

When Mike sat back down, Jacob handed him a copy of an article with "WHAT IS EMOTIONAL PROCESS?" printed across the top. "Here, Mike, take this home and look it over when you get the chance. It'll give you a fuller explanation of what I'm talking about when I use the phrase 'emotional process.' And, hopefully, it will help you understand how powerful and important a force it is in shaping human behavior. I've downloaded this copy from my website, but there's a lot more material there related to what we have been talking about. I've written down the access code for the website so you can get into the online resources section. Between now and our next session, I suggest you might want to check out some of what's there." Jacob paused for a moment and then asked, "How was your break? Were you able to get caught up on your voicemails and emails?"

Mike, shaking his head, started venting. "I just picked up a copy of an email exchange between Craig, one of my area vice presidents, responding to a request for information from Steve, who's in marketing. The request is for some customer data analysis. While the substance of Steve's request was on target, his turnaround time was pretty tight, and he asked to meet with Craig to go over the data in person. Craig just blew Steve off telling him that he should do the analysis himself."

Becoming more animated as he talked, Mike continued, "This happens all the time between the two of them. Whenever Steve gets a bit anxious over something, he wants Craig to hold his hand. And it drives Craig crazy. I spend more time trying to get them back on track and working together than you can imagine. I was about to send them both a follow-up note to straighten out the debate, and then I began to think about our conversation and wondered if there was some of this **emotional process** stuff that you're talking about going on."

"You mean in your reaction or between the two of them?"

Well, I was thinking of them, but now that you mention it, I guess the question could apply to my reaction as well."

Jacob replied, "You're right. The question is just as valid about you as it is about them. And once you're more skilled in this 'New Way of SEEING,'" you will be watching on both levels—your reaction and others as well.

"As far as your reaction goes, I'm curious; what was your first instinct to say to them? If you were going to jump right in to solve the problem for Craig and Steve, more or less like a referee, and if—as you say—you often play that role, I suspect there are probably some forces beneath your conscious awareness that are influencing your behavior.

"On the other hand, the fact that you didn't respond immediately and chose instead to talk it over with me sounds like you are trying to be more thoughtful about your response. How would you characterize what your very first instinct was like?"

Mike thought for a moment. "I guess I just wanted to fix the situation as fast as possible. We need to keep things moving in this business, and I see one of my roles as the driving engine. My inclination was to tell Craig to just get it done and meet with Steve. It's his job."

Jacob replied, "Okay, if you had followed your first impulse, what would have happened then?"

"Well, if I tell Craig to do it, he will jump in, finish the analysis, meet with Steve, and just move on. I won't hear another word from him. Then Steve will come by my office in the next few days to see if everything is okay. He always needs to check everything out to be sure no one is upset. He worries about his relationships with the team all the time, and it drives everyone nuts. If anyone ever gets angry with Steve, or even if anyone gets 'pissed off' at anyone else in the team, Steve gets terribly anxious. He wants everyone to get along and avoids conflict like the plague."

"Mike, there are a couple of things going on here that you could think about," said Jacob. "First, the e-mail exchange between Craig and Steve included a copy to you, ostensibly to keep you informed. But I suspect you recognize that there is more to it than just keeping you informed. Just from the perspective of office politics, people often copy in a boss to referee a debate or to afford them protection in a contentious situation. But there is usually more than that underneath, and the 'New Way of SEEING' that I'd like to introduce you to can help you recognize some of those hidden forces at work. Your being brought into the situation has put you in an anxious triangle, and we will talk a lot more about that in the future.

"Second, if your typical response to this type of exchange is to step in and solve problems as quickly as possible, even with the good intention of keeping things moving, what impact do you suppose that has on the long-term growth of teamwork in your division?"

"I'm not sure what you're getting at. Doesn't it show them

how to solve problems more quickly by just getting it done?"

"Well, what do you think? How much have you learned in situations where someone stepped in and solved a problem for you, instead of letting you work things out yourself? Seems to me you're helping them avoid resolving their own conflict, and that shifts the responsibility to you instead of leaving it with them. I'm not sure how much they learn about teamwork from that."

Mike nodded, "Yeah, I suppose you're right. But it drives me crazy how much time all of this crap wastes."

Jacob smiled slightly and then said, "Mike I wonder if there's a learning opportunity here for you, if you can become more self-aware of some of the deeper stuff driving your pattern of behavior in such situations."

Jacob paused to gauge Mike's reaction, then continued, "To the extent that your own behavior is reactive—what I sometimes call **automatic functioning**—to that extent you lose the opportunity to be more thoughtful in exercising a style of leadership that builds long-term capacity in your team. Your own reactivity actually reinforces a reactive style in those around you. And once you tune in to how **emotional process** is influencing the situation, you will realize how contagious anxiety is. The triangle you're in between Craig and Steve sounds like a pretty anxious one to me."

Mike was following Jacob's words carefully, thinking that this man made a lot of sense after all.

"And third, if you can start looking at how Craig and Steve handle conflict in the team from the perspective of **emotional process**, you will open up a whole new world of insights that will be invaluable to you as a leader.

"You characterize Craig as a self-starter and pretty independent. You like that in him and see the same characteristic in yourself, is that right?"

"Right there," said Mike.

"On the other hand, you see Steve as a worrier. Steve always seems anxious about his relationship with others and tries to make sure that everyone is happy, right?"

"Right again," Mike replied.

"And Steve sort of drives you nuts. You think he spends too much time worrying about his relationships with others and even the relationships between other team members?"

"You got it," Mike nodded.

Jacob went to the white board and drew a line as he began to talk. "Mike, here are some key ideas that will help you get a handle on what I mean by **emotional process**. When watching for **emotional process**, it is helpful to envision a continuum, a sort of line all people fit on. One end of the line represents the primal forces within us that drive us to be an independent self. These are the forces that underlie our individuality needs, which make us want to assert our independence. The other end of the line represents otherness forces, and these drive our need to be connected and in relationship."

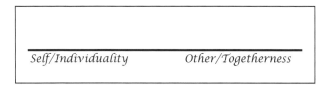

As he spoke, Jacob wrote the words "Self/Individuality" at one end and "Other/Togetherness" at the other. Mike was following intently, and asked, "So, then, which end is it better to be closer to? Or is the middle the only healthy place to be?"

Jacob responded, "It's not that simple, as if there's only one healthy tendency. Extremes are usually a problem, because they produce people who are pretty rigid. But we all have a place on the line that is where it feels natural for us to locate when things are peaceful in our life. That's the place we automatically go to because of a lot of factors. Much of it has to do with how we are raised. If we come from a family where everyone is sort of distant and disconnected from one another, where emotions are rarely shared, we learn at an early age that the world works best for us if we keep our distance and keep our feelings to ourselves. As a result, we wind up more towards the Self-Individuality end of the continuum. Other families are more open with their emotions and everyone is very close, constantly involved in one another's business and sharing one another's feelings. Those are the folks who are comfortable with a lot more togetherness, and they gravitate towards the other end of the line.

"Mike, here is the point: these tendencies are imprinted on each of us at an early age, and the result is that we end up taking our place somewhere along the continuum without even thinking about it. Our place on the line, so to speak, is the result of how **emotional process** operated in our family of origin, and those forces influence our behavior for the rest of our lives in powerful ways that we are usually completely unaware of. Another key point: The more anxious we become, the more we are inclined to move toward one or another of the extremes of the continuum, depending on which direction we tend to lean.

Mike answered with a surprised look on his face, "You got all that out of this one little e-mail exchange?"

"Well I have been watching and learning about human functioning for a long time. There is a good deal of research from Bowen Systems Theory behind my coaching process. When I talk about **Resilient Leadership** coaching, I'm drawing on and applying that research."

Jacob explained that Murray Bowen was a psychiatrist at the National Institutes of Mental Health and Georgetown University Medical School who did groundbreaking work for about forty years after World War II. Jacob regarded Bowen as a sort of a guru of his for many years, and Bowen's insights influenced Jacob's use of the **Resilient Leadership** model in his coaching.

Jacob paused to see if Mike was still with him. "But I see our time is almost up. Do you have energy for a few closing thoughts at this point, or have you had enough for today?"

"Sure, I'm still with you. Go ahead."

"Every person has a need to keep a healthy balance between those two primal forces for self and other. We all have a need both to be separate and to be in relationship. It is a universal law in nature that living beings are constantly balancing these two drives. Loss of a proper balance is a root cause of the various diseases and dysfunctions that threaten healthy life. Have you ever read what happens to infants if they are neglected in their cribs, never picked up and held?"

Mike nodded, "Yes, they don't develop normally. Babies need to be held."

"Right. Babies have a primal need for a certain level of 'togetherness'; they need to be physically close to others to survive. Or, here's another example: why do you think that penal institutions enforce solitary confinement as one of the ultimate forms of punishment? Because it deprives a person of the fundamental urge to be in relationship with others."

Mike was following intently now. "I get it. And for some people too much togetherness can be just as destructive as not enough. I'm thinking of my wife's sister Judy who is constantly 'smothering' her kids. She hovers over them and doesn't give them room to breathe. Karla and I have often said those kids are going to grow up as emotional cripples."

"You've got it, Mike. For us humans, too much togetherness is as toxic as not enough. Overcrowding in our cities gives rise to social problems that are like what we observe in the animal kingdom, when an entire species can suddenly collapse due to overpopulation. It appears that achieving a healthy balance between these two primal forces—self and other—is one of the fundamental challenges in the 'dance of life' at every level."

Jacob was energized, waving an arm to gesture at the white board. "So, here are some questions to think about: Where do you think Craig and Steve fall on the Self-Other continuum? And how do you need to deal with each of them? And how might you help them better manage their struggle to connect with each other, given the quite different comfort zones that they've had since childhood? And what about your own comfort zone? How does that fit in the mix?"

"Stop, stop. You're making my head hurt," Mike said, laughing. "I get the point. Well, I really haven't absorbed all of what you're talking about, but I'm beginning to recognize that there's a world of things to see out there that I've been pretty much tuned out to."

"I think we've covered a good bit of ground, so let's declare victory for today. Give me a call for another appointment after you've spoken with Vanessa."

Mike held up his cell phone and replied, "I'll look over this article you've given me, and I'll check out your website. By the way, Jacob, do you think I should reply to Craig and Steve's emails or not?"

Jacob smiled, pushed his wheelchair back and replied, "Well it all depends on what you SEE in your role as leader. Before we met today you would have automatically shot off a response right away. Now, we have created a space, a moment for you to pause, look more carefully at the issues, and think before you take action. Whatever you choose to do, you will be at least more thoughtful and self-aware."

Mike smiled and immediately knew what he was going to do.

They shook hands and Mike promised he would meet with Vanessa and then call Jacob back to set up the next visit.

Evening Reflection

Mike was excited by how much ground he had covered with Jacob, and he thought to himself, "This guy is on to something. He knows what he's talking about."

Karla was out with real-estate friends for dinner so Mike stopped off at a local restaurant. At home that night, he reached for the article Jacob had given him and began reading:

WHAT IS EMOTIONAL PROCESS?
by
JACOB WOLFE, PhD.

The notion of "Emotional Process" is a foundational concept in the **Resilient Leadership** model, borrowed from Bowen Systems Theory. The phrase refers to a level of functioning that is much deeper than we generally associate with the word "emotions" or feelings. Popular use understands the word "emotions" to refer to feelings such as fear, anger, erotic desire, and so forth. Although we are not always conscious of those feelings, in general they are accessible to our awareness if we focus and get in touch with them in a deliberate manner. "Emotional Process," on the other hand, while including the realm of feelings, refers also to dimensions of our makeup that are too deep for conscious awareness.

The following image may be helpful in illustrating this fuller sense of the phrase "Emotional Process" as it is used in Bowen Theory and in the context of the **Resilient Leadership** model.

Prior to the advent of diving equipment and other modern technologies, a person who saw the ocean had little ability to grasp its true depth and the complexity of the forces that lie beneath its surface. On a calm day, the sea could appear to pre-modern people as peaceful as any shallow pool of water. There was simply no way of understanding the incredible depths of the ocean, nor the vast currents of water, some warmer and some cooler, which swirl in regular patterns beneath its surface. The teeming life forms beneath the surface were only hinted at in miniscule fashion when fishermen hauled in their nets. From time to time a naïve observer would, of course, see how the calm seas can erupt with ferocious waves that reach unimaginable heights and that crash against the shore with thundering force. And a hint of the vast complexity that lies beneath the surface might also dawn on a swimmer caught in a rip tide or other fast-moving current.

The term "Emotional Process" can be compared to the vastness of the ocean itself, with all of its mysterious, hidden depths that an unsuspecting observer might easily miss. The waves that appear on the ocean's surface are like surges of emotion, feelings that only occasionally become the object of our conscious awareness. Sailing across gentle seas, we can become so accustomed to the steady rhythm of the waves that we are oblivious to the way they push our boat up and down. But a rising wind that churns up greater turbulence, or a sudden realization that a current has gradually pulled us off course, alerts the sailor in us to focus attention on those familiar forces to which we had become oblivious.

In a similar way, our feeling states are most often not the object of our conscious awareness, although at some level we realize how they lift and lower us as we float along life's currents. It is usually only when they reach the level of more pronounced waves (of anger, love, sadness) that we attend to them in a focused way. Rarely, however, especially when we are caught in the grip of a period of turbulence, do we stop to remember that the waves are only surface phenomena, and that vast, complex forces lie beneath the waves. Rarely in times of high anxiety and increased reactivity do we remember that to grasp the full significance of those threatening waves we need to understand much more about the depths of the ocean itself.

Ancient mariners came to realize that a boat that appears to be rowed on a straight course can actually be drifting far astray on an ocean current. The best captains were those who became aware of the complexity of the many different, often unseen, forces at work (wind and waves, tides and currents, influencing the course the helmsman was steering) as the ship traversed the ocean. In much the same way, the best leaders today are those who recognize how much people and the organizations they form are being driven by the deeper forces of Emotional Process, not just by the surface winds of a feeling response to the latest change initiative or the anxiety provoked by stormy waves of marketplace competition. The same applies to the leader's own functioning.

Another way of thinking about Emotional Process is that it is an expression of instinctual behavior that we share in common with other living creatures. Just as animal behaviors are driven by instinct rather than the sort of higher cognition we possess, so a good bit of our ways of acting are more instinct-driven than thoughtfully chosen. A friend recently described in glowing terms a two-week vacation on a game preserve in the Serengeti, and how much he and his wife had learned about animal behavior thanks to the privileged, close-up look that their guides had made possible. One of their most striking memories was a scene that unfolded on their last day in Africa, as the afternoon sun was setting. A herd of elephants had come to a river for water, when they suddenly realized the presence of lions on a far opposite hilltop. There was no possibility the lions would be able to cross the river and threaten the herd, but instinctively the female elephants made a protective circle around their young calves and headed for safety in the opposite direction. As the herd lumbered off, a single old female took up a position at the rear and walked away backwards (!), never losing sight of the perceived threat from the lions. What they saw gave new meaning to the military term "a rear guard action," and it left my friends with a lasting appreciation for how much we share in common with other life forms. Instinctive behavior—

rooted in Emotional Process—is deeply embedded in us all and exerts a much more powerful influence on our behaviors than we imagine.

Mike put down Jacob's article and decided to make his evening notes before Karla came home.

Today
- *Craig and Steve need to work things out themselves but I can help by clarifying expectations*
- *Think about self-other continuum and comfort zones*
- *My self-awareness is lower than it should be—what does that mean?*

Issues
- *Jacob is a strong coach—emotional process (EP) makes sense—an important idea.*
- *EP is instinctual, not malicious by nature.*
- *Watch for EP in myself and others.*
- *Is Jacob's coaching really what I need to become a COO candidate?*

Follow up
- *Set up meeting with Vanessa to talk about coaching.*
- *Call Sally to reschedule Boston visit.*
- *Call Richard.*
- *Think about this: "Watch for emotional process—below conscious awareness, imprinted from childhood, impacts all social contacts. Think in terms of relationship systems."*

Karla came home from dinner at about 10:00 and was eager to know how the day went and in particular how the visit with Jacob came out.

"It went very well," Mike told her. Jacob is an interesting

person and he has a lot to offer, but sometimes he sounds a lot like a professor lecturing his students."

"So, will you be going back?" she asked.

"Absolutely," Mike replied. "We will be meeting every week, more or less, for the next few months. If I can make it through all of his jargon, he's got a lot to teach me. I'd like to gather my thoughts over the next day or two and then talk to you about my conversation with him."

Karla got the signal and knew it was better to wait until Mike was ready to talk. She had learned that pushing him to communicate before he was ready never worked well. She smiled and began to get ready for bed.

Mike had grown to appreciate Karla's ability to be patient with things; it was an attribute he admired in her because he knew how impatient he could be. He was not ready to go over everything with her yet while the ideas were jumbled in his head, and he needed to sleep on the day's activities and discussions to better organize his thinking.

A NEW WAY OF SEEING

Chapter 1: Watch for Emotional Process

Review Key Points

- Knowing what to pay attention to is a key leadership competency.
  - **Emotional process** should be a primary focus of a resilient leader's vision.

- **Emotional process** is about more than feelings. It has to do with all of the life forces we share in common with other living beings.

- **Emotional process** frequently operates too deeply for conscious awareness.
  - **Emotional process** is instinctual, reflexive.

- **Emotional process** influences a leader's functioning in powerful ways.
  - **Emotional process** also influences entire relationship networks (families, organizations).

Questions for Reflection and Discussion

1. When she confronted Mike in her office, Vanessa told him that he had "zero self-awareness" and that his style of management was "destroying careers and hammering the culture of CHI." Mike apparently does not recognize any of this about himself. What clues have you picked up on at this point in the story that indicate Vanessa is correct about Mike—that he is unaware of the extent to which **emotional process** forces are driving his behaviors in ways that are destructive?

2. In your workplace, how aware do you think the leadership is of this dimension of human functioning and its impact on the organization's effectiveness? Why do you think that?

3. How much awareness do you have, in general, of the influence that **emotional process** has on your behavior? Can you identify some recent examples of this?

The Practice

Self-awareness occurs when we are intensely present in the moments of our life. When we are aware at this level we become the "watcher" rather than the "doer," and our ego involvement is diminished. Experiencing life at this level of engagement requires us to be of two minds at the same time—"the engaged mind" and the "witnessing presence." At home and at work, begin the practice of witnessing key moments of your life at the same time that you engaged in these moments. Become a present, witnessing awareness. Go up "in the tree" to observe yourself and others that you come in contact with by envisioning yourself on an imaginary tree watching the interchanges that you are having with others. Watch the way in which you are connecting with others at the level of **emotional process** by "seeing" your reality from the point of view of a neutral observer.

1. Anticipate a situation that will potentially trigger an emotional response.

2. Get "up in the tree" to envision yourself as both a participant in the situation and an observer of the situation.

3. Identify "my responsibility" during this encounter.

4. Write a "script" that will help you to manage the emotional dynamics of the situation better.

A New Way of Seeing

Watch for Emotional Process

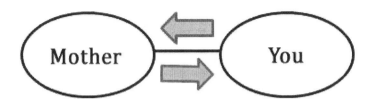

Set boundaries related to advice on taking care of teenage son.

Practice Steps	Events and My Reaction
1. Anticipate the situation.	1. Mom will criticize the way I am raising my son.
2. Get "up in the tree": Observe the situation.	2. *My viewpoint:* defensive, resentful of her input, closed to her suggestions. 2. *Her viewpoint:* eager to help, convinced she knows the answers, cares about both me and my son. 2. *Our interaction:* both getting more frustrated, "up tight" and angry with each other.
3. Identify my responsibility.	3. I can set boundaries she respects without her feeling excluded and hurt; both of us agree that what matters is whatever is best for my son.
4. Write a better script I can use.	4. Mom, I really appreciate your concern about my relationship with my son, but it makes me defensive when you are always offering suggestions that feel like criticisms. I promise to ask your advice when I need it if you'll promise to wait until I ask before offering it.

To learn more, go to www.resilient-leadership.biz.

A New Way of **SEEING**

Chapter 2: Self-Other Forces

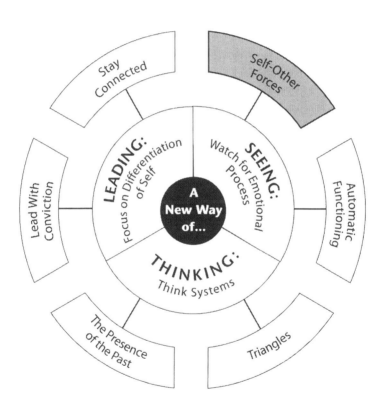

Fast Start

Tuesday morning came quickly. Mike was up at 5:00 a.m., back from the gym by 6:15, headed for the office at 7:00, leaving messages for Sally, Vanessa and Crystal between 7:30 and 8:00, and finally looking at the work for the week at 8:15.

While sitting at his desk, he got a return call from Vanessa.

"I can meet with you this afternoon at 3:00 p.m.," she said.

"That is great," said Mike. "I need to go over a few issues with you and get your input on a few personnel decisions I want to make."

"Okay, anything else?"

"Well, I had my first visit with Jacob Wolfe, and I would like to update you on that meeting and discuss a few of the ideas he presented to me."

"Sure, see you at 3:00. Oh, by the way, Mike. We need to meet with James soon. I will set up that meeting. Are you in town for the remainder of this week?"

"Yes, I am around all week, but I am planning to return to Boston next week if possible."

Vanessa replied, "I'll set up a 30 minute meeting with the three of us this week if his schedule permits."

"Great, see you this afternoon." Mike hung up the phone.

His views about the meeting with Vanessa and Jacob had taken a dramatic turn in the last three days. After his session with Jacob, he was beginning to understand more about what was behind Vanessa's self-awareness comment. He was beginning to wonder about the ways that **emotional process** forces were driving his own functioning, and the extent to which he had been blind to those influences.

"Maybe she really is going to give me a shot at the COO position," he thought.

Just then Crystal whizzed by Mike's door. "Hi, boss," she said as she headed for her desk to pick up messages and get started for the day. Mike knew that she would be listening to his early morning message in the next few minutes.

Sally called from Boston and Crystal put her call right through to Mike.

"Hello, Sally."

"Hi, Mike. Did you have a safe trip back to DC?"

"I did. Sorry again for running out on you last week."

"No problem, Mike. So, I know that you want to review last period's performance for this region, and I am ready to do that whenever you are."

The pair chatted for a few more moments, discussing the possibility of meeting in Boston the following week. Mike agreed to let Sally know by Thursday what days would work best for him.

Sally ended the call with a heavy dose of anxiety at the prospect of dealing with Mike for two whole days next week. Her area had tanked last period and the weekly flash report had not alerted her to the area's mid-week occupancy challenges. She also intended to support her general manager at Newton, Paul Brady, even though Mike was clearly gunning to get him replaced.

Crystal stuck her head in the door to Mike's office. "I got your voicemail about the annual conference in July. As I recall, this is a huge undertaking. Do you want to begin planning this soon?"

"Yes, we need to get going on the conference. We need to check the availability of Vanessa and James for the middle two weeks of July," Mike said.

"Mike, don't forget that July is a really big vacation month for many people. If you call a division-wide conference in July, you are going to make a lot of people unhappy," Crystal reminded him.

"That is a good point. Let me think about this a little more before we take any action. I have a meeting with Vanessa today at 3:00 p.m., and I will talk about timing with her."

"One more thing, Mike. Don't forget this Saturday. Saturday is April 19th."

Mike thought a moment: Karla's birthday. "Crystal, you deserve a raise! I don't know how many times a year you save me from certain disaster!"

Crystal just smiled and said, "Also don't forget what May 9th is, either."

Mike also knew that date: Crystal's birthday.

Vanessa

At 3:00 p.m., Mike went to Vanessa's office. She was waiting for him and was in good spirits.

"Hello, Mike," she said with her warm smile.

"Hi, Vanessa," Mike said as he realized that he didn't really know how to start a conversation about their last meeting.

Vanessa instinctively knew that they needed to go back to the last meeting and pick things up from that point. But she also recalled that Mike wanted to review some business and personnel topics.

"Where do you want to begin?" she asked.

Mike knew that he would not be able to concentrate on his business issues unless he first dealt with their last meeting.

"Let's go back to our last meeting for a moment," Mike said.

"Those 30 minutes last week were some of the most difficult and disappointing moments of my life. I felt betrayed by you and extremely embarrassed by your comments."

Vanessa did not react at all.

"After the meeting, Jacob and I continued our discussion for a few minutes and then he left. I found myself going over and over the meeting in my mind for the whole weekend.

"But before Jacob left on Friday, he went on to say that in his opinion, you took the steps to confront me and involve him because you felt I have what it takes to rise to the challenge. But it sure didn't feel that way."

Vanessa still did not react.

"Well," Mike asked, "Is he right?"

Vanessa stood up and walked to her window. She could see the faint outline of the Blue Ridge on the crisp April morning.

"About ten years ago I was running the Northwest Region working out of San Francisco. The region had grown substantially over the past few years, and I had been credited with much of the success. All the performance indicators were strong and had been strong for several years. The economy was booming, but I was sure my own performance was the central reason for our success. Later I realized I was a very small part of the success we enjoyed in the region.

"The company had grown to the point that James could not effectively handle all of the responsibilities of running the business. The time for establishing the COO position had arrived.

"I was at the top of my game. I thought I was the best of the best. I was 34 years old.

"One of my areas, Denver metro, began to lose market share

both in the transient and contract markets at the same time. The area vice president, Bob Henry, was a veteran and had 20 years on me. He had years of experience and knew how to get through market downturns.

"I began to work with him on a number of improvement steps, but we didn't work together well at all. To make a long story short, I ended up forcing his retirement before he wanted to retire and before we made the changes we needed to make in Denver. I was convinced that Bob was just a tired, worn-out hotel man who was not keeping up with the innovations needed in the business.

"Bob was professional and a gentleman all the way through the process. He left with grace and dignity. It was one of the worst management decisions I have ever made. Later I realized why.

"Bob's idea was to reinvest in the Denver market to bring back business through new value creation. His idea was to work through the downturn by investing in the business. He wanted to spend more money on staff, training, soft goods replacement, guestroom redos, et cetera. The list was extensive.

"I was not willing to wait that long or spend that kind of money. I wanted a quick performance turnaround. I wanted to cut operational overhead and get expenses in line right away. We had several meetings to discuss these two approaches, and in the end I decided that Bob had to go.

"A few months later, I finally realized that the differences Bob and I had were about leadership. Bob was exercising effective leadership in the situation; I was the boss and had the power, but I was a pretty poor leader."

Vanessa turned from the window and looked directly at Mike.

"Bob was interested in providing service and value to CHI customers. Bob was interested in the customer.

"I was interested in pleasing Mr. McMaster by making money for CHI. I was really interested in me—in my track record and looking good.

"Back then I did not consciously know this because I was so sure of myself. I saw things from my own point of view. I knew that I was right."

Vanessa walked over to her chair and sat down.

"But did the Denver area turn around?" Mike wanted to know.

"That depends on how you look at it. We made short-term

financial improvements right away. Then we lost even more market share. I blamed our poor performance on an over-built market; too many hotels and too few customers. I blamed Sheraton, Westin and Marriott for saturating the Denver metro area. But the truth is we lost market share because we had an inferior product at our price point. We were not competitive on customer value."

Mike leaned back in his chair and thought about Paul Brady, the Boston market and his conversation last week in the car with Sally.

Vanessa interrupted his reverie, "I'll bet you're wondering what all this has to do with you—and Jacob."

"You're right, and how did you meet up with Jacob Wolfe?" Mike asked.

"Same way you did, about eight years ago." Vanessa replied.

"I will never forget it. James flew me in from San Francisco for an evening dinner with him and his wife, Helen. At dinner that night I spent the whole evening telling James and Helen all about my accomplishments and experiences. They were very pleasant and very respectful."

Vanessa paused and looked past Mike into the wall as she recalled that evening.

"I acted like an ass."

"The next morning, James invited me into his office right over there." Vanessa gestured to the office across the hall.

"James introduced me to Jacob; the two of them knew each other from their college days. Then James told me that he was taking me out of the Northwest Region job and either promoting me to COO or asking me to leave the company. He had developed a plan for me to work out of DC in finance and marketing for about six months each and then he would decide one way or another.

"After that news, James told me why he was making the move. Without going into all the details, Mr. McMaster told me just about the same thing I told you last week.

"He gave me the evening to think things over. My choices were to relocate to DC and begin a one-year program of executive development and coaching with Jacob or leave the company immediately. There was no guarantee that I would be placed at the end of the year.

"I decided to stay. Then I began one of the most difficult and rewarding years of my life.

"I learned how to look at the company from a national and corporate level in the financial and marketing fields. I learned that my view of business and in fact my view of life was filtered through a very narrow, clouded and judgmental lens.

"I learned a lot technically. But my most significant learning was about myself. I expanded my level of awareness. I began to learn about my reactivity and with Jacob's coaching help I began to see, think and act in very different ways."

Mike was totally silent. He thought about **emotional process** and was beginning to realize that he, too, looked at life through a narrow lens. He was trying to absorb all of this information when Helen knocked on Vanessa's door to ask if James could join them.

"Is it okay with you, Mike?" Vanessa asked.

"Sure," Mike replied.

Vanessa told Helen to let James know that they were ready any time. Helen closed the door.

"Vanessa, I am still a little confused," Mike interjected. "I don't know if I am a candidate for the COO post or not."

"Let's wait until James arrives and talk about the situation," Vanessa replied and suggested a short break.

JAMES MCMASTER

About ten minutes later, all three were reassembled in Vanessa's office. She began, "Mr. McMaster, Mike and I are having our first follow-up meeting since last week's introduction to Jacob Wolfe."

McMaster responded, "I'm glad that you have Jake involved. Mike, have you met with him in a one-on-one coaching session yet?"

"I sure have. We met yesterday."

"I have the utmost respect for Jake and his work." McMaster went on, "Vanessa thought that the two of you should spend some time together. I think that you can learn a lot from him; I know I have.

"Mike, I am hoping that we can talk about your interest in becoming a candidate to replace Vanessa when the time is right. Of course, we will be considering other candidates as well, but we think you are a strong contender."

"Vanessa suggested that we start the in-depth interviewing

in June, and I am really looking forward to getting started." With that, James stood up, shook Mike's hand and left the room.

Mike suddenly realized that Vanessa had not shared with James her views of his shortcomings as a COO candidate. While she had "laid him out straight" in the meeting last week with Jacob, it was clear that she had not yet shared her concerns with James. She actually had cleared a pathway for him to become a viable candidate.

As soon as the door closed, Vanessa began. "Mike, last week, I told you that you had what it takes to lead this organization technically, but that you do not have some critical leadership characteristics needed to lead the business. In simple terms, there is a big difference between leading people and driving people – that difference is what you need to learn."

"In the next few months, you will have the chance to see the difference as you apply what Jacob and I can help you learn."

Mike asked, "Can you tell me some of the things you learned from Jacob?"

Vanessa explained that Jacob helped her to discover that developing the required skills to lead CHI required an understanding of how to manage the balance between what Jacob calls "**self-other forces**." With Jacob's guidance, Vanessa's awareness developed gradually as she became more and more attentive to her own functioning. Becoming more aware of her own functioning gave her firsthand sensitivity to the subtleties of **emotional process**, both in herself and in others.

"But developing my ability to see in this new way took me a lot of time and patience," she continued. "I found that I am caught up so easily in my own stuff that the discipline of becoming more self-aware only came about very slowly."

Mike injected, "I am already beginning to see the need to be more self-aware. I've been thinking through my visit last week in Boston."

Vanessa nodded and continued, "Another thing I discovered is that while Jacob is a wonderful teacher, my real learning happened with my family—by paying more attention to those relationships. And I don't mean just Bill and the kids, but my relationships with my Dad and my sisters. You know how challenging those relationships have been for me over the years."

Mike acknowledged, "Yeah, I remember you had some pretty rough times with them after your mom died."

A New Way of Seeing

Vanessa continued, telling Mike she discovered that the more aware she became of how her family relationships are a constant balancing act between getting too close and too distant, the more she began to see those same things playing out at CHI, with various people and even with the entire organization.

"Taking a clear stand here at work, I discovered, is usually a lot easier than being a 'self' in family relationships that carry so much more baggage. But the work Jacob did with me here at CHI helped me at home, for sure.

"You know, we like to think that at work we operate in a professional manner quite differently than how we do in our sometimes 'messy' personal lives. But on the level of those primal forces where **emotional process** operates, we're pretty much consistent in every setting, and the gains we make in one area spill over into the other."

Mike could hear the impact that Jacob had had on Vanessa's thinking as he listened to her ideas and saw the similarity in their language. He began to think about the challenge he was facing with Jacelyn and Russ. He also recognized that how he chose to resolve this challenge would have a very significant impact on his relationship with Karla.

"As you continue your work with Jacob, he will begin to explore what he calls 'A New Way of SEEING.' This is a very subtle skill to develop. But it pays big dividends, believe me. Not only is each of us as an individual constantly trying to manage the balance between being too close or too distant in our key relationships; CHI itself is a network of relationships that is also constantly seeking to find its own balance.

"The whole company is like a big family that has its own unique comfort zone and that has its own way of functioning that seems 'natural' to it. It's much deeper than what is sometimes called our 'organizational culture,' though that's certainly a place where the signs of **emotional process** and **automatic functioning** show up regularly. Once you begin to see how those forces are influencing the entire CHI organization, you will be able to lead in an entirely different way."

Mike began to think about the relationships in his division and how the cliques and separations between some of his team members were setting the tone for much that was going on between his operating and support staff members. He wondered what influence his own way of functioning had on those who worked for him.

"Mike, one of the things a leader needs to do is be aware of how far off center—how unbalanced—the organization is getting during times when there is lots of stress and anxiety floating around. Whenever people are feeling particularly anxious, you can observe certain behaviors that will tip you off that the balance is getting out of whack."

Mike needed some clarity. "Just how does a leader recognize that an organization is moving too far toward one extreme or the other?"

Vanessa continued, "During the time that I worked with Jacob, I developed a list of things to look for that I can share with you. These are some of the ways that what Jacob calls **self-other forces** can be spotted at work in an organization." Vanessa opened up her laptop and pulled up a file. She printed a copy and handed the first page to Mike to read:

Patterns

Here are some of the patterns that are signs that people are getting anxious and moving toward too much togetherness:

- People get overly interested or involved in what others are doing, sticking their noses in where they don't belong.
- Big waves of emotion ripple through the organization at the speed of light on subjects such as business downturns, an unexpected termination, layoffs, a hotel being sold or bought, etc.
- Outrage erupts over bad news in a distant part of the organization, despondency over the fate of someone judged as treated unfairly, fear of reprisals or layoffs generated by the rumor mill, etc.
- Too much gossip occurs at the water cooler or copy machine, buzzing over the latest events of the moment.
- The use of sick leave suddenly escalates, as people's stress levels are manifested in more physical illnesses.
- Too much drama surfaces over a perceived slight or

injury, especially when it leads some people to feel as keenly about the problem as if it had happened to them.
- There is too much e-mail traffic about a trivial event, with others adding views in a running "blog type" dialogue.
- People try to explore challenges and solve problems by overusing "focus group" discussion sessions, doing more and more market surveys, and generally piling up more and more data.

Vanessa gave Mike a few moments to read over the list. "Does any of that sound familiar?"

"Wow! It sure does. How did you put all of that together?"

"My list keeps growing. Every now and then I add another item to it as I see more clearly the presence of **emotional process** surfacing in the interplay of **self-other forces**. Here is a list of some behavior patterns that I've observed as people express their anxiety by pushing the organizational balance toward being too distant." She handed him the second sheet:

- Withdrawal of groups or individuals from open communication with others in the organization.
- People focus on "distractions" that are actually avoidance mechanisms.
- Empty chatter without substance proliferates so that the real issues are not faced.
- Targeting certain (usually difficult) people for cutoffs, and justifying those actions by placing the blame on them.
- Immersion in tasks/busy work to an extent that precludes routine interactions with the rest of the team/organization.
- People stop answering email or telephone messages or delay their responses for an excessive amount of time.
- Messages between people get distorted; folks just can't seem to "hear" one another easily or accurately.
- Disruptive tactics (e.g., changing the subject or becoming argumentative) when the conversation becomes too sensitive.
- Missed appointments (e.g., forgetting to put them on the

calendar, double scheduling so meetings can't be made).
- "Managing" the boss or the situation by withholding information that might provoke a reactive response.

"Quite a list, don't you think?"

As Mike took in the significance of Vanessa's lists, the impact and reach of her "seeing" tools began to dawn on him. He felt both confused and excited.

"How do you hold all of this in your mind?" he asked.

"I don't hold it consciously in my mind now, because it has become second nature. But in the beginning, I had to make lists to remind myself what to look for. Then I'd go back through situations after they occurred to see what I'd missed. It takes a while.

"But here is a helpful way to think about it: Practice being in two places in your mind at the same time during the events of your day. In other words, be inside the events of your life and, at the same time, be outside in a more objective place, watching the events unfold.

"Imagine being up in a tree looking down on yourself to 'see' the situation from a more objective and removed point of view. And as you look down, pay particular attention to the ways that **emotional process** seems to be surfacing in you and in the behaviors of people around you."

"I can see that I have some homework here," Mike commented, looking overwhelmed.

Vanessa said, "Here is a piece of advice: Begin learning to observe with family issues, because that's where these things tend to surface more clearly. As you deal with interactions involving family members, you will quickly spot your own **automatic functioning**, how those primal **self-other forces** result in excessive expressions of togetherness or separateness.

"Take a trip up the imaginary tree and look down on your family system. Look down on the interactions among your family members and yourself to see what you can observe. Once you start looking, you'll see things all over the place and wonder why you never saw it all before."

Mike's thoughts flashed back to his conversation with Jacelyn in Boston—how she had hung up on him, and how he had avoided calling her back for days. He remembered the struggle between him and Karla to communicate over the years when they were at odds—how both of them tended to withdraw rather than keep working at communicating.

Vanessa stopped and checked her watch. "Mike, I need to either reschedule my next appointment now so we can continue or get back to you on the other business topics you wanted to discuss with me."

"Let's reschedule," Mike said. The topics were not time sensitive, and he had a lot to think about before he brought up the problems at the Newton hotel.

As Mike stood up and walked out, he stopped at Vanessa's doorway and thanked her for all that she had done to give him a shot at the next post.

His thoughts jumped to Steve Alba, his most likely internal competitor for the COO position. Both of them were very talented. Steve was definitely more well-liked in the business. Mike wanted to know if Steve was getting coaching from Jacob or someone else, but he decided not to ask.

He went to his office and packed up his materials for the day to get ready to head home. He recognized that it was now well past time to talk with Jacelyn and Russ and catch up with Karla about what he was learning from Jacob.

Karla and Mike

When Mike met Karla Bennett, she was Sister Karla, a Catholic nun in the last stages of her novitiate, a period when aspiring candidates decide if they should take their lifelong vows. Having been in the convent for nearly six years, twenty-three-year-old Karla had, at an early age, done more than her share of interior reflection; at the same time, a rather sheltered life that was part of her Catholic upbringing, plus her time in the convent, resulted in her being relatively immature in the world of intimate relationships. Mike was attracted to her like a magnet. He set his sights on courting her, and he pursued her with a single-minded focus. Over the course of the next two years, Karla decided to leave the convent, married Mike, and conceived their first child, Jacelyn.

Mike had an idealized image of Karla from their very first meeting, and for Karla the world of courtship was wondrous and magical. The sobering realities of marriage and parenthood took them both by surprise. Not unlike many young couples, the challenge of developing their own relationship in the midst of learning how to raise a child resulted in a measure of growing pains. The first years tested their marriage, but Karla's strong and determined commitment to family and Christian values guided them through those difficult, early times.

Mike went out into the business world determined to make a living for his family. Karla was his anchor, a stay-at-home mom dedicated to home and family. Despite a quick temper and a stubborn streak of her own, she always supported Mike in his career moves, and she managed to see to it that the stresses in the marriage never went unattended for too long.

Mike had really wanted a son as a first-born, but when Jacelyn came along he discovered a capacity for love within himself that took him by surprise. He knew that he wanted more children; and two years after Jacelyn was born, Richard arrived. The birth of their second child involved a very difficult pregnancy and delivery for Karla, and it was clear that the Sampson family was now complete.

Mike was away from home a great deal in the early years of their marriage. His various jobs with Clearview Hotels required night and weekend work as he moved up the ranks from one position to another. Then extensive travel began as he was promoted into positions of greater responsibility, first for a district and then a division of hotels. Steady salary and expense increases always drove him to strive for the next career opportunity. Now, after 26 years, he found himself and one other CHI employee, Steve Alba, as well as two outside hires, competing for the most senior position in the company next to James. Mike really loved his job, and he loved Clearview Hotels. In fact, he often defined himself more in terms of the job than in terms of his family.

The huge ego that had emerged over the course of his successful career had produced a real problem, both for Mike and for CHI. His ambition and the affirmation he received for his successes at CHI had created one of the smartest, most experienced operators in the company—and one who was also an arrogant, self-serving autocrat whom most people feared. Karla had learned to live with the toll that ego took at home, but not infrequently her own strong-willed side resulted in an explosive clash of wills. On those occasions, Mike never won the battle.

Now, Mike's career was threatened at the very moment he was reaching the top of his profession. He recognized that he was at a crossroads, and he was very glad he had met Jacob Wolfe.

Jacelyn

Mike knew he needed to call his daughter to continue or maybe restart their last conversation. It was early Thursday evening, and he decided to check with Karla before calling Jacelyn back. On the way home he reached Karla on her cell phone.

"Hello Beauty," Mike opened. "I need to call Jacelyn back, and I wondered if you have spoken to her in the last few hours."

"She calls me three or four times a day; I spoke to her 15 minutes ago," Karla answered with a crisp edge in her voice.

"She and Russ are looking at places to go for a honeymoon and wanted some advice. I know that she would love to talk with you about hotel and flight arrangements, if you're not too busy."

"Well, why doesn't she call me then?" Mike snapped.

Karla did not respond.

"I will give her a call in the next few minutes," Mike continued, knowing his conversation with Karla was on thin ice.

"I am sure she would love to talk with you, I know she misses you." Then Karla continued in a more conciliatory tone, "Honey, before you give her a call, I suggest that you check on your own emotions and be in the right frame of mind. I know you want the next call to bring you and her a step or two closer together. Are you ready to give her a call now, do you think?"

Mike knew he wasn't ready, but said the exact opposite. "I don't have all day to deal with her moods. I will give her a call, and we can work things out now!" Mike declared.

Karla was silent for a moment, just the right length of time. Then, controlling an urge to lash out at his stupidity, she said, "I know you will do the right thing, Honey. I will see you after my next showing. I'll be home at about 6:30 or so. I love you, Sweetheart."

"I love you too, Beauty." Mike pressed the end button on his cell phone and proceeded to drive home much too fast for the speed limit. He pulled into his circular driveway, popped open his cell phone and pulled up his notes from the previous evening.

Watch for emotional process—often below conscious awareness, imprinted from childhood, impacts all social contacts, Think in terms of social systems

A few minutes ago Mike knew that he was not ready to call Jacelyn. He could sense it, but he did not know why. Now it was written in front of him, in words he had created for himself — **emotional process**. He decided to go for a run.

The Call

After the run, Mike showered and checked his phone and text messages. Nothing urgent had come in. It was time to call Jacelyn.
"Hello, Jacelyn, how are you doing?"
"Fine, Dad, how are you, how is work?"
"Work is great; it is a good year for the most part. Listen, Honey, I want to apologize for my remarks last time we spoke. The conversation has bothered me a lot and I know that I was reacting to your call in the wrong way. I know that you are old enough to know what you want in your life, and I need to do a better job in letting go. I just love you so much and want you to be happy."
Mike wanted to get to the end of his comment to hear how Jacelyn was going to react.
"Dad, I know that you love me and that you mean well, but I am ready to make up my own mind on things. Russ and I are making plans for the upcoming wedding, and I want you and Mom to be a big part of it."
Just then, Mike sensed resentment swell up in his throat—resentment of Russ. For one of the first times in a long while, Mike caught himself before he spit out a response. It was very difficult for him, but he took a deep breath before responding.
"Honey, what can I do to be helpful to you?" Mike slowly replied.
"Dad, Russ and I need help in finding a suitable place for a

honeymoon," she said. "And I want you and Russ to get along better somehow. Sometimes it seems that you deliberately say things or do things to make me think that Russ is not a good choice for a mate. When you do that, it hurts me a lot and makes me very angry." Her voice cracked as she struggled to maintain herself.

Mike felt ashamed. He had been really hard on Russ and knew it. Here was his darling daughter, asking him to be less of a jerk to the guy she was going to marry. No one, not even Karla, could get to Mike like Jacelyn. When his daughter got emotional, Mike nearly always melted. The thick-skinned businessman was nowhere to be found. He had often wondered about this reaction in himself. It was not the same with Richard. The only other person who had this impact on him had been his own mother.

Mike said, "Of course I will help you, Honey. Do you have any ideas about where you want to go?"

"Someplace warm, with a beautiful beach," Jacelyn replied.

Mike said, "I will dig up some information on our hotels and other options and give you a call back. When are you, I mean when are you and Russ coming back to DC?"

"We will be coming home in about three weeks. Russ has a job interview with the US Customs Authority there in DC somewhere."

"Is the opportunity for a position there in Florida?"

"Actually Customs is hiring people for several locations, so we have no idea where this might lead. It's kind of exciting."

"Okay, Honey. I will look up some information about resort destinations here and in Central America and get back to you in a day or so," Mike said. "I promise you that I will work on my attitude about both Russ and your marriage. I love you, Honey."

"I love you too, Dad," she said with a level of joy in her voice that made Mike's throat swell for a moment.

Mike hung up the phone and looked around the house for Karla who was downstairs in the den reading the newspaper and waiting for a call from another sales agent with her real estate firm.

After the Call

"Hey, Beauty, I just talked with Jacelyn. We had a good conversation," Mike started.

"How was she?" Karla asked.

"Great, as always. She and I talked about our last conversation. I hurt her feelings a lot with the comments I made about Russ, and I apologized for my reactions. We did not discuss the wedding very much, but she did ask me to help her and Russ with plans for their honeymoon. I am going to look for locations in California and down in Costa Rica as well.

"She also said that she and Russ are coming up here in about three weeks. Russ has a job interview."

"Yes, she has been talking to me about their trip to DC, too," Karla said. "I am glad to know that you and she are talking again. I get really unsettled when I know the two of you are not hitting it off."

"You make it sound like it happens all the time—like Jacelyn and I are arguing a lot," Mike said.

"The two of you are very much alike, Honey. I get caught in the middle a lot." Karla smiled as she flipped a page of the paper.

"What do you mean, you get 'caught in the middle' a lot?" Mike shot back. He was getting defensive.

"When you and Jacelyn have a difficult conversation or you don't think she is doing things or making decisions the way she should, you complain to me. She does the same thing," Karla said.

"So, you don't want me to talk to you about the way I feel about our daughter?" Mike asked sarcastically.

Karla stopped reading the paper, quietly and neatly folded it, laid it on her lap and gave Mike a cold stare that he knew meant trouble. He regretted his sarcasm immediately. "Mike, I can sense by your tone that you are starting to get angry with me. All I am saying is this: When either you or Jacelyn have an issue with each other, one or both of you come to me to talk about the situation. Much of the time one of you is asking me to take their side in the argument. I don't want to take sides in an argument between my husband and my daughter. It's not fair to me."

"Fine, just fine, I will keep it all to myself," Mike shouted as he walked away.

After a few minutes to cool down in the kitchen, he walked back into the den. "I'm sorry that I blew up again," Mike said. "I guess I'm still dealing with all the changes that are going to take place in our family in the next six months or so."

"Mike, maybe you can talk some of this over with your coach," Karla offered.

"Well, both Jacob and Vanessa have mentioned that I need to work on my behaviors when I get agitated. They both have said that the work I do in my family will pay dividends at CHI as well. But I was warned that doing the family work can be even more challenging than making improvements in the office. I guess I owe it to you to try to make improvements at home as well."

Karla smiled slightly and asked, "Just what are you supposed to do differently?"

"Well, I get caught up in what Jacob calls **automatic functioning**. It's sort of like a survival mechanism when I am under pressure. All people do this sometimes. We have this instinctual side to us—it's the product of evolution or something like that—and sometimes we act out of that part of our brain without thinking. Jacob has said I need to watch out for when I'm on autopilot and reacting without really thinking. He describes it as my feelings hijacking my ability to think clearly."

"That's very interesting," Karla said softly. "What else did Jacob say about it?"

"Well, he said that there are certain behavior patterns that you can learn to spot that tell you when you're acting more from reactive functioning than from thoughtfulness."

"Like what?"

"Like, there's a continuum in our relationships, and it runs from an extreme of being too independent and separate from others to another extreme of being emotionally fused with others—too much togetherness." Mike walked from one end of the den to the other, making an imaginary line as if he were sliding his hand along a clothes line.

He turned to Karla, "Families, work teams and even whole organizations fall into familiar patterns in how they relate to one another. It's like they form a culture in which a certain point on this continuum seems normal and comfortable. But when we're stressed, we tend to move toward one or other of the extremes.

"So, when I get irritated and walk away from a conversation with you like just now, I am moving my position on the continuum toward more separateness. It's how I automatically handle stress—by distancing myself. At the extreme end of the continuum is what's called a cutoff."

"You mean like your cousin Don and you haven't spoken in years—since the argument over your dad's loan to him?"

"That bastard is not worth connecting with," Mike said emphatically.

Karla realized that she had touched a hot button and perhaps gone too far. She recovered quickly and said, "So, tell me more about this separateness and togetherness thing. It sounds fascinating."

Mike shifted in his chair and said, "Vanessa has a whole list of behaviors that organizations and teams and people exhibit when they are under lots of tension, and how their reactivity surfaces when they get too close or too distant on the continuum. She thinks an important element of every senior leader's role is to recognize what's going on around them and work to keep the organization from veering toward either extreme."

Mike paused and became more thoughtful, as if something important had just dawned on him.

"And they do this by self-regulation—by keeping a better balance themselves."

"So how is all this going to help out here at home?" Karla asked.

"Jacob says that even though it can be the most difficult, the best place to learn about this is in our most important relationships. If I can become more aware of how much my behavior is the result of **automatic functioning**, I've made a big step forward. The other step is to learn how to manage my own reactivity when I am under stress. When I can modify my own behavior, then I'm in a better position to help others do the same." Mike became quiet for a few moments. "I think he's right. I'm in here talking to you now, rather than out taking a run to control my frustrations. I can see now that I use running as a form of escape as much as anything else.

"What I am not sure of is whether all this will make a difference at work. Changing things at work is a lot different from changing how I handle discussions with you or Jacelyn."

Mike ended the conversation by saying, "Karla, I will work at not putting you in the middle so much. I know that I will still fail from time to time, so when it happens again, please tell me. I promise to work at handling things in a different and better way."

"I will, Sweetheart," Karla said as she stood up, gave Mike a kiss, and went up to take her shower.

A New Way of Seeing

RETURN TO BOSTON

Early Tuesday morning Mike boarded the shuttle back to Boston. He had made the choice to return for a short trip and was reviewing a number of notes he had made about hotel performance. Mike was looking at the profit and loss statements for year-to-date and period performance and highlighting the units that did not do well compared to last year and compared to the average of the last three years.

He knew that the fundamentals of the business in Boston were solid. The market was not overbuilt; most of the Clearview Hotels were positioned well in the city, and the summer months were always strong in Boston provided the weather cooperated. He was looking through the P and L statements for the biggest performance variation when he came across an electronic note that had been forwarded to him by his controller. It was a paper copy of a note to the Boston area general managers from Sally Harrison—Subject: Mike Sampson's Visit.

> *Mike Sampson will be returning to Boston to complete the visit he started several days ago. I do know some of the hotels that he will visit but not all. To get ready for his visit, I want each of you to be prepared to address your top line sales figures and middle of the page controllable expenses.*
>
> *Put together a clear briefing on the performance of your hotel over the last month, six months and year-to-date. Know your RevPar and ADR against all of your competitors. Have a handle on the next three and six months in terms of projected occupancy. Know your performance on the key indicators of customer satisfaction and employee engagement. Identify food, power and labor cost overages and have a plan to address any problem.*
>
> *I know we are all very busy with our springtime business up-turn but I want you to give this visit with Mike a high priority. He doesn't visit us that often, and we benefit by his knowledge and suggestions. Call me right away if you have any questions. Sally H.*

A very neat handwritten note across the bottom of Mike's copy read:

"DO WHAT HE TELLS YOU TO DO OR LIVE TO REGRET IT"

The handwritten note bothered Mike a lot.

The flight landed, and Mike was on the phone as it taxied to the gate. Nine calls in 55 minutes. He grabbed his overhead luggage and moved along the narrow isle, irritated by all the delays in just getting off a crowded plane these days. He met Sally at curbside and jumped into her car.

"Hello Mike, welcome to Boston," Sally said.

"Glad to be back," Mike answered. "And thanks for picking me up."

"You're welcome. We've been preparing for your return visit."

Mike wondered if Sally really wanted to pick him up or did it because she felt she had to.

"Okay, are we headed for my office first or do you want to go to your hotel to make some calls?" Sally asked.

"Let's go to your office first and then make a plan for these two days," Mike said.

"Sure, that makes sense, but we have appointments set up for this afternoon for Watertown and Chestnut Hill. They are within a few minutes of each other."

"Good, but before we go there, I wanted to talk with you about how the area is doing and also follow up on my last visit."

Sally knew that meant Newton and Paul Brady. They rode in silence for the next few minutes.

The silence was broken by an incoming call on Mike's cell phone. He quickly looked at the caller ID and saw it was from Silverstone Retirement Village. Silverstone was the senior citizen community where Mike's father had reluctantly moved about 18 months ago after a mild heart attack. His mom had passed away about six years ago.

Mike did not want to talk to his dad now. He became slightly anxious and decided to let the call go into voice mail. Dad was given to long talks, unsolicited advice and repetitive complaining.

Mike really disliked talking with his Dad and felt guilty about it nearly every day of his life. Sally saw the change come across Mike as he looked at the call and said, "Is everything all right, Mike?"

Everything was not all right.

A New Way of Seeing

"Sally, let's stop off for a cup of coffee even before we get to the office."

"Do you have a place in mind?" Sally asked.

"Let's go to a quiet sit-down restaurant and talk for a few minutes."

Sally knew where to go, but she did not know what Mike was up to. Usually, he did not stop off for anything, even to go to the bathroom. She pulled into a local diner not far from the office. They got out of the car, went in, sat down and ordered coffee, water and pastries.

Mike was in one of his act-now, think-later moods. With little forethought and no planning, he was about to have a confidential conversation with a person he hardly knew outside of their often strained working relationship of about 18 months.

Sally took a deep breath.

Mike started. "Sally, I want to talk to you about a few things that are going on here in CHI to get your reaction and perspective. I cannot tell you everything because of confidences that I need to hold."

Sally felt excited and afraid at the same time. She really did not trust or like Mike very much, and now she sensed a conversation coming that would slip into areas where she would feel at least odd if not very uncomfortable.

"I'll do what I can to be of help," she said.

"When I left Boston a few days ago I was called back to the office to begin planning for transitions that will take place with Vanessa's departure. We had several meetings and it was decided that there are four candidates to be considered as possible replacements for her. I am one of the candidates, but I am a very distant fourth-place contender. The reason that I am at the rear of the pack is because of my tough, self-centered leadership style. I have been given a lot of feedback in the last few days that lets me know that I am not nearly as effective a leader as I thought I was."

Sally felt a sense of dread come across her whole being.

"Then on the way up here I read a copy of a memo that you sent to the general managers in the area to help them prepare for my visit. It was a good memo, but there was a handwritten note at the bottom of the copy I got that bothered me quite a bit."

Sally was now sick to her stomach.

Mike reached into his vest pocket, pulled out the note, and handed it to Sally.

She stared at the memo, including the handwritten addition at the bottom. She immediately recognized the handwriting and looked up at Mike.

Mike went on, "I don't want to know who wrote the note, but I am wondering if you think that there is a widespread sentiment in CHI about me that is consistent with that note."

Sally had arrived at the moment she had anticipated five minutes ago and now had to decide how to handle Mike. Just how honest could she be with him was the question she was racing to answer during the momentary pause.

"Mike, that is the sentiment the field has about most people from DC," she said, trying to be honest and also sidestep the direct question. But then she went on.

"People both respect you and fear you at the same time. You know the business extremely well. You ask very challenging questions. You make snap judgments that are, by the way, for the most part correct."

Mike interrupted and said what Sally was thinking, "But…"

Sally continued, "Well … but you are hard to work for and you can be very challenging to be around some of the time."

Mike was silent. He was thinking.

Then he said, "Sally, you know I just don't see it. I actually thought that people enjoy having me come to their hotels and their meetings. People tell me that they have learned a lot from me and that they appreciate that I take time to visit with them."

"They do and I do," said Sally. "People do learn from you. They learn a lot about the business. For that alone all of us are appreciative of your time. But you do not leave behind a feeling of being appreciated or valued on our end. There is always the list of what needs to be fixed or corrected without the acknowledgment of what has been accomplished."

Mike tried to sum it up. "So, if I said thank you more and acknowledged accomplishments since my last visit, things would go better."

"Well, that would be a big help," Sally said, recognizing that Mike was just trying to find a "quick fix" solution.

"But what you are telling me is that there is more, right?"

Sally wanted to get out of this conversation.

She said, "Mike why don't you develop some sort of process to gather input on your leadership effectiveness from a number of people? I could give you a lot of feedback sitting here in the diner, but if you collected input from a number of sources you would have a much better sense of how others view you and what could be done to make the adjustments you want to make."

Mike thought that was a good idea and that Jacob could help him with the assessment process.

"Do you think people will give me honest feedback?" Mike asked.

"Well, you will need to find a way to collect the input anonymously, and even then some people will not respond," Sally replied.

Mike suddenly had the feeling that he may have said too much to Sally and wanted to ask her to hold the information they had discussed in confidence. But before he said anything, Sally recalled his request for the discussion to be in confidence and she recommitted herself.

"Mike, I know our discussion was about sensitive issues, and I will not talk with others about this conversation."

As they began to get into the car, Mike looked at Sally and thanked her for the coffee and the willingness to talk. For the first time, Sally saw a side of Mike that was different from his "game face." She recognized how difficult the conversation was for Mike, and she was relieved they were leaving the diner.

BOSTON DISTRICT OFFICE

Mike greeted the employees who were in the office, spending more time than usual saying hello, and then went to Sally's office to review district performance for the recent period. Sally was prepared and gave a good overview of current problem spots in the district in sales and cost controls. Then she summarized her contingency plans that were for the most part cost cutting steps she was planning to take if the business did not show signs of strengthening in the next three periods.

Mike's immediate reaction was to suggest that Sally implement some of the cost controls now, but he began to think about the Denver Metro discussion he had had with Vanessa the week before. He saw a lot of parallels in the two situations.

"Sally, do you think you could get through the downturn here in some way that would build customer loyalty even in the face of lower margins?"

She thought for a moment and then said, "That could cost more in the short term, Mike."

"Sometimes you have to spend money to make money, you know. If you were to take that approach, what might be some of the things you could try that would pay off in the long run?"

"Well, perhaps if we invested in more marketing efforts, more customer service training and even some modest hotel soft goods upgrades? We'd be investing to grow top line sales in addition to taking some of these cost cutting measures."

"Yes, those are great possibilities. Why don't you and your team think along those lines and give me some suggestions that are backed up with facts."

Sally was taken aback with Mike's openness to a different line of thinking and his willingness to ask for input rather than give directives.

"Okay, Mike. We will do that and get back to you in a few days."

A number of other topics were discussed, and then it came time to talk about Paul Brady at Newton. Sally brought up the topic.

"Mike, during your last trip, we had a difficult visit with Paul at Newton. You gave me a directive to replace him after that meeting. I have been working with Paul since your visit, and I feel he has good potential, but he is in over his head at Newton. I want to pull him out of the general manager assignment and move another general manager from the area into the job. I want to place Paul in a second position at another hotel, keep him on my district budget, and provide him some additional training and mentoring."

Mike said, "I don't agree. But, if you have the training dollars and feel it is a good decision, I will sign off on it." The conversation ended abruptly. Sally was relieved yet still apprehensive.

That afternoon and the next day, Mike and Sally visited several hotels. The general managers were well prepared and had good answers for most of the questions Mike asked. He kept throwing the new "invest in the top line" curveball at each meeting. This new dynamic was going to cause Sally and the team to do more work on their contingency plans. It was an assignment that Sally was looking forward to and eager to undertake before Mike changed his mind.

Mike returned home late on Wednesday evening. He still had not returned his dad's call and, as was typical for him, felt guilty.

On the cab ride to the airport, Mike checked in with Karla who reported on the latest plans for the upcoming wedding. She reminded Mike that he needed to follow up on the honeymoon location and also call their son Richard. She was in a positive mood. Mike looked forward to getting home. On the plane he made notes about follow-up actions for each hotel and the Boston area in general. He also checked his calendar for Thursday and saw that he had a visit with Jacob for 10:30 a.m. to 12:00 noon.

As soon as he got in his car in DC, Mike left a message for Crystal to call about hotel accommodations at Mission Bay and San Mateo, California, and Los Suenos, Costa Rica. He knew of fine hotels in all three of the locations and thought that Jacelyn and Russ would enjoy any of them. Before bed on Wednesday night he summed up the day.

Today
- *Sally gave me more information on my lack of self awareness.*
- *"... live to regret it" comment hurts.*
- *Spend cash to make cash is a foreign idea to CHI.*

Issues
- *I can see my reactivity as it relates to Boston Newton GM and my reaction to my dad when he calls or I visit him.*
- *I revert back to my automatic functioning when I get stressed. It is happening all the time.*
- *Boston GMs and even Sally really don't know how to drive revenue in a down economy—need help.*

Follow up
- *Talk with Jacob about the Boston memo and conversation with McMaster and Vanessa.*
- *Go to see dad at Silverstone.*
- *How do I avoid getting Karla caught in the middle of a debate with Jacelyn?*

RICHARD

Early Thursday morning, Mike touched base with Richard, his 21-year-old son. Right out of high school, Richard had chosen to make his living using his abilities and skills related to automotive and home repair. He worked two jobs in the Jacksonville, Florida, area—one as a condominium maintenance employee and the other as a mechanic at an automotive repair shop. Lilly, Richard's fiancée, was working as a dental assistant and had her sights set on a career as a dental hygienist. Richard and Lilly had already saved nearly enough to make a down payment on a first home.

Because Richard and Mike had such different interests and because they both worked almost nonstop, little time had been spent retaining a close relationship since Richard left home. Mike sensed a void in their relationship but really did not know what to do about it. It seemed that Richard was moving through his own life and after all, not much could be done given the limited time and the distance between DC and Jacksonville. It was not as if Mike could just stop by on the way home from work.

But the lack of contact bothered Richard a lot. He dreamed of a family vacation when they could all get away together and have fun. He did not see his mom and dad often, but every time he did he felt reconnected in a way that he really missed. Also, each time they got together, Richard saw his parents getting older.

Recently he had been reading a book on spirituality and wanted to tell his dad about what he was learning. It had become more than a passing interest for him, and he was looking for an opportunity to ask his dad to read a book written by Eckhart Tolle. The book was interesting to him in and of itself, and he also hoped to find a common interest so that he and his father could talk more often.

"Hello Richard, how is the work coming down there?"

"Too much work, Dad; too much work, and too many bills."

"I know how that feels," said Mike. "How is Lilly doing?"

"She is great. Recently she got a raise that was unexpected. Also, we're getting real close to paying off her student loan, and that will be a big relief."

Lilly was several years older than Richard, a smart, responsible young woman who had paid her own way through college. They both were doing quite well for young adults their age.

Mike and Richard exchanged light conversation for a few minutes and then both had to go. At the end of the call, Richard said, "Hey, Dad, when you have a moment I want you to look at a website that has a summary of a book I am reading. I will send you the link in the next couple of days."

Mike said sure and thought nothing more about the comment.

Chapter 2: Self-Other Forces

Review Key Points

- **Self-other forces** are present in every living being and every relationship system.
  - **Self-other forces** are manifested in how the close-distant relationship continuum is managed.

- The individuality-togetherness balance that seems "normal" to us is the result of our family upbringing.
  - The "dance of life" involves an ongoing effort to maintain a healthy balance between these two polarities.
  - Both individuals and organizations are engaged in the "dance of life" at the deep level of **emotional process**.

- Leaders can lead more effectively by "seeing in a new way," i.e., by becoming more aware of how these primal forces operate in themselves and in others.
  - The leader's own family is an important place to learn about and become more skillful in managing **emotional process**.
  - Skills developed in a family setting are transferable to other relationship settings, and vice-versa.
  - Competency in this New Way of SEEING is developed gradually over many years of practice.

Questions for Reflection and Discussion

1. Each of us has a "default setting" on the **self-other** continuum where we feel most comfortable. We all also have subtle triggers that warn us of threats from either side—fear of being left out and fear of being gobbled up. Under stress, we tend to move more toward the extremes of our default setting. From what you know of him so far, would you say Mike's tendency when stressed is to

withdraw or come closer? What details of the story lead you to answer as you do?

2. In general, would you characterize the way relationships operate in your workplace as more in the direction of "close" or "distant"? What are the behaviors that lead you to say this? What happens when anxiety is high in your organization?

3. During stressful times when you were a child, did members of your family tend to move in the direction of more closeness or more distance? Do you continue to follow the same pattern in your significant relationships today? How does this manifest itself? Under what conditions does movement toward/away occur?

The Practice

Self-other forces play a significant role in all relationships. You can more clearly see **self-other forces** in your relationships by constructing and using a simple SOF diagram.

1. Place your name inside a circle in the center of a piece of paper.

2. Around the central circle draw other circles and write inside each circle the name of an individual who plays a significant role in your family or work life. Space these names so that those who seem to maintain a comparatively greater emotional distance from you are in more distant circles than those who seem to be closer to you.

3. Now indicate with a directional arrow which way each person naturally travels (away or toward you) in times of emotional stress or anxiety.

4. Determine what actions you can take to help preserve an appropriate "close-distant" relationship during times of stress with individuals in your network.
    a. At times you will need to take action to prevent fusion when others come too close to you as they attempt to alleviate their anxiety.
    b. At other times you will need to take action to close a widening gap when others move toward "cutoff" in their attempt to manage anxiety.

Does this analysis lead you believe that you need to take action with someone in your SOF diagram at this time?

A New Way of Seeing

Self-Other Forces

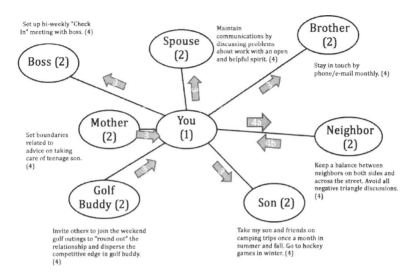

To learn more, go to www.resilient-leadership.biz.

A New Way of <u>Seeing</u>

Chapter 3: Automatic Functioning

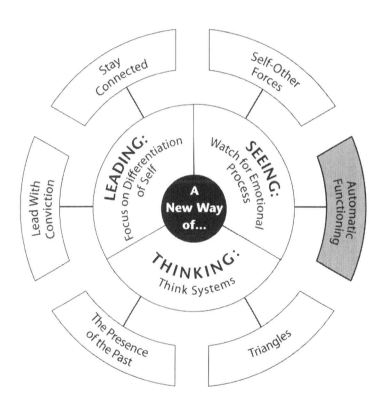

BACK WITH JACOB

Mike was excited to see Jacob. Even though their first meeting was only ten days ago, he had covered a lot of territory since then and wanted to share his experiences and his insights with Jacob.

A fast drive to Red Hill Drive, a knock on the door, and a quick hello ended with Mike sitting across the table from Jacob with a big smile on his face.

"Looks like you had a good week judging by that grin," Jacob said.

"I made some great progress," Mike replied.

Then Mike set off on a 20-minute monologue covering the details of his week. He spoke about his evening notes that now include summaries, although very short, about **self-other forces** and about **automatic functioning**. He summarized his meeting with Vanessa and James McMaster. He shared his growing awareness that Vanessa was really giving him a fair shot at the job of COO. He described his conversation with Jacelyn, including the deep sense of relief he had in reconnecting with his daughter and the follow-up conversation he had with Karla after his call to Jacelyn.

He reviewed his conversation over coffee with Sally and some of the decisions and actions he had taken in Boston. In particular he told Jacob about the inter-office memo he had gotten with the caustic handwritten remark at the bottom and about the suggestions that Sally had made about gathering input in the form of an assessment of some sort. He talked about his call from his father and how that had made him feel anxious and guilty. And finally he ended up with a quick summary of the discussion he just had with Richard before driving to their meeting.

Jacob smiled and said, "Wow, you have been really busy!" After a pause, he continued, "You have told me a lot about what you have done. Let's talk about what you have learned about others and about yourself."

Mike had been aware of some different feelings in himself, but he had not thought to ask himself what he was learning.

Jacob realized that Mike was in the beginning stages of trying to do things differently in his life. He was following the same pattern he would with any new skill he was trying to learn. He studied the materials he was given, looking for tools he could use. He made notes and then experimented to see what worked. He kept what worked and discarded what did not work.

Jacob knew that Mike's next level of understanding would be about the relationship between his own behavior and the outcomes that unfolded in his life. But Mike was just learning about becoming more self-aware. So, at this point he was using the new learning as techniques to manipulate situations rather than as learning points to help him more deeply understand his interior way of being and the behaviors that arose from that level.

"Mike, what would you say were two or three of your key learning points since we last met?"

"I have learned that I resent Russ because I feel like he is taking Jacelyn away from me and changing the dynamics in our family. But I also have learned that I can manage that resentment by slowing down in my reactions and thinking about what to say and how to say it so that I do not anger Jacelyn and embarrass myself. I'm using the metaphor that Vanessa suggested to me recently: the idea of climbing up a tree and looking down on myself and on the situation I'm in."

"Mike, you are right. You are beginning to take the time to think about your behaviors. Doing this enables you to place a space between what happens in your life and your reaction to it."

Jacob went to the flip chart and wrote two word sequences:

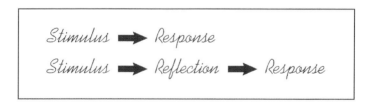

"Here is a quick summary of what you were doing in the situation you described. Rather than simply reacting without thinking when you talk about Russ, you are beginning to be more thoughtful so that you can make a more carefully considered response."

Mike smiled and agreed. "I felt in control of myself, even though I was steamed."

"But here is another question, Mike. Why are you angry at Russ? Why are you steamed at all?"

Mike sat back and was quiet. After a few moments he said, "Well, I really think they are too young to get married. They are just not ready for all the challenges they will face. I don't want Jacelyn to get hurt. And frankly I don't like the fact that they live together now without being married."

"So you have listed the reasons that you do not think they are ready to get married and you mentioned that you don't like them living together. But, Mike, why are you angry?" Jacob asked again.

Mike became agitated.

"I am scared that they will not have a permanent marriage. I have a great deal of anxiety about it and I just react… I guess," Mike said.

"Mike, let me ask you about your dad for a moment," Jacob said, turning the conversation in a different direction. "You mentioned that you have a lot of guilt associated with not returning his calls promptly. It bothers you a lot, yet you do not return calls anyway. Why don't you return those calls?" Jacob asked.

"Well, I am busy and Dad is just not a priority for me. He is the kind of guy who is always upset about something and anticipating the worst in situations. It's like he expects bad things to happen all the time and spends a lot of time worrying about even the most remote potential problems—problems that don't materialize even half of the time. It's exhausting to talk with him."

"Has your dad been like this for a long time or just in the later years of his life?" Jacob asked.

"He has been like this since I can remember, but it has gotten a lot worse since mom died," Mike replied.

"Mike, how would you compare the level of friction between you and your dad and between you and Jacelyn?"

Mike was about to say, "Why there's no comparison at all," but he caught himself as he realized that there was more to Jacob's question than it first appeared. So, instead, he said, "Jacob, what are you getting at?"

Jacob replied, "Mike, here is what I want you to think about. At some level, is it possible that Jacelyn is having a similar experience with you as you have with your dad?"

Mike was stunned. "My God, am I becoming just like my father?" Mike asked himself out loud.

Jacob did not say anything for a while. Then he said, "Mike, let's take a quick break and regroup in ten minutes."

Mike stood up and went outside to think.

When they reconvened, Jacob started off.

"Mike, last week we spoke about **emotional process**. One clue to what is happening on the level of **emotional process**, you will recall, is how a person or group of people work at managing their **self-other forces**. There is another behavior that tells you a great deal about what's happening on the level of **emotional process**, and that is known as **automatic functioning** or reactivity.

"But before we talk about reactive behaviors, I need to focus you on their deeper roots at the level of **emotional process**. It's a kind of **automatic functioning** that Bowen Theory calls "chronic anxiety."

"Sounds something like lower back pain," Mike said with a grin.

Jacob nodded and continued on without stopping. His clients soon recognized that when he put on his "teacher's hat" he sometimes became quite intense, to the point of seeming very academic. Mike was getting a sense of this now, and he rather enjoyed seeing Jacob operate with such single-minded focus. As Mike was reflecting in this fashion, he realized his mind had drifted, and he quickly tuned back into what Jacob was explaining.

"A generic way to think about anxiety is as a response we make to any sort of threat, real or imagined. There are two kinds of anxiety, however. *Acute* anxiety arises when we are faced with an immediate physical or emotional threat, and our spontaneous response takes the form of either fight or flight or freeze. That's the kind of immediate response that makes us swerve to miss a deer that leaps out into the road, for example.

"*Chronic* anxiety is quite another form. It can be thought of as a pervasive and a more free-floating type of uneasiness in our lives. It generally operates underneath our conscious awareness, at the level of emotional process. Acute anxiety comes and goes, but some measure of chronic anxiety is always with us. It's chronic anxiety that I want to talk to you about as the source of your reactivity.

"Have you ever known someone who seems to be anxious all the time?" Jacob asked.

"Yes; me," Mike responded.

"Can you explain that a little? What makes you anxious?"

"I am always uneasy about losing control of situations. I work hard to be on top of everything, business problems and family problems alike. I'm constantly checking on bank balances, credit card balances, phone messages, yard work—you name it, and I worry about it. I want to keep a lid on things."

"And how long have you been living your life this way?"

"I was this way when I was a kid," Mike said. "And it has served me well. I am on top of things and in control most of the time."

Jacob leaned back in his chair, "Mike, here are a few thoughts I have that may be helpful to you in understanding chronic anxiety and some of your own reactive behaviors, both at home and at work.

"First of all, while your worry about losing control is certainly an expression of your uneasiness, the kind of chronic anxiety I am talking about is even deeper and is actually the source of your need to be in control.

"What I have learned over the years through study and practice is that a person's level of chronic anxiety develops from a very early age and is deeply impacted by how that person's family relationships functioned. It is the parents' overall level of chronic anxiety that is passed on, more or less, to their children. You told me just a few minutes ago that your father is 'always upset' and 'anticipates the worst.' Depending on their position in the family and other circumstances while they are growing up, children inherit more or less of the anxiety that their parents got in turn from *their* parents. They carry it with them throughout life, and they will eventually pass a good deal of it on to their own children."

"Sounds grim. Do you really think people are just condemned to live out the family destiny? Don't you think people can change?"

"Of course I do," Jacob said forcefully. "My whole career has been about helping people change and grow beyond their current limits, both personally and professionally. But there's no doubt in my mind that we all start out our adult life at a certain point, based primarily on what we've absorbed from our family of origin. Understanding your starting point is a first step on the road to further growth."

Jacob went on, "Here is why all this matters to you in business and at home.

"The chronic anxiety we grow up with has, in a sense, hard-wired into us certain triggers or hot buttons that we react to with little or no thoughtfulness. These triggers are holdovers from our youth that restart or reawaken our anxiety. And when this happens, there are significant, reactive behaviors that often occur.

"It sounds like one trigger for you is loss of control. When you feel that you are losing control of situations—even comparatively small situations like unanswered phone messages—your anxiety level begins to escalate. This causes you to react automatically, and in some cases to overreact. Your chronic anxiety spills over into your relationships with others, and left unmanaged, you get labeled a control freak. Your reactivity also triggers others' anxiety, and you experience unwanted reactive pushback to your behavior, like Jacelyn hanging up the phone on you.

"Here is the point: recognizing your triggers and then coming to terms with managing your reactivity to these triggers will help you with all of your relationships, both at home and at work. As you figure these triggers out, you will be taking a big step toward greater self-awareness—the kind of self-awareness that Vanessa was talking about the first day we met."

Mike was nodding agreement with everything Jacob was saying. It was making sense to him.

"How can I get a handle on all of this? It's hard to know where to start, and I'm not particularly interested in getting into therapy."

"We're not talking therapy here, Mike; just a growth in self-awareness and improving your self-management. The 'New Way of SEEING' that is part of the **Resilient Leadership** model involves learning to watch for how **emotional process** surfaces in certain behaviors. Recognizing those behaviors and becoming more skilled at self-regulation is what we are going to be focusing on.

The range of possible reactive behaviors is so great that we can't begin to list them all. However..." Jacob picked up from his desk a sheet of paper that had printed at the top in bold letters, **Automatic Functioning: Reactive Behaviors – What to Watch For**. "Take a look at this. It's a few of the typical expressions of reactivity that you're likely to run into—both in yourself and in others. You might also recognize that these patterns are as likely to crop up at home as they are at work. Take a few minutes now to read this over, and tell me what you see."

Mike studied the list intently for several minutes while Jacob made notes at his desk:

Automatic Functioning: Reactive Behaviors – What to Watch For

- **Either/Or Thinking** — Reactivity results in simplistic, black and white categories. There is no grey, no nuance in the midst of reactivity. It's all-or-nothing, you're for us or against us, and anything less than complete agreement is seen as total disagreement. The result of this kind of functioning is a polarization of people and positions, with an adversarial approach to every contentious relationship.
- **Victim Mentality** — Reactivity often surfaces as hypersensitivity, a perennial stance of woundedness in the face of others' behaviors or even just life's outrageous fortunes. The result is a flight from responsibility. "It is never my fault; the other is always to blame and I am inevitably the innocent victim who cannot be held accountable for circumstances beyond my control." Ironically, the flip side of this also surfaces sometimes in the form of blaming self, even though there is no objective basis to do so.
- **Deadly Serious** — Reactivity can mask itself in the guise of a learned, grave attitude where everything is treated with a deadly seriousness. There is no lightness, no humor to offer perspective; rather, reactive functioning can seem to operate in slow motion, as if one were wading through the heaviness of molasses. Another flip side to look for is a kind of (nervous) joking that is actually a way to mask one's reactivity.
- **Impulsive/Thoughtless** — Just the opposite of slow-motion heaviness, another typically reactive way of functioning is to refuse to take time for thoughtful deliberation. Every situation triggers an immediate

response; every new development requires quick action, and judgment comes only by way of an afterthought.
- **Invasive Behaviors** — **Automatic functioning** is often oblivious to the need to respect appropriate boundaries. This can manifest itself in behaviors such as disregard for proper channels of communication, ignoring or subverting the democratic process, refusing to play by the rules, over-functioning beyond one's mandate/jurisdiction/area of competency, offering unwanted advice, and trying to step in and "fix" others' problems whether they want the help or not.
- **Focus on Crisis** — Reactivity is often manifested in an excessive focus on pathology, to the point of ignoring the positive, healing potential present in every situation. This orientation often results in too much time and energy spent on the lowest functioning, least productive, most troubled members of the organization.
- **Narrow Vision** — Reactivity narrows one's range of vision. One gets "stuck" on a preoccupation with rituals, procedures and policies rather than being able to see the big picture. When situations present themselves, reactive functioning results in an exclusive focus (e.g., on the content of the issues), without regard for the surrounding context or the emotional dynamics underlying the issues. At the extreme end of this pattern is insensitivity to one's environment and to other people that amounts to a real blindness. People who are accident-prone (with cars or relationships) may be "blind" in this way.
- **Hijacked Thinking** — Reactivity occurs when feeling processes overwhelm thinking processes. Emotions—whether of anger, sadness, elation, or whatever—can often be so powerful as to make careful thought nearly impossible. This is obvious when it comes to those feelings that we are immediately aware of. But because chronic anxiety is part of our **automatic functioning**, it is often much more difficult to realize the full extent to which our capacity for thoughtfulness has been compromised by anxiety-driven reactivity.

- **Limited Repertoire** — Reactivity limits one's ability to think and act creatively. In the grip of reactive functioning, the range of available options always appears less than it is in reality. Fundamentalism, with its simplistic and reductionist approach to complex situations, is a typical result of reactivity.
- **Easily Stampeded** — Reactive functioning opens people up to the influence of contagious emotions in the same way that a failed immune system makes a person more vulnerable to infection. Reactivity produces "groupthink" and results in people being easily swayed by emotional appeals, mindlessly following the crowd, over-reacting to perceived threats, and so forth.
- **Rebellion/Submission** — Both of these patterns can be forms of reactivity, two sides of a single coin. Stubborn refusal to comply with reasonable requests is as reactive as complete willingness to submit, regardless of the personal price. Both forms of reactivity are usually accompanied by a host of rationalizations that justify why the particular course of action is reasonable or appropriate "given the circumstances."
- **Dominating/Scapegoating** — Again, both of these behaviors are aspects of a particular form of reactivity. When chronic anxiety has resulted in a person feeling a loss of control, either of these behaviors aims at regaining control by claiming a superior position in the relationship.
- **Physical Symptoms** — There is a growing body of evidence that many physical symptoms are a form of anxiety-based reactivity. This is more than just the phantom signals once described as "psychosomatic" illness. Genuine clinical conditions, it seems, are sometimes rooted in an individual's reactive functioning and its negative impact on physical health.

"Wow! That's quite a list," Mike said in a very subdued fashion. "I'm afraid I see a bit more of myself in there than I'd like to admit."

Jacob laughed. "Don't let it overwhelm you, Mike. Remember that I said every one of us carries around a measure of chronic anxiety. And every one of us is reactive to some extent, in various ways. The issue is not whether you engage in reactive behaviors or not. It's how you can begin to develop more self-awareness; and once you recognize the triggers that result in your thinking responses being hijacked by **automatic functioning**, how best to calm yourself and manage that reactivity.

"It's a lifelong process of growth. What you and I are doing is helping you to focus and become more intentional about improving your leadership by embracing the 'New Way of SEEING' of the **Resilient Leadership** model."

"I think I'm beginning to realize there are better ways to lead than just being a steam-roller."

With a smile, Jacob said, "When you're a hammer, everything looks like a nail."

This brought a smile to Mike's face and seemed to ease the tension he had been feeling. "You know, Jacob, remember when I was here and got the email about the conflict between my two direct reports—Craig and Steve—over Steve's request for customer data analysis?"

"Yes, I remember we talked about Steve's over-functioning and his anxiety whenever there is conflict on the team."

"Right. Well, I recognize now that a number of Steve's behaviors fit your description of reactive patterns. This one about invasive behaviors and not respecting boundaries fits him to a tee. And his focus on crisis, his narrow vision—he really fits the profile in a lot of ways."

"What does that tell you about Steve's functioning on a deeper level?"

"That he's a pretty anxious cookie, and that his reactive behaviors are symptoms of that anxiety."

"How would you say, then, he might respond to a manager who puts more pressure on him to change his behavior or meet some goal?"

A light went on in Mike's brain. "I get it! All that does is make him more anxious and more reactive. The best way to manage him is to lower his anxiety, not raise it!"

"And what if you're really pissed off at him about something or feeling anxious yourself when he's not coming through on a crucial task? How will your own level of reactivity influence him, do you suppose?"

Somewhat sheepishly, Mike responded, "I guess I'd need to manage my own reactivity before approaching him, or else I'd just make matters worse."

"Exactly," Jacob said with emphasis. "Now, I don't want to discourage you, but I need to add that it's pretty hard to fake it with someone as attuned as Steve is to picking up the signals of a reactive authority figure. Even when you try to appear calm, you will be sending off subtle cues that he is bound to pick up on. So you really do have to work at calming yourself—genuinely calming down—if you're going to be able to manage him more effectively."

"I'm beginning to see the scope of the personal work I've got to do, Jacob. And I don't mind telling you it makes me feel a bit uneasy."

"So, by talking to you about anxiety I've succeeded in making you more anxious, is that it?" Jacob gave a big smile and both men joined in a hearty laugh.

"Listen, Mike. It's a gradual process and you've made a good beginning. Do the best you can at this stage, and we'll be working on these issues for many months to come. The progress will often be too gradual to see, but if you're lucky you'll have a few more standout successes than your occasional failures. A year from now, you'll be a much better leader, regardless of whether you are the new COO or not."

"Thanks, Jacob, but I realize we've already run over our time. I really have found today's session helpful."

"Good," Jacob said. "Mike, the behaviors on my list are only a sample. I am sure you could add to the list from your own experience, and I encourage you to do so. There is one more reactive pattern that I want to review with you in some depth next time we meet —sabotage. Let's select a date to meet next week."

Looking at his calendar, Jacob said, "How is next Friday at 9:00 a.m.?"

"That's perfect. See you then."

That night Mike was back at his evening notes.

Today
- *I have a lot of automatic functioning and it comes from my reactive nature. My reactivity is,*

at least in part, caused by chronic anxiety that I get from daily life and my family.
- *I am a lot like my dad—ugh.*
- *This Resilient Leadership stuff is not about acting differently—it is about being different—I have a long way to go.*

Issues
- *Manage my own reactivity is a challenge to me. It seems that if I am always measured, always watching from up on a tree I can't really be me.*
- *My success in the past has been related to how effective I have been in getting others to do what I want them to do. I am concerned about the change we are considering.*

Follow up
- *I am going to start a good habit of looking at the materials that Jacob has given to me once a day for five minutes. See how it goes for 30 days or so.*
- *I see how much I favor Craig over Steve in my relationships with both. I will need to work on keeping a better balance.*

CRYSTAL

The next morning Crystal asked for an hour of Mike's time to go over a number of topics.

First, she provided Mike with a summary of the flight schedules, room availability, amenities and costs for each of the hotels on the short list of possibilities for the honeymoon. Mike decided to take the list home to show Karla and then send it off to Jacelyn.

Second, she reminded Mike again about birthdays. Mike asked her to make reservations for him to take Karla to dinner at their favorite steakhouse in DC on Saturday night.

Third, Mike and Crystal returned to the topic of the annual division conference. After some discussion, it was decided that the conference would be postponed until after Labor Day to provide the maximum participation and the minimum amount of frustration. To limit travel costs and get the greatest participation from HQ types, it was decided to hold the conference in DC. Crystal was to check on Vanessa's and James' schedules and get a couple of dates for Mike and his team to consider.

Fourth, Mike discussed an assignment he was going to give Sally Harrison in Boston. He had talked with his division controller and sketched out a report format that had both cost containment options and revenue enhancement options for his Boston area general managers to use when he returned in about ten days. The spreadsheet was being developed in the controller's office, and Mike wanted to send it off to Sally right away. He gave Crystal the general idea of what to put into a cover memo to Sally and when to schedule the second follow-up visit. Crystal would take care of the details.

Finally, Crystal wanted to talk about rumors that she had been hearing. Was Mike a candidate to replace Vanessa? Who else was in the running, if anyone? The intense office rumor mill was focused on two things. First, how would the transition from Vanessa to someone else impact jobs? Second, who will replace Vanessa and when will the announcement be made?

Mike did not give Crystal all the details, but he did tell her that he was one of four candidates for the COO post at this point. He did not cover the specifics of who was being considered or the timing for the transition or the exact content of his coaching with Jacob. Crystal was not a gossip, and Mike knew he could trust her, but he felt a degree of confidentiality was needed.

CHECK-IN WITH VANESSA

Mike decided that he should update Vanessa on the issues he faced in Boston and in the remainder of his division. He wanted her to have the information she needed when she made her quarterly update to Wall Street in the next couple of weeks. She was about to go to New York for meetings with investors for three days, so Mike caught 30 minutes in her calendar on

Tuesday at lunch time before she left for the airport.

"Mike, come in," Vanessa said as he appeared at her office door.

"How are you, how is Boston, how is it going with Jacob?" She asked all at one time.

Vanessa stopped what she was doing, motioned for Mike to sit at the conference table, and they both took a seat. Just as she sat down, her cell phone squawked but she didn't even flinch. Vanessa had a remarkable ability to be present in the moment and this was the moment for Mike. Mike noticed.

"Boston first," Mike said, trying to be efficient. "I had a very good visit with Sally and about six hotels. They are putting contingency plans in place with an eye toward implementation in about 90 days. I noticed that all the plans were about cost management and cut backs; things like taking accrued leave to control wages, cutting back on security, closing pools earlier in the evening, you know, the usual things."

Vanessa smiled and nodded.

"Your story about Denver was ringing in my ears, so I took a lesson from that experience and asked the entire region to focus on top line growth in addition to prudent cost containment measures. The idea was well received, and I am going to go back to get a full report on new ideas for growing as well as cutting."

"Good for you, Mike," Vanessa said. "I am sure you will get some great ideas. Be sure to bring them back to share at our next executive staff. Also be prepared to have to pry good ideas out of some of your people. You will find some of your GMs will be pretty skeptical of any change of direction, and they will probably not put their full energy into the top line growth, thinking that you are really not serious. It's a form of resistance that always emerges when a new direction is attempted."

Mike knew Vanessa was right. He was familiar with the resistance that always surfaced when a change of direction emerged. His typical way of dealing with this problem was, of course, to push harder.

Mike pointed out that this approach gives his people two ways to address their economic challenges: upside growth and middle of the page cost management.

"You are changing the game on them, and the change is unfamiliar to most of the people, uncomfortable for some and frightening for others. Here is how it works: Cutting costs is not fun, but it is a familiar drill for our people. By that I mean, operators have been taught for years how to cut money out of operations and do with less for a time. Then, when things go south in employee engagement or customer satisfaction, they have a scapegoat—I know I did. But if you challenge them to increase top line growth by increasing volume or margin or both on existing retail sales or by creating new revenue streams, they will have to commit to a bigger top line number. That's scary; that's a lot harder. Some of your people will say it cannot be done and find ways to prove it can't. It's a reaction to the game change."

"So how do you handle this form of resistance?" Mike asked.

"Well, first, do not take it personally. That's hard because people tell you that what you are after cannot be done. Stay focused on the target. What matters is your steadfastness.

"Within reason, do not take 'no' for an answer. You know how to do that, Mike. But be careful not to step in and give answers, but rather ask questions. Keep asking 'how' questions. And do not expect their answers to be like yours; give them space to learn by doing and many of them will grow."

Mike realized she was right and also how hard that was going to be for him. He paused and then went on to the second topic.

"My meetings with Jacob are going very well. I have had only two visits, but already he is helping me develop and broaden my perspective."

"That is what he is there for. Tell me, is it worth your time?" Vanessa asked.

"Absolutely; I am putting some of his ideas to work immediately. Some suggestions he makes I use here at work, but a lot of what I am learning I can apply to family situations."

"Well, it sounds like you are off to a good start. When I was working with Jacob, it eventually became clear to me that I was engaging in my life with a much deeper awareness of what was really going on around me. It took me a while. Today I enjoy participating in my life and watching my life at the same time."

Mike scribbled the words "WATCHER OF MY LIFE" on the back of one of his spreadsheets.

"Last time we met, you wanted to talk about one of your Boston GM slots and your division conference."

"I have decided to let Sally move her leaders around a bit

before I get involved in any GM discussions with her. And I am still working on the conference. So I will get back to you later on those points."

"Okay, Mike. How is Karla doing?" Vanessa inquired.

"She is just great; always the best cheering squad for me and the family. Her health is good, and she is happy and selling houses. Life is good."

"Glad to hear it, Mike," Vanessa said. "Anything else?"

Mike sensed that it was time to end the meeting. "No, thanks for the time," Mike said as he stood up and walked toward the door.

BACK TO BOSTON

On Wednesday morning Mike arrived at Boston Logan again, and as his plane touched down he became acutely aware that he would be tested today. The test in front of him was this: "How should I balance the tension between letting my leaders design and implement their own plan, versus giving them advice from my years of experience?" He thought to himself, "How will I know when to ask questions and when to give direction?"

He decided to call Jacob as the plane taxied to the gate to see if he could talk for a few minutes.

"Hello, Jacob; it's Mike Sampson. How are you today?"

"Great, Mike; it's good to hear from you." Jacob paused and then added, "Can I help you with something?"

"Jacob, I am up here in Boston following up on some improvement initiatives that have been developed by the general managers. The market is a little soft right now and we are trying to control expenses and do some things to bring more business into the hotels as well. What I want to talk about is how to handle some of the briefings that are going to be short of the mark without coming across in my usual aggressive, self-centered manner."

Jacob responded quickly, "Mike we have gone over the techniques in the last two meetings, and I know you have made some notes to yourself that are really helpful. I suggest that you start by asking yourself what are the triggers that could set you off in the meetings you will have today. Then identify the reactive behaviors that you need to watch out for, making a mental note to stop yourself when those tendencies begin to crop up. Keep your second mind, the mind that is up in the tree, awake and alert all day long."

Mike made a few quick notes and waited for Jacob to continue, but there was only silence on the line. Mike waited.

"Is that it?" Mike said.

"Pretty much," Jacob replied. "Remember, Mike, the changes you are working on are about making good choices during the process of dealing with people. If I were to give you a list of things to do and avoid doing today you would concentrate on the list rather than work on being present in the moment. Rely on your instincts, Mike. You will know what to do."

Jacob ended the call saying, "Call me at the end of the day if you like, and we can discuss what you learned today."

Mike was disappointed in the response he got from Jacob. He was thinking that he would get a few specific, helpful suggestions from Jacob that he could record and refer to during the day. Instead, he got an assignment from Jacob that he would have to do now, and then think about during the day.

THE PLAN

Mike sat down right after he got off the plane and called Sally's cell phone to tell her that he needed about fifteen minutes to work on something before he could meet her at baggage pickup.

He opened his cell phone to April 28 and the notes section.

He typed in the word "triggers" and thought for a minute. Then he wrote,

Triggers–Briefings short on Creativity, Impact Data, Implementation Plan, Passion, Smart Thinking and Can-Do Attitude

This list was a quick summary of the triggers that would set him off and take him off his game. It struck him that he could start off the meetings by letting people know what his expectations were. Then he wondered if that was a good idea so late in the briefing process. Maybe he should have communicated these expectations when he sent out the spreadsheet format last week. He decided to share his expectations first thing in the meeting anyway.

Then he began to think about his reactive behaviors. He

wrote, *"From the Tree–Watch for interrupting, snap judgments, talking too much, giving answers, not asking questions."*

He closed up his notes section and called Sally.

As Sally pulled up to the baggage claim area, Mike got into the car with a big smile on his face. Doing the work in the last 15 minutes gave him a sense of control; control over himself, which he was excited about.

"Hello, Mike," Sally said. "Did you get your work done?"

"I did, and I am ready to go. Thanks for waiting."

Sally continued as she left the airport, "We really appreciate the opportunity to review our work with you, Mike. The team has been working on a number of creative ideas, and they are eager to share them with you. We have set up a briefing room at our Copley Place hotel and the GMs are arriving there now."

"Great, I am looking forward to the day. Did the spreadsheet help?"

"Yes, it did. We have a good idea of your expectations. We have developed a number of ideas that would not have surfaced had you not given us the challenge to look at new approaches to top line growth."

When Mike arrived at the hotel meeting room, the GMs were waiting. Mike was in for a daylong briefing from about 25 area general managers. It was obvious there was both an air of excitement and anxiety. After friendly greetings around the room, everyone took a seat at the large U-shaped table.

Sally stood up and thanked everyone for coming. Then she quickly reviewed the agenda for the day.

After she spoke, but before the briefings began, Mike asked to have a moment to say a few words.

"First I want to thank each of you for the work that you and your teams have put into these briefings. I will make additional comments at the end of the day, but I want you to know that I sincerely appreciate the efforts you have taken. Second, I want to acknowledge the short turnaround time for such an effort. I was just up here at the beginning of last week and my return visit today gave you only a short amount of time to do a lot of work. Because of that, I anticipate that you will have ideas that are not fully developed and that is just fine. If we do a good job today, we will discuss a lot of things and set some overall direction for the Boston area.

"I have made some notes for myself about today's discussion that I want to share with you before we begin. This is just a short list of what I am hoping to see today."

Mike opened up his cell phone and asked one of the general managers to write these words on a white board in the room.

- Creativity
- Impact Data
- Implementation Plan
- Passion
- Smart Thinking
- Can-Do Attitude

After Mike called out these six points he gave a brief summary of what he meant by each one. As he was talking, it dawned on him that this list could be used as a kind of checklist to evaluate each of the briefings; and, that if he kept good notes on each briefing, he could be more effective in controlling his trigger points.

Then he realized that he was actually being present in two places. He was at the front speaking and at the same time above the room looking down on the meeting. He felt a sense of calm, and he began to relax at a deep level. Mike ended his comments, sat down, and smiled.

A few of the general managers who knew him wondered what he was up to.

MORNING BRIEFINGS

The briefings in the morning were well organized and followed the guidelines Mike had prepared. Many ideas related to cost management were well defined and presented with solid impact data and an implementation plan. Cost controls for labor hours, contract services, energy utilization, food and liquor expense, and preventive maintenance topped the list. The discussion in the room helped the general managers learn from each other as much as anything else.

Throughout the briefings, Mike was able to get most of his ideas out by asking questions for clarification and by making suggestions. In a couple of cases, he felt that the briefings lacked any type of creative thought. It seemed as though the speaker was just going through the motions, making rote report-out.

But overall, Mike found the number and quality of new revenue generation ideas that the general managers came up with very impressive. The ideas included developing an outside catering business in the Boston area, taking in laundry from other hotel operations to utilize unused capacity, building a free-standing dry cleaning business, packaging new eco-friendly tours of Boston, creating evening dinner parties that had themes which linked to the summer holidays, creating a shared pool of banquet servers to rotate among hotels, and offering subsidies to employees taking public transportation. The list was extensive and quite promising.

As the leaders broke for lunch, Mike was of two minds. The revenue generation ideas were very creative, but also long-term. He wondered how they could explore some of these ideas and undertake steps to make an impact on top line revenues in the short term.

Afternoon Briefing

Toward the end of the briefings, two 30-minute discussions became pivotal moments of the day.

Starting at about 2:00 p.m., one longtime, experienced general manager and one newcomer made two very different presentations.

The old-timer, Lamont Sill, the general manager for the hotel at Union Square, began his briefing by recounting the impact that the ongoing renovation was having on the hotel performance. CHI had retained an untested general contractor who had gone bankrupt during the project. The undertaking was plagued by one problem after another. Labor disputes, construction and fire code violations and overall poor project management had put the project way behind schedule. Because of delays in the construction schedule, convention business had been cancelled or moved to other CHI hotels. In some cases, the business had to be transferred to other hotel brands in the Union Square area.

Mike sat patiently waiting for Lamont to get through the reasons why his performance was down to identify what he was going to do to address these issues and get back on a positive track. But Lamont never came out of the downward spiral. The entire briefing was an elaborate excuse for his lack of leadership. Eventually, Sally interrupted. "Lamont, I think you have summarized the challenges you face at Union Square well. Can you move on to the action plan you intend to undertake to minimize the impact of these problems?"

"This year is a washout," Lamont responded, "I am working with my team to think in terms of a grand reopening of Union Square later in the fall. We have decided to focus on next fiscal year, starting in October."

"But that is five months from now," Sally said. "What are you and your team going to do to address the shortfall in these next 150 days or so?"

Mike was sitting up on the edge of his seat staring at the words: *From the Tree –Watch for interrupting, snap judgments, talking too much, giving answers, not asking questions."* He was just barely holding his tongue.

Lamont, who was ten years Sally's senior, began a theoretical monologue about how the strategic intent of an organization needed to accommodate the variability of ups and downs in business. He went on and on. Everyone in the room knew two things:

Lamont was not catching the idea about how today's meeting was different from others in the past, and he did not have an answer that was going to be satisfactory to Sally and Mike.

Mike held on through the discussion without saying a word. Everyone in the room was waiting for the bomb to explode—and it almost did, once.

Just as Sally was asking Lamont to wrap things up, she turned to Mike and said, "Boss, do you want to add anything before we move on?"

All eyes were focused on Mike as he looked up from his cell phone, took a breath and said, "The challenges we face at Union Square are really significant. Lamont and his team are thinking about the future and that is good. We need also to address the short-term problems we face at the hotel. You and your district team, Sally, can help a lot in that phase of planning. More needs to be done, and I have every confidence you guys will figure this out."

A New Way of Seeing

Everyone in the room was stunned and silent. The bomb had not detonated. It was a first.

After a short break, the meeting continued.

The general manager who ran Copley Place, Ken Holt, introduced Sandy Henderson, his marketing manager. Sandy stood up and told a story about how she had an idea to generate significant increased revenue with a new angle on attracting travelers from London, England, Edinburgh, Scotland, and Dublin, Ireland. Sandy had developed a relationship with three tour companies in the UK that were specializing in helping upper middle-class families in these three cities conduct genealogy studies in the New England area. With the strength of the Euro against the dollar, the business was brisk and the additional revenue stream was very impressive. Year over year room occupancy numbers were up about 15 percent over the past three periods and the ADR had moved up 8 percent, well above the CHI target for the year.

It was a great presentation. Sandy was full of life, enthusiastic, and had produced real results.

Then she hit the "home run" of the day. Because of the recent push on top line growth that began with Mike's visit just the week before, Sally had contacted the COOs of two of the three companies, who were good friends, only to find out that they were coming to Boston in May to explore how they could significantly upgrade their offering. They decided to ask for a meeting with Sandy and her general manager and Sally Harrison to discuss opportunities for not only the downtown hotels, but also for other hotels in Boston, Philadelphia, New York and Baltimore.

Sandy passed around a copy of the letters she had sent to both COOs and their enthusiastic response. When Sandy reached this point in the room, the general managers were actually clapping as she went from one point to the next. Sally Harrison was absolutely beaming.

At the end of the very long day, Sally thanked everyone for all their work and asked her controller to review the many follow-up actions they would need to track. She then turned to Mike for his summary.

Mike sincerely thanked everyone for their effort. He asked that the final report be on his desk by the end of the month. He then gestured to the white board where his first words of the day had been written and said,

"Today I saw a lot of creativity, passion, smart thinking and for the most part a real can-do attitude. Underneath all the charts and slides and words I also saw a love for the business and for serving customers. This was a great day."

Everyone stood up, clapped and began gathering their things to leave.

Mike realized that he had turned a very big corner in this meeting. During the day he had managed his reactivity in the face of some very trying moments. It was not a permanent change, but it was a start, and it gave him a measure of confidence in his ability to make even greater strides in the days ahead.

Sally wanted to know how Mike really felt the day went. She was happy with how things had turned out, but she was still cautious about what Mike was thinking. He seemed genuinely pleased as they chatted in the car on the way to the airport, and she gradually felt herself relaxing.

As they pulled up to Logan, Sally said, "Mike, I really appreciated how you let me lead the meeting today. Your input was invaluable. And your style of leadership today was energizing to all of us."

As Mike shook Sally's hand and turned to go into the airport, he felt a sense of accomplishment quite unlike anything that he had felt before. Usually, he felt good about what he had done; today, he was feeling best about what he had *not* done! He wanted to call Jacob, but decided that he could wait until Friday morning.

FRIDAY MORNING WITH JACOB

Mike arrived at Jacob's office right on time, and they began their early morning meeting with a lot of enthusiasm. Jacob started things off, "Hello, Mike, how was the week?"

Mike described the Boston visit. He summarized the different events of the visit including his preparation meeting with Vanessa the day before. Jacob was listening to each component of the story and making a few notes as Mike spoke.

"Wednesay afternoon the briefings in Boston included two

very different presentations," Mike said. "A general manager who has been with CHI for a long time made a presentation that was so weak that I felt he was choosing to ignore the instructions provided to help him prepare for the meeting."

"Has he been effective in his job in the past?" Jacob asked.

"This guy has been with CHI for a long time and has always done fairly well. He was promoted, mostly in the northeast, up through the ranks and has reached his peak at one of our smaller hotels in Boston. He is not a superstar but has always done a respectable job," Mike answered.

"I tell you, Jacob, I was surprised, disappointed and agitated with his briefing. Just thinking about it sitting here makes me mad."

Jacob quickly added, "Tell me more about that part of the day."

"Lamont has been managing his way through a difficult renovation project. His hotel is one of the older units in Boston at Union Square, but it is a goldmine. This part of Boston is in a renaissance of sorts. Because of a number of problems associated with the construction that are out of his direct control, he and his team have just about given up on this year's budget challenge."

"So, what about this part of the meeting made you agitated?" Jacob asked.

"It's not that the Union Square team did not come up with good answers for the challenge they face. It's that they did not even try to find an answer to the challenge. Even if Lamont had stood up and suggested ideas that were not very smart, at least we would have had something. It's like they just threw up their hands and said, 'We give up.'" Mike's voice had taken the turn it takes when he gets really agitated—sharp, satirical and biting.

In a very brief, reflective moment, Mike looked at the palms of his hands and quietly said to himself, "God, how I hate that kind of behavior."

Jacob could see that Mike was connecting to a very deep feeling and waited for the moment to set in a little. Then he said, "Mike, when we stopped last time I suggested that we talk about a form of reactivity called sabotage. You will recall from our last visit that reactivity is the public face of anxiety. We spoke about the fact that your effort to establish and maintain control of situations is your way of managing anxiety."

Mike nodded.

"How did you do during the meeting in terms of managing reactive behaviors?"

Mike smiled and said, "Jacob, I did really well. I made a few notes to myself as you suggested on the phone, and I kept focusing on them when I felt myself getting agitated. The few minutes of preparation before I started the day helped me a lot." Mike paused, "But then I almost lost it during this afternoon session with Lamont."

"Mike, it is one thing to deal with the reactivity within yourself. But it's quite another thing to recognize reactivity in others and then manage yourself in the context of their reactive behavior toward you.

"Let me ask you this: Do you think that Lamont has the knowledge and experience to come up with a plan to get out of his short-term dilemma there in Boston?"

"I know he does, Jacob. I have seen him work his way out of much more difficult situations in the past. That's what was so damn irritating to me. He knows what to do, but is just sitting on his ass."

"Well, it is interesting that we are speaking about sabotage today, because I think you are seeing it in the way Lamont is handling himself in the challenge he faces at his hotel. Here is what I mean."

Jacob went to the white board next to the table and wrote four words:

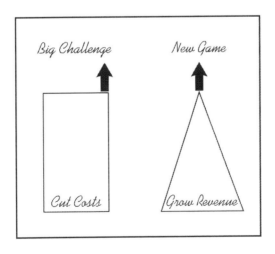

Then he drew arrows pointing at those words, and at the tail of the arrows a rectangle and a triangle. Inside the rectangle he wrote "Cut Costs" and in the triangle he wrote "Grow Revenues."

"Mike, you've told me that your challenge to the Boston team to come up with new revenue was something that no one expected. Everyone pretty much knew the drill about cutting costs, and they expected you to tell them to find some bottom line savings. But no one was ready for you to tell them to do both. Is that right?"

"Yes. I think I took them pretty much by surprise with a new approach."

"Is it fair to say that, in a sense, you changed the rules of the game on them?"

"Well... I suppose so. But I wasn't exactly asking them to do the impossible."

"That's not the point. What I'm saying is that by introducing a new game," and as he said those words Jacob underlined <u>New Game</u> on the white board, "you took them by surprise and asked something unexpected of them. Not only did you ask something new of them, you did it in a new way—inviting rather than demanding. When you did that, you destabilized a familiar system, and that is always sure to trigger anxiety in many people. Some people love a fresh approach and a new challenge, but most people instinctively resist change, even when it's in their own self-interest to comply."

A puzzled look crossed Mike's face. "I'm not sure I know what you mean when you say I destabilized a familiar system."

"I don't have time to go into it today, Mike. We'll talk about thinking systems next time. But for now let's just say your challenge and how you delivered it threw people off guard and made some of them very anxious with this new game they had to play. Apparently Lamont in particular got very anxious over it.

"Mike, here is one way to think about how Lamont is dealing with the challenge he is facing. He has a physical plant that is really struggling and his product, that is his hotel, is facing problems that he does not have control over at this point. You are asking him to find a way to not only cut costs but also grow revenues in an operation that is crippled, at least from his point of view. It seems pretty reasonable to me that his anxiety right now is higher than usual, right?"

"You bet. He's been totally stressed out by one thing after another going wrong, and it's been totally beyond his control to fix the disaster that's unfolded with the renovation project."

"Okay, so he's already very anxious. And now on top of it all, you throw a new challenge and ask him to play a new game. What do you suppose that does to his anxiety level?"

Mike nodded, "I see what you're getting at. My new game pushed him over the edge. His anxiety must have gone over the top."

"Exactly, and when we are anxious we get reactive. But here's something very important I want you to follow carefully." Jacob's voice dropped, and he leaned forward towards Mike. "Remember that we're talking about **automatic functioning**, which is usually beneath conscious awareness, and how it manifests itself in the form of reactivity. That means almost surely that Lamont has no clue his behaviors are reactive, even though it might be obvious to lots of other people—although I doubt that as well.

"Here's a guess at what was going on in his mind: He had two choices. He could have tried to comply with your wishes and work through your challenge. But he had another choice, too. He apparently decided that his situation is so significant that he doesn't have to play by the new rules. In fact, his briefing was so different from all the others because he believed his circumstance is truly different from the others and he doesn't need to be held to the same set of rules."

Mike was listening intently.

"When anxiety escalates, our feeling responses frequently override our thinking responses. In those circumstances, people often convince themselves that they are in a unique situation and their noncompliance with rules or established expectations is justified. This noncompliance is not born out of malicious intent, but nevertheless its effect is to sabotage the new game they are being asked to play.

"Here is an example. Take a mom stopping in a parking space, jumping out of her car, and deciding not to put any money in the meter because she intends to only be gone one minute to pick up the kids from day care. Then she finds out that her little Amanda has lost one tennis shoe somewhere in the day care center and she needs to find it before she can leave. Twenty minutes later she is back at her parked vehicle looking at a $35 parking violation. She knows that she violated the rule but feels like the rule should not apply to her because of her special circumstances. In her mind it feels unfair.

"The same may be true with Lamont. In his reactive state, he may be thinking he is different and his team should be given a pass because of their difficult and largely uncontrollable circumstances. The effect—but not the intent—of his actions is to sabotage your efforts to introduce a new approach to solving the current problems in Boston."

Mike's exasperation spilled out, "We pay this guy over a quarter of a million dollars a year to think a lot more clearly than some frazzled mom running into a day care center."

Jacob replied, "Mike this is not about thinking things through. I am talking about anxious **emotional process** hijacking thoughtfulness. I want you to see how it is linked to reactivity, and one form that reactivity can take is called sabotage. Don't forget we are all susceptible to this type of resistance. Effective leaders learn to **watch for emotional process** and recognize what is going on underneath the reactive behaviors they encounter in their team."

Jacob was quiet for a time, allowing Mike to absorb what he had been saying.

Eventually Mike said, "So, if I understand what you're telling me, I need to recognize that Lamont's failure to accept my challenge was about mindless resistance, not a deliberate refusal to get with the program. He was sabotaging my initiative, but he's totally oblivious to it. Is that it?"

"That's exactly it, Mike. It doesn't mean you give him a pass or excuse him or anything like that. But it does mean that you shouldn't take it personally, since it's more about *his* functioning than about *your* authority being challenged. And if you can keep from taking it personally, you will be better able to handle your own reactivity in the face of his sabotage."

Jacob paused and asked Mike, "How did you handle your reactions in this situation?"

"It was a real challenge. I held my tongue and let someone else address the limitations of the briefing. Sally, the area vice president, did a good job. In the end, it will be up to her to help Lamont address his short-term performance issues. But I am sure my face was red as a candy apple, because I was about to just burst."

"Well, congratulations, Mike. That was a real victory for you," Jacob said. "Here are a few more pointers about how you can deal with this sort of reactive sabotage."

Jacob maneuvered his wheelchair back to the white board and quickly wrote a list of bullets:

- *Don't take it personally*
- *Manage your own reactivity*
- *Lower anxiety*
- *Hold fast to your position*
- *Watch process, not content*

"I've already told you not to take it personally, and we've discussed that you need to be managing your own reactivity. The next tip I'd offer is to lower, rather than raise, the anxiety when you encounter sabotage. Pounding the table or exploding would have only made Lamont more reactive. It sounds like you did the right thing letting Sally deal with him later on. That was a second victory for you!"

Mike couldn't help but break out in a big grin at the praise.

"When you encounter reactive sabotage in response to a change you've initiated, there are forces in the system trying to get you to go back to the way things were. It's very, very important you do not have a failure of nerve and give up at that point. So, calmly restate your position, and hold to it."

Jacob went on, pointing again to the white board, "This last point is more subtle and a lot more difficult to pull off. It is so easy to get hooked by the content of an issue, rather than staying up in the tree, looking down on the process that is unfolding. But as you grow in your ability to do so, your leadership effectiveness will take a quantum leap forward. The phrase '**watch for emotional process**' is the way I try to capture this skill, rather than getting hooked by the content."

"Could you say a little bit more about what you mean by that?" Mike asked.

"If you had engaged Lamont in a discussion of his alleged reasons for not being able to grow revenue, that would have been getting hooked by the content. Or when your team is complaining about something you've done or not done, if you are naïve and think the real issue is whatever they're complaining about, you'll likely miss what is really going on. Frequently, it's just a way of getting your attention when they're feeling neglected. Because these behaviors are usually below conscious awareness, it's often tricky to know exactly what is going on. But you will learn to recognize subtle clues, like a disproportionate anger or upset over a trivial issue, and that will alert you to the presence of **automatic functioning** of which they themselves are totally unaware."

"Damn, it sounds like you want me to become a psychoanalyst or something," Mike groaned.

"Not really," Jacob said. "I'm simply suggesting you might profit from becoming a better, more aware observer of human nature. You already have great instincts about so many aspects of running a business. I'm just adding to your tool chest.

"But I think we're overdue for a break. How about we stop for ten minutes or so?"

They took a ten-minute break, and Mike used the time to record some of his thoughts about sabotage in his cell phone for further review.

He was no longer thinking about calling his office at every break to see what was going on. Now the content and depth of his coaching was taking center stage for him at these sessions. He was beginning to understand what Vanessa had learned years ago and what she was helping him learn today.

UNDERNEATH REACTIVITY

When Mike came back into the office, he said to Jacob, "I was thinking about your congratulating me for not pounding on the table during Lamont's presentation. But what if I'm in a situation where I feel strongly about something and it seems right to let the team know my feelings? Are you saying I can never show my emotions?"

"Of course not," Jacob said. "Your victory was that you contained your reactivity and gave thinking rather than feeling responses. But if you had decided that the most useful strategy you could adopt in order to further your purpose was to pound your fist on the table, you should have responded that way. The key is not to prevent emotional exchanges; rather, it is to ensure that you provide a thoughtful response, which in fact might be done with great intensity."

This was new learning for Mike. Up until this point he had equated controlling his reactivity with keeping his "tough guy" inclinations bottled up inside himself. Now, he was seeing that the key was not emotion versus non-emotion, but rather acting out of thoughtfulness versus automatically reacting with a blind feeling response.

Jacob pointed to a new picture he had drawn on the white board. It was a long horizontal line with the two words, "Societal Regression," written below the line and "Reactivity" written above the line.

Reactivity

Societal Regression

"Mike, the last point I'd like to talk about today is something that Bowen Theory calls 'societal regression.' It is an important concept for you to know about in order to understand the context of much of the reactivity you see around you at work, at home and in the community.

"We've been talking about reactivity as a symptom of chronic anxiety, but our focus has been mostly on how individuals—you and Lamont, for example—express and deal with reactivity. But there has been a huge amount of research done into how entire family systems function reactively when they have higher levels of chronic anxiety. In a nutshell, their functioning becomes more regressive, less mature.

"Because the behaviors of chronically anxious families have been studied in detail, those behaviors can be predicted with a fair degree of accuracy. But the key insight here is that not just families, but organizations of any size demonstrate parallel symptoms when they become highly anxious. And in the same way that families regress, those larger systems show similar symptoms of regressive functioning.

"One of my mentors, Ed Friedman, was a history buff and he did a lot of study of how American society today shows the same patterns as a highly anxious, regressed family system. He drew parallels between contemporary American civilization and predictable behavior patterns of highly anxious families—things like herding—or groupthink—and shifting blame to others and always looking for a quick fix.

"I'm pretty sure those same patterns show up regularly in organizations like CHI when they are caught up in the heightened anxiety of the larger society we are part of. It might help you get a bigger perspective on what we're discussing about reactivity if you explore Friedman's ideas more deeply. He's got a great book on leadership called *A Failure of Nerve: Leadership in the Age of the Quick Fix*, and I highly recommend it."

"Jacob, I'm afraid my brain is on overload. Can you give me the *Reader's Digest* version of this and why it's something I need to know?"

"Sure, Mike. What I want you to be aware of is that this kind of atmosphere makes it particularly difficult for a leader to function in a mature, self-differentiating way. As you become better at watching for emotional process, you should be able to recognize how individuals and entire organizations are increasingly anxious as the society around them becomes more and more regressed. Every leader today is dealing with the fallout of this heightened reactivity, and the challenge of leadership is correspondingly difficult."

"Now I know why Vanessa is jumping ship," Mike said with a laugh.

Jacob joined in the laughter. Then he said, "Listen, Mike. I know I've given you a lot to absorb today, and we can talk further about all of this some other time. I think we need to wrap up our session.

"I've spent so much time talking with you about chronic anxiety and reactivity because I believe it constitutes one of the major challenges faced today by anyone responsible for leading an organization of any size. A colleague of mine recently used the image of a room filled with leaking gas fumes to describe the buildup of chronic anxiety in our world today. All it takes is one match to spark a major conflagration. When that happens, it's usually the person who struck the match who gets blamed, but a more thoughtful perspective realizes that it's the gradual buildup of gas that was ultimately responsible for the problem.

"True leaders are the ones who watch for the accumulating gas fumes, and proactively know how to take action to clear the air before it reaches a critical point. In the face of very, very powerful forces of reactivity, that's about as challenging a task as I can think of. If you're going to be the kind of outstanding leader that I think you are capable of being, then you need constantly to watch for anxious, regressive forces in order to spot trouble before it happens.

"So far we've been working on the fundamentals of seeing the social systems around you through a different lens. This different lens is the lens you are using when you are in your second mind or up in the imaginary tree, watching what is happening beneath you. When you see the systems around you from this more thoughtful and less reactive vantage point, you can more effectively determine the correct action to take to achieve the goals you want.

"As a leader, you have a very powerful position from which to shape outcomes in your organization. When you act out of a thoughtful, self-differentiating stance, you can more effectively direct the output of the system you lead. Your non-reactive behavior will calm those you lead and provide them the stability they need to follow your lead. I am convinced that as you learn how to use the **Resilient Leadership** model to apply the principles of Bowen Theory, you will be better able to counter the regressive forces that infect every organization and every individual today. That's why, in addition to 'A New Way of SEEING,' I want to explore with you next time what I call 'A New Way of THINKING.'"

Mike was beginning to understand that Jacob was introducing him to some very, very important ideas. His understanding, he knew, was still fairly shallow. But he also knew that he was on the right track.

Chapter 3: Automatic Functioning

Review Key Points

- Anxiety is response to a threat, real or imagined
  - Acute anxiety is immediate and transitory; chronic anxiety is generalized, pervasive and enduring
  - Chronic anxiety operates at the level of **emotional process** and is quite often beneath conscious awareness
  - The roots of chronic anxiety are in one's family of origin
  - Different families have different levels of chronic anxiety with which they function
  - Organizations, like families, have their own characteristic levels of chronic anxiety

- Reactivity—a prime example of **automatic functioning**—is the visible expression of anxiety.
  - Reactivity occurs when feeling responses overtake thinking responses
  - Sabotage is a predictable, natural—and rarely deliberate—response to a change that upsets the equilibrium of the system
  - Reactive sabotage is anxiety-driven and generally beneath conscious awareness

- Tips for a leader dealing with reactive sabotage:
  - Don't take it personally
  - Manage your own reactivity
  - Lower anxiety
  - Hold fast to your position
  - Watch process rather than content

- In periods of societal regression, entire societies demonstrate behaviors similar to those of chronically anxious families:
  - Reactivity
  - Herding
  - Blaming
  - Quick-fix solutions

Questions for Reflection and Discussion

1. Mike has come to realize that one of his triggers is loss of control. Can you name anything else that triggers reactivity in Mike?

2. Reactive sabotage is a "natural" systems response to change. Can you identify any such behaviors that have surfaced in your workplace around changes introduced into the organization?

3. As you reflect upon your family of origin, what level of chronic anxiety do you think was part of the family's functioning? Can you identify any particular patterns that you recognize now to be symptomatic of heightened reactivity?

The Practice

Most of our daily thinking process occurs in the form of verbalized or non-verbalized questions. These questions we ask others or ourselves create the reality we see in most circumstances. Consider these two (internal reflection) questions to the same event:

- Why does Sarah always correct me or add her own "additional thoughts" when I am making an important point to our boss?

- How can Sarah and I communicate with our boss in a way that is satisfying to us both?

Which question is proactive and which is reactive? Does one of these (internal reflection) questions create a pathway to anxiety? Which question is more solution-centered? Here is the idea: If you change the question in your mind, you change the reality of your experience.

1. Think about one of the most difficult interpersonal challenges you have faced in the last few months. Draw a

diagram of the system relationship and write a sentence that describes your **automatic functioning**.

2. With as much objective perspective as possible, reflect on how you have handled yourself in the situation. Given the description of your role in the circumstances, determine the underlining assumption (in the form of a question or two) that is guiding your behavior/action.

3. Now closely consider how the "question in your mind" is creating the reality you face in the challenge itself. Then recast the "question in your mind" in a less reactive way. This process of self-reflection will help you begin to see your own **automatic functioning** in the challenge you chose to analyze.

Automatic Functioning

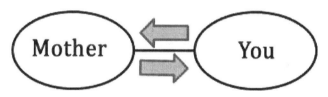

Set boundaries related to advice on taking care of teenage son.

My Automatic Functioning	Questions in My Mind
1. I automatically resent Mom's constant polite but judgmental suggestions about how to gain more control over my son.	2. **Questions in My Mind Now:** Why do I have to listen to Mom's constant judgmental chatter about how I need to be a better parent? 3. **Better Question:** How can I engage Mom in a discussion that would allow me to understand and evaluate her suggestions without feeling judged by her?

To learn more, go to www.resilient-leadership.biz.

A New Way of **THINKING**

Chapter 4: Think Systems

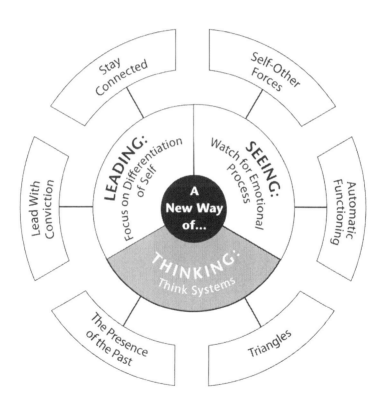

Vanessa Check-In

Vanessa had been thinking about Mike and Steve Alba over the weekend and decided to connect with them both on Monday. She asked Helen to set up two brief meetings.

As Mike arrived at her office, Vanessa was concluding her conversation with Steve, and they passed in the doorway. It was amicable on the surface, but both men knew that they were in quite a competition. Mike wondered if Steve was getting coaching. Maybe he was a client of Jacob as well. He wanted to ask the question but decided against it.

Vanessa looked at Mike expectantly. "Hello, Mike. I hear that the trip to Boston was a big success."

"It was a success with some challenges, as always. Our team in Boston has pulled together and helped each other out a lot. I was especially impressed with the work done by a marketing manager at the Copley Place hotel. She is doing a great job getting group business in Great Britain. I will give you and the team a full report at the next Executive Team meeting."

"Great; let me know if I can help in any way," Vanessa said and then changed the topic.

"Mike, how is your coaching with Jacob progressing?"

"My time with Jacob is interesting and very helpful. We are meeting regularly, and he is continuing to focus our discussions on issues I have here at work and at home. He is a big help. I'm learning a lot."

"That's great, Mike. Have you begun to talk about systems thinking yet?" Vanessa inquired.

"Jacob says we're getting to that topic next. He mentioned systems thinking at the end of our last session."

"Well, Jacob is the pro on the subject, but I can tell you a little bit about the concept. I think it could be a real help in dealing with the challenges you face in Boston. May I spend a few minutes on this with you?"

"Absolutely," Mike said, "I appreciate all the input I can get on this stuff."

"Before your last trip up there, I mentioned that you would need to 'pry open' some of the mental models people will have about new-revenue generation during economic downturns. To some of our people, it seems counterintuitive to spend more money to attract new customers or recommit existing customers when sales and profits are in the tank."

"I ran into some of that in Boston during my last visit, and now I need to follow up with Sally about one particular hotel and general manager," Mike replied.

"One aspect of systems thinking that I find particularly useful is the basic perspective that it establishes. Jacob used the terms 'family systems' and 'organizational systems' in a way that I found confusing at first, until I began to recognize what he was talking about in my own family," said Vanessa.

"At one point during my coaching with Jacob, my sister and brother began what has turned into a long-term argument about how best to care for our aging father. The decision to place a parent in a nursing home is difficult, as I'm sure you're aware from your own situation with your father."

Mike nodded vigorously.

"My brother and sister had very different ideas about when and how to take that step. As I watched the debate explode into a huge family squabble, Jacob was able to help me see the functioning of the 'Jackson Family System' in a larger systems perspective rather than seeing Chantal and Marcus as simply two people locked in a passionate argument."

Mike asked, "How do you see a system?"

"That is what I learned from Jacob. You don't actually see the system—you see the dynamics of the system acted out in behaviors. Here is a good example: Marcus, being the youngest sibling, had a real emotional bond with Dad and he increasingly saw himself as his primary caretaker as he got older, especially after Mom died. Chantal, the middle child, being a practical down-to-earth type, dealt with the decision to place Dad into a retirement center in a more or less matter of fact way. Just get it done, so to speak.

"Well, the discussions about where, when, and how was like pulling teeth. But gradually, as I watched what was happening, I could recognize that the back-and-forth between Marcus and Chantal was just a way of passing the anxiety around the family system. When he got more anxious, she would get calm, and vice-versa. And of course both of them tried to triangle me into the discussion on their side. When the tension between both of them calmed down, my father's anxiety would flare up. It was amazing to watch how they passed the anxiety around the various family triangles. It was a real soap opera.

"Has Jacob talked to you about triangles yet?"

"No, not yet."

"Well, you'll learn a lot about triangles from Jacob, but simply put, the notion of triangles is a way of thinking about relationships and the **emotional process** that is operating in those relationships. Triangles are the basic building blocks of every relationship system."

Mike was trying to follow, but finally he said, "I'm not sure I'm getting the connections you want to make between systems and triangles and what Jacob is getting at."

"Once Jacob showed me how the triangles were working in my family system, it wasn't long before I began to see all of the same behaviors here at CHI. I began to understand and think about what was happening here in terms of triangles that interlock to form an entire network of relationships—a system. It's as if each little triangle creates its own force field—like a magnetic field or a gravitational field—and all of them together create a huge, organization-wide field."

Mike wished he was better prepared to engage on the subject, but he realized this was not the time to fake it with Vanessa. "I'm still not sure I understand what you mean," he said.

"Here's an image that might help: Imagine three people in a room with a gigantic rubber band around the outside of them, holding them all together. They are programmed to maintain the tension on the rubber band, so that it doesn't drop to the floor if they move too close together, or snap if they move too far apart. The tension that holds them together is the force field, the hidden dynamics of the relationship system—what Bowen Theory calls **emotional process**.

"Now, here's the really important part: I began to realize that I could influence the entire field with my own behavior. If I move closer to one person, the other one has to move farther away in order to keep the tension on the rubber band balanced. If I move away, the other two have to get closer together. That's the way triangles work to keep systems in balance, and it gives a leader enormous leverage to influence the system—if he or she understands how it all works.

"In practical terms, I began to understand that my level of

anxiety or calmness dramatically impacts the degree of tension on the rubber band—the emotional climate of the organization and of the people around me. I began to realize that how I function in the system actually changes the field around me. I can cause the tension in the rubber band to increase or decrease by how I function. So if I react to a situation by becoming more anxious, I cause greater reactivity in others; and if I become calm, then people around me decompress and become less reactive. Once I realized all of this, I began to 'think systems' a lot more!

"Jacob uses the terms 'step-up' and 'step-down transformer' as a metaphor for how a person influences the system around him or her."

Mike sat and thought for a moment and then said, "I will need to think about all this in the context of my work with the team in Boston. I am a little concerned about whether I am in triangles up there myself."

"Oh, you're surely involved in lots of triangles, Mike—everyone is. Triangles are a natural phenomenon within any group of people who are in relationship with one another. They're not good or bad, in and of themselves. It's how a person functions within triangles that results in more productive or less productive interactions in any relationship. You need to talk with Jacob about all of this.

"Mike, here is my point. I just want you to begin to recognize what powerful leverage you have in your position as a key CHI leader. You need to start thinking more about how your own behavior—Jacob uses the word 'functioning'—influences people around you."

Mike realized that both Jacob and Vanessa were trying very hard to help him become more self-aware, not just by challenging him to be less of a jerk, but by providing him with new leadership tools and new ways to think about situations.

Mike also began to realize that learning about triangles could be a significant help for whomever was selected as COO of CHI.

"Vanessa, thanks for showing so much interest in my work with Jacob," Mike said.

With real warmth, Vanessa said, "You're welcome, Mike. I'm happy to do so."

Mike stood up and walked toward the door. As he did so, he

noticed how Vanessa switched gears with ease and grace as she began to prepare for her next meeting. He admired Vanessa a great deal.

MIKE SENIOR

In preparation for the Sampson family reunion in June, Mike knew that he needed to return his dad's recent phone calls and also make arrangements for the annual trip back to Pennsylvania. The reunion was always held at his Aunt Mary's 100-acre farm about 30 miles west of Pittsburg. The family all congregated at the farm starting in the early morning of the fateful Sunday in either late June or early July. Save-the-date postcards always arrived in May, and Karla insisted that they attend the outing each year to stay connected to the family.

This was no small reunion. Throughout the day more than 200 relatives arrived from all over the east coast. Mike's family roots went all the way back to a group of five Mennonite families that came to the U.S. from Northern Germany in the early 1700s and settled first in eastern Pennsylvania and later in western Pennsylvania near the Ohio border. Mike knew his family history back a number of generations and having this knowledge gave him a sense of pride about his heritage.

German Mennonites were a tough breed of farmers that had a rather strict and hardnosed way with life. While Mike was nowhere near a Mennonite in his religious affiliation, he always believed that his tenacity and sense of self-discipline came from his Mennonite roots.

On a bright Saturday morning about a month before the reunion, Mike drove to visit his dad at Silverstone Retirement Village, which was about 45 minutes west of Reston in Front Royal, Virginia. Mike pulled up to the main community building, took a deep breath, gauged that he would have to be with his dad for no more than 45 minutes, and went in to the reception area. He walked into the lobby, glanced at the receptionist, turned left, and headed to room 220.

As he knocked on the door and stepped into his dad's room, he noticed that the TV was on, with the volume too loud, and that Mike Senior was not in his chair or bed. Just then the nurse's aide came into the room, said hello and told Mike that his dad was in the courtyard with several other residents. Mike headed back to the reception area and across the lobby to the courtyard.

"Hello, Dad," Mike said with a big smile.

Mike Senior stood up slowly and stretched out his hand to shake young Mike's hand. The two of them had had a distant and formal relationship for as long as Mike could remember, and it was not about to change now.

"Hello, Michael," Mike Senior said. Mike Senior was the only one in the family who called him Michael.

Mike smiled at the four women who were sitting with his father and pulled over a folding chair to the group. Turning to his dad, he asked how Mike Senior was feeling.

"Lonely," Mike Senior replied.

"Well, you are sitting here with these four lovely ladies," Mike replied.

Mike Senior did not answer.

Mike noticed that his father had not shaved in a couple of days and that his clothes seemed clean but very wrinkled. His guilt had already kicked in, as it always did during one of these visits.

"Dad, I've come to check up on how you are doing and to let you know that we are getting ready for the trip to the family reunion in about a month. We will pick you up on Saturday to sleep over at the house, and then we can get an early start the next day. How does that sound to you?"

"Are you sure you want me to come to your house?" Mike Senior asked.

"Of course we do, Dad." Mike replied. "Besides, if you come over the day before we can visit with you that afternoon and have a cookout in the back yard."

"The bedroom you put me in is upstairs and I have a lot of trouble with the stairs. Besides, I don't like sleeping in a bedroom that does not have a bathroom close by. Your house is too big. You don't need all that room now that your kids are gone."

Mike could feel his anxiety beginning to elevate.

"Well, do you want me to come pick you up early Sunday morning so you can stay in your own room here at the Village?" Mike asked.

"I don't care. Do whatever you think is best," Mike Senior said.

"Well, Dad, we have two choices. Either you come with me

the day before we leave for the reunion, or I come here early Sunday morning. Either way, you need to make a decision."

Mike Senior did not say anything.

"How is Karla?" Mike Senior inquired.

"She is just fine. She was busy with shopping or she would have come with me to see you today."

"Shopping is more important, I guess," Mike Senior mumbled half to himself and half so Mike might take the bait. Mike Senior had been argumentative for as long as Mike could remember, but his sour moods had gotten much worse following the death about six years ago of his wife Jackie at the age of 68. Mike Senior was just turning 80 and was one of the oldest living Sampson family members. He was always a center of attention at the annual reunions and always had a great time.

"Dad, Karla loves you and would have been here today if she could have. You know that," Mike argued.

"I want to go back to my room now," Mike Senior said.

Mike had long ago learned that his father had the behavior of just changing subjects when someone made a point with which he did not agree. It was his father's way of controlling conversations and others in general. It was an irritating behavior.

They walked back to room 220, and Mike Senior took a seat in the recliner while young Mike sat in a chair next to the bed. The room was in the assisted living area of the continuing care facility. It was one step above independent living but not yet at the skilled nursing level. Mike Senior's memory was failing and from time to time he would get lost in the facility, so it had been decided about six months ago by the staff with Mike's agreement that his father needed to be moved from independent living to the next level of care.

Mike knew that the best decision for the reunion weekend was to pick up his dad on Saturday evening. He decided to tell his dad how the weekend would go.

"Dad, I think the best thing for us to do is to leave for Pennsylvania early on Sunday morning, so I will come by and pick you up at about 4:00 p.m. the day before. I will give you a call on Saturday morning to remind you and ask you to pack up a few clothes. Does that sound good to you?"

"It will be a surprise if you call me," Mike Senior said.

"Dad, I will call you on Saturday, the day before the reunion and pick you up at about 4:00 p.m. I need to head back home now. Can I get you anything before I leave?"

"No, I am just fine," Mike Senior said in a sarcastic voice. He picked up a magazine and ignored Mike as he turned to walk out of the room.

Mike looked at his watch as he walked away from room 220 and realized that he had spent about 20 minutes at the retirement center and it seemed like three hours. He just did not know how to talk with his dad without getting frustrated at the constant complaining and negative judgment that he always felt. He wanted to sit down and have a friendly and maybe even meaningful discussion with Mike Senior, but he just could never get started in a direction that worked.

As Mike reached his car, he thought about the last visit he had with Jacob and began looking through his briefcase for the list of reactive behaviors that he picked up at the last coaching session. He found it and skimmed down to one section:

- **Victim Mentality** – Reactivity often surfaces as hypersensitivity, a perennial stance of woundedness in the face of others' behaviors or even just life's outrageous fortunes. The result is a flight from responsibility. "It is never my fault; the other is always to blame and I am inevitably the innocent victim who cannot be held accountable for circumstances beyond my control." Ironically, the flipside of this also surfaces sometimes in the form of blaming self, even though there is no objective basis to do so.

He was looking for a way to understand his father's behavior, and it seemed that victim mentality was a good description. Then he thought, "If my dad exhibits a victim mentality, how am I reacting to him?" He looked further down the list and found that a lot of the descriptions fit his own behavior, but one in particular, rebellion, fit him to a tee:

- **Rebellion/Submission** – Both of these patterns can be forms of reactivity, two sides of a single coin. Stubborn refusal to comply with reasonable requests is as reactive as complete willingness to submit, regardless of the personal price. Both forms of reactivity are usually accompanied by a host of rationalizations that justify why the particular course of action is reasonable or appropriate "given the circumstances."

He began to see his reaction to his dad as one of rebellion. He had been a rebellious son for as long as he could remember. He had always taken pride in his ability to be his own person, even in the face of his father's dominating control. The real split came when Mike decided not to attend dental school to carry on the tradition of dentistry in his family. His father, grandfather and great-grandfather were all dentists who had practiced in the western Pennsylvania backcountry.

Then he thought about Jacelyn. More clearly than ever before, Mike could now see the similarity between the two relationships he had with his dad and his daughter. The conversation several days earlier with Vanessa about her family system was becoming clearer as he thought about all the reactivity in his own family. It seemed that every generation had its own version of the pattern.

Mike decided that he would visit with Jacob to discuss this situation before the reunion. He wanted to find a way to recast his relationship with his father, if at all possible, before it was too late.

When he arrived back home, he discovered that Karla was busy all weekend with house showings, so he quickly summarized his visit to Front Royal as they passed each other in the hallway. He decided to talk with her about his deeper insights sometime in the coming few days.

On Sunday morning Mike decided to relax for the day. He ran in the morning and rested all afternoon, dozing on and off with the Sunday paper and movies on TCM. About 8:00 p.m., he made some notes.

Today (Weekend)
- Dad and I just cannot talk to each other without being reactive.
- I have got to change my reactivity toward Dad before I can expect him to change.
- Is Dad really unaware of his reactivity—his vitriol seems so targeted at me.

Issues
- *Does the rubber band analogy apply to my relationship with Don and my dad?*
- *Systems thinking, especially triangles, makes some sense, but I can't see triangles the way Vanessa talks about—let alone emotional systems.*

Follow up
- *Talk with Karla about the fact that Dad has victim behaviors and I have rebellion behaviors.*
- *What are Karla's reactive behaviors?*
- *Find out why the behavior of a leader is so impactful in a family or organization. I think people can have their own agency—I think strong management leaders set their own direction. They often buck the system.*

A NEW WAY OF THINKING

On Monday Mike headed over to Jacob's office to make his 9:00 a.m. coaching session. Jacob had mentioned that they would be changing gears in this meeting and looking more deeply into relationship systems. Jacob had requested that they have two sessions in rapid succession so the material could be covered in a more coherent manner. Today's meeting was to be followed by another meeting on Monday of the next week.

Mike recalled that Jacob suggested that they would be moving from what he called "A New Way of SEEING" to "A New Way THINKING," and he felt a little more prepared because of his conversation with Vanessa a few days earlier. The night before the meeting, Mike had read some material on Jacob's website about chronic anxiety in families, society and organizations, as well as prepared a list of priorities for the day.

Mike knocked on the door and heard the voice from inside say, "Hello, Mike. Come right in." Jacob was in good spirits, as always.

"How are you, Mike?" Jacob asked.

"Terrific. I had a great rest over the weekend and a pretty good run this morning," Mike answered, although he was feeling the aftershock of a fairly severe pain in his left knee joint. The feeling was unlike anything he had experienced before, but he had taken some ibuprofen to dull the pain.

"Mike, today I was thinking we might cover some new territory that I hope you will find very helpful. In fact, I am sure you will," Jacob said with confidence. "But first, is there anything you want to talk about today?"

"Yes, I was hoping we could talk about my dad and the upcoming family reunion."

"Sure," Jacob responded. "In fact, that would fit perfectly with what we were going to cover anyway. It would be helpful to me if you could give me a little more background on your dad and on the relationship between the two of you."

"Okay, but I'm not sure where to begin. My dad and I have had a pretty contentious relationship for years—in fact, as long as I can remember we've butted heads over just about everything. He is stubborn as a mule, and he never misses a chance to criticize me or put me down. Since my mom died and especially since he's been in the retirement home, he's been more miserable than ever. I think he blames me for his winding up there, although the truth is my sister is the one who pushed hardest and finally convinced him it was what he needed to do."

"How does your dad get along with your sister, Mike?"

"Very well. She's always been the golden child. I could do nothing right, and she could do no wrong. She's been very worried about dad since mom died and has hovered over him and really mothered him. He loves the attention."

"Are there any specific issues between you and your father—any major conflicts or any past history of the two of you having it out?"

"No, nothing like that. We've always been too distant for that. We don't fight. He just snipes at me, I feel guilty and avoid him, and that just makes him criticize me all the more. I tell you, Jacob, he's just pig-headed and unhappy and dumps it all on me."

"Mike, do I have your permission to push back a little and challenge you a bit?"

Mike was taken aback, but recovered immediately and said, "Sure, of course. What do you want to say?"

Jacob gave a warm smile and said, "Well, it sounds to me like your assessment is that the problem between the two of you lies pretty much with your dad's bad temperament. Is that a fair portrayal of what I've heard?"

Mike was a bit embarrassed, but nodded, and said, "Yeah, I suppose so. It sounds like I'm blaming him for everything and not willing to accept any responsibility myself. But the truth is that I can usually get along with most anyone, but with the way he is…"

Mike's voice trailed off and he fell silent. It was obvious to Jacob that deep feelings were welling up in Mike as he thought about the painful relationship he had with his father.

Jacob spoke softly, "Mike, most people who experience conflictual relationships tend to think about them in the way that you do. They try to fix blame—sometimes on the other person, and sometimes on themselves. And the blame is generally framed in terms of an individual perspective: 'It's his personality.' or 'I just can't communicate with him,' or something like that.

"What I'd like to share with you is a different perspective—one that I think offers a deeper and more accurate understanding of the complexity of human relationships. We've talked about the 'New Way of SEEING' that the **Resilient Leadership** model teaches, and I think you've made a lot of progress understanding what that is all about. But, as I've hinted along the way, watching for **emotional process**—that is, watching for its symptoms in the attempts to balance **self-other forces** and in anxiety-driven reactivity—is only the beginning. You also need to develop 'A New Way of THINKING' as well. If you do, it will help you understand and manage yourself in your relationship with your dad in better ways."

Jacob continued, "The 'New Way of THINKING' I refer to is learning about emotional systems—learning to '**think systems**.' Let me explain what I'm getting at in that phrase."

Jacob was aware that Mike was getting impatient—that he could not yet see how this had any connection with the conflict between him and his father.

"Bear with me, Mike, and I'll try to show you how this applies to what is happening between you and your father.

"A system, I'm sure you know, is a dynamic environment—one that is constantly making adjustments and compensations aimed at balancing the inner forces that hold it together.

Scientists call this phenomenon homeostasis."

Jacob maneuvered his wheelchair over to point at a four-foot long mobile hanging in the corner of his office.

"This mobile has been hanging here for years. It's a system, an entity with an identifiable shape, and the stable interrelationships among all of its parts keep it in balance, even as it turns in the breeze."

Jacob pushed on one of the metal plates of the mobile and set it to swinging.

"As these parts turn and glide in the breeze, its coherence and unity is perceived immediately."

Then Jacob picked up an alligator clip from his desk and clamped it onto one side of the mobile.

"But if one part of the mobile suddenly takes on added weight, the entire field adjusts and compensates, achieving a new balance in view of the new reality of one of its parts. Only a systems perspective can adequately understand the sudden shift in the entire mobile."

Jacob pointed to the counterbalanced weight that shot up on the left side of the mobile when he added the new weight on the right side.

"A narrow focus on this one element that suddenly lifted its position relative to the whole—without looking to the opposite end where a weight was just added—misses the point completely.

"So, failing to look systemically for the reason why one side has suddenly surged upward risks a misdiagnosis that the 'problem' lies in the unruly part that is throwing everything out of whack!"

Jacob paused, waiting for Mike to make the connection.

Mike just stared at him.

"What I'm suggesting is that you are looking at your father's behavior—the 'unruly part that is throwing everything out of whack'—without understanding the complex balancing forces at work in the emotional system he is part of. You're not looking at the rest of the mobile—the system that he is part of. You are one part of that system, but so are your sister, your wife and children, as well as lots of other people that are part of his network of relationships.

"His foul mood, his attacks on you, and so forth, are connected to much more than you are understanding."

Mike was paying more attention now, and Jacob knew that he had caught his interest.

Mike nodded slowly and said, "Okay, so help me figure out how I'm supposed to understand all of this. What's this 'new way' I'm supposed to be thinking?"

Jacob continued, "My example of the mobile has some limitations, Mike, because it's a mechanical system that follows physical laws. The kind of systems thinking that understands how a mobile works is rooted in principles drawn from physics and engineering. On the other hand, the kind of thinking I am talking about is rooted in evolutionary biology and the natural sciences."

Jacob reached for his portable ant farm and moved it to a place on the table between the two of them. He pointed to the ants crawling around in the sand tunnels, and said, "These little guys have something in common with my mobile over there in the sense that they are also part of a system. But their living system obeys different laws than the mobile, which is a mechanical system governed by Newton's laws.

"For ants—in fact, for all sentient beings—the kind of systems thinking required is more organic, less mechanistic. You've heard me say that Bowen Theory unlocks the hidden chemistry of organizations. When I say that, I am trying to focus attention on the fact that there are primal forces that we share in common with every form of life, from the smallest organisms to the most complex human societies. My approach involves looking at and thinking about those life forces and how they operate to maintain the balance in relationship networks. The **emotional process** I've asked you to begin watching more carefully is the 'dance of life' that constitutes the dynamism of every family—or organizational—system, even this ant farm.

"When I point out the need to **think systems**, I am suggesting that you need to focus on understanding the interactive forces governing **emotional process**, and how those forces surface in our relationship networks, large and small. Remember the mobile over there. If we try to understand how it functions only by studying the shape and weight and color and texture of the individual pieces, our thinking is far too limited. You can get lots of data that way, but it will take your thinking only so far. And when you miss half the story, chances are you are going to misread the whole damn book, so to speak."

Mike held up both of his hands in a T formation, making the referee's sign for "time out." "Jacob, we need to simplify all of this before we go on. Let me see if I am getting your drift."

Mike continued, "The mobile over there and this ant farm, and for that matter all living systems, have some things in common, they sort of work as a unit. But the comparison between mechanical and living systems only goes so far."

"That's right," Jacob responded, nodding.

"And you're telling me that I've been thinking about my relationship with my dad in ways that are too simplistic, like simple cause and effect, when the reality is a much more complex system."

"Right again," Jacob said.

Mike went on, "Okay, then, let me see if I can apply what you're saying to my work systems. You know, since the publication of Peter Senge's *The Fifth Discipline* years ago, it's taken for granted in business circles that a leader has to have a systems perspective as he works to align the various segments of the organization. To do that, I use a lot of tools like Myers-Briggs inventories, and individual 360 assessments and career counseling, and so forth. But are you telling me all of that is missing the mark because it focuses on individuals rather than focusing on the emotional system itself? I always thought it was helpful to know that I am an ESTJ, using Myers-Briggs lingo. What am I missing?"

"Mike, it's not that those assessments and professional development efforts for individuals are wrong or off the point. It's just that focusing on individuals within the organization is only part of the story. What you are missing is the other half of the story. Most of the leadership development efforts used today have some real value. But I'm suggesting that the **Resilient Leadership** model helps to focus on a neglected, crucial perspective that operates on a far deeper and more significant level. The focus on **emotional process** allows you to **think systems** at a much deeper level, and it lets you understand what is happening in the organization in a correspondingly deeper manner."

"Okay," Mike said. Can we take a break now? I need to clear my head a bit."

Jacob smiled, "Sure. Let's take a break."

Field Theory

"Mike, how are you holding up?" Jacob asked after their short break.

"I'm feeling a bit more clearheaded now; let's keep going," Mike replied.

Jacob took a breath. "Okay, here we go."

"Think about the **emotional process** that governs our **automatic functioning** as generating what is called an 'emotional field.' If you remember what you already know about Field Theory from high school science, you might understand better what we've discussed previously about 'A New Way of SEEING' that looks for visible traces—reactive behaviors—of an invisible reality—**emotional process**.

"An electromagnetic field, for example, is an 'invisible' reality that cannot be directly observed. We know that it is real, since we can observe its effects. But direct observation of its reality is a more elusive goal. However, we can learn a great deal about the characteristics of the field by studying its effects, those regular patterns that emerge as it functions repeatedly in a predictable manner. The same can be said of the gravitational field and the laws of gravity. From careful observation, we can formulate certain principles that accurately describe how the field functions.

"For example, Field Theory helps us understand that seemingly unrelated phenomena can often be understood only when we recognize that they are part of the functioning of a larger reality, a bigger system of which they are just a part."

"Say that again," Mike said, clearly losing track of what Jacob was trying to explain.

"What I'm trying to say is that the **automatic functioning** you observe in the individual members of a family or an organization can only be understood adequately when you think in terms of the entire family or organizational system that they are part of. It's not enough just to have each of your CHI team members take a Myers-Briggs inventory if you really want to understand why they're having trouble working together."

Jacob went on, "I have a good example to help you with this point. One of the issues we have been talking about is the communication challenge between the marketing guy—I think his name is Steve—and the vice president, Craig.

Steve and Craig are engaged in a struggle that is an eternal challenge in matrix organizations. It is the inherent tension between line managers who run things and staff managers who try to help line managers run things. I see it all the time in my coaching work. Both line and staff jobs are essential for multiple-unit businesses where there is a need for uniformity across operating units. But the essential need for both jobs does not mean everyone is clear on who has control over what and how people should work together."

"I know," Mike said. "I'm constantly sorting out everyone's roles and responsibilities that are not clear, trying to be specific about lines of authority, and trying to blast people out of their silos. But it just keeps going 'round and 'round."

Jacob smiled slightly.

"Well, it's true that these two guys will work together better if the organizational structure in which they operate is adjusted to accommodate their needs and their responsibilities, that's for sure. But addressing the problems on that level is not enough, even though it's typically all that leaders pay attention to in an organization."

"What am I missing then?" Mike asked.

"You're failing to think about the emotional system that they are part of."

Mike said, "Craig is a bulldozer operator and Steve is an orchestra conductor."

"Fine, but as long as you think the root of the problem is just their particular personalities or work styles, you'll never get beyond the constant clash between the two of them. Here is another principle to remember when you **think systems**."

Jacob wrote on the board:

> - *A field has more power to determine the functioning of its parts than does any constituent part.*

"In other words, the functioning of both Craig and Steve is much more a factor of their positions in the emotional field they are part of than of their own 'natural' personality characteristics or Myers-Briggs profiles. You need to think about how to address the emotional field in which Steve and Craig work, rather than just telling Steve to stop worrying about people's feelings all the time and telling Craig to stop being a bully.

"Let me ask you this: Is Craig a bulldozer operator with you when there's an issue he wants to push for?"

"Hell no; he knows better."

"So, in addition to his recognizing that you are his boss, isn't it also true that the emotional field between you and Craig is quite different than the one between him and Steve?"

"Sure," said Mike. "When he wants something from me, he's as slick as a used car salesman."

"Exactly," said Jacob, who was getting more and more animated. "You need to see that the nature of the **emotional process** between you and Craig brings out different characteristics in him. His behavior is the product of the position he occupies in the larger field between the two of you, more than any of his inherent personality traits."

"I think I'm getting the point," said Mike thoughtfully.

"You will help them at a much deeper level if you can influence the emotional field between the two of them. Your job is not to tell them what to do or stop doing as a parent might advise a child. Your job is to work at changing the larger emotional field in which they operate."

Jacob continued, "I use the expression 'step down transformer' to describe the way a leader needs to function." He propelled the chair closer to the white board and began to write a few bullet points as he explained:

> - *When you are able to calm an emotional system, you step down the anxiety that feeds reactive behaviors.*

Jacob looked over his shoulder at Mike. "When you accomplish this, you create more space and bring a sense of calm to the entire system." He turned back to the board and wrote as he continued:

> - *When people become more thoughtful and less reactive, their thinking is less likely to be hijacked by their feelings.*

He wheeled his chair over to Mike. "When people achieve that state of being less reactive and more thoughtful, you can help them to work their way through their conflicts more easily."

"How do I do that?" Mike asked.

"It's mostly about how you are present—what's going on inside yourself, and how that is communicated simply by the way you are present to the system. One of the best ways to step down the anxiety is to ask questions rather than give directives. But it's important that your questions are asked in a way that communicates a calming presence."

"How do I do that?"

"Your questions should make them more thoughtful and more self-aware—help them become more conscious of their own reactivity and how it is getting in the way of their working together successfully. You already know something about **emotional process**, and as their supervisor you can help them learn about it, too. Maybe you could use some of the information I provided you back at the beginning of our work together."

"Jacob, I have to tell you that in theory I can see the benefit of this approach, but it is a real stretch for me to actually think like this when I am on the battle line. Things move real fast out there, and I am so much into automatic functioning myself that I am really not sure I can ever remember to think like this. When I come to visit with you, this all makes so much sense. But often I leave much of it at your doorstep as I drive away."

"Well, so does almost everybody else, Mike. But you don't leave it all at my doorstep. Over time you will embed more and more of this mental model in your head.

"Mike, we just have a little time left, and I promised we could get into your issues with your dad and the family reunion."

Mike gave Jacob a quick summary of what had happened with his dad and his concerns about how he was going to handle what was coming up.

Jacob responded by saying, "Mike, I'm glad we have another

session or two before you go to the reunion. Let's focus our conversation on that next time, rather than dealing with it here too quickly. Family reunions are wonderful opportunities to help you **think systems** and also to work on key relationships. We need to talk about how you can make the most of the day with your dad and your family by 'thinking systems' and seeing things in a new way."

Mike said, "One last thing, Jacob: Vanessa talked to me about triangles a few days ago and suggested I ask you to talk to me about how they work."

"She did, huh?" asked Jacob with a laugh. "You can be sure we'll get to triangles at our next session," Jacob said, smiling.

Chapter 4: Think Systems

Review Key Points

- A system is a dynamic environment, held in balance by reciprocal forces (homeostasis).
- An organic model based in life sciences (e.g., evolutionary biology) offers a more helpful understanding of emotional systems than a mechanical model based in the physical sciences (e.g., General Systems Theory).
- Field Theory offers two important principles that deepen understanding of emotional systems:
  - The way two seemingly unrelated elements function can be adequately understood only when they are seen as part of the larger system to which they belong.
  - A field determines the functioning of its parts more than the nature of the parts themselves. For example, the earth's gravitational field determines the orbit of the moon more than any quality within the moon.

Questions for Reflection and Discussion

1. Based on Mike's interactions with Craig and Steve, are there any indications that he is "thinking systems" in his work setting?

2. Can you give an example from your workplace of the power of the emotional field to influence individuals' functioning, even to the extent of overriding behaviors that seem more "natural" or characteristic of them?

3. Reciprocal interactions (e.g., one person in a relationship over-functioning while the other is under-functioning) are instances of homeostatic forces at work in a system. How do you see this kind of pattern at work in your family?

A NEW WAY OF THINKING

The Practice

Think about you own family system, including your parents, grandparents and siblings if any. Recall any specific event that caused a "system-wide" disturbance within the family unit. This could have been a death, birth, financial crisis, job loss, etc. During the event or after it occurred, see if you can visualize the reactivity of individual family members as they moved either toward fusion or cutoff to cope with emotional challenge or upset. As one family member moved in the family system, can you recall counter-balancing actions of others to maintain the equilibrium of the family system and thus return to homeostasis?

1. Select a social network that you belong to and draw a simple diagram of the network with names being connected to other names with lines.

2. Find your own place in the network and then identify actions you could take that do not follow your usual pattern and therefore would provoke an imbalance and responding counter-balancing action by others. Observe how the system adjusts to changes.

Think Systems

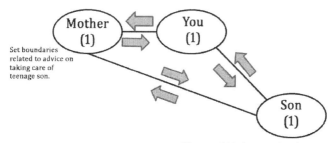

Take son and friends on camping trips once a month in summer and fall. Go to hockey games in winter.

Mom and Son
2. Become unavailable to take son camping and invite Mom to "pinch hit" on a camping trip.
2. Invite Mom to come to family dinners every other month.

To learn more, go to www.resilient-leadership.biz.

A New Way of **THINKING**
Chapter 5: Triangles

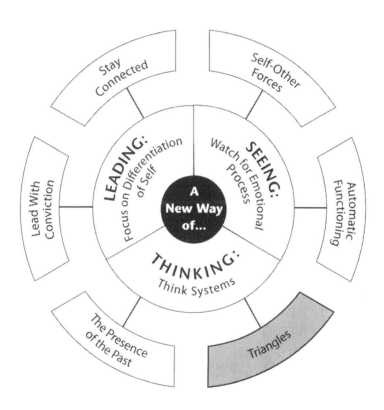

Friday from Hell - 7:00 a.m.

Friday morning began one of those days that come along two or three times a year. In the space of ten hours, Mike had enough go wrong in his life to drive someone over a cliff.

As he walked in from his morning run, Karla mentioned that Steve Parks, the marketing director, had called and asked that Mike call him right away about a problem he was having with Craig Hernandez again. Something about Steve traveling all the way to Pittsburg to attend a meeting that Craig had cancelled without advising him. Steve was really hot about this because it was the second time in six months that something like this had happened.

Karla asked Mike about Steve. "Steve's message seemed almost hysterical," Karla said. "Why is he calling you and why is he calling you this early at home?"

"Do you mean hysterical like funny?' Mike asked.

"No, no, I mean he sounded almost out of control," Karla replied.

"Well, Steve is like that and he and Craig just cannot get along at all anymore."

"I thought Craig was one of your bright stars," Karla added.

"Craig is a sensational operator, but he's very headstrong and hates people slowing things down or getting in his way. He has no tolerance for Steve."

"Are you going to call Steve back now?" Karla asked as she prepared a quick breakfast of oatmeal.

"Not now and not from home," Mike said. Just then his cell phone went off with the signal that he had set only for incoming messages from Vanessa. The note read:

Fire at Monroeville, call ASAP, Vanessa.

Just as soon as he read the note from Vanessa, his cell phone received a second call, this time from Craig Hernandez. Mike hit the receive button.

"Mike, we have a fire going at Monroeville as we speak. The general manager is on vacation and the manager on duty just called me. I am about 20 minutes from the hotel. I don't know the extent of the damage yet, but some employees and some guests are being taken to the hospital."

Craig was great in tough situations, and Mike knew that he could trust him with all the details, so Mike simply said, "Call me as soon as you have information. I'll alert Vanessa and contact the PR department."

"Will do," Craig said and hung up.

Mike's next call was going to be to Vanessa, but just then his phone rang again. Mike looked at the caller ID and saw that it was Steve Parks.

He felt his irritation rising as he answered the phone. "Mike Sampson," he snapped.

His annoyance clear in his tone of voice, Steve said, "Mike, this is Steve. Did you get my message?"

Mike felt like hanging up on Steve. He wanted to call Vanessa as soon as possible.

"Well, Karla just told me about it," Mike said as calmly as he could. "By the way, Steve—"

Steve cut Mike off and said, "I want you to know that I am riding back to the airport in Pittsburg right now, having come here last night to attend a meeting that was, once again, canceled at the last minute. Because of Mr. Hernandez's lack of communication, I am now wasting my time and the company's money just fooling around here in Pittsburg. Do you know how frustrating this situation is to me and also how damaging all of this is to our team effectiveness?"

Mike lost it.

"Steve, shut up for a minute. I just got a call from our Mr. Hernandez, who is on his way to a fire at the Monroeville hotel. I don't have the time right now to listen to the problems you and Craig have with communication. I need to get off the phone with you and on the phone with Vanessa and with our public relations people as soon as possible."

There was dead silence for five seconds.

"So, Steve, I want to see you in my office this afternoon sometime. Call Crystal and set up a 30-minute meeting for when you get back in the city."

Steve said, "Sorry, Mike; I didn't realize—"

Mike cut Steve off by saying, "I need to go now; see you later today." Mike hung up the phone.

Mike immediately called Vanessa, but the call went into her voicemail. He left a message and ran to take a shower.

Friday from Hell – 8:30 a.m.

Mike parked his car in front of CHI and ran into the building and up the stairs to the fifth floor. He went directly to Vanessa's office.

"Hi, Mike. What's the update?" Vanessa asked.

Mike had heard back from Craig twice in the last 90 minutes to find out that the fire had started in the grease duct in the main kitchen and had gutted the first-floor specialty restaurant. Apparently the flame retardant system in the hood had failed to function. The fire had smoldered for some time before flames broke out; the sprinkler system in the restaurant dining area had contained the blaze, so there was not much structural damage, but the water damage was extensive. Smoke had spread up one of the two guest room towers and some guests were taken to the local hospital for smoke inhalation.

The biggest concern now was that one family had not been able to find their 16-year-old daughter in the confusion of the fire. They were in the lobby with police and fire rescue personnel trying to discern what had happened and what steps to take. Finally, local fire officials had decided to close the entire hotel, which was causing the transfer of all guests to other hotels in the area.

Mike gave all the details to Vanessa.

"We need to call James," Vanessa said. She picked up the phone and called James with a brief update.

"Where is the general manager?" Vanessa asked.

"She is in Mexico somewhere," Mike said. "We are locating her now. The area VP, Craig Hernandez, is at the hotel and he is a very capable man."

"Do you need to go out there, Mike?" Vanessa asked him with no preconceived opinion about the correct answer.

"Maybe; it depends on what happens in the next few hours. I will keep you updated."

Mike hurried back to his office to see if anything else had happened.

Friday from Hell – 10:30 a.m.

Crystal knocked on the door of his office and came in to hand Mike an urgent telephone message from Sally Harrison, the area VP of operations in Boston. She also handed him a sealed interoffice envelope with the handwritten word CONFIDENTIAL neatly printed on the outside.

Sally's message read. *Lamont Sill/Union Square Problems – please call ASAP, Sally H.*

Mike opened the sealed envelope and read the following handwritten note:

> *Mr. Sampson, you should know that Crystal is spreading a lot of rumors in the office by telling people that you are going to replace Vanessa and that Crystal will become the senior executive secretary. I do not know if any of this is true but her behavior is really upsetting a number of administrative people who would like to have the opportunity for advancement. And Vanessa's secretary, Helen, is beside herself.*
>
> *Someone needs to provide more communication about what is going on so people can get back to work and stop worrying about all the office politics.*

The letter was not signed. Mike looked up at Crystal, who was staring right back at him. He smiled and asked Crystal to close his door as she left so he could have some quiet to think. It was only midmorning and he already felt like the day had been two weeks long.

FRIDAY FROM HELL - 12:00 NOON

Karla called Mike's private line in the office to tell him that she had just gotten a call from Joyce Bennett, the wife of Mike's cousin Don. On Sunday evening Don had suffered a mild heart attack and was resting comfortably in the hospital near their home in Zelienople, Pennsylvania. Don was the first-born son of Mike Senior's sister Mary. He was 45 years old and did not take care of himself at all. Mike and Don had not spoken to one another in over ten years due to a family disagreement over an unpaid debt to Mike's dad. Mike Senior had long since forgotten about the whole thing, but not Mike.

"So Joyce feels that Don will have a full recovery?" Mike restated his understanding of Karla's summary.

"Well, it is too soon to tell, but she is optimistic," Karla said.

"What else did she say?" Mike wondered if Don was behind Joyce's call. He was always suspicious about the motives of these once in a blue moon calls from the cousin he didn't like and could not trust.

"That's about all, Mike. I will get a card for us both to sign and send some flowers. Joyce did mention the upcoming reunion and wondered if we would have time to stop by and see them as they will not be able to come to the celebration this year. I told her that I would talk with you and one of us would call her back."

"I don't want to visit with them at all," Mike said. "We will have enough on our hands getting Dad to and from the reunion, let alone visiting with Don."

"You know, Honey, if you don't try to keep up contact with your family we will lose what little connection we have now," Karla said.

"That is just fine with me," Mike quickly answered.

"Well, I think we should go by with your dad and visit with Don and Joyce, if even for a short time, because we will be within 45 minutes of them and we don't get back there but once a year. Besides, Mike Senior is not getting any younger," Karla said.

Mike knew from her tone of voice that Karla had dug in her heels on the issue and that she was not going to give up on this point, so he agreed to a short visit.

FRIDAY FROM HELL – 2:00 P.M.

Reports from Monroeville were now beginning to stabilize. The lost 16-year-old daughter was found. She had taken off during the confusion with a boy she had met at the hotel. Two guests were hospitalized for smoke inhalation and related respiratory complications. The hotel was to be closed for about 48 hours and accommodations had been found for all the guests who wanted to stay in the area. All room accommodations charges were canceled.

The cause of the fire was still under investigation, but it looked like there would be a real case for subrogation of the loss because the fire suppression system had failed. There were a lot of insurance representatives taking photos. The public relations team had done a good job and media coverage was well positioned to protect the reputation of CHI while still accurately reporting the incident.

Mike was really glad that Craig was in the area and on the scene.

Mike gazed at his computer and saw a note from Richard. It was unique and caught his eye. Richard was encouraging his dad to pick up a book on spiritual enlightenment and read it so that the two of them could discuss the content. Mike read a lot of business books, but he was not interested in reading about spirituality – at least at this point. This book written by Eckhart Tolle was entitled *A New Earth – Awaking to Your Life's Purpose.* Richard went on to point out that the book was a bestseller and that it had offered him and Lilly some really helpful insights into their own spiritual journeys.

Mike did not commit to buying or reading the book but sent an email to thank Richard for the note and provide an update on the upcoming wedding plans for his sister.

Just as he finished his response to Richard, Steve Parker knocked on Mike's door.

"Come in," Mike said.

Steve opened the door, stepped in, shut the door and walked over to Mike's desk.

Mike motioned for Steve to sit down and he got up from behind the desk and walked around to the front of the desk to sit next to Steve.

Steve opened the conversation, "How is the situation in Monroeville?"

"Well, it was a really unfortunate situation for us. We had a very small grease fire that turned into a major event because of a failed fire suppression system in one of our vent hoods over a deep fat fryer. It never should have happened. We are lucky to have no serious injuries, and for that I am thankful."

Mike paused to see if Steve wanted any more details. He did not.

"Steve, let me ask you a question. Why did you call my home this morning?"

"I had to tell you straight out about the situation. You need to know when one of your leaders is not being a team player. I have tried to work with Craig for almost two years now, and I have had nothing but trouble with him. Today was the last straw."

"What do you mean, the last straw?"

"Well, I am not going to keep working with someone who is completely unprofessional. In fact, it is beyond unprofessional. Craig is downright destructive to our efforts here in CHI!"

"Steve, why did Craig cancel the meeting you were to attend?"

"I don't know. He will not call me back, and he will not respond to my e-mails."

"Why not?" Mike asked.

"Mike, I don't know why. You tell me why," Steve shot back.

"Well, I am quite sure that he has been very busy today," Mike said.

"I am not just talking about today. He doesn't communicate with me any more at all," Steve said.

"Steve, let me give you a few ideas that may be helpful.

"First, I want you to know that I think that both you and Craig are essential to the effectiveness of this team.

"You do a wonderful job in handling a very difficult job in marketing. With all the challenges we face from top to bottom in our marketing efforts, I see you as one of the stars on the analysis side of the discipline. You know our markets and our products better than anyone in the division I manage. What I know about you is that you will have ideas about what to do next to address our competition's moves before the rest of us even know the competition is moving at all.

"Second, you should also know that I think Craig is a great leader. He is bright, fast and a real self-starter. He hates process and wants to go, go, go all the time. Sometimes he goes too fast. That is a sign of young talent needing to be managed, not of a dead weight waiting to be retired.

"Here is what I need the two of you to do. I need you guys to figure out how to work with each other. I need the two of you to do this without getting me involved to take sides because that means there will be a winner and a loser. We can't have that. CHI and I need both of you guys. Besides, I don't want either of you working for the competition.

"Third, I want to tell you about something I am learning called **emotional process**. This is what drives our reactions when we are on autopilot. It is below the conscious level. It's part of your make-up and mine, too. We get this programmed into us, so to speak, from our childhood, and emotional process shows up all the time in how we do things and say things. The **automatic functioning** that I see in you is related to your anxiety about building and maintaining calm and peaceful working relationships. What I see in Craig is the need to have control and to move very fast. The two of you are coming from different places when it comes to working relationships. You want to maintain harmony and he wants to maintain control. How people feel about you and about each other is important to you, and Craig doesn't even think about things like that."

Mike thought carefully as he tried to remember and apply what Jacob had told him about working with this situation. He was trying to remain calm, speaking very deliberately, without letting any irritation creep into his tone of voice. He realized he was talking too much and not asking any questions for Steve to think about as Jacob had suggested. But he needed to plow forward.

He continued, "Now, neither preference is right or wrong. They are just different. Here is what I want you to do. I will send you some information about **emotional process** that I want you to read. Try to think about how it applies to you and Craig. Then come back and see me so we can talk some more about how to make things better."

Mike could see that Steve was trying to absorb the information Mike had just given him.

There was a long pause before he answered. "Okay, Mike. If this is what you need, I'll give it a try. I must admit that I am not optimistic."

"That's okay for now. Just let me get the information to you and then let's talk again. As you're reading it over, ask yourself, 'Where is my **emotional process** getting in the way of working better with Craig Hernandez?' We'll talk more about all of this."

As Steve left the room, Mike thought to himself, "I'm not sure I'll ever be able to remember all this **emotional process** crap that Jacob is asking me to use."

By 4:00 p.m., Mike was fried. It was Friday; he had just finished the day from hell and simply did not have the energy to call Sally Harrison back or have a conversation with Crystal about the confidential note he had received earlier in the day. So he wrote Sally a short email and said he would call on Monday, and he decided to take the note home to discuss it with Karla.

He walked to his car, got in, turned off his cell phone for the first time in over a year, and slowly drove home.

FRIDAY FROM HELL – 7:00 P.M. – RELIEF

After a shower and dinner, Mike showed Karla the confidential letter.

She quickly read the letter and said, "If you get the COO job, will you take Crystal with you?"

"I am not sure how all of it will work, to be honest; and, besides, it's a question that is much too early to consider," Mike replied.

"But what you do know is that everyone in the office that has a job now will still have one after the transition, right?"

"Yes, I am sure we will find a position for everyone who is there now."

"Then I think a good step to take is to tell everyone that and also describe to them how the selection process for new administrative positions will be determined," Karla said.

"It's not quite that simple. For example, I am not sure what arrangement has been made with Helen, Vanessa's current assistant. A deal may have been made with her years ago when Vanessa came into the position. It's possible that the new COO, whoever it is, may have to retain Helen as his or her administrative support person. It's just too early to address this issue."

"But it is not too early to tell people what you do know and also describe the process that will be used to move forward when steps can be taken. You know, Honey, this problem has come to your attention because Crystal is your assistant, but the problem is really an office-wide problem and one that Vanessa needs to address."

Mike had not thought about it in this way, but Karla was right. Mike decided that he would get Vanessa involved, but not until he had a workable solution to suggest when he presented her with the problem. "Thanks for the input, Beauty. I will take it up with Vanessa next week."

Mike thought about making notes for the day but was just too tired to do the work any justice.

Coaching on Triangles

On the drive to Jacob's office, Mike called Sally in Boston. She was out until the afternoon. Mike was relieved. He still was steamed about Lamont and needed to come up with a different frame of mind before he spoke to her.

He pulled up to Jacob's office and noticed him out in the garden next to the office, working with some flowers. Jacob loved chrysanthemums.

"Hey Jacob, are you working with a new emotional system out there?" Mike kidded.

"As a matter of fact, I am," Jacob said as pushed his wheelchair away from the potted plants and smiled. "These guys have an ecosystem all to themselves. Their **automatic functioning** has them reaching for the light. They are hogging all the prime space out here."

Jacob cleaned his hands with an old towel and began to wheel towards the ramp leading to the office to start the session. Mike asked if they could talk outside in the fresh air for a few minutes. In the garden, Mike played back the day from hell for Jacob. It took about ten minutes.

"My God, Mike, it's a wonder you are still standing," Jacob said.

"It was quite a day, and I am glad it's over. I thought it would be good to go through it out here so I could get it off my chest before we began the session," Mike said.

As they went into the office, Jacob began to set the stage for the session.

"As I recall we are going on to a discussion of **triangles** today and also cover a bit more on systems thinking. I think today's primary focus is centered on the family reunion that is coming up. Is it next Sunday?" Jacob asked.

"No, it's in three weeks. I plan to pick up Dad that Saturday afternoon."

"Okay, and the trip to western Pennsylvania will take about six hours?"

"About," Mike said. "And we will be at the reunion about three or four hours, then visiting with my cousin Don and then returning home."

"And then what?"

"Then we are going to stop by Front Royal on the way home

and drop Dad off before we return to Reston," Mike said.

"Wow, that will be a very full day. Are you sure you can pull it off all in one day?"

"It sure will be a long day. I want to get it over all at once," Mike said flatly.

"Sounds like you are not really interested at all in going to the reunion," Jacob said.

"I really don't ever like going, but then when it's over I am usually glad I went."

Jacob began, "Well, before we get into the reunion itself, let's talk a little more about systems thinking. When we left off last time we were talking about the emotional field that is part of every family and organizational system.

"We discussed the idea that a leader skilled in systems thinking will respond to issues quite differently. Rather than rushing to 'fix' a problem, the resilient leader will recognize that problems are symptoms—they provide an invaluable window to learn about the larger system of which they are a part. When the leader is curious about a problem and recognizes it as an opportunity to learn more about the **automatic functioning** of the system, he is positioned quite differently than when he feels threatened by it and feels an urgency to come up with a quick fix."

"I can't say problems make me curious," Mike said. "I just want to fix them as quickly as I can."

Jacob continued, "A systems perspective helps the leader to avoid the error of focusing on any single person, issue or factor when trying to understand the source of a problem. By thinking of problems as symptoms within a system-wide perspective, a leader's horizons are automatically broadened, and the chance of spotting relevant data is significantly enhanced."

"What you're saying makes sense. But I'm still trying to grasp these ideas," Mike added.

"Stay with me, Mike," Jacob urged as he continued.

"When the leader understands the power of an emotional field over its parts, and when he focuses his attention on information that is truly relevant, i.e., the interactive processes at work in the relationship system, he is able to see the bigger picture more clearly. When he asks himself, 'What is going on here?' he is also better equipped to resist being co-opted by those same forces, and hence he can lead the system in a less reactive, more effective manner. Maintaining a systems perspective increases the likelihood that a leader's response will be thought-driven rather than feelings-driven, especially in critical, high-pressure situations."

Jacob continued, "You are already beginning to think like this from what I can tell. In view of what you told me outside today, it seems to me that the way you counseled Steve last week suggests that you knew enough not to try and 'fix' the situation between the two guys. Instead, you placed the responsibility for solving the problem back with Steve and Craig. You were 'thinking systems,' even if it was a stretch for you. Your follow-up conversation with Steve can now focus on his and Craig's **automatic functioning**. You are getting at the emotional field in your division that is shaping the behaviors of both men."

"It's a start," Mike said rather tentatively.

"It's a good start, Mike. Now, let's go right into a discussion about triangles. The notion of a relationship triangle is one of the most valuable resources that Bowen Theory provides a leader who wishes to '**think systems**' in this new way. Bowen called the triangle the basic building block of an emotional system, the smallest stable relationship unit."

"I know. That's what Vanessa told me," said Mike with a grin.

Jacob smiled as he maneuvered his wheelchair over to the white board and drew a triangle, placing the letter 'A' at the top of the triangle and 'B' at the lower left angle and the letter 'C' at the lower right angle.

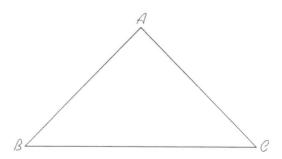

"A triangle consists of any three parts of a relationship network, whether those parts are three persons or groups of persons. Triangles are formed spontaneously because two-person systems are inherently unstable. Here's what I mean." Jacob began to write bullet points on the board as he explained:

> - *Any relationship between two people, no matter how good it is, generates a certain measure of chronic anxiety.*
>
> - *Any two people in any relationship are always working at maintaining balance between their **self-other forces**.*
>
> - *Trying to get their respective needs for closeness and separateness into alignment automatically produces a certain level of anxiety.*
>
> - *To manage that anxiety and stabilize their relationship, the two-person system instinctively spreads the anxiety over a larger geography by involving a third party.*
>
> - *When they create that **triangle**, they lessen their anxiety by redistributing it.*

Jacob looked at Mike. "Does that make sense to you, Mike?"
"Yeah, I think I'm following you."
Jacob then quickly sketched out five additional triangles at other points on the board with the following groupings of names or words at the corners of each triangle in place of the letters 'A', 'B' and 'C':

Mike, Steve, Craig
Mike, Karla, Jacelyn
Mike, Vanessa, Jacob
Mike, Cousin Don, Mike Senior/his unpaid loan
Mike, Sally, Paul Brady

Jacob pushed away from the board and turned to face Mike.

"Now, here are some triangles we can talk about as learning labs, so to speak. Which one do you want to talk about first?" Jacob asked.

"Let's start with Steve and Craig and me," Mike responded.

"Okay," Jacob said, "here are a few basic points." He wrote a few words on the board again as he continued:

- *When **triangles** form, it is typical that two of the parties are closer to one another, while the third party is more distant and has the "outsider" role.*

- *There is comfort in the closeness that the two "insiders" feel, but that also means the third party is likely to feel more distant and will often try to get "closer" to one of the insiders.*

- *If the third party is successful in that attempt, then one member of the original pair suddenly senses that he or she is now in the "outsider" position. In response, that person will make some sort of effort to regain the closeness that has been lost.*

Jacob put down the marker and faced Mike. "This dynamic is constantly in play, with the result that the anxiety that the triangle originally dispersed continues to be passed around to various points on the triangle. **Triangle**s are always shifting—they are **emotional process** in action. In the triangle that includes you Craig, and Steve who is on the outside?" Jacob asked.

"Steve is on the outside for sure," replied Mike.

"Right," Jacob said, and he re-drew the triangle to place Steve's name at the angle distant from Mike and Craig.

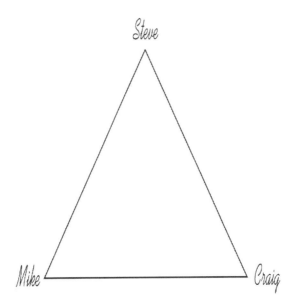

"And when Steve feels left out, his anxiety kicks in and produces reactive behaviors."

"Right," Mike said, "and that is when Steve runs into my office, or shoots me an e-mail or calls me at home."

"Right again, Mike. Let's go back to the call from Steve that started off your morning on that awful day you were describing to me outside my office. Steve's call to you at home arose from a deep level of frustration that he was feeling in the emotional system with Craig. His reactive functioning caused him to call you rather than call Craig. Why do you think he called you rather than speak to Craig directly?"

Jacob stopped and waited for Mike to think about his answer.

"Well, he wasn't getting a response from Craig, and with Craig distancing from him, I guess it was triggering lots of anxiety to be shut out like that."

Jacob continued, "Mike, that's a pretty good educated guess based on what Steve told you and what you know about their relationship. Of course neither one of us really knows why Steve called you and not Craig. Here is the point I want to make."

Jacob turned back to the triangle diagram they were discussing, redrew the triangle and placed an "X" on the side of the triangle opposite Mike's name, between Steve's and Craig's names.

A New Way of Thinking

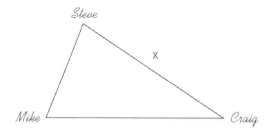

"Steve was describing a frustration he was having with Craig. In our triangle here, the problem is on the other side from your position, over where this X is, between the two of them. That is the side of the triangle that has the most conflict. Steve is trying to reduce anxiety in his relationship with Craig by inviting you to take his side of the issue. Whether he is self-aware that he is trying to bring you closer to him in the triangle or not is unknown, but either way he is attempting to satisfy his need for closeness by getting you into the discussion on his side."

"And being in that triangle is a bad thing for me, right?" Mike asked.

"Well, it's neither good nor bad; it just is what is going on here. The fact is you are in the triangle. How you handle it will determine whether it's going to either serve to improve the situation or make it worse. If you take the bait and side with Steve on the issue, you will be reinforcing the dependence that Steve has on you and you will be doing nothing to reduce the anxiety in the system. If you side with Steve, Craig will begin to feel that he is being left out, and his anxiety will likely increase."

"Damned if I do, and damned if I don't, I guess."

"There's another option open to you: You could explain to Steve that you don't want to be drawn into a triangle between them in the wrong way—that you need to have a positive relationship with both of them. That leaves Steve to work out the problems with Craig himself. If he asks, you can give him some suggestions for how to begin that process. This is what is called repositioning yourself in a triangle—you define your position to each side, but you stay away from the effort to put you in the middle by getting closer to one or the other of them.

"Another thing you might do is explain to Steve how his reactions are getting in the way of developing a more positive relationship with Craig. See how much capacity he has for self-knowledge. You'll need to calm him down a bit so his feeling self stops hijacking his thinking self. Over time, Craig and Steve will either work things out or they won't. If they do not, you may have to get involved, and if it comes to it in the end, you can pull the plug, so to speak, on one of these two leaders."

"I don't want to lose either of them. How can I help them so it doesn't reach that point?"

"You can't fix it for them, and you shouldn't try. What you can do is clarify your expectations of them, as you have, and then hold the team of leaders accountable for results on time and at standard. Remember, if you remain calm and steady while seeing and thinking about the systems of interaction around you, you have a great leverage point. I suggest you might also start to show them how their reactive functioning is getting in the way of resolving their differences."

Mike said, "Let's try another triangle."

"Okay, which one?"

"How about Mike, Karla and Jacelyn," Mike suggested.

"Sure," Jacob said.

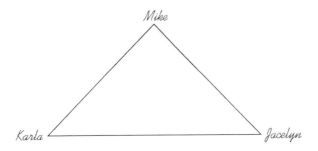

Jacob started, "Not long ago, you told me about an issue you had with Karla that centered on her feeling that you or Jacelyn would often try to put her in the middle of a debate. Do you recall that discussion?" Jacob asked.

"I sure do. Karla gets really agitated when she feels cornered," Mike added. "She generally acts and speaks with grace and ease, but when she feels the stress of our family squabbles, she lets me know right up front."

"So, you tell me, Mike, using this triangle here with the three of your names in the corners, what is going on that causes the reaction you experience with Karla and Jacelyn?"

Mike hesitated a little, thinking about the situation. Then he got up and walked to the board. Pointing to his own name, he said, "When I get frustrated with Jacelyn, it usually has to do with her making decisions with which I disagree. Sometimes I think her logic is just silly and that she is making emotional decisions without really thinking things through.

"When she was little, I just corrected her. But during the last few years, and especially in recent months, she is resisting my input unless it agrees with her own point of view. She simply is ignoring good, solid input."

"And when that happens, how do you react?" Jacob continued.

"Well, I ignore a lot of it because much of the time the consequence of the decision she is making is not terribly significant."

"So what do you do then?" Jacob asked

"I just keep my mouth shut," Mike answered. "But sometimes, a lot of the time, frankly, I end up talking to myself about it under my breath, or I complain about it to Karla."

"Do you actually talk to Jacelyn at these times, Mike?"

"Not really. I guess that I just don't think it would be worth the effort to have an argument over a small issue. I think a person needs to pick his battles."

"Do you hold a lot of built-up resentment from all those times you stayed silent?" Jacob asked.

Mike knew where this exchange was going, and he was beginning to see a side of himself he did not really want to look at, at least not now.

"Jacob, I do hold a lot in, and I suppose it builds up in me and at some point I explode. But if I spoke up every time I disagreed with Jacelyn, we would do nothing but argue."

Jacob said, "Let's get back to the triangle for a moment. You are telling me that you frequently disagree with how Jacelyn is making decisions and that you pick your battles."

"Right," Mike added.

"Right, and at times you loop Karla in the middle of disagreements, and when you do that it makes her upset."

"That is true," Mike nodded.

"So here is one way to look at it, Mike. You and Karla and Jacelyn are in a classic family triangle: mom, dad and child. It's universal. The triangle is not good or bad; it just is there. But when you try to enlist Karla to agree with you in opposition to Jacelyn, Karla feels trapped and Jacelyn feels deserted. When you move closer to Karla, it automatically means Jacelyn is left in the 'outsider' position.

"You are trying to pull Karla to your side because of the built-up anxiety you have in your dealings with Jacelyn. Furthermore, all the small little disagreements you have with Jacelyn that you just stuff down only add to the anxiety that is floating around in the system."

"It's not a good formula for managing this triangle," Mike quietly said, mostly to himself.

"Well, don't be too hard on yourself; this is a very common situation. What do you think should be done about all of this, Mike?"

"For one thing, I need to avoid trying to get Karla on my side."

Jacob held his hand up as if to make a signal to stop. "Well, that is a good thing to do, but it is not the only thing to do." Jacob continued, "Stopping the effort to pull Karla to your side is well and good, but it's only half of the job."

Mike looked at Jacob with confusion.

"You need also to learn how to have conversations with Jacelyn that provide her perspective and advice when she asks for it, and you need to learn how not to give commands or unwelcome opinions. Jacelyn has become her own woman; she is no longer your little girl, and I guarantee that if you make it a contest of wills with her you will always lose."

"That's been the case for many years," Mike said with a note of irony in his voice.

"But, Jacob, sometimes she is dead wrong."

"Of course she is dead wrong sometimes. So am I and so are you. Your job is not to tell her she is dead wrong. Your job is to provide advice and perspective when asked so she can learn to be dead wrong less often. And when you're not asked, just stay quiet.

"Mike, here is the bottom line on this triangle. You can't just stop talking to Karla about concerns for your daughter. It's one thing to share your perspective and quite another to try to get Karla on your side. You also need to be able to share your viewpoint with Jacelyn in a way that is not so demanding, as if you need to be in control of her life. Just state your position, and leave it there for her to accept or not. In the long run, she is much more likely to listen to you if you are not always trying to control her."

Mike was subdued, but managed to say, "Yes, I see what you're saying, and I know you're right, but..." He stopped himself before he said anything more.

"Mike, when you keep open lines of communication between yourself and Jacelyn, the relationship will become much less stressful. There will always be triangles and stress in any family system. But you can manage that stress by gaining perspective, thinking about your position in the triangle, and then asking yourself how best to relate to both Karla and Jacelyn without trying to get either one of them 'on your side.' That's the best way to influence Jacelyn without causing her to distance herself from you. Nobody wants to be around a control freak, you know!"

Jacob ended with a smile and softly said, "You remember the old control freak, don't you Mike?"

Mike's memory of Vanessa's remark was all too clear. "Yeah, I remember, Jacob."

"Let's take a break," Jacob said.

Mike stepped outside and just stood still, looking at Jacob's chrysanthemums. He was beginning to see the impact of his behavior on others in a way he had never considered. Then he thought about Sally in Boston, Vanessa, Steve in marketing, Karla, Jacelyn and Richard. He now saw how his intense desire to control everything around him had made both himself and others very anxious.

His cell phone went off. He reached for it and quietly turned off the unit without even looking at the incoming message. He took a deep breath and turned to go back inside.

"Mike, let's take a look at a third triangle. I suggest that we discuss Mike, Cousin Don and that unpaid debt to Mike Senior."

"Sure," Mike said.

"Now this triangle is a bit different because one angle represents a situation as well as a person—your dad and the unpaid loan. Remind me what is going on here."

"Don borrowed some money from my father in the late 1980s, said he would pay Dad back and has just either ignored the repayment or forgotten about it. And we're not talking about small change here. The loan was for $10,000."

"So this took place more than a dozen years ago, right?" Jacob asked.

"That is right. And it has been a real sore subject ever since the repayment date was missed."

"And when was the repayment date?" Jacob asked.

"Well, I am not entirely sure, but I know it should have been paid back a number of years ago." Mike almost yelled, then smiled and tried to act relaxed with little success.

"Mike, how did you come to know all about the loan and repayment problems?"

"Dad used to talk to me about it all the time," Mike replied. "And now that I have a basic understanding about triangles, I realize that Dad was trying to get me all riled up so I would talk to my cousin."

"Did you?" Jacob asked.

"I sure did. I wrote him a letter and then called him to discuss the loan.

"It was a shouting match. First of all, Don doesn't have that kind of money. I know that he blew through the loan fast and he doesn't have anything to show for it, either."

"Well, how did the shouting match end up?" Jacob asked.

"I told him that he needed to repay the loan, and he told me that the loan between him and my father was none of my business. Don is a jackass."

"What happened next?"

"I decided to take it to the next level. I got a lawyer involved who agreed to represent my dad and write a letter to Don."

"Did that help?" Jacob asked.

"It made Don mad as hell," Mike replied. "He called Dad and really let him have it. I am not sure what was said, but no money has been repaid, that's for sure. I haven't talked to Don since then, and now Karla wants to visit him after the reunion because he's recently had a heart attack."

"Does Mike Senior bring up the topic now?" Jacob asked.

"No, not since they talked. It's like the topic has just gone away. I don't know if my dad has truly forgotten about it or just doesn't want to deal with it."

"So, Mike, why don't you just let it go?"

"Because it's not fair to my dad. The agreement had been

made to repay the loan, and it needs to be repaid. Besides, my dad isn't rich, and he needs that money."

Mike had gotten very agitated, and Jacob could see that he was a long way from settling down on this topic.

Jacob said, "So, Mike, what do you want to do now?"

"I don't know what to do," Mike replied.

"I have some ideas," Jacob said. "Let's begin to talk about getting ready for the reunion trip.

COACHING ON THE FAMILY REUNION

Jacob knew that family reunions, weddings and funerals are great opportunities to observe family systems at work and also make some great progress in relationships. He also knew that if Mike reconnected with his family system with a clear vision of what he wanted to be sure to do and not do, he would be much happier with the outcome.

"Mike, your trip to western Pennsylvania is a great opportunity for you to work on your relationships with Karla and your dad and even your cousin."

Mike added, "Maybe Richard and Jacelyn too."

"Oh really, are they going to be at the reunion too?" Jacob asked

"Yes, they both sent Karla emails several days ago saying they both were coming, together with Russ and Lilly."

"Well that's great. How is everyone getting over to Pennsylvania?"

"We've decided to take two cars. Both kids are coming up to the house here, and we're going up and back from Pennsylvania in a little two-car caravan."

Jacob went to the white board and asked Mike to help him write a few ideas. "Mike, let's think about the combinations of family members who might be able to ride together and spend time together."

After some discussion they came up with the following list:

Car ride to Pennsylvania

1. Karla, Mike, Jacelyn and Russ (car 1), Richard, Lilly and Mike Senior (car 2) (½ the trip)

2. Karla, Mike, Richard and Lilly (car 1), Jacelyn, Russ and Mike Senior (car 2) (½ the trip)

Car ride back to Virginia

1. Mike, Mike Senior, Jacelyn and Russ (car 1), Karla, Richard and Lilly (car 2)   (½ the trip)
2. Karla, Mike and Mike Senior (car 1), Jacelyn, Russ, Richard and Lilly (car 2)   (½ the trip)

Mike looked at the list and said, "I am not sure I can get everyone to agree to all this moving around."

Jacob encouraged him, "Try making a game out of the day. See what you can do. I suggest that you really try to get these combinations into the vehicles. If you do this, you can have some important conversations with family members. It's a real opportunity to work on your family system.

"Mike, I'm going to give you a little homework assignment to help prepare you to make the most out of this visit. Would that be okay with you?"

"Sure. What is it?"

"I want you to make a list of the one thing you most want to accomplish in how you relate to each person whose name is here on the board. Keep in mind that in order to achieve that one thing, you will have to manage your own reactivity and not let them push your 'hot button.' Do you think you can do that?"

"I guess so. Can you give me an example?"

"Well, it's just an example, and you can probably do better. But suppose you decide to talk with Jacelyn about some wild idea she's got for her wedding that drives you crazy. Your whole focus will be to bring it up and remain calm and nonjudgmental. No matter how wacky her ideas get in your opinion, your energy will be devoted to staying calm and not giving advice unless she specifically asks for it. And even then, just offer your viewpoint in a matter-of-fact way that indicates you don't really care that much whether she follows your advice or not."

"Sounds challenging, but I'm willing to give it a try."

"Okay. And if you don't mind, send me your list before you leave for the reunion, and we can talk it over after you return. Be sure to pick issues that tend to make you a bit reactive so the exercise will be worthwhile.

"This is why I'm suggesting you arrange very carefully the configurations for the car ride both ways. It can be a time of very active engagement for you. You'll have time with both of your children and their mates, and that will provide a golden opportunity for you. You will be able to travel to the reunion without having your dad in the car with you, so you can focus on the kids without distraction. He will be with you on the return trip when he is tired and will probably be easier to deal with. He'll also most likely sleep a little in the back so you can have time with Karla."

"What about my visit with my cousin Don?" Mike asked.

"What do you think would be most helpful?"

Mike was quiet for a time, then said, "Jacob, I'm really stuck. Can you give me some suggestions about how to get started with him?"

"Since you've made the decision to see Don, be sure to call ahead to set up the visit. While you are visiting with Don and his wife, don't by any means speak about the debt he owes your dad. If he brings it up, pause and become an observer of your own reactivity. Watching creates distance, and that pause will help you better manage your **automatic functioning**. You can just tell him you've decided it's between him and Mike Senior.

"Mike, what would it take for you to walk away from the debt issue entirely?"

"Jacob, I just don't think that would be right. I have a responsibility to look out for my father's interests."

"You know, Mike, your dad drew you into the drama of this triangle years ago. Most likely he did this out of his own **automatic functioning** and without any malice or forethought. This family triangle makes you very reactive, and it's a no-win situation. Whenever you are in a triangle with two people and you get in between them and their issues, it's guaranteed to raise your own anxiety level. You are absorbing the stress of their relationship, and it's causing a lot of needless anxiety in you."

"So you are telling me to just forget the whole thing—act like it did not even happen?" Mike responded with an incredulous look on his face.

"I am suggesting that you recognize the issue is not yours and accept that fact. Here is the real situation, as I see it anyway.

"Don will either pay your father back or he won't. They've obviously reached some understanding between them, even if it's just a tacit standoff. Your involvement in that decision has no direct bearing on the outcome. By accepting a role in this triangle you are absorbing stress that creates anxiety in you. That anxiety is showing up as anger and a family 'cutoff'—a sure sign of reactive behavior. Because you are filled with this anxiety, you are no doubt transmitting it to others in your family system as well. Because of your feelings, I'm sure Karla and the kids are absorbing the tension in the relationship between you and Don, and that will increase the anxiety they carry as well."

Jacob added Karla's name, making another triangle that interlocked with the Mike-Don-Mike Senior one. This new triangle was Mike-Don-Karla.

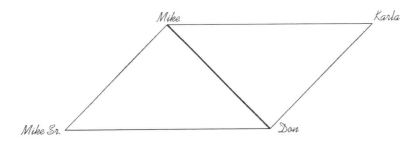

"Mike, look at this interlocking triangle that now includes you and Don and Karla."

Then Jacob quickly drew two more interlocking triangles—one by adding Jacelyn's name at one corner, with Mike and Karla at the other corners, and the other by adding Richard's name to form a triangle with Karla and Don.

A New Way of Thinking

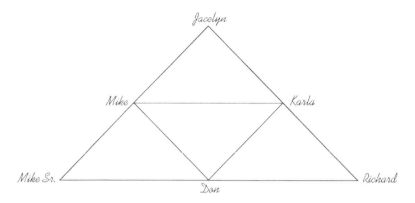

"Now look at this. The whole family is connected to this issue that started out between just Mike Senior and Don. That's what happens with anxious family systems." Jacob went on to explain that:

- *Anxiety heats up in one relationship.*
- *Soon everybody is triangled into the situation.*
- *This produces higher and higher levels of reactivity.*
- *This same dynamic happens in organizations.*

Jacob continued, "Eventually you'll be able to spot how it is operating at CHI. Knowing how to influence a system through its interlocking triangles is a powerful weapon in a savvy leader's arsenal."

Mike realized that he had created new triangles with all three of his family members over the years as he described what a terrible injustice Don had done to his father. But he was not ready to give in quite yet.

"Jacob, you can draw all the triangles you want, but the fact is that Don is still taking advantage of my father and I hate that; my dad is an old man and he deserves to be treated well."

Mike moved to the edge of his chair and with both fists clenched, he pounded the table and said,

"For God's sake, if something doesn't happen soon, Dad will die and the debt will never be repaid! SHIT... That is just dead wrong! BULLSHIT!"

Mike rose from the chair and stood stiffly as he glared down at Jacob.

Jacob calmly looked up at Mike. The room was silent.

Mike walked to the door and said, "I will call you in a few days." He opened the door and walked out of Jacob's office.

Jacob got his gardening gloves and began to head back to the garden. He stopped in the middle of a thought and went back to his computer. He wrote Mike a quick note.

*Mike – enjoyed the session today. Good progress. I am pasting a page that has some "universal laws" that describe how emotional **triangles** function in family and organizational systems. THIS MAY BE THE SINGLE MOST VALUABLE PIECE OF BACKGROUND MATERIAL IN MY FILES! It will help you in working through both CHI and family issues. I recognize the language is a bit dense in places, but working your way through this material will pay real dividends, I guarantee you. Take a look at these "laws," and let me know what you think, especially about number 12. Jacob*

1. Not all triangles are the result of poorly functioning relationships. As a natural phenomenon, they are simply the way that any relationship system works through and contains its anxiety.
2. Leaders can be triangled in a number of ways: for example, by becoming the focus of unresolved issues of two others, by getting caught in a position of being responsible for two others' relationship, or by becoming responsible for the relationship of another and his/her symptom or problem.
3. Triangles are often more difficult to spot when they involve more than one person in each corner.
4. Leaders who are triangled have a more difficult time healing from whatever ails them, and they can find their functioning hindered through no fault of their own.
5. Efforts to change the other two sides of a triangle generally produce the opposite effect.
6. The more the third party of a triangle tries (unsuccessfully) to change the relationship of the other two, the more likely it is that the third party will absorb the stress of the other two.

7. *Stress and burnout in leaders has less to do with hard work than with being emotionally triangled.*
8. *Because of the interlocking nature of triangles, efforts to change any one of the triangles will be resisted by the others.*
9. *One side of a triangle tends to be the source of more conflict than the others.*
10. *To the extent a leader can maintain a calm presence in a triangle, the more likely will that leader be able to reduce chronic anxiety in the others.*
11. *The most triangled position in any system can be the most powerful, as long as the leader understands the laws of triangles and acts accordingly.*
12. *Repositioning oneself in a triangle holds the potential for effecting real change in the system. What is necessary is for leaders to keep the focus on their own functioning and not get "hooked" by the red herring of "content" or other anxiety forces in the system.*
13. *The greater a leader's ability to maintain a focus on the process/system level—rather than ascribe causality to persons, problems or events—the easier will it be for that leader to remain neutral about the relationship process; and, the leader's efforts to reposition will be correspondingly more effective.*

Mike sat outside Jacob's office for ten minutes trying to cool down. As his wits returned, he wondered if he had offended Jacob and decided to call him later in the day. He started the car and turned on his cell phone to see incoming messages.

He saw Jacob's message and quickly scanned the list that Jacob had just sent him. When he read universal law 12, he stopped on these words:

What is necessary is for leaders to keep the focus on their own functioning and not get "hooked" by the red herring of "content" or other anxiety forces in the system.

He realized what had just happened in Jacob's office. He had been hooked by a red herring all right. He also realized how deeply into his own mouth the hook had been set.

As he put the car in reverse and began to pull away, Jacob appeared at the door, heading for the garden. He gave Mike a great big smile and a thumbs-up sign.

Mike worried that he had conducted himself very unprofessionally over the last 15 minutes.

But Jacob knew Mike was making great progress. Later that night, Mike reluctantly sat down to write his evening notes. He did not want to write about the day, but knew he should.

Today
- I lost it at Jacob's. More reactivity. I got caught up in anxiety around the content of our discussion.
- I am really defensive when it comes to my relationship with my dad.
- Learned about emotional systems and a lot about triangles.
- Our whole family is caught up in emotional triangles.

Issues
- How do I really help Craig and Steve make progress?
- Have I damaged my coaching relationship with Jacob?

Follow up
- Make appointment with Steve to discuss emotional process handout from Jacob.
- Offer Jacob an apology.
- Talk with Karla about the reunion.
- Jacob's universal laws of triangles suggest I am in a very powerful position to drive change. How do I find out more about this?

Chapter 5: Triangles

Review Key Points

- A **triangle** consists of three persons in a relationship network.
    - A triangle is the smallest stable unit of a relationship network, the "basic building block" of an emotional system.
    - **Triangles** form because a two-person relationship is inherently unstable; it generates anxiety and automatically seeks to relieve that anxiety by focusing on a third party.

- **Triangles** are a "natural" phenomenon, rather than a problem to be avoided.

- **Triangles** generally have two persons who are "insiders" while a third person is the "outsider." Efforts to move to what is perceived to be the more favorable position result in a triangle being constantly in motion as alliances shift and members attempt to find the **self-other** balance that is best for them.
    - Anxiety shifts among the members of the triangle; if the anxiety becomes too intense, interlocking triangles are formed to disperse and redistribute it among a larger number of people in the system.

- Repositioning oneself in a triangle (sometimes called "de-triangling") is achieved by managing one's anxiety, becoming more thoughtful, and adopting a more neutral stance to the relationship process that constitutes the triangle.
    - Since a leader is usually the most "triangled" member of an organization, he or she exerts tremendous influence by how well or poorly he or she manages self in the network of interlocking triangles that make up the system.

Questions for Reflection and Discussion

1. The interlocking nature of **triangles** is one reason why systems resist change so stubbornly. What level or type of resistance do you think Mike might anticipate if he tries to change his relationship with his cousin Don?

2. Efforts to change the other two sides of a triangle generally produce the opposite effect. Give an example from your workplace that illustrates this "law" of triangles.

3. Identify a time when the "insider" and "outsider" roles shifted back and forth among the members of a triangle in your family.

The Practice

Triangles occur naturally in social systems and are easy to see in family and work relationships. Remember that triangles can involve three people but it is also possible that one angle of the triangle can be an inanimate object or behavior. For example a young married couple may have a triangle in their relationship with the third angle being the wife's professional career.

1. Identify one of your most troubling triangles. Draw a picture of the triangle and label the three angles.

2. Write a descriptive sentence or two to describe why you have identified this triangle as troubling.

3. Working on the two sides of the triangle that you are connected to, identify what actions can be taken to change the way you relate to the "trouble." Also identify what actions you need to eliminate or avoid so that you will no longer take responsibility for the relationship on the "other side" of the triangle.

Triangles

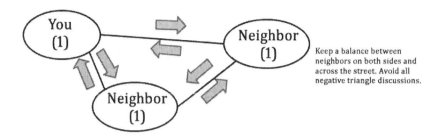

Keep a balance between neighbors on both sides and across the street. Avoid all negative triangle discussions.

Neighborhood Triangle
2. Both neighbors are friendly with me but have a habit of gossiping about each other. The gossip is mostly harmless but will build resentment eventually. I believe they must also gossip about me in my absence.
3. Build a friendly relationship with each neighbor individually. Have periodic social activities with each individually and with both together.
3. Avoid any gossip or conversation of a judgmental nature about either friend with the other. If either friend brings up a topic of gossip do not engage in the dialogue—change the subject. Honor both of my friends in their absence.

To learn more, go to www.resilient-leadership.biz.

A New Way of **THINKING**
Chapter 6: The Presence of the Past

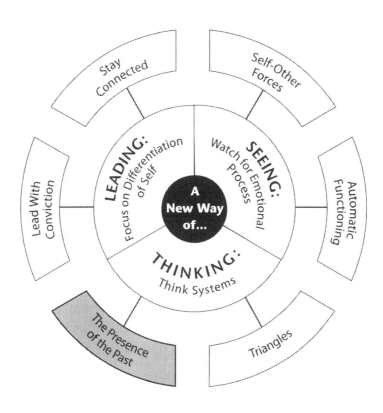

LAMONT REVISITED

At 2:30 a.m. Mike awoke to severe pain in his left knee. He had been noticing that the knee was getting very tender after running and recently he was in discomfort after his workouts. Now the area around his kneecap had swollen to the size of a small grapefruit. Something was definitely wrong and getting worse. He had to get up and take something for the pain. He'd make an appointment with the doctor when he had a chance.

At 5:45 a.m. he pulled up outside his office to sit in his car. Mike had arranged to have a conference call with Sally and Lamont at 8:30 a.m. He opened his cell phone to review materials about the plan Lamont was going to discuss on the call. A brief cover note had been sent to Sally and him yesterday but the briefing, the real substance of the correspondence, was not attached to the memo. Mike shot off a note to Lamont asking him to forward the attachment ASAP so that he and Sally could review it before the call at 8:30.

Mike knew that Sally had challenged Lamont to become more proactive in improving sales and customer service at his hotel. Rather than using the disruption of construction delays as an excuse for missing this year's performance plan, he needed to find a way to reach for the plan goals.

Some time had passed, and Mike had cooled down a lot. He was ready to hear a solid, well-thought-out plan. In preparation for the call, Mike had drawn a triangle on his notepad with Lamont, Sally and himself at each angle. He wanted to be sure he retained his proper position in the discussion.

In just a few minutes, the attachment arrived, and Mike felt good that Lamont was up early attending to issues at his hotel.

At 8:30 Mike dialed in to the conference line that Sally Harrison had set up, and there were four people on the line: Mike, Sally, Lamont and the marketing director for the Union Square hotel, Remi Keys. The briefing was handled by Remi rather than Lamont. That was a mistake. Mike needed to see Lamont take some initiative himself, and not keep passing things off to his assistants.

Mike quickly realized that he had to think in terms of additional triangles now that Remi was on the phone too. He did not have the time to think about all the additional triangles, but he at least knew that one of them was Sally, Lamont and Remi. He needed to be careful.

The briefing that Remi did was solid and the suggested short-term actions to bolster sales and control costs made a lot of sense. But when asked how he was going to take an active role in the plan, Lamont pointed out that he was going to be focusing on the construction challenges while his team would deploy the short-term sales and cost management plan. Further discussion revealed that the plan had been created by the Union Square team while Lamont was on vacation.

It was clear that the plan was not a priority for Lamont and that he had gone through the motions of having the plan created but did not intend to lead his team in its execution.

Mike realized the problem almost immediately and began to think about the leadership system he was trying to influence. He knew that he should not criticize the plan or explode about the absence of the personal involvement of the general manager in the implementation steps. He waited to see what Sally would say.

She picked up on the problem right away and critiqued the plan with intensity. Mike realized that Sally was covering all the bases and at the right moment suggested that a follow-up phone call should be scheduled for the following week to review the revisions that Sally had suggested. He also knew that Sally would want to deal with Lamont one-on-one before that call. All agreed. The conference call ended, and Sally called Mike back in 30 seconds.

"Mike, thanks for being on the call today. I can't believe what we just heard. It's like Lamont just doesn't understand the significance of his responsibility in the short-term financial challenge he faces. I think I have the wrong guy at that hotel."

"Don't worry about what happened today. Just focus on getting it on track in the next week or so. Let me know when you want me to be on the next call."

CHI EXECUTIVE LEADERSHIP TEAM MEETING

Mike sat down next to Irwin Briggs, the senior vice president for the Southeast Division. Irwin was a long-timer with CHI and a close friend of James McMaster; he also hadn't had an innovative thought in years. He admired Vanessa Jackson but did not much like working for her. Vanessa was not tough enough for Irwin. She needed to "just make a damn decision"—a phrase he used often and with great enthusiasm.

Vanessa formed the CHI Executive Leadership Team when she took the job. The ELT structure included four division senior vice presidents of operations plus six senior staff vice presidents, one each for finance, human resources, diversity, strategy, marketing and communications. The ELT total head count was 11 including Vanessa, and they met every month for two days, or more if needed.

It was the third week of June. The agenda had been created several days before the meeting date and included follow-up discussions on a number of projects and priorities underway as well as two new priorities. One topic was the national reservation system that was going operational in January. The second topic was the review of a very large new business opportunity for a nationwide contract with several UK travel agencies. The afternoon session was devoted to this topic. Review materials had been provided in advance of the meeting.

INSIDE CHI

Vanessa began the briefing by making the point that this opportunity was significant from a guaranteed room occupancy standpoint, but that there was an added challenge of balancing long-term fixed price contract business with the flexibility needed to adjust rates to take full advantage of market conditions. A lot was riding on the price point that the UK agencies were willing to guarantee for the huge room block they were trying to secure. The solicitation would stimulate responses from other major lodging chains in the US.

Luke then reviewed the specific elements of the UK solicitation and the response he was recommending that CHI provide. In simple terms, the proposed response that Luke developed made good business sense for CHI as a whole and for the Northeast and the West Coast, but it would really hurt the Southern and Central divisions.

The briefing took Luke a little over an hour to finish, and it was followed by a break. At about 2:50 the discussion resumed in the CHI board room between Vanessa's and James McMaster's offices.

Steve Alba, the SVP for the Central Division, spoke first. "Luke, thanks for the hard work. It's pretty clear that the impact of this business opportunity will benefit CHI as a total system, but the numbers also indicate that Irwin down there in the Southeast and my Central area will really take a beating if we agree to submit a proposal for this opportunity in our areas.

"Our Northeast and West Coast properties are newer, bigger and much more upscale than the south or my older units in St. Louis and Chicago. We don't cater to upscale international travelers in my 'neck of the woods.' For the most part, the Midwestern area of CHI is an early 1980s hotel operation."

Everyone in the room agreed. CHI had no real core identity as a company. The problem was longstanding and seemed to dominate almost all of the national level marketing discussions. Ever since the beginning of CHI, it was clear that the business model was "sell whatever people will buy," and while that short-term approach served local market needs, it really created problems as CHI grew to a national presence in the US.

The problems with national group business had become more and more severe. CHI had failed to capture any large national contracts in the last few years. Opportunities had been missed in the lucrative airline crew business and the pharmaceutical and computer sales markets. In every case, the Midwest and Southern regions of the company simply could not compete with other hotel chains.

Alba was describing the historical problem when Vanessa interrupted him and asked, "Steve, what do you suggest we do?"

"Well, we need to find a way to take advantage of this opportunity for CHI in locations where it will work, but minimize the downside impact on the Central and Southern Divisions. To do that, I suggest that we explore two options. We could eliminate the Central and Southern regions from our proposal or underbid the offer in these areas to be more competitive."

Neither of these ideas was very satisfying. The room was silent for a moment. Next, the newly hired SVP of strategy, Max Case, spoke up.

"How did we get to the point where we have such an

imbalance in our portfolio? Why are we behind in the Southern and Midwestern regions?"

The operational veterans all looked at each other to determine who would talk next. They all knew that the Midwest and Southern regions were a mixture of very dissimilar units that had been acquired in the 1980s during a period when CHI had investment dollars and was trying to quickly build market share. From old, tired conference center hotels built in the 1960s to even older hotels in the downtown areas of St. Louis, Minneapolis and Chicago built in the late 1800s, the CHI portfolio of hotels in the middle of the country was eclectic. Many of these hotels were in declining sections of the cities. In contrast, the CHI hotels in the Northeast and West Coast were newer, located in more desirable locations and more competitive against the bigger and more well-known chains.

It was as if there were two CHI's. Until Vanessa put a stop to it several years ago, people attending internal company meetings often referred to themselves as either the "New CHI" or "Old CHI." The problem was getting much worse in recent years as new upscale and smaller boutique hotels began to challenge these older units in many metropolitan areas.

Then Max, the youngest and most outspoken of all the staff leaders, asked the million-dollar question.

"Why are we not pruning our portfolio to prepare for the future? It's pretty clear that we need a strategy to reposition CHI as a national brand if we hope to compete for business on a national scale. What am I missing?"

What Max was missing was that James McMaster had held a firm grip on which hotels to buy for the last 30 years, and his model of deciding how to invest also had not changed in 30 years. James had some very strong beliefs about business that were deeply formed in his mind as a young man who grew up as the country was emerging from the Depression. These beliefs were outdated, and everyone knew it except James McMaster.

As a youngster, James went to work for pennies at a local hotel in order to help his widowed mother pay the bills. Over time, James worked in all the departments of the hotel as he learned the business from the ground up. He saved his money, only bought what he could afford and never borrowed money or used credit to finance anything. His mantra "cash is king" served him well in earning a living for his mother and brothers and eventually his own family. As he moved from working in hotels to owning hotels, his simplistic view about how to operate the business remained about the same, and it made him one of his generation's most successful entrepreneurs.

The problem with James' "cash is king" mantra is that it can become a very short-term strategy—and it had at CHI. Profits are important, but so is growth. James could never really come to the point where he saw the wisdom of selling an operation that was making money, even if the market was declining.

Irwin would always sum up the situation this way, "My good friend James McMaster sees CHI as a collection of hotels, not a chain of hotels. He loves each one as a father loves his children; they are all part of his family."

Irwin turned to Max and said, "I'll tell you what you're missing. We've been through this a thousand times before. Let's not waste time going over all the core strategy stuff again. We never get anywhere when we debate how to form one company, and we never will. We, or James that is, has some fundamental assumptions about CHI, not unlike any other organization, and they are not going to change any time soon."

Irwin continued, "Luke, you've been here long enough to know that we really have two distinct groups of hotels, right?" Luke nodded slight agreement, but did not say anything. "So just go to the bottom line on this proposal. Will we make money at the corporate level or not with the South and Midwest involved? And if so, how much upside potential do you project over our budgeted domestic business for the next two years?"

Just as Luke was about to come up with an answer, Max jumped back into the conversation. "In the short run that is the right question, but in the long run we need to ask a different question. In the long run we need to decide how to create, communicate and operate so that we maintain uniform service and quality."

Irwin had heard this discussion too often and his impatience was growing. "Max, we have heard all this before. We know that CHI needs to be more consistent across its divisions and we also know that the only way to accomplish this is with a dedicated effort to eliminate or refurbish some of our hotels—a lot of our hotels in the South and Midwest—and acquire or build more units, too. We also know that James McMaster will simply not agree with this approach."

But Max was not done yet.

"We may have addressed this issue in the past. But the fact that we have not dealt with it in the past does not mean that we should ignore it now."

Knowing he was right, he pushed even harder.

"Besides, the purpose of this team is to ask hard questions and find the answers to move the business forward. We can't just pretend that this issue is going to solve itself."

Irwin decided to give Max a history lesson.

"Look, Max, everyone here in the room knows you are right. It's simply not a question that we can successfully address. Our company has a deeply embedded culture that is over 50 years in the making. That culture is strong as steel, and one pillar of that culture is a dedication to some of our most prestigious and long-standing hotels. We will never sell the Great Southern Hotel in Savannah, Georgia, period. End of story, and we have not made a dollar of profit at that hotel for the last four years."

Vanessa began to interject a point, but Irwin was on a roll and plowed ahead.

"And here is another fact. In the last 15 years, I have seen five or six of you new hires try to come in with fresh ideas about how to reposition the company. I can even remember one or two meetings where we brought the old man himself in for the discussion.

"Those guys are not here in the room today, as far as I can see. You have a choice to make here, Max."

Irwin's last comment was said in a threatening tone, but Max was unaffected. He then made the comment that stopped everyone in their tracks, even Vanessa.

"The problem seems not to be about old versus new hotels, but rather old and outdated thinking. If Mr. McMaster cannot effectively deal with the changes we all know must be addressed, we need to go around him. We need to go to the Board of Directors."

A hush fell on the room.

"And another thing," Max added, "This is not about me; it's about us as a leadership team. And it's about Vanessa's responsibility as COO."

The silence in the room deepened, as everyone pondered whether Max had crossed a line.

Irwin knew it was time for him to bow out of this conversation. Mike realized that he had been thinking along the same lines as Max for years, but had never really cut to the chase as incisively as Max had just done. Vanessa finally broke the silence. "Max is right. James and I have had discussions about this topic a number of times in the past few years. I am not prepared to decide next steps here in the heat of the moment, but I will assume responsibility for figuring out what to do next. Let's put the UK discussion on the follow-up list, and I will get back to all of you about the path forward."

Vanessa concluded, "Thank you all for your contributions today. This has been a very thoughtful discussion."

As Mike stood up he felt a terrible shooting pain in his knee again. He had to stand straight for a few moments holding on to the table before he took his first step. He had several ideas about how to move forward, and as soon as he got back to his office he sent Vanessa a quick note to set up a meeting. He also needed to talk to Vanessa about the anonymous note he had gotten about Crystal, and he wanted to debrief with her on the situation with Sally and Lamont in Boston.

GETTING READY FOR THE REUNION

As Mike was pulling up to visit with Jacob, he wanted to review his homework assignment for a few moments before he knocked on the door. Sitting in the car, he took out the list he had drawn up and reviewed his notes for each person:

> *Karla – Revisit the issue of placing Karla between me and Jacelyn and discuss what I am learning about emotional triangles.*
>
> *Jacelyn – Talk to her and Russ about their wedding plans and the honeymoon, and be supportive of their plans even if the ideas seem stupid to me.*
>
> *Russ – Discuss his job search and try not to show my anxiety about getting married to Jacelyn without even having a job.*

Richard – Connect with him on the book he asked me to read. Ask him questions about his life and listen at a much deeper level than I usually do.

Lilly – Get to know her better. Ask questions about what she likes and does not like.

Dad – Good luck! Ask how he is doing at Silverstone. Don't get hooked by his criticisms. Stay positive. Avoid any guilt trips.

Don – Just ask about his health and the family. Sum up the reunion. Don't bring up the loan. If he lashes out at me, work at not striking back (good luck here, too).

Satisfied that he had done a good job on his homework, Mike got out of the car and knocked on Jacob's door. Jacob immediately called out, "Come on in, Mike."

As Mike walked in, he was startled to see Vanessa just ending a discussion with Jacob. She smiled at Mike and waved a quick hello, then shook Jacob's hand and stepped toward the door. Mike wondered what they were talking about but quickly changed his thoughts to the conversation he wanted to have about the reunion.

"Jacob, I will set up a visit with James, you and me for early next week," Vanessa said as she opened the door to leave.

"Great," Jacob replied and turned his attention to Mike.

"Hello, Mike. Getting ready to head to Pennsylvania?" Jacob asked.

"Yep, and I just checked my homework," Mike handed him his notes.

After studying the list for a moment, Jacob said, "These look real good, Mike. What is this 'good luck' comment you have here next to your dad and Don's names?"

Mike smiled and said, "Well these are the two conversations I have the most anxiety about, to tell you the truth. Oh, and I am sorry I stormed out of the meeting so quickly last time."

"Don't worry about it," Jacob said. "By the way, that was a great demonstration of one of our favorite topics, right?"

Mike thought for a moment and then it struck him that his abrupt departure during the last coaching session was typical of his way of dealing with his reactivity. "It was a cutoff, I guess."

Jacob smiled and said, "It was a beauty of a cutoff, Mike. I wish I had it on video!"

The lightness of Jacob's tone of voice dispelled any tension, and they both laughed at the idea of capturing Mike's reactivity on tape.

Jacob continued, "Mike, let's be sure we cover all the bases on your family so we don't miss any opportunities at the reunion. He wheeled over to the flip chart and began to draw a diagram as he asked Mike to give him names and ages of family members. In a short time they had constructed the following genogram:

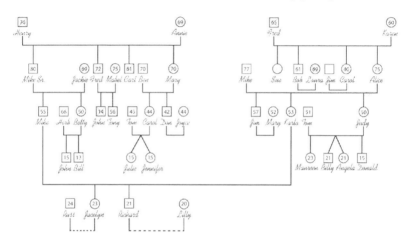

Jacob pushed his wheelchair away from the flip chart and said to Mike, "You really know a lot about your family members—Karla's too."

"Yes, I'm sort of a history buff, and I've always been interested in knowing about previous generations of the family. But I'm not sure how this diagram is going to help me at the family reunion."

"Right now it helps me to understand the bigger picture, but it may be useful to you as well, especially when we debrief after the reunion. Don't worry about it for now, okay?"

"Sure," replied Mike. He hesitated before adding, "Jacob, putting together that list got me in touch with how much I dread going to the reunion. But you seem so positive about what a wonderful opportunity it will be for me. Can you help me see it like that?"

"Sure, Mike. Reconnecting with your family of origin can be an opportunity to work on your own functioning—what Bowen

Theory calls '**differentiation of self**.' Reconnecting with key family relationships in a different way can help you to practice new behaviors, rather than just falling back into reactive patterns in a 'script' you've been using since childhood."

"But how do I keep from repeating those old patterns? You call them 'automatic functioning,' and for me they really are!"

"I understand what you're feeling, Mike. But you may be surprised that when you approach the reunion as an observer—someone who is there to watch the way family interactions work—you are much less easily hooked into the old patterns. Make it a kind of research project to find out all you can about your family. Ask questions of people, and think of yourself as a kind of anthropologist doing field studies."

"What kind of questions do you mean, Jacob?"

"Well, for example, you might talk with your Aunt Mary about a couple of things. Ask her about your father's behavior of just changing subjects when he does not agree with something that someone else says or does. Find a way to determine if this form of cutoff is something that your dad always has done or if it is a more recent behavior. And inquire about other similar patterns in other members of the extended family."

"That's going to feel pretty strange if I just start cross-examining her."

"Make it more natural. Just be curious. Ask her to tell you some stories about how people interacted, especially when there was stress or disagreements over any hot button issues.

"Also, will your sister Betty be at the reunion?" Jacob asked.

"She will be there. I can talk with her, too."

"You might want to check out if she sees your dad in the same way you do. How do you and Betty get along, Mike?" Jacob asked.

"We get along fine. Betty is five years younger than me and was always the joy of mom's life. She married late, and Herb is a full 16 years older than she is. They have a good marriage, but Herb is just too old to be raising teenage boys in this day and age."

"How did your sister and dad get along with each other?" Jacob asked.

"Quite well, actually," Mike replied. "Betty was an extremely compliant child, and she liked to please people a lot. I am sure Mom and Dad found her much easier to raise than me."

"That's interesting, Mike. Remember that list of reactive

behaviors I gave you? One of them described how both rebellion and submission can be two sides of a single coin, both of them a form of reactivity."

"Wow! I never made that connection. I just focused on the fact that I was the rebellious one. But I missed completely that Betty's submissive style was also a kind of reactivity."

"Well, I'd be wary of making a quick diagnosis about someone else, but it might be a good idea to ask her about family cutoffs, too," Jacob said.

Jacob continued, "Let me make a few points about how all this fits into systems thinking. To **think systems** is counterintuitive, and it requires us to be very deliberate about broadening our horizons in order to arrive at a deeper level of understanding. In order to do that, the first step—as we've discussed—is to practice 'A New Way of SEEING' so that you begin to notice dynamics that you previously missed. Once you have become more watchful and start to become more aware of your own and others' **emotional process**, the next step is to make sense of it in a new way as well."

Mike was following carefully and thought to himself that when Jacob launched into one of his explanations, his manner of speaking reminded him of lectures given by his college professors. What was different now, Mike mused, was that there were no grades to worry about, and he was infinitely more motivated to follow what his instructor was explaining to him.

Jacob went on, "In order to **think systems**, the notion of triangles is a pretty useful tool, since it immediately gets us thinking about how **emotional process** operates in systems. But there is another layer of insight that lets you include what you know about triangles within a framework that is even bigger, and this is where your family reunion will be so helpful.

"The layer of insight I am referring to is how our **emotional process** is the result of patterns that are passed on to us from previous generations, usually without our even being aware that our ancestors are influencing our present-day functioning. When you think that way, it's not long before you recognize **the presence of the past** nearly everywhere in your current reality."

Mike interrupted, "Are you saying that emotional patterns are genetically based? Then how come members of a single family can be so different in how their emotional makeup works?"

"To understand what I'm saying, we need to go back to what you learned about how triangles operate to transfer anxiety around in any emotional system. Remember that the classic, primary triangle that most of us know firsthand is the one that exists between us and our parents. No matter how healthy and good the relationship might be between two parents, they each carry into their marriage a certain level of chronic anxiety. As they relate to one another in the ups and downs of married life, there are times when the anxiety in their relationship escalates and creates more than usual tension. Automatically, beyond conscious awareness, they discover that by focusing on a third person—their child—their relationship becomes more calm and easy. This is simply what happens in families, and there is nothing necessarily pathological about it. Nor can even the most savvy and well-integrated parents avoid doing it, since it is how we humans operate in all of our relationships."

"But does this kind of process also apply to businesses?" Mike interjected. "It seems a stretch from parents and children to what I'm dealing with at CHI."

"Yes, there are very real parallels. We will get to that later, but it's easier to understand by first looking at how these processes operate in our own families. We will talk about the business version of this later."

Jacob went on, "So back to family systems. The anxiety of a two-person relationship is instinctively 'off-loaded' onto a third party, and a triangle is born. What varies from family to family, and situation to situation, however, is the *amount* of anxiety that is transferred to a particular child. Some parents contain the anxiety between them in the form of marital conflict, or even physical illness. But very often, it overflows onto the children. The more anxious the parents are, the higher the general level of chronic anxiety experienced by their children."

"Great," Mike chuckled. "I was hoping I could blame my problems on my parents."

Jacob laughed, too, and nodded, "Exactly. But it doesn't stop there. Even within the parameters of what is the typical amount of anxiety in a given marriage relationship, it happens that some children become a particular focus of their parents' concern and attention. The reasons why this happens are many: sometimes the child is the firstborn family 'standard bearer'; or at times a child reminds her mother of a sibling or aunt or grandmother with whom she had a problematic relationship, and the subliminal associations stir more than usual anxieties; another time a child is challenged or particularly gifted, and either case can trigger higher than usual anxiety in the parents."

Mike responded, "Well, I know for sure I was supposed to be the family standard bearer. When I decided not to pursue the family trade of dentistry, it was like I had betrayed every Sampson dating back a hundred years!"

Jacob smiled, "I think you're getting it, Mike. The key insight here is that the result of a child being focused on more than usual is a greater degree of the parents' chronic anxiety being transmitted to that child. That is one reason why not all of the children in a given family turn out the same. Each child is focused on in different measure by his or her parents. Other factors enter in, of course, but it is certainly the case that each child in the family grows up with his or her own degree of 'baggage' from the amount of chronic anxiety off-loaded by the parental triangle."

"Does that mean that I got more baggage than my sister? Because Betty was always able to fly under the parental radar. She was so sweet to everyone, she could get away with murder and nobody ever bothered her."

Jacob answered, "I can't really speculate about that, Mike. But in general, the child who has less parental focus escapes to a greater degree the negative effects of this transfer of anxiety. We have not yet talked about the notion of differentiation of self, but I will add here that a person's capacity to be a 'self' is directly influenced by the degree of chronic anxiety inherited from his or her parents. A child who becomes the focus of anxiety from his or her parents receives a disproportionate share of the family system's anxiety, and healthy functioning is proportionately impaired as a result."

Mike jumped in, "Well, I can tell you for sure that in my family it was me—much more than my sister—who got our parents' attention. I was a much more difficult child to raise, and they were always worried about my getting into trouble at school, and so forth."

"If that's the case, then it may well be that you got more of the anxiety of your parents' relationship than she did. Tell me, apart from what you said earlier about her being very compliant, would you say she's less reactive as a person than you are?"

"Absolutely, nothing seems to faze her. She's always laid back, and nothing seems to stir her up."

"Well, differentiation of self is a much more complex notion than that, but at least I think you're getting the point about how one generation passes on to the next various patterns of **automatic functioning** that are rooted in chronic anxiety. The handoff from one generation to another goes back a long way, when you stop to think about it."

Mike was thoughtful for a bit, and then said to Jacob, "You know, it's sort of spooky to think about what Karla and I have passed on to our kids, and how much I've probably given them from my own dysfunctional patterns."

Jacob smiled. "I know what you mean, Mike. I'm a parent, too. But it's not worth wallowing in any parental guilt. We all do our best, and hopefully each generation will improve on what we give them. That's the great circle of life."

"I know," said Mike. "There's nothing I can do about it anyway."

"That's not exactly true, Mike. It's never too late to do something about it. All of this work you're doing with me will yield some very positive benefits to every member of your family. In the measure that any one member of a family works on his or her own differentiation, the entire family system is that much better off. The work you're doing on being a better leader will have real payoffs for Jacelyn and Richard, believe me."

Mike was quiet for a time and then said, "You know, Jacob, I can't quite articulate it right now, but I think I'm beginning to see why this family reunion is so important. It's something about the generations of Sampsons, and how I can become a more proactive—rather than reactive—member of the family. And, hopefully, how my kids will benefit as a result."

Jacob smiled, "For someone who doesn't know how to name it, I'd say you're pretty close, Mike. But before we run out of time, I want to move on to discuss what all of this talk about parents passing things on to their children has to do with your exercising more effective leadership in CHI."

Jacob paused before continuing. "We've been talking about **the presence of the past**—the way that one generation passes on to the next certain levels of anxiety and certain ways of functioning to manage that anxiety. The patterns are transmitted from generation to generation, whether in a family or in organizations. Let's look more closely at CHI.

Can you identify any patterns, any distinctive ways of functioning, that you've seen repeating themselves at CHI?"

"I'm not sure. What kind of patterns do you mean?"

"Well," Jacob answered, "You might want to look in particular at issues that provoke anxiety and how that anxiety is typically handled, e.g., who gets reactive, who gets the self-other balance out of whack, and so forth."

Mike was quiet for a long while. Then he looked up at Jacob and said, "Maybe this will work. Just the other day at our Executive Leadership Team meeting, we dealt with a hot button issue that got everyone pretty anxious, and it's not the first time it has come up, either."

Mike then gave Jacob a quick recap of the longstanding issue of how James McMaster's outmoded business strategy was compromising CHI's ability to compete on a national level. He spoke of the tension surrounding Max's assertion that something needed to be done about it, even if it meant going around McMaster to the Board of Directors.

"That really got everyone's anxiety up," Mike concluded.

"It sounds like James McMaster is the subject of very anxious focus in the CHI leadership team at this point in time. You say that the growth curve for CHI has slowed to a crawl. People, perhaps even including Vanessa, seem to be directing a disproportionate share of their reactivity at him as CEO, and no one has been willing or able to address this issue with him over a number of years."

"That's not completely it," Mike corrected. "The issue has been raised with James in the past, but had not gotten anywhere, and most of the people who brought it up are no longer with the company. But, yes, she did seem fairly anxious about it, and she shut down the discussion, saying she would take it up later and get back to us. I've got some ideas about it, and I want to see if she's open to what I have to say."

"That is fine, Mike, but I want to caution you to be very thoughtful and very careful about how you are going to approach this issue. If it really is a matter of James' reactive functioning that has become embedded in the organization, then no quick fix solution is going to adequately address it. You said that Mr. McMaster has held onto a certain philosophy about new acquisitions and renovation or disposal of old hotels, despite a more common-sense approach that has been suggested to him?"

"Right, the old guy has been as stubborn as a mule about the issue, and he can be pretty touchy when someone challenges him. Irwin Briggs reminded Max at the meeting that we've gone through quite a few people who have challenged the status quo on this issue."

Jacob was quiet for a bit, deep in thought. Then he said, "I know James, and he's no dummy. So if he's ignoring some common-sense advice, it tells me that perhaps the system has become very anxious, to the point that his feeling responses may have overtaken his capacity for clear thinking."

"It seems that way," said Mike. "And unless and until he and his Board of Directors and the leadership team come to terms with the changes needed to bring CHI into the future, the company is at significant risk. I would guess that James and the next COO have probably two to three years at most to pull out of the downward trend before CHI is in serious jeopardy."

The room went silent. In the space of a few days, Mike had felt the dull headache he always had about CHI grow into a full-blown migraine. He considered the idea that he was competing for the position of COO at a time when the company would either step into the future or begin a downward spiral. He felt excited and sick to his stomach at the same time.

Jacob interrupted the silence and said, "This is important, and I want to come back to it with you. But today is not so much about CHI as it is about getting ready for the reunion. I think you are ready to go; what do you think?"

Mike smiled and said, "I am ready to go. And while I'm not exactly looking forward to the trip now, neither am I dreading it like I was before."

"Why is that, Mike?" Jacob asked.

"That's a good question," Mike said and then thought for a moment. "It's because I have a better understanding of myself, I guess. I think the idea of becoming more self-observant and self-aware is helping me be more effective in working and living with people."

Jacob smiled and said, "That's the whole idea."

Today
- *Relationships always include a third person to decompress emotional field.*
- *The emotional system in both my family and CHI need my balanced, controlled and low anxiety involvement.*

Issues
- *James is the focus of a lot of anxiety—has been for a long time— issue is "cash is king" short-term thinking.*
- *Be really careful in how I approach James on my ideas about CHI transition.*

Follow up
- *At the reunion I need to check with Mary and Betty about Dad's cutoff behavior when he was younger.*

Vanessa's Office

A few days later, Mike went into Vanessa's office to keep the appointment he had made after the recent ELT meeting.

"Hello Vanessa. I was surprised to see you in Jacob's office the other day."

"Well, I haven't seen Jacob for a coaching session in a long time, but I think I might work with him again for the next couple of months as I prepare my transition."

Mike nodded and waited to see if Vanessa wanted to be more specific. She did not.

"Vanessa, I have three topics to discuss with you. The first one is related to this anonymous note I received last week." Mike handed the note about Crystal to Vanessa.

"I have been aware of this issue for a few weeks," Vanessa said, looking over the note. "Helen has asked me about it, too. It's too early to make any decisions, but I am aware that the rumor mill is beginning to spin as we move toward my departure date. Helen asked me if she should begin looking for another job, and I told her to make that decision based on whether she wanted to stay in the position after I left. She said that she needed to think about it."

Mike picked up the note from the table. "This note is really not so much about what Crystal is or is not saying as it is about the increased anxiety that is present in the administrative ranks," Mike said. "I think that we need to tell people what we know and also tell them what they can expect as we move closer to the transition date. The system is getting anxious, and we need to calm it down as best we can."

"You are beginning to sound like Jacob," Vanessa said with a smile. "You're right. I will talk with Helen again and then communicate with the whole staff in the next few days. I'll write a memo to the admin team and then hold a question and answer session soon. You might want to talk with Crystal after I send it out to bring her up to speed on what you know and encourage her not to feed the rumor mill."

Mike nodded. "I also wanted to talk with you about the meeting we had last week. The discussion about the UK opportunity was a rehash of old discussions, but we also broke new ground. Max spoke with a level of intensity that was refreshing about issues that we really do need to address."

"I totally agree," Vanessa said. "I admire Max for his candor and directness, and I also appreciate the risks he is taking with his teammates."

"Vanessa, I have thought a lot about this situation, and I feel strongly that you and the senior team and the incoming COO must find a way to get James and the Board of Directors to grapple with this issue soon."

Vanessa sat back in her chair. She had broached the subject in a very preliminary way with Jacob during her recent visit and knew that the time had come to press the issue.

"Mike, I want to discuss this more thoroughly with you and Steve Alba. I will set up a meeting in the next couple of days."

At first Mike thought that it was odd that Vanessa wanted to meet with both him and Steve at the same time. But then he realized that from her point of view, having two COO candidates in a room together would give her the chance to see what each was thinking on a critical issue.

Then it dawned on him that sometime in the last few weeks,

Vanessa had decided that he was a viable COO candidate. Sitting there in her office, he finally realized that he actually might get the job.

"Anything else?" Vanessa asked.

"Yes, let me quickly bring you up to speed on the situation up at Union Square in Boston," Mike said. "Sally Harrison is doing a very good job addressing the downturn in the Boston market. She has taken steps to challenge each of her hotels to develop a contingency plan that includes not only cost containment steps but also revenue enhancement activities. This idea arose from the coaching you gave me several weeks ago. One of the biggest challenges is Union Square, which is well behind their year-to-date sales and profit goals. The general manager up there is Lamont Sill."

"He has a big challenge with the renovation up there, I bet," Vanessa replied.

"The renovation of the hotel is a whole story in and of itself," Mike said. "Lamont has become so anxious about the renovation problems that he's completely lost his focus on the big picture. He and Sally are going back to the drawing board to establish the accountabilities for Lamont to lead his hotel out of the problems they now face."

"What is the real problem up there?" Vanessa asked.

"The central problem is the lack of day-in day-out supervision by the general manager in order to get thing moving. They have a decent plan, but accountabilities to implement the plan are weak. The general manager is not taking aggressive steps to pull the team together."

"What are you going to do about that?" Vanessa asked.

I asked that they revise their plan and get back to me within ten days as to what is going to be done by whom and when. Sally is handling the details."

"Mike, let me ask you something," Vanessa said. "How would you have handled this situation a year ago?"

"I would have flown up to the hotel, met with the hotel executive committee, developed a plan with some input from them and flown home in about 48 hours."

"Well, why did you not do that this time?"

"Because I realize that a quick fix solution to the immediate problem does not provide the opportunity for the team to grapple with how to remedy its own problems. By taking this approach I am giving Sally the opportunity to grow and address the problems as she sees fit. I also create a triangle of interference when I inject myself into the process with the wrong level of involvement. I want to be sure that the management system is working to improve itself for its own good, not in order to please me down here in DC."

"Did Jacob teach you something about a triangle of interference?" Vanessa asked.

"Well no, I just sort of thought up that name. He has taught me a lot about triangles and how not to get involved in what belongs to the other two people. I call it a triangle of interference to remind myself not to interfere."

Vanessa smiled and said, "Thanks for the update on Boston. It seems that you are really picking up some good ideas from Jacob."

"It is helping a lot," Mike said as he stood up and headed for the door.

Vanessa had seen some growth in Mike over the last few months, but now she could see a major shift in his overall leadership style. She was confident that she now had two very strong internal candidates for her replacement.

GETTING READY FOR THE REUNION

On the Saturday before the reunion, Mike and Karla drove to Front Royal to pick up Mike Senior. They talked about the weekend on the ride over.

"At my last session with Jacob, we discussed this weekend," Mike said. "He and I have been talking about the transmission of behaviors from one generation to another in families. He calls it **the presence of the past**. It's been a real eye-opener."

"What have you learned?" Karla asked.

"Well, I have learned that I am becoming my dad," Mike said, and then laughed after seeing Karla's expression.

"What I mean is that I have some of the same behaviors, albeit updated for our generation, which my dad has; especially when I am frustrated. I am prone to want to control everything, to triangle people in stressful situations and also to just cut people off when I get anxious or don't agree with them."

Karla didn't say anything.

"Well, don't you agree?" Mike asked, looking for confirmation from Karla.

"We are all somewhat like our parents, Honey," Karla replied. "But the big difference between you and Dad is that you try to understand yourself and make improvements. Believe me, that is worth its weight in gold. I am glad you are learning about all of this, but be sure to keep it in perspective. You are a wonderful husband and father."

Mike smiled at his wife. "Jacob and I talked about the value of my having specific conversations with family members. And I could do that by rotating people in the two cars as we travel to Pennsylvania tomorrow. Here are the specific topics I want to discuss with each person."

Mike handed Karla the list he had prepared for Jacob. Karla looked at the list and then stared out the rider's side window. She said nothing for a moment.

"Honey, we need to have a fun time on this trip. I don't really want to have therapy sessions as we drive around the country. I just want to enjoy the weekend."

Mike realized that he was beginning to control the very process of learning how to manage his own controlling behavior. He almost reacted but caught himself and said, "I can see your point. I don't intend to make the trip a therapy session. I just want to be sure I have specific conversations with people so I can build a better relationship with them. It's also about my learning to manage my own reactivity in better ways."

"Okay, Honey, let's talk about the driving arrangement with the kids tonight," Karla said as they pulled up to the retirement center in Front Royal.

Mike Senior was waiting outside for them as they arrived.

5:00 A.M. REUNION DAY

As the family piled into two cars to head west, Mike suggested that Jacelyn and Russ ride with him and Karla for the first leg of the trip. The plan was to reach the reunion by about 1:30 p.m. Everyone agreed that it was going to be a long day.

Karla would do most of the driving of car #1 during the

daytime. In the family, the stories about her driving had achieved a legendary status. She could get to places in half the time that Mike could because she knew back roads and also had a heavy foot when it was needed.

As the trip began, Mike only asked one question about the wedding plans and Jacelyn was off and running for 45 minutes on everything from flowers to dresses to the reception to the honeymoon. Mike, Karla and Russ just listened. Mike noticed that a lot of Jacelyn's initial plans that had seemed to him to be unnecessary and downright crazy had somehow passed away. As he listened to her, it seemed that she was making a lot more sense until she got to one subject.

"Wait a minute," Mike said. "You want to hire a photographer *and* a videographer to record the entire wedding and reception?"

"Yes, Dad, I want to have a complete record of our wedding so we can have it to watch after the ceremony and also to show our kids. Don't worry. We will have a copy made for you and Mom, too."

Mike was not worried about getting his own copy. He held his tongue.

Karla said, "Honey, I think this is a great idea. We never look at our wedding pictures, but if we had a video we could watch it from time to time and show it to others. Plus, it's a great record that can be passed on from generation to generation."

Mike thought that this was an absolute waste of money. He wanted to ask how much the recording would cost, but knew when he heard the number he would get even more steamed up. "I think you should consider the cost and true usefulness of the video and then ask yourself if it really makes sense. If you still want to do it, then we can."

The car was silent for about 15 seconds. The decision to move forward with the wedding video had already been made and everyone knew it. The discussion was over.

Russ and Jacelyn had come up to the DC area to attend the reunion, but Russ also had a job interview with US Customs.

"Russ, how did the interview go this week?" asked Mike.

"It was a great interview. The opportunity to work for US Customs has a lot of pluses. They are looking to hire people for positions all over the country. I didn't realize it, but there are customs posts all over the country, even up and down the Mississippi River. Import inspections by Customs and other governmental agencies are done not only at port cities but also at locations within the US borders. It's really quite interesting."

Russ continued. "And with all the imports coming from the Middle East, the work will be steady and there would be a good chance for promotion if I took the job and performed well."

Mike was encouraged and relieved to hear his future son-in-law talk about a job opportunity with enthusiasm. "So what happens now?" Mike went on.

"Well, I told them I wasn't interested in the job; too much office work. I would be glued to a computer all day long. I want to have a job where I can be moving around a lot and not be cooped up in a cubical. It was a good interview, but the work is definitely not for me. I like being outside."

If Mike had been driving the car at this moment, he would have swerved off the road. Here was a great opportunity to get a solid job with the federal government and the husband-to-be of his only daughter was not going to take the job because the opportunity would not let him be out in the sunshine every day. He clutched the armrest with his right hand, very hard. "So, what's next?" Mike asked, trying to sound calm.

"Well, I have some ideas about starting my own import business," Russ replied.

"Oh, really, what kind of imports, Russ?" Mike asked.

"Well, I'm not sure yet, something from China. I want to figure out how to import items in volume and with low weight factors, something I can import for retail distribution."

"Well, do you have any ideas about where you would do this, who would buy it from you, or what you would import?"

"Not yet. But I'm working on it."

Mike actually had the mental image of turning around in the front seat of the car and choking Russ.

"Well, I hope it works out for you," Mike said. He wasn't sure he was making any progress at all.

There was an uncomfortable lull in the conversation. Breaking the silence after several long minutes, Russ said, "Mr. Sampson, I know you are worried about me getting a job and taking care of Jacelyn after we get married. I want you to know that I am clear on what I am responsible for and I will find a way to not only make a living, but give Jacelyn a great life. I appreciate your patience with the situation and your support of me. It means a lot."

Mike said, "You're very welcome. I know you will be a great son-in-law." Just after he said this, he felt a great release in his chest and quietly thanked God for Mr. Jacob Wolfe.

9:30 A.M. REUNION DAY

As the two-car caravan arrived at Cumberland, they stopped at a fast food restaurant. After a quick bite to eat and a fill-up at a nearby gas station, they switched cars and were off. This time Karla and Mike were up front in car #1 and Richard and Lilly were in the back.

"How is the trip going in car #2?" Karla asked.

"Great," Richard answered. "Grandpa is a lot of fun. He is really looking forward to the reunion. He also told us a lot of stories about his work and the family when Dad was young, living back in Steubenville."

Mike wondered what kind of stories Mike Senior was spinning now.

Lilly added, "I really like the one about the time your grandpa was called in on a weekend to meet a woman in his office who had just decided that her dental pain was too much to bear. She wanted all of her teeth pulled out—every single one. When he took the call, he headed for the office bound and determined to convince her that teeth needed to be saved, not pulled. When she sat in the chair and opened her mouth, to his surprise, she had only two teeth left. He pulled them both in three minutes and sent her on her way."

Actually, that was a true story, because Mike knew Sarah Hinton himself. The story was true except the part about three minutes. Every year that Mike Senior told the story, the time frame for the tooth extraction got shorter.

Lilly and Richard had been living together in Orlando for about eight months, and this was her first trip to the DC area. It was also the first time the Sampson family had met her. She hit it off with Mike Senior right away when she told him that she was a dental assistant down in Orlando.

"Lilly, have you been working for the dentist for a long time?" Karla asked.

"I have been there about three years. Dr. Smoot is a prosthodontist and has been in the Orlando area a long time. I plan to go to dental hygienist school in about 18 months, as soon as I get my student loans paid off."

Mike liked Lilly a lot already. She had her head on straight.

Lilly went into her family history, her interests in music and theater and how she met Richard at a Snow Patrol concert.

"Wow, I have been talking too much," she said, "one of my biggest faults."

Both Mike and Karla thought she was a delightful young woman.

"So, Richard, how is your life going?" Mike asked.

"Great, Dad, I have good work every day and I am really enjoying learning about auto mechanics with my new boss."

"Seems like that is a lot to keep going—landscaping during the day and working on cars at night and on the weekends," Mike said.

"Well, I love the work and the people. Time goes by fast, and I have a lot of bills.

Anyway, I don't like just sitting around the house watching TV. It's a big waste of time."

Richard went on, "Dad, did you ever go to the website I sent you information about?"

"Not yet. What is it about?"

"It's a book written by a man named Eckhart Tolle. Basically, the idea is that the best way to achieve happiness in life is to always be present wherever you are. When you are thinking about the past or trying to plan the future, you mind is preventing you from fully experiencing the current moment of your life. He has also written a book called the *Power of Now*."

Mike wasn't impressed. "Well, if we all walk around being present we won't get very much done."

"Tolle does not suggest that you don't plan. It's that you don't waste your time brooding over the past or suffering the future. Make plans and then take action," Richard said.

"Now that makes some sense," Mike commented.

"Dad, I can't do the book justice, but I really think you would benefit from reading it."

"Why are you so interested in me reading this book? You

have never asked me to read anything before," Mike observed.

"I thought it would be good to have something to talk about; we don't really talk like we used to," Richard said.

Richard's quick and very direct answer hung in the cabin of the car for a few seconds.

"Okay," Mike said. "I'll get a copy of the book."

Richard pulled out an extra copy of the book from his travel bag and handed it over the seat to his dad.

1:30 P.M. REUNION DAY

The caravan pulled up into the grassy field on Aunt Mary's farm that was serving as a parking lot for the day. There were already close to 100 cars, trucks and vans parked in the field. A big sign was draped over the front porch—SAMPSON REUNION.

There were hundreds of people milling around the farm. Mary and Ben had pulled out all the stops again. There were hayrides, horse rides, three moon bounces, nature walks for the city kids that included tours of several barns and more food than could be eaten by 600 people.

As was the case every year, there were many people Mike hardly knew because most family members were either raised here in the valley and had never left, or they were from different areas of the East Coast. Nevertheless, he knew that the only way to get started was just to walk up to people and say hello.

Mike's first stop was to find Aunt Mary and Uncle Ben so they could see Mike Senior. As he moved with his father through the crowd looking for either one of them, the remainder of the family headed for bathrooms and refreshments.

Aunt Mary was standing behind one of the serving tables under a shade tree, just behind the house, when she saw Mike and Mike Senior.

"Hello, Brother Mike," she yelled as she saw them walking toward the line of food tables. She ran over and threw her arms around her older brother.

Mike Senior teared up. "I didn't know if I would see you again."

Mary laughed. "Mike, you say that every year. I am always here and you will always come to these reunions."

A New Way of Thinking

Mike knew that whatever happened for the remainder of the day, it would all be worth the effort to have this moment.

Just then Betty came up and hugged them both. Mike Senior grinned from ear to ear in a way Mike had seldom seen. Betty was still her dad's little girl. Herb, Betty's husband, was there, too, and looking a lot older than last year. They all sat down in the shade and began to catch up on the year's activities and events. The conversation and laughter went on for two hours. Several comments were about Don and his health and how everyone missed him and Joyce this year.

At about 4:00 p.m., Mike began to realize that in previous years, by this time he would be starting his good-byes and preparing for the ride back to Virginia. But now the trip to Don and Joyce's house was looming in front of him. He also wanted to talk for a few moments with Betty and Mary about Mike Senior.

He caught Karla's attention and took her aside to talk.

"Honey, we really don't have time to head over to Don and Joyce's house and then get back to Virginia today. I think we need to skip that visit."

Karla would have none of it. "Absolutely not," she said. "If you want to go home, you take one of the cars and go by yourself. Don and Joyce need a visit from us this year more than ever. He's recovering from a heart attack, they have missed the reunion, and they are sitting in their house 45 minutes from here waiting to see us. I am not going to disappoint them."

Karla was a mild-mannered woman, but she had her moments, and this was one of them. Mike actually thought about taking a car and going home but realized that it was not a good idea no matter how he looked at it.

"Okay, well, let's get on our way. This is going to be a hell of a long day."

Karla was not adept in leaving a party quickly, and Mike knew that it would be another hour before they were in the cars headed for Don's. He decided to talk with Aunt Mary and Betty.

He caught them at the dessert table.

"Can I talk with the two of you for a moment?" They all stepped away from the dessert table and pulled up three chairs.

"Mary, I wanted to talk to you about my father. I've been noticing that he has been getting more and more forgetful and agitated with me and others in the last few months."

"Do you think he's in an early stage of Alzheimer's?" Betty asked, "Have you had someone at the home examine him?"

"They watch him all the time, and they haven't said anything along those lines. But he has been getting lost from time to time in the home, and he is always irritable with me."

Betty said, "But it is a big home, and a lot of the hallways look the same to me. He has certainly seemed fine to me today."

Mary added, "Yes, I agree with Betty. He seems fine to me. And he and I talk on the phone almost every week, and I haven't noticed any problems with his memory. Keep us posted if you see anything serious develop, but for now I think you're worrying too much, Mike."

"Mary, what about the way he always cuts people off when he doesn't like what he's hearing? Was Dad always like that?"

"Are you kidding? He's always been that way. Our brothers Fred and Carl and especially our father Henry were all the same. The Sampson men have never had many social skills. They dislike parties with anyone other than family; they're suspicious by nature, and they can cut you out of their world for years if they disagree with you. I don't see that behavior in the women of our family, but it is sure a part of the way the men operate."

Betty chimed in. "Mike, don't you remember that Dad has always been like that? He's the least patient man I know. I remember how impatient he always was with you when you were slow doing your chores. I could always get around him by charming him, but the two of you just locked horns constantly."

"Really?" Mike was stunned by the emphatic way that Betty spoke. He wondered how tuned out he had been to many other family dynamics.

Mike thought about sharing what he was learning about **emotional process** and even spending some time talking about Jacob, but he didn't know how to start and decided against the idea. He wanted to be ready to leave whenever Karla had finished saying goodbye.

He did continue for another few moments, "So, Aunt Mary, tell me more about the Sampson men folk. Are you saying they were prone to cutting people off?"

Mary burst out laughing. "That's an understatement. Of course, your grandfather got mad at his parents at 16, ran away from home, and never spoke to them again. And he eventually got into fights with every one of his business partners and refused to speak to them ever after. And your uncles Fred and Carl, God rest their souls, were as ornery and reclusive a pair as you'd ever want to meet. Why ever would you ask about that?" and she laughed again.

Mike was embarrassed, but he mumbled, "Well, I guess Dad has handed down some of this legacy to me, too. In my work I have to be so careful not to cut people off when I don't agree with them. It's really important for both me and others in the world where I work."

Betty said, "Mike, I never see you like that when we are together."

"Well, Betty, that's because you always agree with everything I say," Mike said with a big grin. They all laughed, and Mike hugged both his sister and aunt as Karla approached and said they were all ready to leave for Don's.

4:30 P.M. – REUNION DAY

The family began to load up into both cars to head for Zelienople, which was about 40 miles north of the farm. Once in the car, Karla called Joyce and Don to let them know they were on the way. The trip was interrupted by heavy showers just outside of Pittsburgh near Beaver Falls, and all the traffic had to pull over for about 20 minutes to wait for the storm to pass. They finally arrived at about 5:30. As they pulled in, Mike realized that the trip back to Virginia was going to be impossible to finish that evening.

Don and Joyce were truly glad to see the Sampson family arrive. They had prepared a light snack and offered refreshments to everyone as they arrived. It had been more than 12 years since Mike had been in their home, and he remembered it as much larger than it appeared now. The house was an older, small colonial on Elm Street that had been built right after World War Two. It was a typical two-story home set among large old trees, with a big front yard and a huge back yard. They sat in the backyard screened-in porch, and a number of conversations all began at once.

Karla asked Don how he was feeling, a question that launched a 20-minute discussion about his recent heart attack.

Don was now on a strict diet and exercise routine. He appeared to be recovering well and looked a lot better than Mike remembered him even ten years ago. Beyond that, Mike sensed that there was something else quite different about him. It seemed that he was more self-assured than Mike had remembered.

After a few minutes, Mike found himself climbing up his imaginary tree to a point above the circle of conversation. He noticed that Don and Mike Senior had a particularly warm and cordial conversation going, and he wondered about the subject that he was not going to bring up—money. He also noticed how much both Richard and Russ were drawn to Joyce. He thought to himself that the distance and time of separation between him and his relatives had caused him to feel even more removed from them. He was beginning to recognize some of the ways that the Sampson family's pattern of reactive functioning ran through himself and his extended family. He also thought about all the interlocking triangles that were at work there on the back porch.

At one point he tuned in on Jacelyn talking with Karla and Joyce about the upcoming wedding. "On the ride over, I asked Grandpa if he would like to speak at the reception, and he said he would really like the chance to talk about the family. You know, it was so much fun seeing Grandpa and Russ having a great laugh over some of our family stories."

Karla beamed as she listened to her daughter talk with such enthusiasm and joy about her wedding plans. It was clear from comments that both Jacelyn and Lilly made that Mike Senior was having a great time traveling with the younger generation. Mike realized that he felt one way about his dad, and it seemed that everyone else, at least on this trip, felt another way.

After a while the group gradually broke up, and people drifted off to different spots in the small house; the yard was still too damp from the rain for anyone to go outside. Mike took the opportunity to talk with Don, resolved to follow the plan sketched out in his homework for Jacob. The heart attack had definitely changed Don's overall perspective on life. In times past, Don would speak about boats, fast cars and hunting. Now his focus was much more on family. He spoke about his sister Carol and her husband Tom, and how much he and Joyce enjoyed their twin nieces Julie and Jennifer. He talked about frequent visits to his parents' house, and about an upcoming vacation they all were planning in October to Kill Devil Hills, North Carolina.

It was obvious that Don had moved on in his life from a focus on possessions to enjoying time with his family. Mike was envious of the transition he saw in Don. Standing in the hallway of their modest home, he saw Don as a simple and happy man, living an uncluttered life. Mike could feel that his heart was beginning to lose some of its hardness toward Don. The unpaid debt didn't seem very important any more, and Mike felt embarrassed at how much it had once mattered to him.

Mike realized that it was already 7:30 p.m. and time to make a decision about going back to Virginia. If they left now, they would not be able to get Mike Senior to Front Royal until 2:30 in the morning. They would have to take him back to DC and then get up on Monday and drive back to the retirement center or keep Dad at home for a few more days. Besides, it would be dangerous to travel in the dead of the night after such a long day. They had to spend the night somewhere, and Mike announced that they should probably be heading out to find a place to stay for the evening.

Joyce would hear none of it, of course, and insisted that they spend the night there and get an early start in the morning. The house was not designed to sleep seven additional adults, but the decision was made to make the extra two bedrooms and the living room couches work. It was clear that Joyce and Don were very pleased that the change of plans included them, and they were genuinely happy to offer their home. Everyone was in bed and asleep by 11:30 p.m.

Monday Morning

Don was up early for his morning exercise walk, and the slow pace allowed Mike Senior to tag along with him. Karla, Joyce and Jacelyn were sitting at the kitchen table. Mike's knee was killing him. He knew that he had something much worse than a just a muscle pull. Russ and Richard and Lilly were still asleep. By 8:00 a.m. everyone was up and moving, and Mike announced that the departure time was 8:30.

Breakfast and goodbyes were quick, and the two cars pulled

away on time. Mike had been successful in rearranging seating again, so car #1 was now carrying Mike, Mike Senior, Jacelyn and Russ and car #2 had Karla, Richard and Lilly. Mike wanted Karla to lead the drive so he stayed back as she pulled away.

Riding in the front seat of car #1, Mike Senior immediately asked a question as they pulled onto the highway, "How long are you two staying up in DC?"

Jacelyn was not paying attention and did not realize that her grandfather was speaking to her and Russ. Mike Senior asked the question again and looked back at her.

"Oh, well I am not exactly sure, Grandpa, maybe until Thursday or Friday," she replied.

"Michael, could I stay at your house to visit with the kids while they are here?"

Mike was startled by the request. "Sure, Dad," he said. "We would be glad for you to visit for a while."

This was a first. Mike Senior had never asked to stay with him and Karla, although they had had him over a number of times during the past few years.

The drive went on for a few minutes and then Mike Senior started again.

"Michael, are you traveling this week while the kids are in town?"

"I'm not sure, Dad. A quick trip may come up at the end of the week."

"Well, it sure would be good if you could stay in the area when the kids are here."

"I'll be here all week if I can. Do you have something in mind that you want to do?"

"Maybe we could go to a ballgame or something," Mike Senior said. "But of course if you are all tied up with business, we won't be able to fit it in, I guess."

Mike could see his father setting a trap, and he was bound and determined to avoid stepping into it. "If I'm not available, I am sure Russ and Richard would be happy to take you to the park."

"Well, I guess that would be all right," Mike Senior said.

"Grandpa, Russ and I would love to take you to the ballpark. Do you mean the Baltimore Orioles?"

Mike answered, "No, Dad loves going to the Hagerstown Suns games. They are a part of the Toronto Blue Jays' farm system. Going to a baseball game there is a real treat."

"I love going out there to a baseball game. They play ball the way the game was meant to be played," Mike Senior added.

"Michael, I really would like you to come, too," Mike Senior said.

"I will if I can, Dad," Mike said cautiously.

"I don't have much time left. Family is important to me, and it should be more important to you, Michael."

The comment was a direct verbal hit. Mike had a choice to make. He hesitated a moment, then he said, "Dad, tell us about some of the games you played down in Florida when you were young."

The deflection was successful, and Mike Senior began to tell some of the often-repeated stories of his successes as a pitcher and second baseman with several American Legion teams in south Florida in the 1950s. The stories were old favorites for Mike Senior. Mike had heard them often, but a few were actually new to Jacelyn.

The remainder of the trip to Cumberland was all about baseball and family memories as Mike Senior and Jacelyn exchanged stories and laughter. Mike was quiet for most of the ride and Russ slept nearly the entire trip.

At the halfway mark, the team filled up the gas tanks and had a quick sandwich. They rearranged seating again, by now finding it a lot of fun to keep switching. For the final segment of the trip, Mike, Karla and Mike Senior were in one car and all the kids were together in the second car.

As they pulled away, Mike spoke up. "Honey, Dad has asked to stay with us for a few days while the kids are visiting."

"That's a great idea, Dad," Karla said with her usual warmth.

Mike noticed that his father was as polite as he could be when Karla was in the car. It was clear that he knew when to turn on and off the charm.

Rather than continue to judge his dad, he decided to listen carefully to the topics and flow of conversation between Karla and him. Karla had an authentic interest in his father's life, and it was obvious she cared for him deeply. Mike thought to himself that the big difference between Karla's relationship with Mike Senior and his own was more about the differences between Karla and himself. Karla loved and attended to his dad. Mike loved and competed with his dad. Even at 80 and 55, the same old tension over who was in control was present in their relationship.

They arrived home Monday afternoon. Jacelyn ran inside to get on the computer to see if the Hagerstown Suns were at home or on the road. There was a Thursday night game at home.

Mike went to his home office to check in on work.

REUNION DEBRIEF

On Thursday of that week, Mike returned to Jacob's office to discuss the reunion and also discuss the upcoming meeting with Vanessa and Steve Alba. He launched into the first subject, telling Jacob that the reunion had gone well.

"So, it must have been pretty boring this year if there were no fistfights," Jacob replied with just the right note of irony in his voice. Both men laughed, and then Mike seemed to settle in and focus on Jacob very intently.

"Actually, Jacob, it was quite a different experience, at least for me this year. I was a lot less resistant to going, and so I was more relaxed, despite the fact that I had all that 'homework' to do for you."

"The homework wasn't for me, you know. It was for you."

"I know, I know. It was a surprising trip in many ways. I've been thinking about it since I got back, and it seemed like I was connecting to people in a different way—more relaxed and at the same time more alert and more aware. I came home with a better sense of who I am, or what I really mean is a sense that I am connected to something bigger—to a family with hundreds of members who all trace back to a handful of pioneers. I can't quite put my finger on it, but do you know what I'm getting at?"

"I think so," said Jacob. "You got in touch not only with your roots, but also with some of the people who form the living fabric of the family in today's world. All of that helps you to have a clearer sense of self, and that is a huge plus. But before you get into the details of the visit, tell me a little bit more about how you were feeling going up there, what you felt while you were there and afterwards."

Mike thought for a few moments and then said, "I had mixed feelings before I got there. Part of me was looking forward to it, but part of me also had my usual negative feelings, and I was also just a bit on edge that I had this homework to do. It felt a bit threatening, to tell the truth. But once I got there, all of that just faded. I really enjoyed seeing a number of people, and I especially had a great visit with my Aunt Mary and my sister Betty. The visit to Don was probably the biggest surprise—and a pleasant one. And since returning, I've just been curious to think about it and figure out what I should be taking away from it all."

"Sounds good. Let's go through your homework, and I'd like you to tell me about each of the conversations that you had planned." Jacob picked up the genogram they had constructed on the previous visit and taped it to his flip chart. Then he relaxed back in his wheelchair and seemed genuinely interested in what Mike was about to tell him.

Mike pulled out his notes and reviewed the list he had written for Jacob earlier. A smile crossed his face as he said, "Well, I am just now realizing that the top of the list—Karla—never happened. We just never got around to talking about my triangling her or anything to do with the systems work. I completely forgot about it. Or, maybe I deliberately forgot about it, because when she saw my list she wasn't exactly enthusiastic about the trip being a big 'therapy session', as she put it."

"Okay, what about the next person on the list?"

"Jacelyn, and I was supposed to talk to her about her wedding plans without blowing up."

"How did that go?" Jacob asked with a grin.

"Pretty well; mainly because she had dropped a lot of the craziness that she had talked about earlier. The only really stupid thing was some big elaborate plan to make this a Hollywood event with film crews recording everything. It's going to cost me an arm and a leg. But I bit my tongue and just told her to think it over. It was clear she already had her mind made up, so I dropped it. It was also clear to me that she had Karla on her side, so I just shut up."

"Smart man," Jacob quipped. "How did that make you feel?"

"Not bad, really; a part of me is really delighted to see my only daughter having so much fun. And the fact that she's so open with me about it feels like a breakthrough of sorts. I get caught sometimes by worrying about out of control costs, but then I figure I can afford it and what the hell, this is a once-in-a-lifetime event."

Mike paused briefly and then continued, "You know, it's funny, but both my parents and Karla's parents eloped to get married because of parental opposition to their marriage, so neither couple had a real wedding. I'm glad I can give Jacelyn a big shindig."

"That's interesting," Jacob said. "Why were their parents opposed to their marriages?"

"They felt they were too young. It was wartime, and things were so unsettled, and they just wanted to get married no matter what their parents thought."

Jacob leaned forward in his chair, "Mike, do you see any interesting patterns here?"

"What do you mean?"

"Well, I remember you telling me that when you first heard about Jacelyn wanting to get married, you felt she was way too young, and that Karla had reminded you of the age that you and she were when you got married—despite concerns on the part of your parents. And now I hear that both of you had parents who themselves encountered resistance over the issue of being too young at the time of their marriage, even to the point of eloping. So Jacelyn is the third generation to face opposition from parents over being too young. Isn't that a remarkable coincidence?"

Mike worked to take in what Jacob was suggesting. "Are you saying that there's something in our family system driving this?"

"**Emotional process** is a tricky thing, Mike, and it's often impossible to assign a high degree of certainty to patterns that emerge. But when I see three generations in a row where the kids got married young over parental objections, it makes me wonder how many previous generations that was also true of. If you knew some of that background, you might discover that there is a history of parental objections, but maybe the objections were not necessarily over the age issue. You might discover that the real pattern is simply parental objections, or perhaps lots of anxiety over fear of loss when a child goes out on his or her own. It takes a lot of careful thinking about possible patterns, but my guess is that it's more than coincidence that Jacelyn is repeating what looks like a family pattern."

"Oh this is just great, so what am I supposed to do with this now?"

"Nothing, because there's no hard proof that there's anything more than coincidence at work; but it might also be possible for you to use this to become more aware of the power of **emotional process** that we inherit from previous generations. **The**

presence of the past can be very powerful. And sometimes being more aware of **emotional process** can be helpful as we try to manage our own reactivity. Does that make sense?"

Mike was quiet for a long time. "Jacob, one of the things my Aunt Mary told me is that my grandfather ran away from home at 16 and never again connected with his parents. We were talking about cutoffs in the Sampson family, but now I'm connecting that with this business about parents objecting to the marriage of their children."

Jacob nodded, "So now we have four generations where there seems to be a lot of intensity around cutoffs, whether it's being a runaway or eloping or just getting married too young. Very interesting, don't you think, Mike?"

"Wow, this is scary stuff."

"Not scary. It's just illustrative of how **emotional process** can result in familiar patterns that are passed down from generation to generation. Remember, a major driving force in **emotional process** is chronic anxiety, and a lot of that anxiety is from the challenge of managing the self-other balance in a healthy way. Without offering this as a diagnosis, I'd like you to think about the possibility that your family system has some recurring patterns that center on that balance, whether it's in the case of a runaway, or elopement, or early marriage, or just a propensity to engage in cutoffs under stress. In every instance it's an issue that says there's lots of anxiety in your family system about how close is too close and how distant is too distant. Are you with me on this, Mike?"

"I sure am. And I'm thinking of what Aunt Mary said about my uncles Fred and Carl, who were apparently cutoff kings, and how I have not wanted anything to do with Don over the money issue that was none of my business, and how I deal with the stress that comes up between Karla and me from time to time. Wow!"

Jacob was quiet for quite a while as he observed Mike processing a whole new set of insights. Finally, he added, "Mike, I wonder if you're able to make any connections with how this pattern surfaces in your other relationship network—your work setting. Do you think there are situations where your inherited tendency to overemphasize one part of the self-other balance gets in the way of your being a more effective leader?"

Mike was nodding before Jacob even finished his sentence.

"Absolutely. I'm realizing how I operate whenever I get anxious about a stressful relationship. I head for the hills and avoid the situation as much as I can. I just hate the feeling of being smothered when relationships get so damn complicated."

"And of course avoiding the issue or the people solves everything and makes it all go away, right, Mike?" Jacob laughed, but Mike was only able to grin slightly at the obvious truth Jacob was pointing to with his rhetorical question.

"Yeah, right," he muttered.

Jacob shifted in his wheelchair and said, "Mike, let's get back to your list. Who's next?"

"Russ, and you'd be proud of me. I got a slam dunk on that one, although maybe I can't take full credit for it."

"What happened?" Jacob asked.

Mike described Russ's foolish approach to employment and his assurance that he understood his future responsibilities as a husband. "I just swallowed and kept my cool, and I think I came off looking real good. Blind luck!"

"Sounds good to me; sometimes silence is golden, especially when anything you say will be held against you. How did you do with the other kids?"

"Nothing special happened. Karla and I loved getting to know Lilly. She's a gem—hard working and a solid head on her shoulders. She'll go places, and she really charmed my father because she's in the dental field. Richard is a great kid, but he wants me to read a book so we can share something in common. I guess I'll have to read the damn thing to keep him happy."

Jacob said, "Sounds like maybe he's working on getting a person-to-person relationship with you. Maybe he wants to overcome some of that distance the Sampson men are so famous for."

Mike felt sheepish. "I hadn't thought of it in those terms. I guess I need to be more open to Richard."

"If you think so, that's probably the right direction to take. Go with your gut on that one, I'd say." Then Jacob added, "What about your father? How did you two Sampson men do with each other?"

Mike shook his head softly, "I'm not so sure. I was on edge with Dad the whole time, just waiting for him to lob his little bombs my way. But, to be honest, he really was on his best behavior. The kids loved him. He even asked if he could spend a few days at our place while the kids were there, and said he wanted to go to see a ballgame with them. Of course, he couldn't help trying to guilt me about working too much, but I didn't go for the bait, thank God."

"You know, Mike, weddings are very powerful times in a family system. Relationships are in play, and it's actually possible to rework some of the difficult relationships for the better because of the way the system opens up. Of course, it's also a time when relationships can get worse if they're not handled right. My point is, you need to think about making the most of Jacelyn's wedding as an opportunity to better things with your father."

"For God's sake," Mike retorted, "the man's 80 years old, and he's not about to change at this point in his life."

"You're probably right, Mike. But I was thinking about *your* capacity for change. If you can manage your own reactivity with him in better ways, then the relationship will change, even if he's still the same person. But never say never because he might surprise you with his capacity to show you a different side, even at age 80. It sounds to me like he still pushes your buttons pretty easily."

"Yeah, I'm afraid so, all too easily. But what pisses me off is that he can be so different with everyone else. He and Don were like bosom buddies, no mention of the money. The young folks at the reunion treated him like a venerable figure, and he played it for all it was worth. With Karla and the kids, he's as sweet as molasses. Why can't he just relax and treat me like he does them?"

"That's a good question, Mike," Jacob said. "But let's rephrase it and ask, 'Why can't *you* relax and just treat *him* like you do the others?' It's a two-way street, you know."

"Touché," Mike said with just a note of irony in his voice.

"Mike, I think it's a good time to take a little break. Let's get together again in about ten minutes."

MIKE DIGS DEEPER

After the break, Jacob pointed to Mike's genogram and said, "Mike, let's take a look at this picture of the generations of your family from the systems perspective we've been trying to think about. Is there anything else from the reunion you want to add by way of insight into how your family functions, especially when it's on autopilot?"

"I don't know how this fits in, but our visit with Don and Joyce was a real surprise. We even wound up spending the night there, and it was an entirely pleasant visit, from end to end."

"You mean you didn't grab the little chiseler by the throat and make him pay up?"

Mike couldn't help but laugh at the image Jacob conjured up. "No, the money never came up. I barely even thought about it. Don was like a different person, calmer, more thoughtful, very much at peace, even though he's still in the early stages of his recovery. It appears he's taken a look at his life and sees everything differently now."

"And how were you feeling during the visit, Mike?"

"Very calm, and I just was amazed at the change in Don. It made it so easy to be around him, it was incredible."

Jacob nodded, "You know, Mike, it happens often to people after a wakeup call like a heart attack. Obviously something has shifted in him and he's changed. But what I want you to observe is how the change in him has transformed the relationship dynamics between the two of you, and how that has made it so much easier to be around him."

"That's for sure," said Mike emphatically.

"Good," said Jacob, "I want you to note how one person can change the dynamics of the entire relationship system. It's why Vanessa sent you to me, because she knows firsthand how personal change results in a leader being more effective. The key is that you can change the functioning of the entire relationship system—the organization you're leading—by making changes in your own functioning.

"That's why you're working on becoming more self-aware, watching for **emotional process**, and understanding more deeply your own functioning by learning to **think systems**. By understanding how the triangles in your family have been passed down from generation to generation, you can learn to manage your own functioning in better and better ways."

"Jacob, can we talk a little about how all of this can help me at CHI? I can often follow what you point out in my family, but making the translation to CHI is sometimes hard for me."

"Certainly, Mike. In fact, last time we were talking about the marketing opportunity from the UK, and you touched on some very significant points that I wanted to explore with you in more depth. Today is a good time to do so, especially in light of what we've been focusing on with how relationship systems pass things on from generation to generation. You said some things I would like to pursue."

Jacob was thoughtful for a moment and then said, "As I recall, Mike, you said something about the fact that the issue we discussed has been addressed by others on various occasions, and that they are no longer with the organization. Can you tell me more about that, or am I remembering it wrong? Have people been fired because they brought the topic up?"

"It's not that simple, Jacob. But in a way, maybe it is. What I mean is that over the past 20 years we have had five or six directors of marketing and a lot of turnover throughout the entire discipline. No other part of the organization has seen that kind of turnover. CHI has a very good record of talent retention, and so for one department to experience so many turnovers has truly been unusual."

"Why have they left?" asked Jacob.

"There were different reasons given, as I recall. Some people just didn't fit; others didn't develop a strategy to ensure the field had what it needed to meet growth targets; some felt they weren't being listened to. It's pretty hard to know the inside story unless you're directly involved. But I do think one of the major issues they all struggled with was James McMaster's intransigence on the question of what our core identity really is. He just refuses to let go of his loyalty to old hotels he bought decades ago even though they are no longer profitable. When he's pushed on the issue, he starts telling stories about how he made CHI the great company it is today, and he's not about to change his business model at this stage of his career. Come to think of it, more than one of our marketing people probably left because they saw the handwriting on the wall in terms of James McMaster's refusal to do what was needed to market CHI as a national brand."

"Mike, I've known James for a long time, and you've been with the company for a long time too. James is tough, smart and shrewd in so many ways. Is this really a significant blind spot for him, and if so what do you think is going on around this issue?"

"It's a total hot button issue for him. He's not open to anyone challenging him on what he considers to be a core identity issue. The irony, of course, is that it's precisely his intransigence on this matter that is keeping CHI from developing a profitable core identity."

Jacob was leaning forward in his wheelchair, encouraging Mike to continue his line of thought. "Mike, is it fair to say that James is functioning anxiously on this issue, that he's more reactive than thoughtful around this one topic?"

"You betcha," Mike said with emphasis.

"Okay, then," Jacob continued, "fill me in on the recurring pattern that you see operating at CHI—how the reactivity, the **automatic functioning**, is being transmitted from generation to generation in that organizational family."

"Well," Mike said tentatively, "It looks to me like James gets very anxious whenever he's got to make major capital investments. I've seen him become very agitated when he makes a connection between some business decision we're discussing and his very early history at the start of his career. I think certain situations trigger his anxiety, and his reactive behaviors cause everyone around him to get nervous. Depending on the personality, some shut down, some become aggressive, or others act out foolishly in some way or other. That's when he gets into a confrontation with someone, and that person is usually not around much longer after that."

Jacob probed more deeply. "And you say this is a pattern you've seen recur over a period of years?"

"Yes, now that I'm looking at it in this way, I can see how several generations of top staff—especially in marketing—have all had their encounters with this pattern, and very few of them are still here to talk about it."

"Mike, remember last time I told you to be very careful about how you approached this topic, and to remember that there is no quick fix solution to reactive functioning that is deeply embedded in an organization?"

"Yes, I remember. I had some ideas that I wanted to share with Vanessa about how to go forward on this, but today's conversation has shifted my thinking a bit. I'm thinking that the issue is clearly James McMaster's reactivity. And unless I want to join the list of those who are no longer here because they pushed his hot button, I'd better figure out a way around his anxieties. I have a business solution that offers us a way out, and that is what I was going to share with Vanessa. But I realize now that I've also got to figure out with her how we can get past James' reactivity on this issue and that how I handle this issue could well make or break my career."

"You may be right about that, Mike. And on that happy note, I'm afraid I've got to end our session and get ready for another client who is due any minute."

"Just as well," Mike said. "Any more of this, and I think my head would explode from all it's trying to process. Thanks, Jacob, this has been a mind-bending session, and I am going to think long and hard about all that we've covered today."

Chapter 6: The Presence of the Past

Review Key Points

- In any relationship system, **automatic functioning**—how much there is, how it is manifested, and how it is managed—follows patterns of seeing and being in the world that are passed on from one generation to the next.

- Parents are the recipients of those patterns passed on to them from their respective families; they, in turn, inevitably transmit to their children some measure of what they have inherited.
    - Each child in the family receives his or her own distinct amount of chronic anxiety from the parental triangle.
    - For a variety of reasons, some children become the focus of parental anxiety more than others, and when this happens they end up with more than their share of chronic anxiety passed down from previous generations. The more anxious focus a child receives from his or her parents, the more likely that child's functioning will be impaired due to a lower level of differentiation of self.

- A genogram, which is a graphic way of mapping family relationships, can be a useful tool for someone seeking to understand how previous generations have shaped the relationship system they belong to at present.
    - Recognizing recurrent family patterns leads to deeper self-understanding and self-awareness and helps an individual identify reactive behaviors they wish to improve upon.
    - Reconnecting with one's family of origin with a deliberate plan to be less reactive in familiar triangles is an excellent way to work on one's own differentiation of self.

A New Way of Thinking

- Organizations, like families, also have ways of transmitting **emotional process** from one generation to the next. This is one important source of the distinctive features that make up the organizational culture and its repertoire of reactive behaviors.
    - Leaders who learn about the multigenerational patterns of the organization they lead are in a better position to function more effectively without being hooked by those forces. They are also in a better position to improve organizational performance by lessening the amount of anxiety passed on to the current and succeeding generations.
    - When an individual within an organization is the focus of the system's chronic anxiety, it becomes difficult for that person to continue functioning in a healthy manner. Leaders are particularly vulnerable to becoming the recipient of an organization's anxious focus, and so they need to be particularly alert and proactive in maintaining healthy ways of functioning.

Questions for Reflection and Discussion

1. Mike's grandfather, father and two uncles—and Mike himself—have strong patterns of cutoffs as a way to deal with anxiety. In light of this, how would you assess Richard's efforts to get closer to his dad by inviting him to read the same book? What do you predict will be the likely outcome?

2. Are you able to identify any multigenerational patterns associated with how anxiety is handled in your workplace? What do you know about the history of this pattern of functioning that might give you a deeper understanding of its origin and transmission?

3. Study of extended family systems usually reveals that some "branches" of the family become less functional

over several generations, while others seem to flourish. Can you identify this phenomenon at work or in your own extended family system? [Note: "less functional" can be expressed as symptomatic behaviors, broken or conflictual relationships, recurrent physical illnesses, career or business failures, etc.]

The Practice

A group (work, sports, community or family) has cultural patterns that develop over time and evolve across multiple generations of leadership.

1. Draw a diagram of a group you belong to today and identify the 3-5 patterns of behavior that are functional (helpful, inviting, constructive).

2. Then identify 3-5 patterns of behavior that are dysfunctional (limiting, elitist, destructive).

3. Write the core tenets or beliefs handed down from the past that are embedded in the group which give rise to these patterns of behavior.

A New Way of Thinking

The Presence of the Past

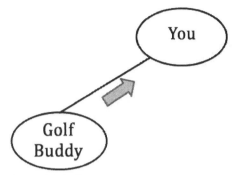

Invite others to join in the weekend golf outings to "round out" the relationship and disperse the competitive edge in golf buddy.

1. Functional Pattern	2. Dysfunctional Pattern	3. Core Tenet of Group
1. Spirit of competition pushes some of us to improve our game.	2. Some team members are very skilled at golf and they want to win more than have fun. Their approach to golf outings makes others feel uneasy.	3. Improving performance and winning is the purpose of playing golf.
1. Spirit of team work builds a sense of camaraderie between team members.	2. But because winning is now the purpose of our weekend outing, we no longer have fun because of the imbalance of skills.	3. It is important to develop skills in golf in order to compete and win.
1. The less skilled golfers are improving their game.	2. The more skilled golfers are feeling that they are wasting their time.	3. Getting better at golf is more important than having fun playing golf.

To learn more, go to www.resilient-leadership.biz.

A New Way of **LEADING**

Chapter 7: Focus On Differentiation of Self

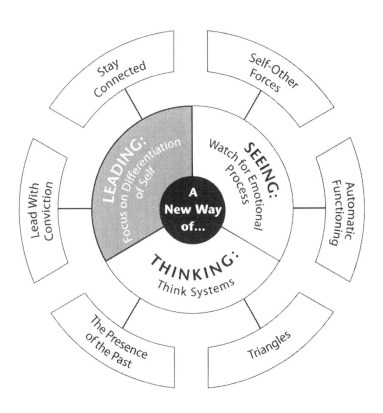

Loose Ends

Early the next morning, Mike arrived at the office with the realization that he had a number of loose ends to tie up. First and foremost he needed to make an appointment to have his knee examined. A number of business issues had piled up too. Several of them were connected with actions that Vanessa had taken.

She had written her note to the HQ staff about her transition and announced that Helen had decided to leave the company, leaving the position of executive administrator to the COO vacant. Vanessa pointed out that Helen's decision would create an opportunity for others in the office who were qualified to apply for the position once the new COO was in place. Vanessa also pointed out that all administrative people in the office would be afforded an opportunity to apply for new positions before any outside hires would be sought.

The memo served to calm down the rumor mill somewhat. Mike spoke to Crystal about the fact that he was only one of the candidates for the COO position and that he agreed with the process outlined in the note from Vanessa. Mike also advised Crystal that it would be in her best interest and his too if she would not speculate about what was going to happen. He also asked her to encourage others to talk with their supervisors if they had questions or comments. Crystal agreed and got the point. Mike ended the conversation with praise for her work, which was very much deserved.

Vanessa and James also dropped a small bomb. They decided to hold a CHI National Conference for all general managers and senior leaders in the fall of the year. National conferences happened in CHI every other year and this was the off year. The timing coincided with the departure date for Vanessa, so it was clear that the conference was being called to deal with the change of leadership. Mike immediately cancelled plans for his division meeting in light of this news.

Mike also returned a call from Steve in marketing. Steve had been reviewing the information Mike had given him on **emotional process** and wanted to talk about what he had read.

"Mike, I've reviewed the article by Jacob Wolfe and the list of reactive behaviors that you sent me a few days ago."

"What did you think about the information?" Mike asked.

"Well, the information was interesting, but I was hard pressed to see how these concepts could be helpful to me or Craig," Steve replied. "What are you suggesting I do next?"

Mike quickly realized that the materials he sent to Steve still did not have sufficient context for Steve to know what to do. As they spoke, it became clear that Steve thought the information was too academic and he did not have a good sense about how to apply it to his situation. Besides, the only way to get at this problem and really to address root causes would be by working with both Steve and Craig. Mike determined that spending time on this over the phone with only one of the two leaders would be wasted effort.

"Steve, thanks for reviewing the materials. I think we need to sit down with Craig and talk about the working relationship we all have. It's my job to set that up and I will soon. You don't need to take any further action before we have a three-way meeting."

Steve was obviously relieved and covered a few other tactical issues before the call ended.

Next, Mike made an appointment with his physician, Kevin Hill, to have his knee examined early the following week. He ended the morning by asking Crystal to order an audio book of *A New Earth* by Eckhart Tolle so he could listen to the book during the next few days of driving.

By 11:30 a.m. Mike was ready to begin planning for his meeting with Steve Alba and Vanessa. He stopped for lunch and got back to the office a little after noon.

FACING THE FUTURE

As Mike sat at his desk, Jacob's words of caution rang in his ears. *This is a crossroads for your career. Be careful yet forthright.*

His idea about how to transform CHI was bold but simple. It was not simply about positioning a proposal to a group of travel agents in the UK. CHI had to change its entire focus and clarify its business proposition. Mike believed that CHI should sell off prime real estate holdings and use the significant capital generated from the sale to refurbish remaining hotels in major Midwest and Southeast cities including Chicago, Detroit, St.

Louis, Atlanta, Miami, Orlando, Tampa and another dozen smaller urban areas where CHI had a presence but not a competitive product. Many of the older and larger convention properties could be sold to investment firms, which would then offer opportunities for other hotel chains to expand their portfolios. Or the big old hotels could be torn down so that the real estate could be used for other purposes.

CHI wholly owned some prime properties in these downtown areas, but Mike did not believe that CHI had the infrastructure to build a competitive convention hotel network. He also knew that convention business was in the early stages of major transition with the advent of greater connectivity via the Internet and the escalation of fuel prices in the US. Spending limited cash to move to a dominant position in such a competitive market did not make sense in the early 2000s.

In addition, Vanessa had mentioned that there were two or three international investment firms that were in constant contact with James and her on various acquisition schemes.

But James was steadfast in his resistance to the idea of selling any CHI holdings.

Mike decided to draft a brief overview of his idea and send it to Vanessa before the meeting with her and Steve. He developed the concept paper, then put it away. On his second review a few days later, he prepared a list of key points against which to evaluate the overview. He wrote seven points:

1. Position CHI to focus on weekday domestic business, transient and weekend escape and family business segments. Move away from large-scale convention hotels and convention business.
2. Move CHI to greater profitability by reducing operating expenses and focusing on key markets and customer bases. Grow the business at margins no less than 15% above the average CHI margin of the last 5 years.
3. Completely renovate the CHI guest rewards program
4. Sell 15% of company-owned assets (estimated at 6.5B)—17 properties.
5. Reinvest capital into 45-50 company-owned properties, mostly in the Southeast and Midwest.
6. Determine what triggers James McMaster's anxiety and

find a way to help him become more thoughtful and open to change.
7. Link this proposal to my interest in assuming the COO role. Bottom line: If we do not make significant changes to CHI core services, I am not going to take the COO slot if offered.

Mike checked his overview a half dozen times and decided not to reference point #7 in what he was writing to Vanessa. He felt confident that he had decided how to approach the upcoming events related to his own career. And, after all, he realized that he might not be offered the COO position anyway.

He sent off his overview and suggested that Vanessa share his ideas with Steve Alba before they meet, which she did. The next day Vanessa set up the meeting for the following week. Not surprisingly, Alba had also prepared an overview. Vanessa sent it to Mike who opened it up as soon as it arrived.

The scope of Alba's overview dealt with the revitalization of the existing lodging properties in the portfolio of CHI and a total makeover of the marketing function. Steve had written a very comprehensive overview of how to reposition CHI with its current portfolio. He proposed a significant renovation effort for well over half of the existing hotels, after which a refocused marketing effort would be needed to recast CHI as a head-to-head competitor with larger multinational hotel companies. Steve had retained the services of an outside consulting firm to complete some high-level analysis of market conditions and to lay out a rough idea about how such a large-scale transition could take place. It was a very well-documented overview.

Steve Alba had prepared a very thought-provoking overview that was as promising as Mike's in many ways and much more aligned with the views held by James McMaster. Steve had obviously had a number of people working with him to develop his overview. Mike had prepared his overview alone in just a few hours of work.

In a nutshell, Mike advocated slimming down CHI by selling off older hotels and renovating remaining hotels with assets gained from the sale. He also advocated making a choice in the market by focusing on transient weekday and destination weekend business and by walking away from convention business.

Steve advocated keeping all CHI hotels and investing heavily in much-needed renovations funded by a line of credit against existing company assets. He also advocated keeping all lines of business, including convention business.

It was time to meet.

KEY MEETING #1—STEVE ALBA, MIKE SAMPSON AND VANESSA JACKSON

All three had thoroughly reviewed the overview materials ahead of the meeting.

At the meeting Vanessa asked them both to review their approaches in detail. Alba began. He brought a lot of supporting documentation and went through his overview in about 90 minutes. Mike and Vanessa had a number of questions of a tactical nature that Steve answered with ease. The briefing was excellent and advocated an expansion of all the current business.

They took a break.

Mike began his review after the break and finished in about 20 minutes. His overview was brief and unlike Alba's represented a huge shift in the direction of the business.

At the end of both presentations, Vanessa spoke about the central differences of the two overviews.

"First, thank you for all this work. You both have obviously done some excellent thinking about the future of CHI, and you have prepared very interesting overviews. My first reaction is that both proposals are viable.

"Steve, your proposal is on the mark. Your ideas are just emerging, but it seems to me that you have created a blueprint that will keep CHI on a steady growth track. However, your plan requires significant borrowing against assets, and there's a great deal of risk in doing so.

"Mike, your approach is very interesting. The ideas you have proposed require a change in focus for the business in that you are advocating stepping away from one key element of our model—convention business. Your ideas will be very difficult for James to accept, although I predict that some of the Board members would strongly endorse your line of thinking."

There was a short moment of silence. Mike had been

preparing for this moment for years and knew exactly what to say and do. Taking a cue from all the meetings he'd had with Jacob, he stood up and stepped to the white board.

"I also think both proposals are viable—but only in the short term. Steve's ideas make sense and for good reason. His ideas are very smart. My ideas make sense, too. But neither approach is a long-term answer—yet. That's because the way forward must be created with a participative process that starts with concrete answers to four questions."

Mike wrote the four questions on the board and sat down.

---

1. What is our organizational passion?
2. What are the markets and who are the customers we choose to serve?
3. What is our value proposition for those markets and customers?
4. What structure do we need to have and what competencies do we need to develop and nurture to excel in our value proposition?

Steve and Vanessa studied the questions for a moment, Then Vanessa asked, "Steve, what do you think?"

"First, we need to see how James McMaster would answer these four questions," Steve replied. "Getting a read from the boss will save a lot of time and let us know which pathways will produce results and which will not."

Then Mike said, "I don't agree. In my mind, first, we need to have a dialogue with Board leaders, including the boss and senior team leaders to see how they would collectively answer these four questions."

After a few moments Vanessa said, "Any other thoughts?" At that point Steve went back to his overview and pulled out several key elements, making special note of the fact that he was sure McMaster would agree with his line of thinking.

"Steve, how are you so sure James would be supportive of these marketing ideas?" Mike asked.

"I reviewed them with him yesterday," Steve said.

Mike was shocked. "Wait a minute. Are you telling me that you have already reviewed your briefing with McMaster?"

Steve said, "Sure did, for about two hours."

"Well, if the new direction is already baked, why are we going through this exercise, Vanessa?" Mike asked incredulously.

"I did not know that Steve had reviewed his overview with Mr. McMaster. But it sounds like a smart thing to have done, don't you think?" Vanessa said.

"Well, that depends on what you intend to do with our work," Mike said. "If McMaster has already signed off on Steve's briefing, you might as well throw mine in the trashcan."

"Hold on, Mike. Nothing is going into the trashcan," Vanessa said. "Do either of you have any other questions or comments?"

No one spoke.

"Okay, I will get back to you both," Vanessa said as she stood up, signaling that the meeting was over.

Both COO contenders left the room saying nothing to each other. Mike was mad as hell.

Mike had been brooding in his office for about 30 minutes when Vanessa called and asked him to return to her office.

He walked down the hall and into her office still visibly irritated.

Key Meeting #2—Mike Sampson and Vanessa Jackson

"Mike, please take a seat," Vanessa said.

Mike sat down, a sense of dread began to overtake his irritation.

"Mike I have decided to withdraw Steve Alba's name from the short list of COO candidates."

Mike just looked at her. "What? Why would you do that?" he said.

"There are a number of reasons that will remain between Steve and me, but I have advised James of my decision and he agrees. I just spoke to Steve a few minutes ago."

Vanessa paused for a few seconds, and Mike sat in his chair absolutely flabbergasted.

"I want to begin working with you to set up two meetings in the next 30 days. One meeting will be between you and James and me. You and I will design the agenda and discussion flow together. The purpose of this meeting is to continue preparations for the Board of Directors meeting and to discuss the topics you and Steve and I talked about earlier today.

"The second meeting is already scheduled for five weeks from this Thursday and Friday. It's the quarterly CHI Board of Directors meeting in Scottsdale. This regularly scheduled Board meeting will also be attended by you and some other senior team members. In addition to the agenda that is already set, we will be discussing the future direction of CHI."

Mike gaped. "Vanessa, what is happening here?" he finally said.

"Well, Mike, you are one of two candidates remaining for the COO post. There is you and one remaining outside hire. She will be in Scottsdale also. Both of you will be meeting one-on-one with Board members and also attending most, but not all, of the sessions. Within a few days of the Board meeting, we will be making our final selection."

Vanessa had a very big smile on her face. She was just delighted with this moment.

"Mike, do you have any initial thoughts on the meeting with James?" Vanessa added.

"Absolutely," Mike said. "We need to carefully and respectfully go directly at James on the need to transform CHI. To do that we will need to help him understand the longstanding impact that he and his mental model of 'cash is king' has had on the identity of CHI. We need to help him see that he, as the founding father of CHI, has created a multi-generational challenge that must be managed—if not overcome in order for the business to thrive in the future."

Mike stopped for a moment to see if Vanessa had any reaction.

"Go on," Vanessa said.

"We need to ask Jacob Wolfe to attend this meeting," Mike added.

Vanessa smiled and knew that she finally had the right guy for COO.

"Let's do it," she said as she stood up and shook Mike's hand.

COO Candidate

Mike decided to call Karla on the way home to break the news to her, and as he started to dial, he drove through a red stoplight. He put down the phone and immediately slowed down once through the intersection and felt lucky that nothing had happened. A jolt of adrenaline coursed through his body, and he became momentarily sick to his stomach.

Just before he reached the driveway, he also called Jacob to tell him about the news but got the answering machine. He left a message with a very quick summary of the day. When he got in the house, he and Karla sat down at the kitchen table and Mike told her the whole story, starting with his meeting earlier in the day with Steve and Vanessa.

"Honey, this is amazing news. I am so proud of you," Karla said.

Mike wiped tears from his eyes. He had been through a lot since the day Vanessa told him that he was an autocratic SOB.

"So there is one other candidate?" Karla asked.

"Yes, I don't know anything about her except that she lives in London. I will meet her in Scottsdale at the Board meeting in a few weeks," Mike said. "Let's go out to dinner to celebrate!"

The evening was filled with excitement and anticipation as they both tried to imagine what might actually take place in the next several months.

No Running — Now What?

The next morning Mike kept his appointment with Kevin Hill at 8:30 a.m. to have his knee examined. Kevin, being an athlete himself in addition to a fine doctor, knew what the problem was right away.

"Mike, you have *chondromalacia patellae*. It is essentially a bruise to the cartilage behind the kneecap. You will need to stop running to let it heal up and also do some physical therapy."

"Why am I getting this problem now? I have not been running any more than usual lately."

"Well, you are not 23 anymore for one thing, and for another you have not been doing enough lateral exercises with your knee to hold everything in alignment. You are a wobbler," Kevin said with a smile. "You wobble when you run. You need to strengthen the tendons in your knee to hold everything in place, to minimize lateral motion. You will be okay in a few months if you stop running and get the physical therapy I recommend."

Mike listened carefully and knew that he would have to follow Kevin's advice closely. The knee really hurt and had swollen so much that it made his whole leg stiff. He had trouble bending his knee and had had to walk stiff-legged at work on several occasions recently.

"How long?" Mike asked.

"Probably eight weeks at least; try some other form of cardio exercise like bike riding or elliptical work," Kevin said. "I'll give you a prescription to take the pain down a bit and also reduce the swelling."

Mike thanked Kevin, paid at the front desk, and went outside to call Karla.

He reached Karla as he was driving to the office. "Honey, Kevin told me I have what is called a bruised kneecap. I need to stop running for a while and get some physical therapy. He told me I'm a wobbler when I run."

Karla, knowing how important Mike's runs were to him, expressed her sympathy for his predicament.

Mike continued, "So I'm going to pick up a prescription on the way to the office, and I will be home at the regular time tonight. I'm worried that I can't run for a while because it really helps me with stress management."

"You will just have to ride a bike for a while, I guess; and, besides, the work you are doing with Jacob will also be a big help to you in the coming weeks."

"I don't find anything helps me like running," Mike replied.

"Change is in the wind, Mike," Karla said. "You will handle whatever comes up; you always do."

Mike told Karla he loved her and hung up the phone. As he drove to the office, he thought to himself that he could not do any of this without her at his side. She was a constant source of energy for him.

When he arrived at his office, Craig and Steve were waiting to speak to him. Craig was at HQ for some business, and Mike had asked Crystal to set up a meeting soon between the three of them. Craig would return to Pittsburgh right after the meeting.

Mike had sent them Jacob's article, "What Is Emotional Process?" so they could look over it over before they met with him.

"Hello, guys, come in and have a seat. Can I get you something to drink?" Mike said as they all walked into his office together.

Both declined and took a seat at the table in Mike's office. Crystal closed the door.

After some casual conversation, Mike said, "Well let's get started."

"Have you had the chance to read the article by Jacob Wolfe that I sent to you?"

Both said yes and nodded. "It was pretty short," Craig said. "I like short articles."

Mike smiled and Steve frowned.

"Here is the point of the article and the reason I asked you both to visit with me today," Mike said. "According to Jacob, the author of this article and my coach, there is an ocean of factors that drive all of us which is way below our conscious awareness. These factors are real, not imaginary, but so deeply embedded in us that we are not aware of their existence except that we see the visible manifestations of them.

"Let me give you an example. I generally am more comfortable in conversations with men than I am with women. I really did not know that until sometime in the last few months. I am not sure why that is; maybe I am always trying to impress or entertain women, I don't know. Who knows; maybe I am afraid of them, but what I do know is that the number of women I can talk with in an easy way includes my wife and daughter and maybe three or four other women on the whole planet. One of the most frightening ideas I can think of is to walk into a room full of women."

Craig and Steve were listening to Mike and wondering why in the world he was talking about this topic.

"Here is my point," Mike said. "Each of us has a set of these factors that are buried in us, built into us from our early days and amplified through our family experiences. These factors shape our behavior just like the instinctual rear guard behavior of the elephant in Jacob's article. Can either of you think of any instinctual behaviors you are demonstrating toward each other that are impacting your relationship and also the team I manage?"

"Mike, I am confused. If you are having a problem with me or my work or how I talk with you or Steve or anyone else, just tell me and I will deal with it. I don't have the time for a counseling session."

Mike just listened to Craig and when he finished did not know really what to say. So he didn't say anything.

Steve spoke up, "I agree with Craig. What are we doing here anyway?"

Mike was at a loss for words but finally said, "You know what, guys, maybe you are right. I am sitting here trying to be helpful and neither of you think it is worth the time. If I were a real coach, maybe I would know what to do now. But I don't. I am, however, your manager, and in that role I do know what to say."

Mike stood up and went to his white board. He drew a triangle that had all three of their names, one at each angle. Then he drew an oval around the side of the triangle between Steve and Craig.

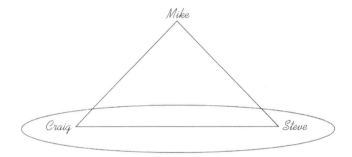

"There are three lines of communication on the board here; one between me and each of you, and one between the two of you. The communication between each of you and me works fine from my point of view. How do you see your communications with me?"

After a short pause, Craig said, "You could get out into the field more often. You could quit asking me for information that I either don't have or have to work with staff back here in this building to send to you. But you are really good at speed and quality of response."

"Okay, can you give me a specific example of when I asked for information from you that I could have gotten from someone in the building?"

"Sure, every quarter you ask me for an analysis of my customer complaints, and Steve here has all that information. When you write to me I just send your note to Steve and ask him to give you the information."

"Then what happens?" Mike asked.

"Well, then Steve gets pissed off at me for sending him work he thinks I should handle," Craig said.

Steve interrupted, "Wait a minute; you are the one who needs to know the primary causes of both satisfaction and dissatisfaction for your hotels, not me. And when—"

Craig cut Steve off and said, "I know the causes of my customers' satisfaction and dissatisfaction before anyone does. That's why my hotels are always ranked in the top five for customer service."

"There you go, cutting me off again," Steve said. "What I was going to say is that when you report your follow-up actions to me, I can identify trends across our region that help us know how to set priorities and adjust expenditures for training, incentives, capital investments and communications. Craig, you manage your district like it was a free-standing company with no connection or obligation to the enterprise we are trying to manage."

"Okay, okay," Mike said, trying to calm things down.

"Steve, how would you describe your communications with me?" Mike said, pointing to the triangle.

"Well, Mike, you grew up in the field and you have a strong bias to side with operators when there is a debate. This example is a good one. I have an arm-wrestling match with half a dozen general managers every quarter. I have told you about this problem repeatedly, and you always send me back to my office to figure it out for myself."

Craig exploded, "For God's sake, Steve, what the hell do you really want me to do with the request I get from Mike each quarter? The customers fill out a response form, which gets sent to consumer affairs, then they collect and scan the forms and generate a report that is sent back to you and me and half the world. What do you want me to do?"

"I want you to tell me and Mike what you are doing to make improvements in the performance of the hotels," Steve said, almost screaming.

"Fine—fine. I'll do that from now on. If you would have made your request clear in the beginning, I would have been happy to reply."

Mike just sat down.

"Well, how would you describe the effectiveness of the communications you two have on the other side of the triangle where I drew this oval?"

"We need to do better," Craig said.

"I agree," Steve said.

Then Mike asked, "What do you need from me to make progress?"

Steve replied, "Craig and I will take this discussion off line and get back to you."

"Okay, let me hear back from both of you together within a week," Mike said.

With quiet disgust, both visitors got up and left the room. Mike realized that his attempt to use the materials that Jacob had provided him had not gone terribly well. It would take some practice and deeper understanding on his part to effectively use Jacob's materials on **Resilient Leadership** with others in CHI. This would be a long, slow process, and he realized more than ever how important it was for him to keep working with Jacob as his coach.

Keeping Up

Mike had a number of major events going on in his life. The wedding was coming up in just over two weeks, and events related to the COO opportunity were moving very fast. Mike would be preparing to attend the Board of Directors meeting in Scottsdale just ten days after the wedding. In just a few days, he would also learn about yet another big assignment Vanessa had in store for him.

Office politics were also stepping up in intensity. There are really never any secrets in large companies, so a number of people began to ask him about the COO post. He noticed people were starting to treat him differently as the politics of the potential change were beginning to set in place. Mike was in and out of Vanessa's office frequently each day, which was the cause for even more speculation. Finally, he decided to talk with Crystal to confirm some rumors and quash others. When asked about any other candidates, Mike told Crystal all he knew, which wasn't much.

The existence of an external candidate was only a mysterious rumor to many in the CHI office. It never occurred to anyone that a complete unknown might actually get the COO post. But Kelly O'Reilly was a lot more than a rumor; she was a very real and very qualified candidate. Kelly was a 38-year-old division-level CFO with All Britain Airways who had lost out in a head-to-head contest for the corporate CFO post when the incumbent retired. She decided that she was being overlooked and resigned the day after the decision to select someone else was made.

Kelly had attended Exeter College in the heart of Oxford University for her undergraduate work in economics and management and had earned her MBA at Harvard. She was smart, articulate, experienced and very self-assured, with a warm and gracious manner. Kelly was very smooth and she was out of a job. She knew her way around service industries, but had never worked in the lodging industry. She was the final candidate left after an exhaustive external search that had taken six months to complete.

Mike did not think that the COO post was his for sure, yet his confidence was growing. He did not yet realize what he was about to face in a one-on-one competition with Kelly O'Reilly.

Late one afternoon Vanessa called Mike into her office to prepare to meet with Jacob and James. It was time to talk with James about either selling some CHI hotels or splitting the company up into two segments so that a more focused brand identity could be created. As Mike walked in, Vanessa was just reviewing another offer, this time for the purchase of 17 CHI hotels.

"Hello Mike; come in and take a look at this overview," Vanessa said as she handed him a summary that had been prepared in the finance department. The overview described a 90-day due diligence process whereby an assessment would be thoroughly conducted to review legal, financial, technical and marketing factors for each property. Vanessa had finally prevailed with James, who reluctantly agreed to have a due diligence process completed because the offer was so appealing. He had never agreed to this step before, and Vanessa saw this moment as a real opportunity to advance the discussion.

The due diligence process was going to be a comprehensive and exhaustive activity for CHI. It would require a coordinator to interface with all the inspection teams from the investment company itself as well as an outside independent firm. The coordinator would be responsible for ensuring all materials required and all interviews requested met deadlines and went forward with a minimum amount of disruption.

Visits to each hotel site would be made, and once that process began, the expression "buyout" would race around the organization, producing an immediate negative impact on CHI. Steps to coordinate the work and plan the communications with the media, investors and employees would take the full-time attention of several headquarter staff members who would work with the coordinator. Even with James' agreement, the due diligence process would only commence when authorized by the Board of Directors.

Vanessa asked Mike to assume the role of coordinator for the due diligence process. It would be a great opportunity for him. Mike agreed without any hesitation, knowing full well that the commitment was significant. The meeting in Vanessa's office covered the due diligence process, the tentative Board agenda and preparations for the preliminary meeting with James.

"What role do you see Jacob playing in our meeting with James?" Vanessa asked.

"I think that Jacob can set the stage for a discussion about how CHI will need to change to be successful in the future. He can help James see that today's CHI culture has been shaped by its longstanding heritage and set of core beliefs that he, himself, crafted during the early days of the company. Then it's our job to help James see that some of these core beliefs continue to serve us well and others do not. We will need to focus on changing his conviction that 'cash is king.' This is critical because it is an ideology that fosters actions that undermine a commitment to long term customer value. Once we get to that point with James, we will then have common ground on which to base a decision about how to handle this current offer from Europe."

Vanessa thought for a moment. "You know, the thing that gets James really excited about this business is deal-making, not running hotels. After the deal is done, he pretty much turns over the operation of the company to me and the executive team.

Maybe I have been doing him and the company a disservice by not bringing him into operational discussions and issues more often. If we are going to expect James to make the connection between poorly performing, outdated hotels and his most strongly held central belief, I will need to spend some time connecting him to the current problems we have in operating most of the hotels targeted for sale."

"I would have thought that you had been doing that all along," Mike said.

"No, I have chosen not to communicate individual hotel performance to James for the last couple of years. He doesn't care for that level of detail, and so I didn't bother. It was a mistake on my part."

They both agreed to a plan of action. Before the meeting, Vanessa would brief James on operating challenges at each hotel that would be involved in the due diligence process, and Mike would visit with Jacob to discuss the upcoming meeting.

"Oh, by the way, I got the wedding invitation in the mail last week. How is the wedding planning coming along?" Vanessa asked as they stood up to end the meeting.

"Things are coming together. I know where I am supposed to be and when. Beyond that, I am pretty much in the dark. Will you be able to come to the wedding?"

"I sure will, and thank you for inviting me. I mailed my RSVP this morning on the drive in to work."

COO Thinking with Jacob

Mike pulled up to Jacob's office with a goal for the coaching session that was brand new. He wanted to continue his learning about **Resilient Leadership** but also ask for Jacob's help in opening a doorway of new thinking for his old friend, James McMaster.

After a quick knock, Mike opened the door and stepped inside.

"Hello Mike," Jacob said in his usual upbeat manner.

"Hello Jacob, are you ready for me?"

Jacob smiled, "I am always ready, but I am even prepared today."

"Prepared for what?" Mike asked.

"Well I got your voicemail, and I am prepared to talk with the next COO of CHI," Jacob said with a grin.

"Not so fast, Jacob; I don't have the job yet," Mike said with a big smile.

"You're right. It's a bit premature, but I am excited for you and Karla and really for all of CHI too," Jacob said with his characteristic genuine delight.

Jacob and Mike both sat down and Jacob dove right into the conversation.

"Mike, today we have a few loose ends to tie up from our last session, and I also want to start in on the third part of the **Resilient Leadership** model: 'A New Way of LEADING.' Frankly, it couldn't come at a better time with the pace and scope of change unfolding in CHI."

"Great, I am interested in moving forward. I also want to ask for your help with a meeting that Vanessa and I are planning with James. We want you to help us think through the meeting and also attend it as well."

"Tell me more about the meeting," Jacob said.

Mike told Jacob that Vanessa had been discussing with James the sale of some CHI properties to a foreign investment firm. He gave Jacob the details, and then continued, "When we last met, Jacob, you helped me see that the intensity of James' focus on the idea that 'cash is king' really is a form of reactive, **automatic functioning**, and it is buried deeply within him from his youth."

Mike had built up a head of steam now, and he thumped the table as he spoke. "For God's sake, in today's world, cash is *not* king—customer value rules."

"Mike, how do you propose getting James to see this situation the way you and Vanessa do?" Jacob asked.

"That's where you come in. "I was hoping that you could attend a meeting with Vanessa and James and me and help set the stage for our discussion with James." As Mike spoke about how Jacob might be of help, he realized that he had not really clarified in his own mind just how Jacob's involvement would be useful.

"I guess I'm not exactly sure how you could help us, to be honest," Mike said.

Jacob spoke, "Well, Mike, asking me to attend a meeting with Vanessa and James may make some sense, but it's obvious that a long-held belief in a 72-year-old man's mind cannot be changed in one meeting.

"Let me ask you a question. Since you are the final internal candidate for the COO post, don't you think it makes sense for you to have an in-depth discussion with your potential new boss about the way both of you see the future of CHI? And by the way, doesn't it seem a little odd that you have not had that conversation by now?"

Mike began to feel uncomfortable.

Jacob went on.

"Mike, let me ask you this question," Jacob said. "If James were to decide not to sell the hotels we have been talking about, or if the Board recommended against that move, would or should that turn of events impact your decision to take the position of COO if offered?

"And as you are thinking about that question, here's another one: Even if the sale of the hotels in question did go through, suppose James and/or the Board decided to invest the fresh supply of capital in a way that did not position CHI for long-term success as you envision it. Would or should that series of events impact your thinking about the COO post? I include the words 'would or should' to make an important point."

Mike shifted several times in his chair as he thought about these questions. He knew that Jacob had asked the right questions. He struggled with his answer because his intellectual response was different from his emotional response.

"Well, the answer is yes to both questions when I use the word 'should.' But I am not really sure about the other two answers. I know I can add a lot of value as the next COO, and I have a vision for a revitalized CHI. But I cannot do it alone; I cannot do it without the backing of James and the Board."

"Exactly," Jacob said. "Knowing you the way I do, I am sure that you want the COO position for several reasons. One of the top reasons is that you want to make a long-term contribution. You want to advance CHI."

Jacob paused and then added, "If I am right, just like CHI, you too are also at quite a crossroads. What do you want to do now?"

"Well, it's pretty obvious that I need to have some one-on-one time with James," Mike said.

"What would be the purpose of the meeting in your mind?" Jacob asked.

Mike answered Jacob, but his response was directed as much to himself as to Jacob. "I need to find out how he sees the future of CHI, what his plans are, how serious he is about the potential sale of these older hotel properties. I also need to see what he thinks about my idea of focusing CHI by eliminating major convention business and selling off any remaining convention hotels that cannot grow on local or regional convention business. We simply do not have what it takes to have a national convention network."

"Mike, that sounds like a good plan. I think it would be helpful if we talk about the idea of differentiation of self in preparation for the meeting with James. Are you up to it?"

"I am," Mike said with a renewed sense of direction. "Let's go."

They took a short break and then began again. Mike knew before he spoke that Jacob had already switched into his "teacher" mode.

"Mike, several times before I've mentioned to you the term 'differentiation of self,' but we've never really explored what that is all about. It is one of the central concepts of Bowen Theory, and it holds a similar importance in my **Resilient Leadership** model. Given your decision to visit with James as a next step, it's a good time to take a careful look at what it means and exactly why I say that to **focus on differentiation of self** is 'A New Way of LEADING.' In many ways, it sums up a good deal of what we've been talking about up to this point.

"I suspect that you read a good many books about how to be an effective leader—I know I do—and I daresay that most of them tell you how to influence other people and how to get them to change in various ways so they will follow your leadership. It must have dawned on you by now that my concern has been primarily with how *you* are functioning, not with how you can get *others* to change. There's a pretty significant reason why my approach to leadership is different from others, and it's backed up by considerable research indicating the enormous influence that a leader exercises on any organization just by the way he is present to it."

Mike was following intently, and he broke in, "Jacob, I know the focus has been mainly on my functioning, but I figured that was just because I needed so much help getting my act together."

Jacob shook his head, "No, Mike. Most of the literature out

there on leadership assumes that a leader's effectiveness is the result of such things as personality factors, mastery of a particular set of competencies, better communication skills, role-modeling certain behaviors, or implementing strategies and techniques that promote organizational change. All of those approaches have some real value, but I see them operating on a more superficial level. When I talk about this 'New Way of LEADING' that I call **Resilient Leadership**, I'm convinced that there is a better, more effective way of exercising leadership. And that way is to focus on your own functioning as the primary factor that spells the difference between a great leader and one who merely manages. Bottom line: Your main focus—if you want to practice **Resilient Leadership**—needs to be on *how you are being,* rather than on *what you are doing.*"

Mike said, "Okay, so let's apply these few first thoughts to the decision I need to make about the COO position, assuming it is offered to me."

Jacob responded, "You have a very clear vision in your mind about how CHI should operate in the future. That vision is based on a lot of past experience, as well as current awareness of the state of the industry and CHI's capabilities and limitations. Your views are well-informed by facts, not just impressions, and finally you have Vanessa's support."

"Agreed," said Mike.

Jacob went on. "Well, here is the key question. Given all of that, is there any way you should accept the COO slot, if offered to you, under circumstances in which you could not implement your vision?"

Mike hesitated.

"Mike, this is not a hard question; it's either yes or no," Jacob said.

"The answer is no," Mike said emphatically.

"All right then, you are ready to **lead with conviction**," Jacob said.

"Jacob, what are you trying to tell me?"

"Mike, you are clear on the fact that you will only lead CHI under a certain set of circumstances. You have told me that and Vanessa that, and now you have told yourself that. Next, you need to tell James that."

Mike looked at Jacob and saw the wisdom and simplicity of it all. He had worked months to refine his leadership skills to lead CHI after the fateful day in Vanessa's office. After hours of study, coaching and internal reflection, he had grown a lot and had now been selected as the top internal candidate for the COO position. But to take the final step, he had to tell the CEO that the only way he would take the COO position was with the understanding that significant changes would be made in asset ownership and business strategy.

"This is not easy," Mike said.

"Of course not," Jacob said. "It's simple, not easy. If it were easy, then anyone could be a COO or CEO. You've heard me say on a number of occasions that a resilient leader is one who actually *becomes* the change he wants to see happen, in business or in life, if you prefer. When you visit with James, you will not be trying to change his mind about anything in CHI at all. What he believes is what he believes. What you will be telling him is what you believe. You will be telling him what you believe and why. Through the strength of your conviction, you will speak about a future CHI that you intend to create by building on the great foundation that he laid. Your words will be spoken with such deep resolve that he will ask himself the central question that he must answer."

Jacob paused for a moment. "And that question is, 'Can I trust Mike Sampson to guard and protect my people and grow the organization I created?'"

Mike knew that Jacob was right. He thought back to times when he saw the old man put up walls and fight with others who wanted him to change things in CHI. Under all the squabbling and debate and downright anger was a fear in James, a fear that he could not trust the new ideas or the people promoting them.

Jacob leaned forward in his wheelchair, caught Mike's full attention, and forcefully added, "What is the answer to that question, Mike Sampson?"

Mike looked at Jacob for a long time. Perhaps only once or twice in his life had he felt as completely challenged as he did at that moment.

"Absolutely, as COO I will find ways for CHI to grow and prosper. We will provide employees with opportunities as never before by finding new ways to develop, promote and reward them. The legacy of James McMaster will be safe in my hands," Mike said with resolve.

Jacob knew that Mike had crossed a threshold that few of his clients would achieve. Mike's courage and firm resolve—both essential elements of self-differentiation—were obvious.

"Let's go on," Jacob said.

"In recent weeks, I have seen you **think systems** a lot more as you address issues and problems at CHI. It may not be immediately clear to you, however, that it is the *position* of the leader in a system that explains why his or her influence is felt so strongly throughout the organization. It's the nature of how systems function for the leader to have a disproportionate impact on the organization, one that far outweighs the influence of any other single individual. That impact is not the result of any inherent quality or personality trait in the leader. It's the *fact of being a leader* that makes you so powerful, the position you occupy.

"Remember, bad leaders are influential too—just in the wrong direction. And that's why it's so important for us to talk about the need for you to focus on your functioning at the deepest level, since that is ultimately what will make the difference between your influence being positive or negative. It's by your continual **focus on differentiation of self** that you can grow towards being a great leader, more than by doing any skill training or by introducing any bag of organizational tricks you might bring into the COO position."

Mike shifted in his chair. "Jacob, I think I'm following what you're saying. But I know if you asked me to explain what differentiation of self is about, I'd be at a loss for words to describe it."

"I understand, Mike. The notion of differentiation of self is a tricky one to grasp, since we are tempted to think of it much like the psychological notions of maturity or self-actualization or individuation. But those categories are different, because they describe a certain developmental level or stage of growth that can be arrived at once and for all. Differentiation of self, on the other hand, is never a point of arrival or a goal that can be reached. Rather, it's a lifelong process; it's continual and ongoing, a way of being in the world that never ceases."

"This makes me all the more aware of why Vanessa was adamant that I work with you as a coach, given her view of my style when we began," Mike added.

"Right," Jacob responded.

"Do you remember when we first started talking, how we discussed the constant balancing act between those primal forces for self and other, and how the effort to keep things in balance never ceases? There's an inevitable tension within us from the competing demands of those polarities, and the anxiety in the systems around us also contributes to our need for constant vigilance, because it can make us exaggerate towards one extreme or the other. Different people and situations can call forth either tendency in us, so it is really tricky to remain alert to the proper balance.

"Take your recent visits to Boston. As you began to work through the business issues in Boston, you also began to work through your relationship issues with people in the field. You started working at balancing those **self-other forces** with Sally and the general managers in the district. You did this by setting targets and then coaching and helping the team to reach those targets. It was important to strike just the right balance between letting them figure it out on their own and over-functioning by telling them how to do their jobs. And you were able to do that better and better the more you managed your own anxiety and reactivity, isn't that right?"

Mike nodded vigorously. "Yes, and you really helped me by being there to process all of my feelings and give me pointers on better ways to handle those relationships."

Jacob continued, "Differentiation of self involves many balancing acts. One of its primary components is how well we are doing with our attempts to be a separate 'self' without cutting off from others; or, from another perspective, it's about how well we **stay connected** to others without getting too close and becoming fused with the others emotionally. Maybe I can illustrate the idea for you better by drawing it."

At that, Jacob wheeled his chair over to the white board, where he drew a long, vertical line. At the bottom of the line he put a zero, at the middle a 50, and at the top he wrote 100.

```
100


 50


  0
```

"There are many considerations that go into where any person might be placed on an imaginary scale of differentiation. Don't think in terms of someone at the higher end of the scale being perfectly healthy and well adjusted and symptom free, since we're all human and no one is perfectly differentiated. But you can think of it as a balancing act, and those who manage it better wind up a bit higher on the scale. However, as I said, there are many factors that determine our level of differentiation, and our ability to maintain a healthy balance of closeness and separateness in our relationships is just one of them."

"What are some of the other factors?" Mike asked with interest.

"Another balancing act is between our thinking and our feeling responses. You know from our previous discussions about reactivity how easily **automatic functioning** can hijack a person's ability to think through carefully any situation where there is a lot of anxiety present. How well we manage our thinking and feeling responses is another ingredient contributing to where a person might be placed on the scale. Someone who is consistently feelings-driven, with very little ability to think objectively, would be here," Jacob pointed to the bottom third of the line, "much lower on the scale than someone who may be in touch with his feelings but still remains able to think through the situation in a more objective fashion."

Mike interrupted, "Jacob, can you explain this in terms of James McMaster for a moment?"

"Sure. I haven't spoken to him in months, but I bet he feels a real tension between his commitment to the decisions he made to buy the hotels now being considered for sale and the pressure being applied by forces in the organization that recommend selling those hotels. If I am correct, right now James' feelings and emotions are competing strongly with his ability to think clearly. How well he can manage his thinking-feeling balance depends on where his basic level of differentiation falls on the scale.

"But placing someone on a scale of differentiation somewhere between 0 and 100 is much more complex than calibrating any two or three factors. It's really about how well a person functions overall in every dimension of the dance of life. If you were going to try to figure out where a person's basic level of differentiation might be, you'd need to look at a whole host of issues: things like health, both physical and emotional, success or failure in relationships, career success and social standing, ability to achieve life goals, and so forth. Bowen would even look at how a person's children and grandchildren were functioning to make that determination. Those are all indicators of a very elusive quality—differentiation of self—that has both interior dimensions as well as external manifestations."

"How does a person wind up at a higher or lower point on the scale?" Mike asked.

"A person's basic level of differentiation is, like so much else in life, the result of the family he or she is born into. We've just recently been talking about how the past is present in patterns of **emotional process** that are passed down from generation to generation, both in families and in organizations. Each of us has pretty much reached our basic level of differentiation by the time we leave home. And that level is the product of a process that was handed down to us from the many generations that preceded us, inherited most immediately from our parents and whatever level of differentiation they received from their families of origin.

"For a variety of reasons, each of the children in a family gets a bit more or less of the parents' freedom or constraints than their siblings, and that is a significant factor influencing the child's level of differentiation. That's why levels of differentiation of self are not the same for every child in a given family. It's really not as deterministic as it may sound, but there's no way of denying the influence of our families in shaping who we are as persons."

Jacob paused to let Mike absorb what he was saying.

Mike said, "Yeah, I think we talked before about my sister being a lot less reactive than I am, and it probably had to do with the fact that I was a difficult child and got a lot of anxious attention—mostly unwanted—from my parents. I guess Betty would be a bit higher than me on that scale."

"Not necessarily, Mike. There are so many factors that go into determining a person's level of differentiation. Basically, what this scale is trying to portray is how much of a 'self' a person has, and how that 'self' is manifested in a variety of ways that make up the whole of a person's life." Jacob turned again to the board and wrote,

> *Differentiation is about our ability to claim a unique identity in the world and to be responsible for and manage our functioning, both internally and in external relationships.*

Mike wrote the statement down word for word. "Jacob, you have slipped into a lot of jargon again. Do some translating so I'm sure I get it."

Jacob laughed and continued, "Okay, suppose you are curious about one of your managers whom you are evaluating for a promotion. You're trying to figure out how effective he will be in a more significant leadership role. One of the issues you'd want to look at is how differentiated he seems to be. Here's some of what you would pay attention to in order to get a better handle on that." Jacob wrote on the board again:

> *1. Is he able to distinguish between what he's feeling and what he's thinking?*

Jacob pointed to the board and said, "If every feeling response is immediately translated into a firm conviction or belief, without any testing, then you've got a big red flag suggesting he can't distinguish what he feels from what he thinks." He wrote another point on the board:

> *2. Does he make choices more on the basis of what he's feeling or what he's thinking?*

"I'm not necessarily suggesting that trusting your gut feeling is a bad idea," Jacob explained. "What I'm warning against is something like this: For example, the guy who has such strong feelings of friendship for someone that he can't bring himself to do what he knows is best, such as passing over his friend for a promotion when he doesn't deserve it, or giving him a reprimand when he needs it.

"It's one thing to be able to separate out your feelings and thoughts; but when it comes down to making choices, there's another step needed so your behaviors are not being driven more by your feelings than by what you know is best." Jacob then wrote a number three on the board. "A third thing to look for as a sign of a person's level of self-differentiation is how much he sets his life course on the basis of fundamental values and principles, rather than being tossed to and fro by every pressure or resistance he encounters." He added a third point:

> *3. How much is he goal-oriented and led by a consistent vision and set of priorities in life?*

Mike replied, "I think I'm getting the point now. You're talking about someone who knows how to manage his anxiety, to reduce his reactivity enough that he can figure out the right course of action, and then follow through on it.

"I think Karla is a good example of that," he continued. "She always seems to be balanced and able to make rational and well-considered decisions. In our relationship I can sense that she instinctively monitors the 'too close' versus 'too distant' dimension. If she has any weakness, it is in being so welcoming and nice to people that she can lose her boundaries sometimes. But that typically doesn't go on for very long before she makes an adjustment."

"Karla is a good role model for you in many ways," Jacob said. "But before you put her up on too high a pedestal, it might interest you to know that people typically marry someone of roughly the same level of self-differentiation. Maybe your choice of her as a mate shows just how shrewd and self-differentiated you are!"

Jacob gave a hearty laugh and then said, "Mike, we have been at this a long time. Let's stop here and quickly review next steps."

"Okay," Mike said. "I am going to meet one-on-one with James after I talk with Vanessa about all of this. Then I will have a better idea about if and how to involve you in a meeting between the three of us."

"Great," Jacob said, "we'll meet again next after you have had a chance to talk with James and Vanessa."

As Mike drove away from Jacob's office, he picked up his messages and called Vanessa. He summarized the meeting with Jacob, and she agreed that a one-on-one meeting between Mike and James was a good idea. But she needed to brief James on the YTD performance and projections for each hotel being considered for sale before Mike met with him. Her meeting was set up for the morning of the next day, and she wanted to have that meeting alone with James.

One of Mike's messages was from Jacelyn who wanted to talk to her dad about the wedding plans. Mike knew that Russ was going to be out with some college buddies that evening, so he decided to take her and Karla out to dinner if they were available.

Chapter 7: Focus on Differentiation of Self

Review Key Points

- To **focus on differentiation of self**, rather than trying to change others, is a more effective way to exercise leadership.
  - The *position* of a leader within any system gives him or her great leverage to influence the entire system.

- **Differentiation of self** is a lifelong process of keeping one's being in balance by self-regulation and self-definition.
  - Bowen Theory's scale of differentiation from 0-100 suggests the continuum of functioning that is possible.

- Many things contribute to one's basic level of differentiation on the scale, most importantly certain factors within one's family of origin.

- The more a person maintains a healthy balance of **self-other forces** in relationships, the higher that person's basic level of differentiation.

- The more a person regulates feeling responses with thinking responses, the higher that person's basic level of differentiation.
  - A person's basic level of differentiation is reflected in the ability to:
    - Distinguish thinking from feeling
    - Choose on the basis of thinking rather than feeling
    - Engage in principle-based behaviors

Questions for Reflection and Discussion

1. What indications do you see that Mike is beginning to focus more on his own functioning—on becoming more of a self—as he prepares to convince Mr. McMaster that

CHI needs to make a significant change in its business strategy?

2. As you think back on times when the people in your organization were experiencing heightened levels of stress/anxiety, were there some people who consistently seemed prone to get caught up in a pattern of escalating reactivity? How were the behaviors of those people different from others who seemed to manage their functioning better and remain more calm/thoughtful?

3. As you think back on life in your family when you were growing up, can you recall the kind of situations/experiences that regularly made it easier (or more difficult) for you to develop a healthy level of self-differentiation?

The Practice

1. Identify a relationship in which you would like to take a more differentiated position. Describe your role and relationship to the other person (e.g., father to Chester, sister to Rhonda, neighbor to Pam).

2. Next create a two-axis chart and label the vertical axis Self Regulation and the horizontal axis Self Definition.

3. Place a mark on both axes to identify where you find yourself in this relationship. For this exercise:
   - Full Self Regulation means able to be both engaged and observant in all interactions while striking a healthy balance between close-distant and thinking-feeling.
   - Full Self Definition means able to be open/honest and at ease in all interactions, comfortable enforcing appropriate boundaries and respectful of the differences in others.

4. When you find yourself below your preferred level of Self Regulation or Self Definition, identify the specific interactions (types of activities or topics of discussion) or circumstances during which you are typically not able to be fully your best self.

5. Based on your observations, identify behaviors you can practice to become more self aware and more your true self.

Focus on Differentiation of Self

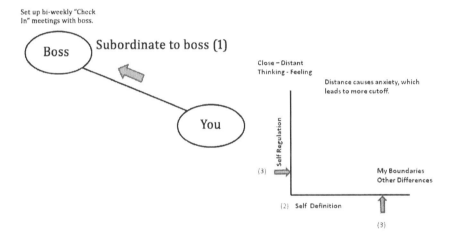

Self Regulation	Self Definition
4. I avoid my boss when I have not been in meetings with him regularly (cutoffs).	4. I don't hold my ground in contentious discussions. I "give in" almost all the time.
5. Stay in touch at least weekly so I keep a good close-distant balance.	5. Prepare for tough meetings by anticipating opposing opinions and remembering to be "up in the tree" to control my anxiety.

To learn more, go to www.resilient-leadership.biz.

A New Way of **LEADING**

Chapter 8: Lead With Conviction

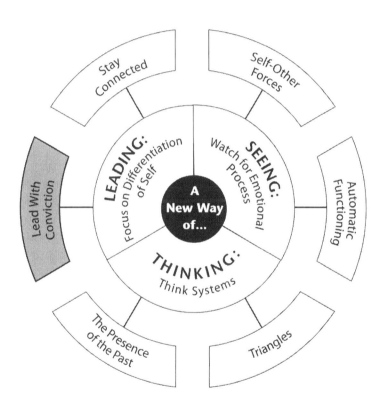

Wedding Plans

Karla and Jacelyn jumped at the chance to go out for dinner, and they decided to head for a favorite local Italian restaurant for a quiet meal. After they ordered, Jacelyn started to review plans for the wedding. She went through the whole event, starting with rehearsal dinner on Friday night, followed by the wedding on Saturday afternoon, which was to be followed by a sit-down dinner with entertainment, and then a Sunday morning breakfast. Then they would be off to their honeymoon to Costa Rica.

Mike just listened, smiled and asked one or two questions. Jacelyn even sought his opinion on a few minor details, which he gladly provided with no expectation that his views made any difference at all—which they didn't.

Mike reflected on the fact that this might be his last time to enjoy his two wonderful Sampson women as the only guy at the table. Soon there would almost always be another man with them. That still bothered Mike a little, but at this point he could observe the emotion within himself and manage it, rather than have it spill all over the evening.

Karla was also listening a lot, and she was deep into the many details that make weddings the unique experience they are. It seemed to Mike that women love weddings and that men observe weddings.

"Jacelyn, Granddad will be talking at the reception, as I recall," Mike said. "Have you talked with him about what he will be saying or when or how?"

"No. I thought about it, but realized the moment to help Granddad with his speech is about five minutes before he gives it," Jacelyn said. "I'm going to be pretty busy at that point, so I think you or mom should help him."

Mike looked at Karla and said, "Can you do it, Honey?"

"Sure. I'm happy to help Dad say whatever he wants to say, but I think I need to talk with him a little earlier than five minutes ahead of time. I'll take care of it."

Russ had called Jacelyn four times during dinner and it was clear that she was getting more and more distracted.

"Honey, do you need to go home?" Karla asked at the end of the fourth call.

"I do. Russ has had a small accident in the car and wants me to pick him up at the auto repair shop."

"Is he all right?" Mike asked.

"He is fine, just a dent in the trunk," Jacelyn said. "Let's go home and I'll take my car over to pick him up."

On the way home, they discussed the accident. Someone had failed to stop at a red light and slammed into the rear of Russ's car. The other driver had been charged with failing to yield at a stoplight.

When they got home, Jacelyn jumped into her own car and headed out to pick up Russ.

Mike still had some lingering questions about Russ, but they were quickly dissolving. Russ was young and so was Jacelyn. But the more time he spent with them both, the more he recognized his younger self and his own bride of 25 years.

Mike's Conviction

His most recent coaching session with Jacob had stopped Mike in his tracks.

As a very accomplished, tough-minded baby boomer, he had accepted a challenge many men his age and with his track record would have dismissed. He had swallowed his pride and taken the steps needed to increase his self-awareness. He had submitted to a series of difficult and time-consuming coaching sessions, occasionally thinking he was wasting his time. In the end, he had done what it took to gain the support of James and Vanessa as a candidate for COO. And along the way, he began to see an amazing transformation in himself. He felt that he was growing as a person.

But not until the last few days had he begun to fully appreciate the difference between his view of the future and James' view of the future. More than an inconvenience—if he was going to be honest with himself—that difference was a huge roadblock. He had three choices: Either remove the roadblock by overcoming the differences between James and himself or ignore his own convictions or withdraw his name from the COO candidate list.

He looked at the cell phone note that he had taken during his last coaching session. It read:

Resilient Leadership

Differentiation is about our ability to have a unique identity and be responsible for and manage our functioning, both within ourselves and also in our external relationships.

With mixed feelings, Mike came to realize that after all his effort to secure the opportunity, he was going to have to make his candidacy for the COO slot contingent on factors beyond his control.

Early Thursday afternoon Mike met with Vanessa to hear how the financial briefing with James had gone that morning. James understood the circumstances in each hotel in question and the gravity of the problems presented by the competition in these locations, the downturn in business in general and the deteriorating conditions at these 17 hotels. He was quiet during the meeting, and at the end restated his commitment to the due diligence process that would be presented at the upcoming Board meeting.

At 3:15 p.m., Mike was making his final preparations for his 3:30 appointment with James. He pulled out his bulleted list of next steps that he had shared with Vanessa and Steve Alba:

1. What is our organizational passion?
2. What are the markets and who are the customers we choose to serve?
3. What is our value proposition for those markets and customers?
4. What structure do we need to have and what competencies do we need to develop and nurture to excel in our value proposition?

He decided to use these questions to frame his discussion with James and quickly made a photocopy of the page.

Then he headed for James McMaster's office. As he walked along, he said "shit" to himself under his breath. He stopped and walked back to his own office and looked out the window for a moment, took a deep breath and started back. This time he said to himself, "I can do this."

"Hello, Mr. McMaster, how are you today?" Mike said as he walked into the CEO's office.

James stood up and walked to meet Mike and shook his hand. "Just great, how are you? How are Karla and the family?"

"I am doing fine, and the family is preparing for Jacelyn's wedding that is just around the corner." As he said those words, Mike realized that he did not know if an invitation had been sent to Mr. McMaster. He could not remember if he had decided to invite James and his wife or not.

"Great, there is nothing like a wedding to bring families together. I love going to weddings."

Mike wanted to change the subject quickly.

"Mr. McMaster, I am honored and very excited to be a candidate for the COO post."

"Well, we are excited too, Mike. I am glad that things have worked out the way they have. Both you and Steve Alba are wonderful leaders and great contributors to the company, but I am confident that you have what it takes to follow Vanessa and keep CHI on track. By the way, we do also have a final outside candidate, as I am sure you know."

"I do know, and I think it is smart to look both internally and externally for the best candidate," Mike said.

"Well, I have interviewed her several times. She is quite well qualified in many ways. If I had my way, I would hire both of you today. Too bad there is only one COO position," James said with a smile.

"Mr. McMaster, I would like to talk with you about your vision for CHI over the next ten to 20 years. And I'd like to share my thoughts with you as well."

"Great," James said with a chuckle, "I can pretty much assure you that in 20 years I'll be pushing up daisies."

Mike didn't know whether to laugh or frown, but James quickly went on, "Let me give you a quick overview as I see CHI's future."

James began talk about hotel deals. "CHI has been in business for about 40 years now and has steadily grown. The last four or five years have seen slower growth due to a lot of competition and the fact that funds for deals have become pretty scarce with the economic downturn. We have got to grow at a faster rate.

"I think we need to double or even triple our development pipeline and go after some smaller markets that we have overlooked in the past. The development people say places like Raleigh-Durham, Jacksonville, Memphis and Wichita are good opportunities for site acquisition and hotel development. They have a list of over 40 cities that we should be thinking about. I am working with Bob Church in development to identify at least eight locations that we can take to the Development Committee next month for approval. We also have some room additions that need to be reviewed and approved."

Mike took a deep breath and then said, "How do you reconcile the decision to add units when we are at the same time considering the sale of some of our bigger and older hotels?" Mike asked.

"Well, the only way it makes sense to me is if we are able to retain a presence in these markets that is financially stronger than the one we hold now. It would be a big mistake to lose our position or presence in any of these markets. Some of the property we own is simply irreplaceable, and that's why we keep getting these big dollar offers. To begin with, I don't like the idea of selling American assets to foreign ownership.

"Secondly, the property we own is so unique, it is insulated from market fluctuations. We own property within a quarter mile of the Wrigley Building, Bush Stadium, Houston Galleria and the River Walk in San Antonio. We are within a mile of the Disney World entrance off of I-4 in Orlando and right on the beach in Miami South Beach, Fort Lauderdale, Marco Island and Destin. We can't give up any of these locations."

Mike wondered what McMaster was thinking. Vanessa had indicated that James was agreeing to a process to consider bundling these hotels for sale. But this conversation seemed to suggest that he had no intention to sell anything at all.

"But from what I understand, we are planning to undertake a due diligence process to respond to an offer from anonymous investors in London," Mike said.

"I am willing to explore an agreement with an investor that will give us both what we want. I will not agree to sell much, if any, of the property we are talking about. But I am willing to make arrangements with the right people."

James smiled. "Think duplex. CHI will own the land the duplex is built on and a portion of the duplex itself. Our partner will own the other side of the duplex and for that privilege they will pay to have the existing facility either renovated or torn down and for the construction of the entire new facility. That sounds like a great deal to me."

Mike now saw the nature of the deal that McMaster was cooking up in his mind. James would allow an investment interest that wanted to build a building on Miracle Mile in downtown Chicago, for example, to lease the rights to build and operate a multiple occupancy building for themselves as long as they also built a hotel property that CHI would own and operate. Mike had no idea if such an arrangement would be possible. James was sure it could be done.

"Will investment groups consider a deal like this?" Mike asked.

McMaster's response was animated. "I don't know. It probably depends on how much someone wants to be here in the US. It also depends on how much money they have to invest. But I tell you one thing, a Euro is worth 40 percent more here in the US this year than it was just six years ago. 40 percent! Today the USA is a great buy, so I am okay with having someone else build, own and operate a building on CHI land. But I am not going to sell any of this prime property, period; end of story.

"I am confident that only foreign national interests would be willing to consider such an arrangement, and then only if they cannot buy what they want here in the States. I do know this—there is intense interest in these properties, and there is a lot of cash out there."

The conversation paused for a moment. Mike realized that James had formulated some non-negotiable points related to potential deals. Mike wanted to talk about operations.

"Mr. McMaster, let me talk about operations for a moment," Mike said.

James said, "Sure, go ahead, Mike."

Mike began, "You and I have had many conversations over the years about hotel operations, and I know that we have the same dedication to service, employees and profitable growth."

"We have had a lot of conversations, Mike, and they have been good ones, too," James added.

Mike continued, "In the last nine months, I have been working with several industry consultants to get a better handle on the trends over the next ten years or so in the domestic convention market. I got started on this topic as I was working with my team in New York to sort out the best way to position our hotel located near the Kell Convention Center in Manhattan.

There is quite a debate going on between New York and Albany about how to grow revenues at the convention center; lots of politics are involved. As I was getting into the details of the challenge we face in New York, I became aware of very similar problems in Baltimore, Boston and Knoxville.

"In all of these cities over the last three to five years, huge public and corporate tax subsidies have been levied to support the convention centers' operational shortfalls. In these locations and others around the country, a number of convention centers are in peril due to the huge debt service and high cost of operations. In addition, we now have the challenge of reduced travel in the US, coupled with oil prices going through the roof. There is a perfect storm brewing.

"I believe that convention business in the US, already down six to eight percent annually for the last three years, will take another big nose dive in the next three to five years. There will always be the AMA, the NRA, the NAACP and other marquee type national conventions in the coming years, but the industry is overbuilt in general and the hotels that heavily rely on convention business are at significant risk. This is particularly true for hotels actually built inside the footprint of a convention center.

"Furthermore, some of our biggest competitors have national and international recognition and a convention network that we cannot hope to compete with in terms of product quality or range of services."

James was sitting quietly, watching Mike closely and listening carefully.

"Mike, I am aware of these problems, at least in general. People always characterize downturns as worse than they really turn out to be. I expect Vanessa and the COO who replaces her to find a way for CHI not only to address these issues but to thrive in this environment. We have a lot of convention business, and each of our hotels will need to address its market challenges and operating budgets to succeed. You and I have been through this many times before."

Mike realized that the time had come.

"Mr. McMaster, I am personally convinced that CHI must exit the convention market to succeed in the future. We have an opportunity right now to redirect the focus of the business toward the luxury, quality and moderate transient business segments. We need to maximize our efforts on our existing markets, invest in markets where our product needs to be renovated, and then penetrate new high-potential markets.

"But it is my personal conviction that my views, although based on well-researched facts, should not drive the business decisions we are considering; nor should yours, Mr. McMaster. What should drive our market focus and site development strategy and operational decision-making in the coming years is embedded in the answer to these four questions."

Mike leaned forward and handed a copy of his four questions to James.

1. What is our organizational passion?
2. What are the markets and who are the customers we choose to serve?
3. What is our value proposition for those markets and customers?
4. What structure do we need to have and what competencies do we need to develop and nurture to excel in our value proposition?

James looked at the questions and said, "Anybody that has been a part of CHI for a year knows the answer to these questions."

"I am sorry, Mr. McMaster, I can tell you that is not true because I don't know the answer to these questions."

James just looked at Mike. Mike wondered if he had just disqualified himself.

Mike went on, "Of course, I have an answer to these questions, and I know you do, too. But I can tell you there is no clear and common understanding to these fundamental questions."

"Well, if the organization has no common agreement on the answer to these basic questions, what does the organization have as a common agreement?"

Mike took a notepad and wrote CASH IS KING in bold letters. He turned the pad around so it faced James and slowly moved it directly in front of him. Mike waited a moment and then softly said, "Cash is king."

James looked at the paper. Then he held Mike's gaze for a moment before looking out the window for a long time.

He then turned back and looked directly at Mike and said angrily, "What would you do if I told you that the idea of getting CHI leaders together to answer the four questions you showed me is a waste of time? Suppose I told you that they should know the answer to these questions, and so should Vanessa and so should you?"

Mike now stood directly at the crossroads of his future. He paused for a moment and realized that he was present in the room in two ways; he was right there with James, and at the same time also above the conversation watching. He said, "Then I would tell you that you have the wrong internal candidate for the COO post."

The room went silent for a long time. Then James slowly stood up, "Is there anything else you want to say, Mike?"

It took everything Mike had in him not to ask another question; he wanted to ask, "Do you agree?" or "Are you angry?" or "Did I just disqualify myself from the COO candidate list?"

But in a self-defining moment, Mike smiled and simply said, "No."

They shook hands and Mike left James McMaster's office. He went directly to the elevator and down to his car. He took a long route home, thinking about what just happened. Vanessa, he hoped, would let him know in the morning what really had happened in his meeting with James McMaster.

Aftermath

As Mike reached the house, Karla was standing outside talking with a neighbor. Mike waved and pulled into the garage. Karla walked up the driveway and hugged Mike as he got out of the car.

"How was your day, Honey?" she said.

"It was a good day and a difficult one, too," Mike said.

With that Mike began to review the whole day with Karla as they walked into the kitchen. He described the meeting with Mr. McMaster, including the abrupt manner in which he ended the meeting.

"What do you think will happen now? Karla asked.

"James will talk with Vanessa tonight or tomorrow morning about our conversation and she will get in touch with me."

"Are you worried about how your discussion with Mr. McMaster turned out?"

"I am worried for CHI. We don't have any more time left to make important changes. I may have been too direct with McMaster for my first meeting as the potential COO, but it is time that we call out this problem in the culture of the company. A lot is riding on the conversation that James has with Vanessa."

Mike was tired and his knee was burning with pain. He wished he could go for a good run to let off steam, but instead he took a shower and relaxed with a book before going to bed early.

James McMaster went home after the meeting with Mike and shared his perspective of the meeting with his wife, Helen.

Helen had always been a good sounding board for James over the many years of their marriage. She knew that James really was married to two "loves": herself and CHI.

Tonight he was very distraught.

"Helen, you know that Mike Sampson is the man that Vanessa and I have selected as the best internal candidate to replace her. Mike and I just had a very disturbing conversation."

James recounted the conversation that he had with Mike.

"Well, what is it about Mike's viewpoint that you do agree with?" Helen asked.

"I agree that he is right about the need to change the direction of the company. I just don't agree with the specific changes he is suggesting."

"James, I think you should talk with Vanessa and also Mike about the way you feel as soon as you can," Helen said. "You are having a difficult time letting go of the development side of CHI. You need to get comfortable with Vanessa's replacement now so you feel that you are turning the company over to capable hands. The way you ended the meeting today did not help things.

"Dear, you need to learn how to trust someone else with CHI and begin to let go."

"I know. I know. But now I don't know if I trust Mike Sampson to do it," James said to himself as he went upstairs to change his clothes.

The next morning both James and Mike left messages for

Vanessa by 7:30 a.m. As Vanessa listened to both messages, she recognized the emotional triangle that she was in. James wanted her to support his perspective and so did Mike. She decided right away to get together with both of them at the same time. She spoke to James first, suggesting that all three meet the next morning. After he forcefully summarized his views, James agreed to meet mid-morning. She then spoke to Mike and made arrangements for a 10:00 a.m. meeting in her office. Mike inquired about James' reaction to the previous day's meeting, but she declined to give him a direct answer. "Let's talk tomorrow," she said.

By 10:30 a.m. on the following day, it was clear that both men had hardened their positions. The meeting in Vanessa's office enabled both men to state their thinking, but Vanessa realized that she had made a mistake. She had given them both the opportunity to restate their views and in so doing highlight their differences.

Near the end of the meeting, she said, "Well, we have done a good job identifying how the two of you see things differently. What do you think we should do now?" No one said anything.

Finally Vanessa said, "I think we need to challenge ourselves to find a third alternative that works—really works—for each of us, myself included. We need to continue this dialogue at another meeting or two with the objective of finding that third alternative. I want your agreement to meet one or two more times before we get to Scottsdale."

Both men agreed, and this time there were smiles and handshakes as they broke up the meeting.

WEDDING WEEKEND

The weekend schedule was hectic as friends from around the city and country arrived for the wedding. Jacelyn and Russ had five bridesmaids and five groomsmen. Along with the best man and maid of honor and several close friends, the rehearsal at St. James and the rehearsal dinner included about 40 people. The practice at the church went as well as could be expected, and the air was filled with laughter and great anticipation.

The rehearsal dinner was held at a local CHI hotel. Karla and

Jacelyn had spent hours selecting the menu and making the arrangements in the specialty restaurant Serene located just a short distance from St. James in Falls Church.

To make the dinner conversations comfortable and interesting, the tables had been set with place cards so guests sat at a table with several people they knew and several that they did not know. Russ' father made the traditional welcome speech, thanking everyone for coming and toasting Russ and Jacelyn. The dinner went on until about 9:00 p.m. and then the older crowd began to drift off for the evening as the wedding party and their friends changed their plans at the last minute and went in a variety of directions.

Karla and Mike visited with Russ' parents, Joe and Beth. They had met only a few times before the wedding, and both couples felt the need to become better acquainted. They sat in the lobby bar and spoke mostly about the bride and groom and their other children until they called it a night around 11:00 p.m.

The day of the wedding was a whirl of activity. Karla was up at the crack of dawn, going with Jacelyn and the bridesmaids to the hairdresser and preparing to get dressed for the 2:30 p.m. wedding. Mike picked Richard up for breakfast at about 9:00 a.m. It was a good time for them to catch up. They had not had much time to talk with one another since the reunion trip. After getting a plate of food at the breakfast buffet, they had a chance to have a quick talk.

"Dad, are you excited about the wedding or a little sad to have your favorite daughter getting married?"

"Well, it's a little of both, I guess. She really loves Russ, and it's time for them to get married."

Richard added, "I got to know Russ a lot better during the reunion weekend. He is a great guy and very interesting to talk with. He is pretty smart and fun, too. He has a million ideas about inventions."

"What kind of inventions?" Mike asked.

"He has an idea about how to make money with advertisements in bathrooms," Richard said.

Mike knew about this advertising venue. Several vendors had approached his general managers with the idea. "We don't advertise in our bathrooms."

"Sure you do," said Richard.

"No we don't," Mike said.

"There is an advertisement in the bathroom at the hotel restaurant where we ate last night," Richard reported.

"What the hell does it advertise?" Mike asked.

"The Soft Touch Health Spa down the street from the hotel," Richard said.

"Are you sure?"

"Yep, saw it last night; three times at the urinal," Richard said with a smile. "It's a great ad!"

Mike wondered what the ad must look like for Richard to comment on it with such enthusiasm. He made a mental note to follow up with that general manager on Monday. During breakfast Richard waited for his dad to bring up the book by Eckhart Tolle, but he did not. He decided not to push the topic any more.

After breakfast they headed down to the hotel to get dressed with the other men in the wedding at about 12:30 p.m. As they were driving Richard noticed the cover for the audio book—*A New Earth*—in the disc holder.

"Hey, Dad, are you listening to this on disc?" Richard asked with excitement in his voice.

"Yes, I am. I'm just getting started," Mike said.

"What do you think so far?"

"Well, it's a difficult concept to get your mind around, but I am working on it," Mike said. "Right now I'm working on the chapter related to ego. I have a big one," Mike said and laughed.

"I have read that chapter at least 20 times. It has so much in it," Richard said.

Mike looked at Richard. "Are you exaggerating?"

"Actually, I am not, Dad. What I am trying to really experience is the difference between the spiritual self and the unconscious or illusionary self. But, Dad, you can't—or I can't—get our minds around this stuff. We have to experience it, not think it."

Mike looked at Richard again. "How do you learn about something without thinking about it?"

"That is what I'm trying to figure out," Richard said.

By this point they had reached the hotel where they were going to meet the groomsmen in a suite that Russ had on the top floor of the hotel. Mike pulled up to the hotel entrance, got out, left the keys with the valet, and headed straight for the restroom across from the Serene restaurant.

There was the advertisement all right. Mike took a photo of it with his cell phone so he could have a visual to use when he talked with the general manager of the hotel on Monday morning.

They headed up to the top floor with their tuxedoes in hand.

The wedding ceremony was perfect. Mike was beaming with pride as he walked Jacelyn down the aisle. The wedding party was dressed in black. The women wore gold sashes and the men gold vests. The ceremony included both mothers lighting candles, lovely music sung a cappella, wedding vows written mostly by Jacelyn and hundreds of photos taken before, during and after the wedding.

The reception was held in the ballroom of a nearby CHI hotel with about 250 guests attending. A full-course dinner was served with several types of white and red wines. Speeches were made by each father and Karla, as well as several other family members.

The highlight of the toasting belonged to Mike Senior, who made a brief speech that was funny, well organized and very heartfelt. Karla had obviously done a lot of work in helping him prepare. Mike Senior dearly loved his granddaughter and it showed as he expressed his pride for her as well as his whole family. His remarks were so moving that he got a standing ovation. It was a perfect ending to the ceremonial part of the dinner and set the stage for lots of fun. Listening to his father speak, Mike realized how smart it was for Karla and Jacelyn to push for a video of the whole wedding.

Breakfast the next morning was at the hotel, and most of the wedding party showed up. A few of the groomsmen had to leave early Sunday morning to return home and a few just could not get up for breakfast. Jacelyn and Russ visited with everyone to thank them for coming to the wedding. Just a few minutes before the bride and groom left for the trip to Costa Rica, Mike and Mike Senior had a brief conversation at one of the tables.

"Dad, you made a great speech yesterday at the reception," Mike said.

"Thanks Michael, I meant every word of it. I am very proud of my family and all they have accomplished. You and Karla have done a great job with your children."

Mike Senior continued, "It was a real treat to see our family having so much fun together. We need to do more together as a family."

Mike wondered where his dad was going with the comment. "What do you have in mind?"

"Well, I am not sure, but I do know that I feel really isolated at the retirement center these days. I would like to be more involved with your family in some way, as long as I'm not being a nuisance."

Mike did not know how he felt about that comment at first. Being around his dad for long stretches of time had never been a good idea.

"Michael, I know that we can only take each other in small doses. I am set in my ways, and you have been headstrong since the day you were born. I am just saying that maybe we both ought to try a little harder, that's all. We should try to do something with the family sometime. I will be on my best behavior."

Mike was stunned by his father's comments. He had never heard him talk about his feelings like that before. He decided to chalk it up to the atmosphere of the event. He remembered something Jacob had told him about family systems "opening up" around weddings and funerals. But Mike had convinced himself that his dad was not going to turn over a new leaf at 80 years of age, even though he talked about being different. Being critical of others and self-absorbed was in his dad's make-up.

Before Mike could respond to his father, Jacelyn and Russ came up to the table to say good-bye as they were on their way out the door. Jacelyn hugged her dad and granddad and Russ shook everyone's hand.

"Dad, thank you so much for a wonderful weekend and for all your support. We are off to Costa Rica and will be back next weekend."

"Granddad, thanks for your speech and thank you for my dad, too. You two mean the world to me. Russ and I will be back here at Christmastime and I want to get together for a great week with all the family."

Mike Senior looked at Mike who grinned and said, "You bet; we will need to review the wedding video."

Later that evening, Mike went to his office to make a few notes on a wonderful day.

Today (Jacelyn and Russ's wedding weekend)
- What a wonderful two days. Everything was perfect.
- Getting on top of my own reactivity is making a big difference.
- Dad did a great job with his remarks at the wedding.
- Dad's request to come to the house is a big change for him and a signal that he wants to get closer now.

Issues
- Having a breakthrough with Dad. He is beginning to talk with me, not at me.
- Need to keep working on the triangle between Karla and Jacelyn and me. Now Russ is involved in a big way. How do I feel about that addition?

Follow up
- Keep moving through the Tolle tape.
- Richard is trying to rebuild a relationship with me—I need to attend to this to build my relationship with him.
- Thinking ahead—get ready for the conversation with James and Vanessa by checking the strength of my conviction.

More COO Thinking with Jacob

Mike was very eager to visit with Jacob. During this coaching session, he wanted to get help figuring out how to handle a number of family and professional challenges.

"Hello, Mike, welcome back. I was just looking at my records before you arrived and noted that we are at the six-month mark in our work together. You have come a long way in six months."

"I sure have, with your help," Mike replied.

"What is on your mind today?" Jacob asked.

"Top of my list is to review the one-on-one discussion I had with James and the follow-up action that Vanessa, James and I have planned. Then I also want to review the wedding with you. It was wonderful, and I had a very interesting discussion with my dad."

"That's great, Mike," Jacob said, "I want to hear all about both events. Also we need to continue with our review of **Resilient Leadership**. We are in the middle of concepts and tools related to 'A New Way of LEADING,' and I want to continue with that discussion as well if we have time."

Mike provided a detailed summary of the conversation with James.

He ended his report with, "After I made it clear that my candidacy for the COO position was contingent on decisions about company strategy which James disagreed with, he became angry then silent and then just ended the meeting. It was a classic cutoff move that had the impact of making me feel like I just lost my candidacy for the COO position."

Jacob asked, "Then what happened?"

"I had a strange evening where I bounced between a feeling of calm resignation to the situation and anxiety that I was about to get fired. I called Vanessa early the next morning; she listened to my summary and then called me back several hours later to set up a meeting with her and James to iron things out. She had obviously talked with James, but she wouldn't tell me his reaction to my meeting with him.

"When we met, we basically restated our views to each other and Vanessa. We didn't make much headway, and Vanessa ended that meeting with the suggestion—really it was a challenge—to meet again in order to find some middle ground. She called it a third alternative."

"Mike, let me ask you this," Jacob said. "How would you describe your state of mind in the follow-up meeting with James and Vanessa?"

"Well, I had not slept very well that night, so I was irritable. I had thought over the meeting with James a lot and basically got pissed off, at myself and him and at the situation. I also was preparing for the wedding, and frankly I was distracted by all of that preparation as well. Karla was tied up with handling a million details, so we barely had a chance to talk."

"Okay, I have a good idea about your state of mind. Now, how did you act in the meeting? Were you reactive, or would you describe your behavior as self-differentiated in the way we discussed it last time?"

Mike tried to remember what self-differentiated actually meant. He tried to recall the discussion at their last meeting, and Jacob could see that he was struggling.

"Let me ask the question a different way," Jacob said. "Were you centered in the meeting and calm in your position? Did you engage in the dialogue with a level of clarity about what you felt was right for CHI? Or would you say that you debated James in a sort of reactive 'dog fighting' fashion?"

"Well, I was surely not relaxed inside. But I was self-controlled. You know, the idea of refining our strategy at this point just makes all the sense in the world, and if we do not engage senior management in the process we will be making a huge mistake. In fact we really have no choice if we want to survive and prosper."

Jacob could see the determination in Mike and he knew that James and Vanessa must have seen it too.

"Mike, I'm also wondering how well you were able to listen to James' viewpoint as he was restating his position. You know, a well-differentiated person not only states his own position clearly and with conviction. He is also able to listen with respect, and non-defensively, to someone who has an opposite viewpoint."

"Hmm, I'm afraid I only got a 'C minus' on that score."

"And how do you feel now about the stand you are taking and the consequence of your actions?"

"Well, I feel like I am doing the right thing for the company without a doubt. But I am not sure I am doing things in the right way. For example, maybe I am being too open with my views at this point in the process. Maybe I should be less candid now and concentrate on getting the position before I start talking about making such far-reaching changes."

"Mike, here is a way to think your way through this question," Jacob said. "When you wonder if you should be forthright at this point in the process, are you dealing with anxious feelings you have or calm thoughts? Are you having self-doubt about how to behave because you are anxious about your candidacy or because you actually think that the best approach to success is perhaps to be less straightforward in sharing your views?"

Mike realized immediately that he was dealing with his anxiety and being reactive.

"I need to continue being forthright with my views," Mike said.

"Forthright, but open and flexible, too," Jacob said. "Hold on loosely to you views. Be strong in your conviction, yet open to input from others who can take your ideas and make them better," Jacob said.

"I wish James was here right now to hear you speak," Mike said.

"James knows this as much as you or I do. Mike, do you think you have earned James' trust?"

"I think he trusts me as a person. I just don't know if he still has confidence in me as his COO."

"Do you have confidence in yourself as COO?" Jacob asked, "Confidence down in your bones?"

"I absolutely know what to do in the position, and I am very confident I can do the job," Mike said with the right mixture of self-assuredness and humility.

Jacob knew he was ready for the job.

"In the meetings you have from now on with James and Vanessa and others for that matter, try to put yourself in your thoughts and your feelings at just the point you are at right now. When you speak and act from the point you are at right now, you are exhibiting strong self-differentiation. And don't forget to listen deeply to other viewpoints."

"I need a little more clarity on how to recognize and further develop self-differentiation," Mike said.

"Okay, let's take a short break and we can talk about that."

Mike stood up, stretched and walked outside for a moment. Jacob wheeled over to his computer to check on messages. Both men returned to the table in Jacob's office after about ten minutes.

Mike started, "I think I've got the basic idea about differentiation of self. In my case it seems like I was born into a family that did not have much of it baked into our DNA. Once you get your dose, are you stuck there for the rest of your life? Isn't there any way to become more differentiated?"

Jacob answered, "There are two possibilities: One is easier, but the other, even though more difficult, is more permanent. The easier way to operate at a higher level of differentiation is to see to it that you're part of a higher functioning relationship network and that your environment is less anxious. Neither of those conditions may necessarily be within your reach; but if they are, you will find that you tend to function at a higher level of differentiation. That higher level would be what we call your *functional* level, as opposed to your *basic* level."

"I'm not sure I follow. Can you explain the difference between those two levels?"

"Sure. We all have what is called our *basic* level of differentiation of self, and that is like our default setting that we operate out of 'all things being equal' when we run on autopilot. But there is also something called our *functional* level of differentiation, which is variable and highly influenced by our surroundings. If we're lucky enough to be part of a high-functioning system, we find it easier to function at higher levels of differentiation. In a sense, we 'borrow' a bit more 'self' from those around us in the system."

Mike nodded and said, "When I am around Vanessa, I get the sense that I am with a person who is very differentiated. I see it in her words and actions, and I feel it in the room when I am with her, too. It is hard to put a finger on what it is. She just seems to be calm and in control. And she makes me feel calmer too.

"On the other hand, I also know many CHI people who are reactive and cause a lot of stress in the areas they manage. In the past I would have never thought of their behavior as being reactive or poorly differentiated. I would have used the term 'up tight' or 'anal' or in some cases 'being a hard ass.' When I'm around those folks, I know I tend to be more quick-tempered, that's for sure."

Jacob asked, "How about outside of work? Can you think of people who seem to be more or less differentiated?"

"Karla is the poster child for self-differentiation," Mike said.

Jacob smiled, "Yes, we talked about Karla briefly last time we met. I think it's fair to say, from what you've told me about Karla, that she operates as a calming influence on you, because she is less reactive, more thoughtful, than you tend to be. She manages her relationships in a very balanced way, and she seems to be less influenced by immediate crises that come up. You've told me often that she's been a real anchor for you on many occasions in your life."

Jacob continued, "Do you remember when we spoke some time ago about societal regression, we agreed that the overall anxiety level everywhere in our world today is making it much harder for people to be thoughtful about their choices?"

"Yes, I remember that conversation."

"Well, that's a fairly dramatic example of how systems dynamics can inhibit higher functioning in people. But on a much smaller and more hopeful scale, one implication of this distinction between basic and functional levels of self-differentiation is that the new COO of CHI will be able to help the people within the organization to function at higher levels by being more self-differentiated himself.

"You see, whether at home or at work, a person can influence entire systems by exercising leverage as a formal or informal leader. That's what resilient leaders do: They contribute to calmer, more thoughtful systems by their way of being present; those who are poor leaders escalate the anxiety of everyone around them by spreading their own contagious anxiety."

Mike said, "I have a neighbor who puts everyone in our neighborhood on edge by her constant harassment of a young neighbor. She calls the cops, calls city home ordinance authorities, writes anonymous threatening notes, gossips and basically causes stress up and down the street we live on. She definitely influences the entire neighborhood system. People get reactive to her and every issue is constantly escalated, with shouting matches and all sorts of divisive stuff that goes on. Sometimes the functional level on our block is pretty low, I'm afraid."

"Well, don't be too judgmental of her, Mike. Remember that she has a family of origin, too, and we both know what that can mean." Jacob smiled. "Here is a thought that might be of some help.

"The lower a person's *basic* level of differentiation, the more susceptible they are to having their *functional* level raised or lowered by the system they are part of. That's because by definition those who are lower on the self-differentiation scale are more easily influenced by others' functioning. The higher on the scale someone is, the less easily are they influenced by those around them. As a consequence, those who tend to be less differentiated have the most to gain by being part of a healthier system."

Mike seemed to be getting the point now. He said, "Now that I think about it, I saw this take place two summers ago, when Betty and Herb's two teenage sons spent two weeks with us. These kids are just terrors at home where they get everything they want and go absolutely nuts when they don't. When they arrived at the house, they were just terrible until Betty and Herb left. Once Karla got them to herself, they calmed down in one afternoon."

"What did she do to calm them down?" Jacob asked.

"Now that I think about it, she did nothing different than when the boys were not in the house. She has a commanding but calm presence and did not overreact to them."

"That's very interesting," Jacob said. "I recall that at a recent session you were saying your sister Betty is probably more self-differentiating than you are, since she appears less reactive. But perhaps she is just more passive and compliant. Not knowing how to enforce boundaries with one's children is usually a sign of higher anxiety levels and lower self-differentiation. That's what I meant when I told you last time that there are many factors to be considered when trying to figure out where a person is on the scale of self-differentiation."

"I see your point," Mike answered. "But can you tell me more about how I can work on my own level of differentiation?"

Jacob said, "Sure, remember I said earlier that there are two ways to raise our level of self-differentiation—one easier and one that is more difficult. Connecting with a higher-functioning system is the easier way because it raises our *functional* level of self-differentiation. The more difficult route is to work on increasing our *basic* level of self-differentiation. That route is harder, takes longer, but it is also more permanent and yields longer-lasting dividends in our overall life."

"I need to know more about this if I am going to be successful in my meetings with James and the Board of Directors in a few days."

Jacob laughed, "Well, I don't have any tricks that will do it for you in a few days' time. But I do have another handout that will give you some ideas about how it's done over the long haul. We've almost run out of time, but if you can stay a bit longer I can go over this with you before you leave."

"Sure, I am okay with my time."

"Good, I'd like to finish this topic with you today." Jacob handed Mike an article from a folder on his desk. "I need to make a quick phone call, Mike, so I am going to go outside while you look this over."

"No, no," Mike said. "You make your call, and I will take a little walk while I read this. It's pretty short. I'll be back in five minutes."

"Fine, you can read the first three sections, but we really don't need to discuss them now because you are already well on your way with these activities. We do need to talk about the fourth section, 'Gain More Self.'"

Mike headed for the door, already engrossed in the article Jacob had handed him:

DIFFERENTIATION OF SELF: THE ONGOING CHALLENGE OF RAISING ONE'S BASIC LEVEL

by
JACOB WOLFE, PhD.

Our basic level of differentiation of self is generally set by the time we leave home and begin our life as an independent adult. The factors that go into determining that level are complex and varied, but in general they include the following:

- multi-generational patterns and influences from our family of origin
- the basic level of differentiation of our parents
- how much anxious parental focus we receive, which is related to our sibling position
- situational factors and particular events occurring in the family system at our birth and as we are growing up

- the degree of emotional residue still unresolved in key family relationships as we embark on our independent adult lives

For most people, that basic level of differentiation does not change significantly over their lifetimes. However, for a person who is committed to his or her own growth and development, it is possible at any age to begin an intentional process of working on raising the basic level of differentiation. There are four dimensions to this process of intentional growth:

1. Learn the Theory. When someone has a deeper and broader understanding of the many forces that influence human functioning, that person is better equipped to focus on the elements that are most critical for personal growth. It can be enormously helpful, for example, to understand what a large role **automatic functioning** plays in our everyday life, and the incredible extent to which we are influenced by the emotional systems we are part of. The work of Murray Bowen offers a strong theory—one that can help you make sense out of yourself, other people, your relationships, and the larger systems you are involved with. Those increased understandings, in turn, provide new insights and guide a person's choices according to sound principles.

2. Manage Anxiety. The second dimension in the process of raising your level of differentiation is to work on managing your anxiety, and the multiple ways that it manifests itself in your functioning. Recognizing the pervasive influence of chronic anxiety in our everyday functioning is the first step. The **Resilient Leadership** model highlights how our struggle to keep the primal **self-other forces** in balance is a key factor generating anxiety.

But there are external sources of anxiety as well, not least of which is the period of societal regression that we are currently living through. Once we learn to watch for the signs of **emotional process** and spot more readily the influence of anxiety in our lives, we can more easily manage it. This involves developing a range of personal calming techniques and working to eliminate or at least minimize our reactive behaviors. By becoming more self-aware, we gradually learn how to integrate our feeling and thinking responses, and our reactive behaviors can be gradually reduced.

There are no quick fixes—it's a lifelong process of working on issues, one after the other—with some modest successes and a few spectacular failures. But if a person continues to put forth the effort, the progress will be real. Working with a professional coach has been a valuable resource for many people who wish to commit to this kind of intentional growth.

3. Clarify Your Vision. One of the essential tasks for people who wish to develop their basic level of differentiation is to be clear about the "big picture" of their lives—what their goals are, what core values really matter to them, what guiding principles shape their choices large and small. The more clearly and deeply you probe within yourself to clarify these factors, the more will you be able to take actions that are consistent with your vision. This step needs to include all of the significant spheres of a person's life—work, family, faith, whatever are the areas that really matter. Differentiation of self is ultimately about a way of *being*, and that requires work on every area of one's life. Many people find the process of writing a personal mission statement helpful in this regard.

4. Gain More Self. Each of us has some measure of unfinished business with members of our own family. Since that is the system where our basic level of differentiation was originally shaped, that is the best place to go to work on raising it. However, the attempt to engage with our family of origin in a less reactive manner is extremely challenging work, and often requires professional assistance.

The more difficult it is to remain calmer and less reactive in any relationship, the more valuable that situation is for you. This means that whenever you are in a relationship that is emotionally significant to you to any degree, you have the opportunity to work on raising your basic level of differentiation. If reengaging with family of origin is impossible or seems too difficult, practicing to gain more self in a work setting is usually easier because there is generally a reduced emotional investment in the workplace.

Whenever a person chooses to try to gain more self in relationships, it is a good idea to prepare by anticipating the predictable interactions that might trigger one's reactivity. By developing a carefully crafted "game plan" before engaging in challenging situations, one is better positioned to remain neutral and less reactive, more able to focus on taking an "I-position" that is as clear and less anxious as possible, rather than reacting to the other person's anxiety. Focusing on facts as one gathers more information about your relationships is one very useful way to remain less anxious in such situations.

Mike stuck his head back in the door several minutes later. "Ready?" he asked. Jacob was waiting for him at the table.

"Mike, the fourth way to work on raising your basic level of differentiation is the most difficult of all: It requires gaining more 'self' in the relationship networks that are most significant to you."

"Can you explain what you mean by 'gaining more self' in my relationships?"

"Sure. For example, when you interact with your dad, you have the option of relating to him not only as his son, but also as a mature adult, the successful husband and father of your family and a businessman who is widely respected in your field. You can interact with him out of that clear and calm space, respecting any differences of viewpoint between the two of you, while still holding your own in the conversation. Or, on the other hand, you can interact with him as his little boy who is still rebelling after 50 years, albeit in more covert and intricate ways. In the former case you are being more of a 'self,' while in the latter there is much less 'self' that you bring to the relationship."

"That helps a lot, thanks, Jacob."

"As the article you just read says, each of us has some measure of unfinished business with members of our own family.

Trying to 're-enter' our family of origin and function in less automatic ways is probably about as difficult and challenging work as you can get. Of course, your family relationship system is not the only place where you can make gains. The relationships you have at CHI are generally much less intense because you are less emotionally invested there, and so that is probably an easier place to take some steps toward defining more of a 'self.' I'd guess that it's easier for you to remain non-reactive with James McMaster than it is with Michael Sampson, Sr."

Mike laughed and nodded vigorously.

"Obviously you've already done some significant work in that regard. As you know, the more difficult it is to remain a calmer and less reactive presence in any situation, the more valuable that situation probably is for you to work on your own differentiation of self. But I don't want to minimize how important your meetings with Vanessa and James in the coming days are for your development and personal growth.

"Whenever you are in a relationship with someone who is emotionally significant to you in some degree, you have the opportunity to work on raising your basic level of differentiation. Your efforts to clarify your position with James are a great step forward for you in this area.

"Here is the key, and this is critical, Mike: James is trying to decide if he can trust you with the operation of the company he spent his life building. For him, it is about two points: do you have the right ideas, and are you are the right person.

"Now, you are sure you have the right ideas. You are the expert on the business and you have done your homework and you even have Vanessa's support. James will eventually see and appreciate this.

"But are you the right person? That is what you and he will find out soon. You are standing your ground with James in a way he is not accustomed to. I dare say no one has ever written the words, 'CASH IS KING' on a piece of paper and stuck it under his nose while identifying the impact of that belief as detrimental to CHI. That rang a bell he has never heard before, and it was surely a hard pill for him to swallow."

"Do you think I was too blunt with him, Jacob?"

"No, I'm not saying that. But whenever you are making an important move in the direction of becoming more of a 'self,' there is a predictable response from others that you can anticipate. You are getting that response from James now. It's not a deliberate or calculated attempt on his part to block your growth. It's just another manifestation of how **automatic functioning** works in any system, as he tries to maintain a familiar and—for him—comfortable equilibrium in CHI.

"If you are alert, there is a predictable pattern you will learn to spot as you move toward greater differentiation of self. The reactions you will encounter from those around you will go something like this," Jacob moved his wheelchair toward the white board and wrote:

> 1. *You are wrong!*
> 2. *Change back!*
> 3. *Here is the price you'll pay if you don't change back!*

Jacob turned to Mike. "These reactions will rarely be stated in such a direct way, but it is a very familiar pattern you can anticipate. Think about the reaction you had the night Jacelyn called you in your hotel room to tell you she was getting married. I'll bet in some form or other, what you said—or wanted to say to her—went something like this: You are wrong! Change back! Here is the price you'll pay if you don't change your mind!"

Mike was amazed and a bit embarrassed at how closely Jacob had named his emotional response that night. But he admitted, "I'm afraid you're right. I was really reactive, and that's exactly what I wanted to say to her. I don't remember if I did or not. I think she just hung up on me before I got there. I can see it so clearly now, but I sure couldn't see it then."

"In your discussions with Jacelyn or James or in most other emotionally charged conversations, the responses are never stated so blatantly. But the pattern is almost always present and represents the essence of the dynamics that a person encounters whenever he changes the system's homeostasis by making a move in the direction of more 'self.'"

Mike's expression showed his struggle as he thought through the implications of what Jacob was explaining to him. Finally, he blurted out, "Damn it, Jacob, it's not fair to have to deal with so much resistance when you're just trying to be a better person. Why does it have to be so difficult?"

Jacob smiled, "Mike, it's human nature to prefer what is comfortably familiar in relationships, rather than to have to deal with the challenge of negotiating a new way of being in the relationship—especially if it may require functioning at a higher level than we are accustomed to. In fact, it's not just *human* nature—it's the way all of nature has evolved across every life form. I'm sure it wasn't too comfortable for that first amphibian to crawl out of the water onto dry land. Leaving behind the familiar school of fish and striking out alone as an independent self must have been hard and scary. The others surely warned that first amphibian to stay put! But that is the way life pushes forward to higher levels of growth and selfhood."

"Wow, I never thought of it that way. That's really helpful, Jacob."

"And now you, the singular choice for the new COO position—at least from the inside of CHI—have struck out on your own and challenged James in a way he has never experienced before. No wonder he stood up and ended the meeting. He perhaps was so surprised that he shut down emotionally and did not know what to say; and, he may have reactively done the only thing he could think of at the moment: he cut you off.

"Mike, it's important that you learn not to take such reactions personally. '**Think systems**' and just be ready to deal with the predictable resistance you will encounter. It's only when you are able to withstand the pressure to return to familiar patterns that you can claim to have made a real change in your basic level of differentiation.

"At some level, James will recognize and respect this in you."

Mike absorbed this information for a few moments, not saying anything. He realized that his anxiety about being too forthright in his conversation with James was really only a concern for himself. His conversation with Jacob was well-timed in the bigger game of helping CHI survive and succeed. James needed to deal with the problems at hand in a new way. Just building more hotels in smaller, less-developed markets was not going to help CHI in the long run.

Jacob interrupted Mike's train of thought. "Mike, we are out of time for sure now, but I know that you also wanted to talk about the wedding. Let's cover that at the next session."

"Sure," Mike said as he looked at his watch and realized it was time to pick Karla up at the auto repair shop on his way home. He picked up his handout, smiled at Jacob, and turned to leave.

MORE ABOUT DIFFERENTIATION OF SELF

Mike picked Karla up at the Acura dealership and suggested they go to dinner. She thought it was a great idea, so they headed for their favorite deli. They loved the little out-of-the-way restaurant—especially the barrels of free kosher pickles that were always stocked to the rim.

After they ordered, the conversation turned to events at Karla's work.

"We have closed only three homes and two condos in the entire office this month," Karla said. "The average length of time on the market for homes has gone up from about 22 days two years ago to over six months. A lot of our younger agents at Hale are starting to take second jobs to cover monthly bills, especially the ones with families."

"What do you have on the market now?" Mike asked.

"I am the listing agent on six homes at the moment, and I have two contracts in the works," Karla replied.

"It sounds like you are doing pretty well."

"Well, I have two couples who have moved and are renting apartments in other cities while they are waiting for their houses to sell. They will lose their patience soon."

"What are you doing to move your inventory?"

"I've decided to target market my little portfolio of homes to people in the UK, France, Germany, Spain and Japan."

"Really?" Mike stopped stirring his iced tea and focused on Karla. "How did you come up with that idea?"

"Well, I decided to find out who purchased the last fifty or so homes in the price range and location I work. The search covered the last 24 months. It turns out that there is a growing market for foreign nationals wanting to buy homes in several large cities in the US, and the DC area is among the top three."

"What are they using these homes for?" Mike asked.

"Almost exclusively speculation, so these buyers are really interested in a home in my price range with an occupant who is renting the home. They are looking for homes between $500,000 and $800,000 with renters who can carry about 75 to 100 percent of the PITI. They can put about 50 percent down. It's a great little formula, at least for now."

"Honey, that approach is very creative," Mike said.

"Well, we have to do something. The market is really slow."

"Are you having any problems?"

"The whole office, really the whole company, is upset with me for taking this direction. In fact, I have been asked by my boss and Hale leadership to stop using this tactic, or at least run it through their national marketing program."

"What are they so upset about?" Mike asked.

"I don't need their national marketing to reach people in other countries. And I am sharing part of my commission with realtors in these foreign countries as a finder's fee. It's my decision and a good one. I can't find people in Munich who want to buy a house in Falls Church, Virginia, but I know a woman in Germany who can."

"Karla, you don't seem worried about this situation," Mike said.

"Well, what is there to worry about? I am just trying to figure out how to sell homes. I am not really concerned about the national program at Hale, to be honest. I really do want to work with the leaders in the company. I've been there a long time. But I am not going to let them dictate where I go to find my buyers or how I set up the arrangement of the fees that are mine anyway.

"I love finding homes for people, especially young families with kids. The way I see it, I am helping about five groups of people by doing what I am doing. There is the seller, the buyer, the renter, the international agent and my family. And Hale gets a cut, too. That's pretty good."

Mike was thinking about the recent coaching sessions he had been having with Jacob as Karla was talking.

"Do you recall the concept of differentiation of self that I have been telling you about?" Mike asked.

"A little," Karla said.

"Well it seems to me that what you are doing at Hale is the

work of a very self-differentiating person," Mike said. "Jacob recently gave me some insight into what it takes for someone to be more of a 'self' in key relationships."

"Really? Like what?"

"I can't remember everything, but here are a few points he made. Differentiation of self requires not only great clarity about the vision you have for your life and the core principles that you wish to guide your behavior. It also requires considerable persistence and stamina, because your efforts will inevitably meet with some measure of resistance.

"Jacob was telling me about his mentor, Ed Friedman, who did a number of historical studies on the early explorers from the time of Columbus on. Friedman would often point out the single-minded tenacity that characterized their leadership. To others around them, such steadfast behavior in the face of seemingly overwhelming odds often seemed foolhardy, even ruthless. But the witness of history is pretty clear that these men exhibited the courage of their convictions and a bold spirit of adventure that allowed them to accomplish remarkable things."

Karla laughed. "Mike, I am not Christopher Columbus; I am just trying to sell houses in Falls Church, Virginia."

"Honey, it's the principle I am talking about."

"Okay, okay," Karla said.

"Jacob went on to point out that he was not talking only about the heroism of Christopher Columbus. In fact, he made the point that knowing your limitations—that is, having a realistic awareness of your strengths and weaknesses—is a very important characteristic of someone who takes a self-defining leadership position. Otherwise the charge of being delusional might be on target."

Karla burst into a full laugh. "Most everyone at the office thinks I am delusional when I talk about getting calls late at night from Osaka, Japan."

"I wondered what the hell all those late night calls were about," Mike said with a smile.

He continued, "Someone who leads with conviction is not unaware of his or her limitations. On the contrary, Jacob says there is a vulnerability that great leaders often display. They are not afraid to expose their ideas to ridicule or critique by others. They know they are fallible, but they still have the courage of their convictions and are willing to take risks for what they believe is the right course of action."

"Honey, you are making too much of all this. I am just selling homes, not conquering a new land."

Mike leaned forward and spoke with an intensity that Karla recognized whenever something mattered deeply to him. "Karla, you don't understand. I am not talking about the scope of the impact you are having. I am talking about the characteristics of leadership you are displaying—what Jacob calls differentiation of self."

Karla now saw how important this topic was to Mike, how passionate he had become. She shifted seamlessly from light dinner conversation to a much deeper level of discussion. She focused intently on Mike and what he was saying.

Mike continued, "In the challenges I face at CHI, Jacob has been helping me see that I must stay on course, see things through with James and Vanessa, even when James is skeptical or downright opposed to my line of reasoning. Doing so will be a stretch. It will require me to be a more differentiated 'self' than I am comfortable with. I see this same intentionality in what you are doing at Hale, and I want to learn from it."

"I see," Karla said softly.

"Jacob frequently reminds me about societal regression and how much reactivity there is in our world today. Being risk-adverse, losing the spirit of adventure, and always preferring to 'play it safe' are all symptoms of a regressed society.

"True leaders need to be bold enough to innovate, take risks, and hold steady, even when the going is tough. In order to pull that off, a leader has to have the capacity to step outside of the reactive emotional climate that surrounds him in order to keep the big picture in view.

"Jacob points out that knowing how to become a better observer of **emotional process**—in yourself and in those around you—is an essential skill for a leader who wishes to separate from the maelstrom of reactivity that swirls everywhere around us today. A leader has to be able to see it, and then step back from it, or else he will be captured by it like everyone else. Only someone who has a strong sense of self is capable of that kind of behavior, and that's why Jacob keeps insisting that to **focus on differentiation of self**, rather than on changing others, is the way to be a more effective leader."

Karla recognized that Mike was talking through these concepts as much for himself as for her. He was trying to integrate them more deeply into his own thinking in order to face the next 30 to 60 days at CHI.

"Does this make sense to you?" Mike finally asked.

"It does, Honey. It's just that I see these ideas and concepts applying to the work you are doing at CHI more so than to my work." Karla continued, "It seems that Jacob has a real gift for describing the deeper level of what goes on during the interaction between people."

Mike had caught his breath and launched out again.

"Let me tell you about respecting boundaries and how your actions at Hale really exemplify this key element of effective working relationships. People know how to respect boundaries when they have a good awareness of where their 'self' ends and the 'self' of others begins. This means that you know your limits, how far you are willing to go on an issue, and what you are not willing to do.

"When I hear you talk about your relationship with the Hale leadership team, I really hear you describing a delicate dance between the boundaries that you set for yourself and what you require of others where you work.

"I'm sure it's tricky and very subtle sometimes when you are negotiating and trying to be flexible. But you reach a point where you realize that if you go any further, you will be compromising a core principle, and I so admire how you always seem to know that point."

Karla added, "Well, I learned about what you and Jacob call boundaries when Jacelyn was two years old and I was expecting Richard. With a two-year-old like her, you better set up boundaries fast or you'll be done for. There were times, though, Mike, when the kids were little, that I felt like I had lost any sense of 'self.' I didn't know who I was—just me, or your wife, or the kids' mother, or whatever. The children were always demanding more, and pushing the boundaries is just what kids do. So I had to set limits to survive. I just called them 'ground rules' back then."

Mike responded, "Well, it's been my experience that in the business world it can be just as confusing and tempting to cross boundaries. Disrespecting a colleague's boundaries—or your own—can mean getting a big deal or contract or even a promotion. But in your gut you know that doing so will diminish your strength as a person and a leader. That's when the challenge of being more of a 'self' really costs something.

"Leaders inevitably come to times when they must stand alone on an issue."

"Leaders and parents," Karla added with a smile. "You know, Mike, you've always lived your life with great integrity. It's one of the things I most admire about you. I hope you don't think that Jacob is teaching you a brand new set of skills."

"No, I recognize that I came to him with a certain level of differentiation of self. I am realizing now, however, that often I was confusing a puffed up ego with the assertion of a strong sense of self. I just want to do better, to be a better person and leader. Jacob has also been very helpful to me in understanding the need to respect the boundaries of others. He pointed out that one of the most telling situations that reveals a leader's level of differentiation is whether he respects others when they disagree with him and take an opposite position.

"I learned a lot about myself on this point, and how easily I was caught up in my own ego. In the past, I often would have problems with people who disagreed with me. I would label them as stupid or hostile or close-minded. I would dismiss them and not take them seriously. In effect, I was refusing to respect the 'self' they were projecting because it conflicted with my own preference.

"I know I did that a lot with Jacelyn in the last 12 months."

"Honey, don't be so hard on yourself. You've been a great dad to Jacelyn and Richard."

"I think we've done a pretty good job—together—with the kids. But these days at work, I am much more able to handle disagreements without taking it personally or without ascribing motives to those on the other side of the issue. It hasn't been easy, but I have made progress. And on a practical level, I see that I am benefiting from a richer flow of ideas within the organization now. Instead of hearing only what subordinates think I want to hear, I am now cultivating an atmosphere where respectful disagreements are encouraged and even welcomed."

Karla interjected, "Jacob has been so helpful to you, Honey.

Will you be able to continue working with him after the decision, one way or another about the COO post?"

"Yes, I am sure I will want to continue with him—one way or another."

The check came for the dinner, and Mike pulled out his credit card. As the card was being processed, Karla asked Mike if Jacob had any other insights about differentiation of self.

"Jacob sums all of it up with the expression '**lead with conviction**,'" Mike said. "My take on it is: Be humble, listen respectfully and deeply, set and maintain your boundaries, respect the views and boundaries of others, take responsibility for your own part of the mess, do not take things personally, and don't be anxious even in troubling and difficult conflicts."

"Tall order," Karla said.

"Tall order," Mike repeated thoughtfully.

He signed the credit card voucher, put his wallet back into his pocket, and stood up from the table. Just then his cell phone rang. He looked at his watch to note it was 10:45 p.m. The call was from area code 724, western Pennsylvania. He did not recognize the number, but the caller ID read Memorial Hospital. It was Joyce.

Don had just had a massive heart attack. Mike got the basic facts and then put Karla on the line so Joyce could talk with her.

Chapter 8: Lead with Conviction

Review Key Points

- It is possible to distinguish between a person's *basic* level of differentiation and his or her *functional* level.
    - It is easier to influence the *functional* level of those whose *basic* level is at the lower end of the scale than it is those with a higher *basic* level.
    - A person's *functional* level of differentiation can be raised by:
        - Being part of a high-functioning system
        - Being in an atmosphere of lowered anxiety/reactivity
    - A person's *basic* level of differentiation can be raised by:
        - Learning more about Bowen Theory
        - Managing anxiety
        - Becoming clearer about life direction/goals
        - Gaining more self in key relationship systems
    - Raising one's *basic* level of self-differentiation is a gradual, long-term process that requires ongoing effort.

- An attempt to become more of a self will encounter a predictable pattern of resistance and provoke typical reactions such as the following:
    - You are wrong!
    - Change back!
    - If you don't change back, you will pay a price!

- One who **leads with conviction** displays certain characteristics:
    - Tenacity/steadfastness, even in the face of resistance and sabotage
    - Willingness to be exposed to ridicule
    - Adventurous, bold spirit, willing to take risks
    - Able to step aside from the surrounding emotional climate

- o Knows where the boundaries of **self** end and those of the **other** begin
    - Able to disagree with others and still respect their viewpoints
    - Willing to take responsibility for one's own contribution to a problem
    - Maintains a sense of personal limits

Questions for Reflection and Discussion

1. What behaviors did Mike demonstrate in his interactions with James McMaster that indicate continuing progress in his efforts to be a more differentiated self? What indications are there that he still has work to do?

2. In your work environment, what situations present the greatest challenge for you to maintain boundaries of self as you feel you ought?

3. Which relationship within your family of origin is characterized by the most intensity for you? Can you think of an example of how you typically revert in that relationship to a pattern where you display less self than might be the case in other relationships?

The Practice

1. Identify a relationship in which you have not set and effectively maintained boundaries and, as a result, your voice or your self is not fully established.

2. Specifically identify the circumstances or situations that most often cause you to lose your voice in this relationship.

3. Explore what might be some of the underlying issues that result in a lower functional level of self-differentiation in this relationship by becoming a more objective observer and noting, "What is happening in the relationship when this occurs?" Look for the recurring patterns that emerge from your observation of your loss of self. Determine some modest, practical steps you can take to transform the relationship into one in which you have more self.

Lead with Conviction

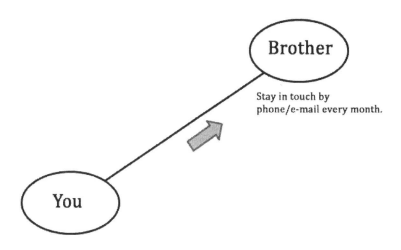

Stay in touch by phone/e-mail every month.

1. My brother and I argue about everything. I find it frustrating so I avoid talking with him.
2. When I talk with him, he declares his viewpoints as fact and quickly begins to argue if I have an alternative viewpoint on all but the most benign topics—weather, latest TV show episodes, etc. I end up "losing my voice" in conversations with him because I don't like to argue. So I seldom talk with him and when I do I hardly say anything in order to avoid a verbal confrontation.
3. I need to talk with my brother more often and begin to assert my own views about topics by pointing out to him that his point of view is interesting but I see things differently. I also need to recognize that bantering with him is a communication approach he enjoys and see that type of dialogue as engaging rather than unsafe and threatening.

To learn more, go to www.resilient-leadership.biz.

A New Way of **LEADING**

Chapter 9: Stay Connected

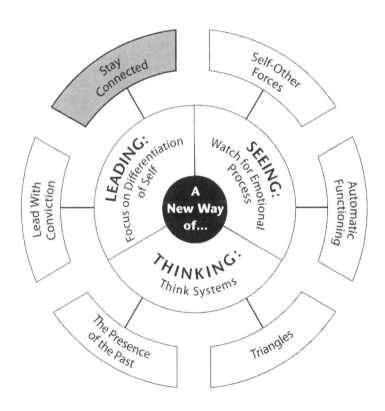

DON

Karla took the phone from Mike. Joyce filled her in on the events of the day. Don was tired all day and had taken an early afternoon nap. When he awoke from the nap, he ate a little bit of cereal and sat in front of the television for most of the afternoon. He was in good spirits although unusually quiet. They had a dinner engagement at a friend's house, which he decided to take a pass on. After a spirited discussion with Don insisting that she go on her own, Joyce went to dinner at about 5:30 p.m. When she got home a few hours later, she found him on the bathroom floor and called 911. His heartbeat was faint and erratic and he was unconscious.

As Karla and Joyce were talking on the phone, the emergency room physician interrupted and asked Joyce to come to Don's room as soon as possible. Joyce said goodbye to Karla and rushed back into the emergency room.

Don died at 11:10 p.m. without regaining consciousness.

The next morning, Karla took off for Zelienople while Mike stayed home to contact a few relatives, Jacelyn and Russ, Richard and Lilly, and then his dad. After some discussion, all four kids decided not to return north to attend the funeral, but Mike Senior wanted to go. Mike also contacted Vanessa and asked that the upcoming meeting with James be delayed until his return from the funeral. Crystal helped Mike rearrange his schedule for the next three days.

The funeral was held on a Thursday morning at 10:00 a.m. Mike drove to Front Royal early on Wednesday to pick up his dad on his way to Pennsylvania. The ride over was the first time that the two had spent more than 30 minutes alone with one another since Mike was a young boy living at home. Once the shock of Don's unexpected death and the impact that it would have on his family was discussed, Mike Senior began to talk about his younger days, retelling many of the stories that he had told many times before. Mike was mindful that the number of days he had left with his dad were numbered, and he listened patiently. He had been thinking about a remark that his dad had made at the wedding just before Jacelyn and Russ left for their honeymoon. In his mind, Mike replayed the comment as best he could remember it:

"We can only take each other in small doses. I am set in my ways, and you have been headstrong since the day you were born. We both ought to try a little harder."

"Dad, how upsetting is Don's death to you?" Mike asked.

"Well, I am sad for his family more than upset. It is so difficult to have a child die before you do, and I think Ben and Mary and of course Carol must really be suffering. Don was really young—44 or 45, wasn't he? Have you spoken to any of them?"

"No, I haven't, but we will see them at the wake tonight," Mike replied.

They went for a long time without saying anything before Mike spoke again.

"Dad, let me ask you a question. Is the care you are getting at Silverstone meeting your needs now?"

"No one really likes living there, but it is not a terrible place. It's just that you do not have a reason to get up in the morning when you live in a place like Silverstone. After my heart attack, it was good to get a rest so I could recover. But I am tired of resting now. I wish I had a job to get up and go to every day, or almost every day."

Mike noticed that, for some reason, his dad was much less judgmental in his thinking and speaking on this trip than in recent visits. The conversation was not burdened with innuendos and sideway accusations. It seemed to Mike that some of the feistiness was gone out of the old guy. Maybe his dad was different because they were alone in the car and there was no need for a performance. But he still kept his guard up.

At Cumberland they stopped for gas and Mike Senior offered, in fact insisted, that he pay to fill the tank up. Mike finally agreed and asked his dad why it was so important that he pay for a tank of gas. Mike learned that Mike Senior had just recently gotten a big check from Don as final repayment for the old loan. His dad had finally gotten his money back, and he was trying to use some of it.

"When did Don repay you, Dad?" Mike asked.

"Oh, about two weeks ago, I guess."

Mike wondered if Don had a sense that something was going to happen to him. He then thought that maybe Joyce now wished they had kept the money or maybe she was glad that the loan was repaid before Don died. He did not know exactly how to think about the set of circumstances. He finally realized that it was the wrong time to even think about such things.

The drive continued with amicable talk, no accusations and there was a sense of comfortable companionship in the car. Mike was beginning to think his dad had actually changed—for the better.

The wake that evening and the funeral the next day were attended by many local family members and friends. Mike, his brother-in-law Herb and his cousin Tom, along with three close friends of Don were pallbearers. A graveside service followed the Catholic Mass. The women of St. Patrick's hosted a reception at Joyce and Don's house to conclude the ceremonies of the day. Mike was very glad that he and his family had visited with Joyce and Don just a few months earlier. It seemed that a lot of issues had been settled before Don died. Karla had helped Joyce with a number of decisions during the days since Don's death and Joyce was very appreciative of her help.

Mike began to lower his defenses and open up to his father more and more over the two days between their ride to Pennsylvania and the return trip. They began to talk a lot about everything from baseball to current events. Mike was now convinced that his father was really turning over a new leaf, and Mike Senior was convinced that his son had done the same.

As he reflected on the shift, however, Mike began to understand more clearly that it was not simply a case of this father changing for the better. Mike realized that the work he had been doing on his own automatic functioning was somehow involved in the changed relationship with his dad. He recalled that Jacob had often stressed to him that when a person begins to "**think systems**," he or she recognizes the extent to which relationships involve reciprocal functioning. Mike saw that in some elusive but real way his growing ability to manage anxiety was allowing more space for his father to regulate his reactivity, and the result was a much less stressful dialogue between them. It gave Mike a new perspective on his tendency to blame the other person whenever his relationship with that person was stormy.

When they said good-bye at the retirement center, Mike Senior shook his son's hand longer than usual and placed his other hand on his son's shoulder for the first time in over 40 years. This act of compassion was the closest either of them would ever come to a hug, but they both noticed the difference.

Third Alternative

Over the next few days, Mike began the due diligence process in earnest. Three teams of internal and external auditors were visiting each of the hotels to develop a summary prospectus for further research. Before this step, a response to the initial tender describing the fundamental elements of James' "duplex" concept had been provided to the mystery suitor in London and was met with enthusiastic agreement. It was soon learned that Universal Holding was the company interested in the deal. Their business development and legal team was working out of London, but the parent company and the decision makers were in Stockholm. They were very capable of delivering on the financial commitment should an agreement be reached.

Vanessa was preparing to work with Mike and James to find the third alternative they spoke about at the last meeting. She knew that alignment needed to be achieved if at all possible before they arrived in Scottsdale. Both men had mellowed somewhat from their recent meeting with Vanessa, and they were ready to meet and try to find common ground. Vanessa had thought a lot about this meeting and decided to be sure that all three of them had the same financial data as a basis for their discussion. She and the CFO compiled a comprehensive summary for CHI YTD and for the last five years. In addition there was a detailed summary of the financial performance for the 17 hotels that was emerging from the due diligence process. The information was distributed ahead of time. Vanessa invited the CFO, Mercedes Zito, to the meeting with the approval of both James and Mike. They started at 9:00 a.m.

During the first 45 minutes of the meeting, Mercedes ran through the financial overview and answered questions. Comparable business unit sales were basically flat over the last three years. Comparable unit margin growth was about four percent year over year for the entire company and there were a number of geographical areas that were down by as much as eight percent. Only six metropolitan areas showed substantial real growth year over year. All in all the company was growing, albeit slightly, only because of new unit openings or room additions to existing units. The core of CHI was in trouble.

Vanessa asked Mike to review with them his thinking about

how to move forward. Mike quickly restated his belief that the company was basically sound and that they should have a four-point plan:

1. Work with the top 100 CHI leaders to redefine the business strategy. Start by answering the following four questions:
   - What is our organizational passion?
   - What are the markets and who are the customers we choose to serve?
   - What is our value proposition for those markets and customers?
   - What structure do we need to have and what competencies do we need to develop and nurture to excel in our value proposition?

2. Enter new markets and refurbish units in existing markets with a focus on local and regional group, contract and transient business.

3. Exit the large national and international convention business if supported by a new business model for CHI.

4. Aggressively pursue the emerging deal with Universal Holdings. Find a way to make the deal work utilizing James' strategy.

Then Vanessa asked James for his reaction. He agreed with Mike's four points in general, but had questions about point #1.
"We discussed this list before; my question the other day was, and still is, about the first bullet point. I do not understand what we are talking about when we speak about organizational passion."
To emphasize his point, James began to count on his three fingers as he spoke.
"Our passion is, one—providing customer service, two—taking care of employees and three—make money. Isn't that how you both see CHI? What am I missing?"
Mike was ready.
"James, I believe that CHI has a corporate passion for only one of these concepts: making money."

Mike went on, "Let me say it another way. Throughout CHI today, any of our hotel operators will do whatever they can, short of breaking the law, to maximize profits. The pressure we place on them is so great that they will lower their standards, cut corners, take advantage of their employees and in the end even reduce customer service to meet their number one priority—make money."

"But you make money by taking care of customers, not by cutting corners," James exclaimed.

"Well, over the long run you do, but in the short run taking care of employees and servicing customers may cost you money," Mike said.

Mike went on, "I have learned a lot about anxiety through my coaching with Jacob. He has taught me how to recognize and understand chronic anxiety in my own family and in my CHI family as well. In CHI there is a constant current of anxiety tied to quarterly profits.

"James, from my work with Jacob I have come to believe that this chronic anxiety has been passed down through the decades from the beginning of our company. You have so often spoken of your intense focus on making money for your own family as a young man, and I can't help but think that some of that sense of urgency has been passed down in the way we operate CHI."

James leaned forward across the table and Vanessa was afraid he was going to explode at Mike before he finished. Mike seemed oblivious to James' body language.

"James, you have often told the story of how you learned to run your business with a clear focus on the principle that 'cash is king.' And no one can dispute the success you have had here at CHI. But there has been a hidden, unseen cost we have paid because of the anxiety that has accompanied that mantra as it has been passed on in the organization."

James could not contain himself any longer. "What the hell are you talking about, Mike?"

Mike's face reddened, but he remained calm and even managed to smile at James, hoping it would ease the tension. "Now, calm down, Mr. McMaster, and hear me out. The impact of your mantra has been both positive and negative. We need to have an intense focus on making money, but not to the extent that we make emotional and reactive decisions about how to run the business. You know that, of course, but some of the people at other levels in this organization become anxious and focus too narrowly on just showing a profit. Jacob has shown me that too much chronic anxiety causes fear; and fear causes people to make short-sighted or even irrational decisions."

"I still don't know what the hell you're talking about, Mike."

James McMaster was visibly shaken, but it was clear that he was listening intently to what Mike was saying. This gave Mike further courage to continue.

"Here is a recent example. At our hotel in Baltimore near the airport, the increase in gas costs resulted in the management deciding to run the airport shuttle twice an hour rather than every ten minutes during peak check-in and check-out times. It seemed like a good idea on paper when the controller quickly penciled out the savings. It may be a good idea, too. It depends on how it is implemented, however. When your weekday transient business traveler is depending on a shuttle every ten minutes and you make this type of a change with no notice, it causes a lot of disruption, a lot of unhappy customers.

The people who run that hotel are smart people. When I asked them why they made the decision, I could see that it was a knee-jerk reaction to several periods of poor financial performance. They did not think—they reacted. They reacted out of fear—probably fear that I created as their VP of operations and my constant focus on the bottom line."

"So, what does this have to do with the way I've run this company?"

"Mr. McMaster, because we do not have a clearly defined corporate vision that is shared by every employee up and down the chain of command, we rely in our decision-making on our best understanding about how things really work around CHI. People watch how more senior leaders make decisions and expend resources, and they decide that is acceptable here at CHI. For the most part, that decision-making is centered on making money far more often than taking care of employees or customers. We simply do not have a counterweight to our 'cash is king' mantra."

Mike was beginning to worry that he had gone too far. He turned to Vanessa for help. "Vanessa, you remember the situation you described to me early on in your career, with the

VP in Denver who clashed with you over short- and long-term fixes for a downturn in business. Wasn't that an example of you looking for a quick-fix solution that produced cash, rather than making a calmer decision about what was best for the business in the long run?"

Vanessa realized Mike was looking for her to throw him a lifeline. She also realized that this was one time that she did not want to be triangled into a disagreement between James and Mike. She was not going to take Mike's side and further escalate James' resistance. She said, "Mike, I understand the point you are trying to make, but I think it's important that you and James come to a common understanding of the issue you are trying to highlight."

Mike knew he was on his own, and so he turned back to James and tried to further moderate his tone, which he feared had become too aggressive.

"Mr. McMaster, the other day when I wrote those three words on a sheet of paper and stuck it under your nose, I believe I offended you. If I did, I sincerely apologize. What I was trying to do perhaps in a clumsy way was share with you my perception that your model of thinking as a young man—which has been so successful for you—has been effectively passed down from one generation of CHI leaders to the next.

"This is only my interpretation, and I may be off base here for even suggesting it, but it seems to me that, along with the mantra, the anxiety that you surely felt as a young man struggling to feed your family and launch a successful business has also been passed down as part of CHI's corporate culture. If I am right about that, then that anxiety has guided a great deal of the functioning of CHI for a long time. It's what Jacob **calls the presence of the past** in a system."

Mike paused, gauging James' reaction to what he had been saying. Then he added, "I'll keep quiet now if you tell me I'm out of line here."

"No, Mike, I want you to continue. I'm not sure I agree with your analysis, but I want to hear you out. Please continue."

"Thank you, Mr. McMaster. It seems to me that during the years this deeply embedded belief has had positive consequences for our company, and CHI has benefited from this belief in many ways. But there have also been a few huge problems created by our sometimes anxious, singular focus on short-term cash flow.

"Here is another example of what I mean. This problem has shown up time and again in our marketing function. We have had a revolving door in our marketing department because of this problem. Marketing professionals and consultants come and go here at CHI because they cannot get us to define ourselves, beyond wanting to make money. So they fail at creating a marketing strategy. They try for a year or two, and then they leave because of conflict with you or because they run right into a cultural brick wall.

"We cannot continue to operate CHI this way. Your influence in the company is stronger today than it ever has been, even if you do not travel to operations very much anymore. The impact that you have on CHI's **emotional process** is so strong because of your powerful leadership and sustained focus over the years."

Mike paused for a long moment. Vanessa was staring intently at James, trying to read his reaction to Mike's impassioned presentation.

Mike continued, "In my view, 'CASH IS KING' is only one-third of the vision that we need to guide us. The other two-thirds are: 'EMPLOYEE IS KING' and 'CUSTOMER IS KING.' From working closely with you in the last few years, I know that you personally think in this broader context. But I have got to tell you, Mr. McMaster, people out in the field only have the first third of the vision in mind when they make decisions. If we are to broaden their vision to match your own, then you and I together will have to work on lowering the chronic anxiety over profits that has been part of the CHI culture for so long. I can help you do that, but I can't do it without your strong support."

James put both of his hands up to stop Mike. He looked at Vanessa. "Vanessa, how do you see it? I need to know your honest thinking on this issue."

Vanessa realized she could not longer keep her views to herself any longer. She said softly, "James, he's right. I could not have said it any better."

Mike was looking down at the room, as he had learned to do since working with Jacob, and he felt a deep calm, regardless of the outcome of this crucial meeting. He knew he was being true to himself, and at that point little else mattered to him.

"Mr. McMaster, I will simply add one more point," Mike said. "I have the utmost regard for all that you have done to bring CHI to the place it is now. Please do not misinterpret my comments. I am deeply committed to the company and to you as the founder. Furthermore, I am confident, if you choose me to help you lead the company, together we can utilize the strong foundation that you have created to forge a bright and very profitable future. We have so much going for us, and while we need to make significant changes, the opportunity to succeed is standing right in front of us. We can do this."

Vanessa spoke again, "James, Mike is right about the current situation in CHI and about the need for change—big change—right now. He's also right about the opportunity we have ahead of us."

James McMaster knew that he could no longer dismiss the point that Mike and Vanessa were making. But he was still not willing to give up completely. He asked only one question. "Mike, how can you be so sure that we should leave the convention business in all the key locations we operate today—places like Chicago and Orlando and New Orleans? I know we have all the industry data that tells us that the segment is headed for a difficult time, but we are in these cities now, and we have premier locations, and we have business on the books for the immediate future. I just can't see why you want to walk away from such a sizable portion of our bread and butter business."

Mike realized that this issue was a major sticking point for McMaster. He had already carefully reviewed the facts and projections that led to his recommendation. James was in a reactive mode and his emotions were very strong on this issue. He also remembered Jacob's warning that he needed to work on listening more deeply to the viewpoint of those who disagreed with him.

Mike said, "James, you are making a very good point, and I don't want to walk away from assets that we will someday regret losing. If we take the steps I am recommending, we will need to use our full leadership team to develop a refreshed CHI business strategy. Let's put the review of the data and the decision in their hands and trust they will help us make the right decision. They may see some aspects that both you and I are missing."

James forced a smile and said, "Fair enough. I never have been able to win an argument with that damn Jacob Wolfe! Tell him I said so, Mike."

Both men realized they had reached a workable compromise, even if they had put off making any final decisions. They smiled at each other with the satisfaction of dealmakers who have arrived at a win-win solution.

Then James added, "I'm ready to develop our briefing for the Board, based on the four points that you have discussed with Vanessa and me."

Vanessa sat back in her chair and felt a heavy weight slip off her shoulders.

PHOENIX AND KELLY O'REILLY

Mike had not yet completed the full due diligence process, but it was already clear that there was a solid basis to enter into serious discussions with Universal Holdings. The remainder of the Board agenda was set, and briefings were prepared and distributed ahead of time. The schedule would be hectic. It included one-on-one interviews with the Chairman of the Board, Martin Flowers, whom Mike had met before, and with the Review and Nominating Sub-Committee. James, Vanessa and Mike were traveling together on a chartered jet, and they were to meet Kelly O'Reilly for dinner at a popular Scottsdale steakhouse.

Mike thought it a bit odd that he would be having dinner with the person who was his biggest competition for the COO position, the last person to beat out, so to speak. As he thought about it, however, he could see how awkward things could get during the three days if they were not properly introduced. Plus, he was really interested in meeting her and sizing her up.

The flight to Phoenix was wonderful; Mike mused that there is nothing like traveling on a private jet. The three arrived at Sky Harbor International Airport and took a taxi to their hotel in Scottsdale. They went to their rooms, freshened up and met back in the lobby to travel to the restaurant. It was a short trip, and they arrived before Kelly and took a quiet table in the back of the restaurant.

They ordered wine and made small talk as they waited for Kelly. Most of the patrons were businessmen in their later forties and early fifties. When Kelly entered the restaurant, you could actually see conversation stop around her. Kelly was more than six feet tall in her bare feet and she had very high heels on. Her long, red hair, bright-green eyes, beautiful smile and elegant, statuesque appearance caused the patrons in the room not only to stop talking; they almost broke into applause. It was as if Miss Universe had just walked into the restaurant. Even the waiters stopped to look at her. Mike felt himself flush when he stood up to say hello. She was unbelievable. Mike's self confidence sank like a rock.

But as dinner unfolded, it became clear that in addition to her stunning appearance, she was also gracious, warm, witty, self-assured but most of all a genuinely kind woman. She was also smart as hell, a lot smarter than Mike, by his own observation. Yet her true attraction was her fun-loving Irish character. She had a wonderful Irish brogue and an infectious smile and laugh. Mike ended the evening liking her a lot and feeling very comfortable with her. And she had taken a real shine to Mike, too. Dinner turned out to be a great deal of fun.

That night Mike reviewed the day's activities with Karla over the phone. When Mike described Kelly in such enthusiastic terms, Karla felt a burst of jealously bubble up, but it lasted for only a few seconds. She asked the key question: why on Earth was a woman like Kelly not selected for the COO position at the British airline she just left? It was not Mike's place to ask such a question at dinner that night, but it certainly was a good question. Mike concluded that Vanessa and James must know the answer.

CHI BOARD OF DIRECTORS

The logistics of the three days were such that Mike and Kelly were to attend and interact with the full Board during the first two days of the meeting and interview with the eight nominating committee members in the evenings. The Board meeting would continue for a third day, but Mike and Kelly would not attend the meeting that day. Both decided to leave Phoenix early in the morning of day three.

All three days of the Board meeting were extremely taxing. The schedule was packed and the Board members worked hard both day and night. The agenda for the first and second day included presentations on CHI Operational Challenges and Solutions, Long Term Growth Strategy, including the due diligence process Mike had nearly completed, Labor Union Issues/Contract Terms, and a review of pending Congressional Legislation that impacted the hospitality business. Mike assisted with the due diligence report-out on the first day, and both he and Kelly attended most of the other discussion sessions.

On the third day, Board members participated in an activity they were unaccustomed to, but one they were excited about. They provided feedback to James on the two COO candidates. Four interview sessions had been arranged for the late afternoon and early evenings of both days. Over the two days Kelly and Mike individually had interviewed with a total of eight Board members. Each of the four interview sessions included two Board members and either Mike or Kelly. The interviews were cordial but intense and wide-ranging. Mike's confidence grew with each passing interview.

On the evening before the third and final day of the meeting, James called Helen to talk about the Board meeting and his thoughts on continuing as CEO. They had been having ongoing discussions about this for months. He had been considering retirement for some time and while Vanessa was a very effective COO, she did not have an interest in assuming his role. Some months ago he and Vanessa sat down and discussed the subject and agreed it was time for Vanessa to move on. CHI needed a new COO who had the capabilities and interest to eventually assume the CEO role. The decision being made there in Scottsdale was, for all intents and purposes, a decision about the most likely candidate to succeed James as CEO. During the conversation that night, Helen and James reached the decision that he would retire from active involvement two years from the time the new COO was in place. During these two years he would work to build his trust and confidence in that person and prepare him or her to assume the CEO role.

The full morning of the third day was devoted to discussions about the two candidates. An advocate for each candidate presented the credentials and interview findings for his or her charge, one for Mike, and one for Kelly. The conclusions of the Board would result in a recommendation to James and the foregone conclusion was that the recommendation would be accepted. In practical terms, only if James and Martin Flowers agreed to reject the Board's recommendation would a different decision be made.

After three hours of intense and thorough debate, the Board recommended that James hire Kelly O'Reilly as the new COO to replace Vanessa Jackson. Their line of reasoning was clear. A change in direction was needed for CHI. Kelly had the business and financial acumen, strategic thinking abilities, and senior-level experience needed to make deals and drive the business. Mike was a great operator, but he was not a highly skilled strategic thinker. Two days earlier the Board had agreed to begin discussions with Universal Holdings; and to a person, they felt that Kelly would be much more effective than Mike in this setting.

The meeting ended with James thanking the Board for all their work and mentioning that he was taking their recommendation to hire Kelly very seriously, but his mind was not made up yet. He and Vanessa discussed the events of the week as they flew back to Reagan National Airport. He asked Vanessa what she thought of the Board's recommendation. She said she thought Kelly would make a wonderful choice to succeed her. Then she paused and added, "And Mike would make an even better one."

James knew he had to make a decision quickly to accept or reject the Board's recommendation about Kelly. During the flight, he called back to the office and asked Helen to set up a one-hour conference call with Martin Flowers for 10:00 the next morning. He also called and left messages for Mike and Kelly thanking them for their excellent participation during the week's activities.

CRUX OF THE DECISION

"Hello, Martin, how was your trip home yesterday?"

"It was just fine. Flights in and out of Atlanta and Phoenix are often troubled by bad weather, but last night was very calm."

Martin was the president and CEO of Flowers Incorporated, a large investment company operated out of Atlanta, Georgia.

James got right to the point of his call. "Martin, first of all thank you for conducting a very successful meeting in Scottsdale. I am excited about the decisions we made, especially related to our growth plans."

"We did have one of our best Board meetings, James," Martin said. "But I also can tell that you are unsettled about the recommendation of the Board to hire Kelly. Tell me what you are thinking."

"Well, it's really not that complicated. Kelly is a truly remarkable candidate, but I don't know her well at all. I have spoken with her probably ten times in the last six months and met with her three times. The headhunter did a great job in finding her. They did what we asked them to do. I just do not know her very well."

"I can tell it's more than that, James. What else is on your mind?"

"I have as much confidence in her as could be expected for such a short period of time. She is certainly more experienced in a corporate setting than Mike and has much stronger credentials. She will pick up the specifics of the business in a matter of a few months. But here's what is really troubling me: She doesn't have the hotel business in her blood. It's one thing to have a person of her abilities in the CFO post, but another to have her as COO and perhaps eventually as CEO."

Then James broke the news about his retirement plans to Martin. They had been talking about James' desire to retire for some time, but now a timeline had been established.

"James, you must be completely comfortable with the person you place in this role and believe that he or she has what it will take to replace you in only two years; that's not a long time."

"I simply am not settled on this decision, Martin. I realize I need to move quickly."

"Take your time. Think it over. I also suggest that you consider a couple of other possibilities. You could hire Kelly and promote Mike at the same time. Right now you have the COO, CFO and Chief Legal Counsel reporting to you. Suppose you create a new position for Kelly, a senior strategic development position of some sort, and also replace Vanessa with Mike. Something like that may work."

James and Vanessa had discussed just such a possibility on the flight home. After thoroughly discussing the option with Martin, James ended the call. "Martin, I will get back to you on my thoughts sometime tomorrow if you are available."

"I will be in my office all day tomorrow; call any time."

James hung up the phone and asked Vanessa to come in to discuss options. In the course of several hours, it was preliminarily decided to offer Kelly a position as chief strategic officer, with an additional interim assignment for one to two years as senior vice president for the Northeast Division. In the strategic planning role she would report to James and in the temporary operational role she would report to Mike. James realized that he could postpone the decision about selecting his successor for some time if he had both candidates working together in leadership positions. He could spend the next year or two working with both of these leaders to get a deeper awareness of who would be the best person to replace him. He spoke to Helen and to Martin several times to bounce ideas off both of them, and by the end of the day he decided to sleep on his final decision one more night and take action the next day unless he changed his mind.

James was up early the next morning. His first call was to Jacob Wolfe. He had one question for Jacob. After he reviewed the basics of the situation he asked, "Jacob, is Mike ready to be COO of CHI?"

Jacob hesitated and then responded, "James, you know if I answer that question it would be a breach of confidentiality."

James laughed, "I knew you'd say that, Jacob. I was curious how you'd respond. What I really want is for you to help me formulate the key questions I need to answer to make sure my decision is the right one."

Jacob was silent as he mulled over his response. Then he said, "James, here are some questions you need to answer:

"Do you trust Mike to carry on your legacy at CHI? Can you trust him with what you've built?

"Does he have the courage and the stamina to face the resistance he will surely encounter as he leads the organization in a new direction? Will he **lead with conviction**?

"Is he the kind of leader your employees will want to follow? Does he inspire confidence in the people whose efforts will ultimately make or break the success of CHI?"

After Jacob finished speaking, there was a long silence between the two men. James completely trusted Jacob's wisdom and admired his forthrightness. He never pulled punches, not from the first day they met at Cornell over forty years ago. "Thank you, Jacob," he said. "I knew that whatever you said would make it very clear to me what I needed to do."

After hanging up with Jacob, James reviewed his thinking and decision with Helen, called Martin to provide a quick summary, and with all in agreement dialed Kelly O'Reilly in London. He explained that he wanted both her and Mike on his leadership team, and felt that Mike's experience with CHI better suited him for the COO position. After he thoroughly explained his offer to her, Kelly enthusiastically accepted the dual position. James was very pleased and advised Kelly that he would need to contact several people and get back to her later in the day about some further details.

When he arrived in the office later in the morning and brought Vanessa up to date on his decision, she pointed out the impact this decision would have on those people inside CHI who would have wanted to be considered for a promotion behind Mike. It was decided not to communicate the temporary nature of the operational job, at least in the beginning of Kelly's role. They would have to manage the negative impact of this decision, but they were sure that Kelly possessed the skill and determination to deal with the internal resentment she would inevitably encounter.

By midday, James called Kelly back and reached a final agreement on compensation, start date and several other issues on which she had needed clarification. He turned over all remaining specifics of the offer to Vanessa. It was now time to talk with Mike.

James asked Mike to come to his office to meet with him and Vanessa. When Mike walked in, he knew that this was the moment he would either relish for a long time or suffer for a long time.

James offered Mike the job and described how they made the decision. He also described the arrangement they had reached with Kelly. Mike was stunned and excited at the same time. The meeting did not last more than a few minutes. They agreed to meet the next morning to begin preparations for announcements and transition planning. Mike shook James' hand, and with a great deal of warmth Vanessa hugged Mike and told him how proud she was of his accomplishments over the last year.

Mike left James' office, went into his office, closed the door and called Karla. She did not answer her cell phone, so he left a message asking her to call back as soon as possible. He sat down in his chair and stared out the window. He was filled with excitement and dread at the same time.

He quietly whispered, "My God, what have I gotten myself into?"

He then picked up the phone and called Jacob.

Brief Celebration

Mike gave Jacob the good news. Jacob was excited and congratulated Mike for his remarkable accomplishment. Mike knew that Jacob had a lot to do with the progress he had made, but he would never find out that James had called Jacob to ensure his instincts about Mike were on target. They went on to make two more coaching appointments in the next two weeks so that they could complete their discussion about the final element of the **Resilient Leadership** model: **stay connected**.

When she called Mike back, Karla was ecstatic and wanted to call both the kids as soon as Mike got home. She also suggested that they celebrate by going to their favorite bed and breakfast inn, which was on the eastern shore of Delaware about four hours from their home. She made a reservation for the weekend as soon as they hung up the phone. When Mike got home, he told Karla that he wanted to call his father first. The two men had a brief but moving conversation, as his dad told Mike how proud he was of him, and Mike—suddenly and surprisingly teary-eyed—told his father how grateful he was for all that he had done for him over the years. Next, Karla called Jacelyn and Russ and then Richard and Lilly to give them the news and just catch up on other events going on in their lives.

The next three days Mike met with Vanessa and James to map out next steps. First and foremost, Mike and Vanessa needed to inform key investors, advisors and analysts about the new COO and chief strategic officer/division vice president.

A number of other administrative issues were discussed and resolved or delayed for discussion later. Mike was just getting a taste of the significant scope change of his new position. The biggest difference he could see in the first three days of discussions was that he was giving up a lot of the day-to-day operational issues and beginning to focus on external CHI relationships.

By Friday afternoon Mike was exhausted. He drove home at about 5:30 p.m. He and Karla quickly decided to delay their plans to visit Lewes by one night so he could rest on Friday night and get up early Saturday morning to head to the eastern shore.

The weather was spectacularly beautiful on Saturday and Sunday in Lewes. On weekends, the small coastal town is a haven for people escaping the pressure of DC.

On Saturday afternoon Karla and Mike walked the main streets, visiting some small art studios and a favorite shop that sells nothing but puzzles. They stopped in a coffee shop, and Karla told Mike that she had some important things she wanted to discuss with him.

After they ordered, Karla said, "Honey, you know how proud I am of your accomplishments at CHI, but I want you to know that you have also grown so much as a father, son and husband, too. Over the last year or so I have seen you really begin to examine your own actions and invest in the efforts needed to improve your family relationships. It has had an impact on Jacelyn and Richard that is very apparent when we get together as a family. But the biggest change I see in you is in relation to your dad. Somehow the two of you have decided to talk with one another instead of at one another, and it is wonderful to see. The change the two of you have made in your relationship affects all of us. When the two of you are easier with each other, it creates a much safer and more open environment for the rest of us."

Mike was surprised that the tensions he had felt with his father had been a burden for the rest of the family, and he felt embarrassed at the same time as he felt good over Karla's affirmation of the improvements he had made.

"Thanks, Sweetheart," Mike said. "I'm really sorry for being such a jerk in so many ways in the past. I have been trying to be a better person, but I know that I slip backwards on occasion. I have benefited from this change more than anyone. I can see how my own approach to things—Jacob calls it my functioning—makes all the difference in the response I get from others. It is not as though I have learned an entirely new way of acting, but I am just so much more aware of myself and more in control of my own anxieties. Jacob has done a good job just 'waking me up,' so to speak.

A New Way of Leading

"One area of family where I still seem to be falling short is reading the book that Richard asked me to read. I have it on audiotape, but never find the time to listen to the tape in the car. Typically my commuting time is too short, and I am almost always on the phone when I am driving anyway, except in the District."

Karla suggested that they both listen to the tape on the way back from Lewes on Sunday evening. She concluded, "I have enjoyed your coaching with Jacob, too. I have learned a lot from you as you have studied and talked about your work with him. Sometimes I feel like he is coaching me, too."

The conversation turned to other subjects, but Mike thought a lot about what Karla said and began to wonder how he would continue to find time for Jacob with his new role. He worried that he might slip backward and somehow lose the gains he had made.

Early Sunday evening they began the ride home and listened to the tape of *A New Earth*. They both agreed that Sunday evening was not the best time to listen to a tape on spirituality that was as deep as the Tolle book, but Mike listened to the tape as Karla fell asleep.

COACHING THE NEW COO

Mike was late for his appointment with Jacob. His schedule was so busy now that everything was getting cut short. As he drove up to Jacob's office, he wondered if Jacob would consider coming to CHI now to save time. He decided to wait until another day to ask the question.

"Hello, Mr. COO," Jacob said with a big grin as Mike knocked and opened the door. They shook hands a little longer than usual as Jacob made sure that Mike knew how proud he was of the accomplishment.

"So, do my fees get to go up now that you are the COO?" Jacob asked with a laugh.

"Sure they do," Mike agreed with a smile. Mike thought about the fact that he did not even know what Jacob's fees were.

Jacob continued, "Well where do we go from here?"

"I want to stay focused on the **Resilient Leadership** model," Mike said.

"That's the right idea, Mike. We are arriving at the part of the model that can really be of a lot of help to you as you begin the work needed to help CHI continue to succeed. Are you ready to go?" Jacob asked.

"I am ready," Mike said with enthusiasm.

Jacob began, "Mike, we've been talking a good deal lately about the need for a leader to focus on his own differentiation. Can you give me your thoughts about differentiation? How would you define it?"

Mike thought for a minute and then said, "Differentiation is the state of mind and set of actions you take when you maintain a balance between what we have been calling cutoffs and at the other end of the line, fusion."

Jacob went on, "Good, that's a fine way to summarize the first half of differentiation. The second half is about a person's ability to keep the right balance in their thinking and feeling responses. I've indicated what it means to **lead with conviction**, but as you know, my **Resilient Leadership** model also includes another aspect of differentiation, which I refer to as the ability to **stay connected**. I suspect you've already noticed that these two phrases represent yet another version of the kind of balancing act we've spoken of so frequently in the past. In fact, both of my phrases—**lead with conviction** and **stay connected**—are simply a practical application of the **self-other** continuum we've been working on from the beginning. Staying connected is a practical application of how togetherness works, and leading with conviction is about individuality, being a 'self' able to take clear I-positions.

"I'd like to explore several aspects of what it means to **stay connected** as a resilient leader. But before we get into the details, it's helpful to remember why this is such an important topic. The fundamental insight is that you can only influence a system to which you are connected. And you realize, of course, that I'm referring to the emotional system—the relationship network—that is the underlying dynamic of any organization."

Mike responded, "I like your phrase about **emotional process** being the *hidden chemistry* of an organization. That's an idea that has stuck with me and really helped me understand why it's so important to pay attention to that level of systems dynamics."

"Exactly. The other thing that is important to recall is how powerful your presence is when you occupy the position of leader in any system. Your emotional field, if you know what I mean by that expression, is extremely contagious, and how you are functioning at that level exerts an influence on others throughout the system that is hard to exaggerate."

Mike added, thinking out loud, "So, it's not just the *fact* that I am staying connected, but the *way* I'm connected that is important?"

"Right again! We've often talked about how detrimental it is when an organization has high levels of chronic anxiety and becomes very reactive. Many of the situations we've dealt with over the months have basically been the result of reactive functioning on the part of individuals or whole segments of CHI. There's no way to get around the cost to an organization that has to deal constantly with symptoms of heightened reactivity. That's why one of the primary roles of a leader is to lower anxiety and reactivity within the system."

"I know what you're going to say," Mike jumped in with a grin. "That the way a leader is best able to lower the reactivity of the system is by managing his own reactivity."

Jacob laughed, "Sounds like you're ready to graduate. You've got it figured out."

"Sure, but we both know that it's one thing to understand it in your head, quite another to practice it regularly. Thanks for the affirmation, but I think I need to work with you a bit longer, especially now that I am in the COO post, if I'm going to keep on applying these principles on a regular basis."

"Well, you're right, Mike, that it takes a long time before this level of new learning becomes second nature. And I hope that my coaching continues to support your efforts. There's really not a lot of theory left for me to teach you, but of course there are always new insights and applications of the theory. I'm still working at and learning myself how to be a more differentiated self."

"That's reassuring," Mike said, laughing. "Now tell me more about this idea of staying connected."

"Right," Jacob nodded. "Do you know what an electrical transformer does?"

Puzzled, Mike said, "I guess so. It steps down the current of the electricity so that it delivers 120 volts, or 220, or whatever is needed."

"Yes, but transformers can also step up the current as well. My mentor Ed Friedman used to say that each of us is, in a sense, a 'transformer' of the energy in the emotional field we are part of. When I think of this analogy, I am reminded of the hot triangle that Craig, Steve and you are caught in from time to time."

"Boy, you're not kidding," Mike added. "You know a few days before I went to Scottsdale I had a meeting with those two guys to review your material on **emotional process** and try to help them work on their interaction."

'Really, how did it go?" Jacob asked.

"Well, it blew up in my face more or less. I am not that good a coach, I guess," Mike said.

Mike went on to describe the situation to Jacob who made some suggestions for how Mike could handle the next meeting that was coming up later that afternoon.

"The Craig-Steve interface is a good example, Mike. There are some people who seem always to bring a calming influence—Vanessa for example—and others who are always stepping up the anxiety and reactivity. It is very important that a leader be a step-down transformer. You will do that if you are less anxious than those around you, if you bring a less anxious presence to the system."

Mike laughed, "That's easier said than done, Jacob."

"I didn't say that you need to be totally non-anxious. None of us are. But you need to try to be less anxious than those around you, even if the best you can do is to be just a little bit less anxious than others. Of course, the lower your own level of anxiety and reactivity, the better it is for everyone involved. You know, generally speaking, a system is unable to rise above the level of differentiation of its leader."

Jacob stopped and asked, "Would you describe James as a step-up or step-down transformer?"

"He can be both. Sometimes he can calm a meeting down, but often he exhibits a degree of anxiety that we all pick up on. When you see the boss so anxious, it makes you very unsettled."

Jacob nodded and added, "And when an organization is anxious and reactive, its creativity and productivity both suffer mightily. When people are anxious and defensive, they are less flexible, communication within the organization suffers, team spirit breaks down, problem solving is impeded, and all sorts of other symptoms crop up that impact the bottom line."

"Thanks for making me feel even more responsible for the health of the company, Jacob!"

"Welcome to leadership, Mike," said Jacob with a grin. "You are and you are not responsible for the company's health. I think I've mentioned before that a leader is like the immune system of the organization he leads. If the immune system breaks down—that is, if the leader becomes overly anxious and reactive—then the entire organization is likely to get sick. That's why it's so important for you to **stay connected** in just the right way—as a less anxious presence—so that you help the entire system to remain more calm and healthy. You need to be the step-down transformer at CHI, just like Vanessa was for so many years."

"Vanessa is like a rock," Mike said. "Over the last few weeks, especially at the Board meeting in Arizona, I saw her determination and bearing so many times in dealing with our Board members, some of whom are very anxious. She patiently listens, summarizes the key points made by someone who is fussing at her, and then just answers the questions with a polite but direct and no-nonsense manner.

"When I think about replacing her, it hits me how many people will be depending on my ability to function in a more differentiated way. You know me pretty well, and you've seen how often I fall short. Every time I think about being a less anxious presence, I start to get a bit anxious!"

Both Jacob and Mike burst out laughing at the irony of Mike's statement. The laughter broke the tension, and Jacob continued, "Mike, I know you feel responsible, and that's a good thing—to a point. Ed Friedman used to say that the classic burnout position for leaders is when they feel overly responsible for those they lead. You need to remember that ultimately you are responsible only for your own functioning. The rest will take care of itself, and you can't become overly focused on trying to fix everyone else."

"I know that," Mike responded. "But I want to make sure I am doing everything I can to manage my own part in the best possible way."

Mike glanced at his watch. "Jacob, I need to run back to the office for a meeting."

"No problem, Mike. We are at a good stopping point anyway.

Let's pick up with your last point here when we resume next time."

STEVE – CRAIG – MIKE TRIANGLE

Later that afternoon Mike's follow-up session with Steve and Craig took place. Jacob had helped Mike realize that his role was primarily to lead and teach through how he was present—he was to be an observer of whatever the two men came to the meeting with as their answer to the question, "How can you improve the way the two of you interact?" Rather than try to be their problem-solver, Mike was to focus on remaining calm and keep from getting triangled by the anxiety of the two men.

Steve and Craig had done a lot of work and came up with a scheme of roles and responsibilities that was essentially a listing of what had to be done by whom and when. They presented the data to Mike with guarded enthusiasm. It was clear that these two men were never going to be the best of friends, but it seemed they had reached a workable agreement. Several times in the course of the conversation, one or the other of them made comments designed to get Mike "on their side" of a contentious point, but he remained consistently neutral and responded with questions rather than answers:

- How will this delineation of duties help you function better with each other?
- What else, if anything, is needed?
- How will you monitor the level of improvement you have made in your interactions?

As they worked through answers to each of his questions, Mike observed that the anxiety between them seemed to subside gradually, and eventually they reached common agreement on the key points. At the end of the meeting they waited for Mike to say something that would let them know whether they had done a good job or bad job. It was almost as if they wanted some sort of a grade—did they get an A or a B or what on their assignment?

Mike gave them neither a grade nor his approval. They were doing this to improve their interaction, not to gain his approval.

Instead, he said, "You will know if you have done good work in creating this plan and in implementing it if your interactions improve. For the most part, the two of you will be the judge of that. Let me know how it goes."

With that, the meeting ended. Craig and Steve were left somewhat perplexed at the different dynamic they had experienced, while Mike reflected on the fact that understanding how triangles work really does make a difference. Things were beginning to change.

That evening Mike made more of his usual notes.

Today
- *You can only influence a system you are connected to. Watch your tendency to cutoffs.*
- *Good meeting with Craig and Steve. They are clear on their charter but I need to be of more help. I remained balanced and handled both sides of the triangle well.*
- *Emotional process = "hidden chemistry."*

Issues
- *Stay connected is the central point here—how do I do that with someone who is holding me at a distance?*
- *I will need to begin working with Kelly in a supervisory capacity. She is far superior to me in her command of the financial issues of the business. I need to lower my anxiety on this point.*

Follow up
- *Step down transformer—hold on to this idea when dealing with James.*
- *For next time with Jacob —how can I become more self-differentiated? What preparation can I make to be in the "right space" under fire?*
- *Be sure to secure a coaching contract with Jacob for the next 12-18 months.*

Karla Incorporated

Early one morning as Mike was arriving at work, he got a call from Karla. She had just come out of a meeting with her supervisor. Shelia Hunter had informed her that she must either stop independently contacting and working with international real estate agents or Hale would be forced to take disciplinary action.

Shelia had not taken the right approach in delivering the message to Karla Sampson and had underestimated her resolve.

Karla quit on the spot. After packing her belongings, Karla went back into Shelia's office and said goodbye, thanked her for her leadership and explained the simple reason she was leaving. She had no intention of stopping her approach to selling homes and while it was certainly Hale's right to provide direction to their sales agents, it was her responsibility as a sales agent to either comply with the directive or leave. She was not going to comply so she was going to leave, period. She went to a nearby coffee shop and called Mike on her cell phone as she fired up her laptop.

"Hello, Honey. I am calling to say I just quit my job—probably just a few days before they would have fired me anyway." She told Mike what had happened.

Mike could picture the scene. No one ever messes with Karla that way.

"You didn't punch Shelia in the nose, did you?" Mike said half seriously.

"No, I missed her on the uppercut swing," Karla said with a laugh.

"Are you okay, Honey?" Mike knew the answer.

"Yes, yes, I am fine. I am going to finish my coffee and get on the Internet to see what I need to do to set up my own little business. I need to sell some houses to people in France and Germany as soon as I can."

They talked a little more. Mike could sense that Karla was just fine. They said good-bye and he walked into the office. It struck Mike that Karla could stop selling real estate and go into competition with Jacob Wolfe as an executive coach, listing herself in the yellow pages as a "self-differentiation coach." At the same time, he wondered to himself if Karla's abrupt decision was an example of reactivity more than self-differentiation. Was it an example of a cutoff or a thoughtful step? "This is really complicated stuff," he mused as he plunged into the day's activities.

More Coaching the New COO

"Jacob, when we last met you gave me some very good advice on how to work with the Craig-Steve-Mike triangle. I had a follow-up meeting with them that went very well; the advice you gave me to ask questions instead of give answers worked perfectly."

"Good, Mike, I am glad it worked. When you are present to them in this new way, I think you will find that it creates more space for them to be thoughtful and to solve their own problems in their own way. It can seem at first like you have less control, but in the long run you will see that it is much more effective in focusing their energies productively.

"Now, I believe when we left off last time, we were about to discuss some actions a person can take to work on differentiation of self."

Jacob moved to the white board and wrote the words:

Mike quickly opened his cell phone to take notes.

"Mike, one of the best ways to remain a less anxious presence is to adopt the stance of an observer, a researcher, who is interested in the process. Your anxiety is automatically lowered whenever you stand apart from a situation enough to become an observer. It is important, however, that you try to be a neutral observer, suspending judgment or bias and just watching for the ways that **emotional process** is surfacing. That is difficult, because usually the content at issue is of interest to you, and you usually have a stake in it and an opinion about it. But when you put on your observer's hat, you want to try as best you can to suspend those biases and simply watch the process. You've already been working on that as you've gotten into the habit of climbing up an imaginary tree to observe the scene you are part of."

Jacob continued, "Remember a few months ago when you were upset because of the criticism the folks in Boston were directing at you over finding ways to increase revenues by generating top line sales rather than cutting costs? I urged you not to get hooked on the content of their criticism, but rather to focus on how the relationships were unfolding. Eventually, we recognized that the Boston district leadership was feeling neglected by you, and what was really behind the criticism was an attempt to get your attention back on them and to bring you back into a closer relationship with them."

"Yes, I remember that. I was so concerned about fixing the problem that I totally missed what was behind the criticism. As soon as I gave them more of my attention, the problem that had appeared so serious just seemed to go away."

"That's what I mean by saying it is essential to watch the process rather than the content. You were hooked on the content at first and getting more and more anxious. As soon as you watched what was underneath the criticism, you calmed down, connected better to the whole district, and then everything seemed better all of a sudden. The key, I hope you see, is that as soon as you became an observer you became less anxious. That allowed you to understand how better to respond—by staying connected rather than working on the red herring."

Jacob went on, "I'll share with you another little trick from my coach's toolbox. Whenever you are dealing with a person or a group that is caught up in an anxious, reactive stance, your best bet is to be curious about how they see their situation and to ask them what they think of it. When you had your hotel-by-hotel district report-outs up in Boston, you were actually asking those kinds of questions of all the general managers. When you do this it immediately puts people in the position of being the observer; and, as soon as they are in that position, their anxiety tends to lessen. Isn't that what happened with Craig and Steve last week?"

"It worked with them for sure."

Jacob continued, "Even in our coaching relationship, if you stop and reflect on how you and I have interacted over issues where you were a bit anxious, you may recognize that pattern at work."

A light seemed to go on in Mike's eyes, "Yes, I get it. In the beginning, especially, I was bringing you all sorts of issues that got me upset, hoping you would give me the answer or at least help me strategize my way out of them. I especially remember a call I made to you from the Boston airport. I wanted you to give me an answer. But you just asked me what I thought about the situation, asked me to describe what I saw going on in it. You asked lots of curious questions and drew out my insights—insights that I would never have thought about on my own.

"When I hung up the phone, I was really energized by those insights. I was more thoughtful, and my anxiety was lower. It was magical!"

Jacob laughed, "Well, I don't know how magical it is. But sometimes it can seem to work like magic. Other times it's not that helpful and you need to keep working at it. Remember, I said that an important aspect of differentiation of self is the ability to integrate your thinking and feeling responses. As a general rule of thumb, the more intensely you are involved in an emotional relationship with a person or situation, the more difficult will it be for you to stand aside and observe your own anxiety and reactivity. You'd think it might be otherwise, since to an outsider a person with high levels of reactivity is so obvious. But when it's you—well, you know how difficult it can be when you're too close to a situation. That's why you need to increase the range of responses available to you when you are faced with situations that elevate your anxiety."

At this point, Jacob moved again to the white board and wrote the words:

> *Expand your repertoire*

"Most of us, when we're caught up in emotionally charged situations—especially when we are part of an intense relationship—tend to fall back on one or two default settings. Unfortunately, those default settings do not always reflect the highest possible level of functioning. Learning to manage your reactivity better, so that you can **stay connected** as a less anxious presence, involves expanding your repertoire of responses. It takes time and practice, of course, but like any other skill, the more you work at it the greater mastery you will achieve.

"Learning to be playful is one of the ways that I have found to be particularly helpful whenever I sense myself getting anxious. It not only helps to unhook me from the grasp of my own reactivity, it also helps those around me to be less anxious as they catch my own playful spirit. Whenever you encounter someone who is overly serious—deadly serious—you can be pretty sure there is a high level of reactivity. Such seriousness comes from the reptilian brain—the part rooted in our evolutionary past where our most primitive **automatic functioning** resides. You've never seen a reptile act playfully, have you? With snakes and lizards it's all about instinct and survival, not much more. It's our ability to be playful that sets us humans apart and makes possible a presence marked by a lightness that immediately encourages others to be more calm."

"I think I know what you're getting at," Mike responded. "But too often when I try humor it comes across as sarcasm."

"Well, obviously, that is not what you want. But irony and paradox are just one notch removed from sarcasm, yet they can be a very positive part of your repertoire. In fact, they are particularly helpful in getting people to reframe their perspective and move towards the stance of observer. When we are being paradoxical with people, it interrupts their linear, one-dimensional way of thinking and requires them to step back and shift perspective in order to figure out what we are getting at. It's a great skill to develop, and it will support your efforts to remain less anxious when those around you are overcome with anxiety.

Mike's mind turned back to his dinner with Kelly. She had the playfulness skill that Jacob was identifying, and it was very effective and charming.

Jacob wrote a third line on the white board:

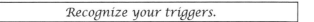

Recognize your triggers.

"Mike, this may sound like an obvious way of managing your anxiety, but it's not that simple. The reason is that most of your triggers were planted in you so early on in life and are so far beneath your conscious awareness that they seem as natural as breathing by now. The brain stores every bit of data that has come into it throughout our entire lives, and it is constantly evaluating new experiences as they unfold in light of that stored data.

"I had a client once who at the age of five was raised for nearly a year during her mother's illness by two maiden aunts. Those aunts were quite heavy and evidently very cruel to the little girl. At least that was her perception of it. In any event, for many years until we talked about it, and she finally recognized what was going on, older women who were overweight triggered all kinds of negative reactions in my client. It reached a boiling point when she got a transfer and her new boss was the mirror image of one her nasty maiden aunts. The trigger was still there, but once she recognized it at work, she could manage her anxiety in a much, much better way whenever she had to interact with her boss.

"We will never recognize all of our triggers, since those unconscious associations operate too far beneath the surface. But with persistence and attention, we can come to recognize many of them. Body language, facial expressions, certain tones of voice or physical situations, how some people dress or carry themselves—all of these and more can be triggers for our anxiety and catch us unaware.

"I'll tell you a little secret about one of my triggers: When I was about six years old, I fell asleep at the beach, and while I slept hundreds of ants from a nearby anthill swarmed all over me, into my hair and everywhere. I was so traumatized when I awoke that for many, many years the mere sight of a little ant would send chills down my spine. I decided it was silly, and so I got my first ant farm and started to read up on them and study them, and so forth. The fear turned to curiosity, and now as you know I'm really fascinated by the little creatures."

"That's really amazing, Jacob. I've never thought about the role that any 'triggers' play in making me more reactive, but I'm sure there are some significant ones. I'll bet Karla already knows what they are."

Both men laughed, understanding that Mike had just said a great deal in very few words.

"Mike, there's one final suggestion I want to offer to help you manage your reactivity and remain a less anxious presence." He wrote on the board:

> *No quick fixes*

"There is no reaction more understandable or natural than to want relief from anxiety. And the more the anxiety, the greater the urgency we feel, and the stronger our desire to eliminate its cause as quickly as possible. Unfortunately, however, it's almost always true that the quick fix is the wrong way to go, at least when you're talking about how to deal with reactive functioning within a relationship network.

"Many leaders, because they care about those who work for them, are particularly vulnerable to the trap of moving too quickly to relieve the pain of those in the organization who come to them for relief. We tend to do it with our kids, too, as you well know. What parent wants to see a child in pain? What boss wants to see his employees unhappy? The problem is that if we act too quickly, the growth opportunity that is embedded in the painful situation is lost. A very unhelpful reciprocal pattern can take root if we intervene regularly and too quickly to comfort whenever someone is in pain. What often drives us to act too quickly is our own anxiety, more than the pain of those in need.

"When you **think systems**, you understand that the more a leader increases his own capacity to tolerate the pain of those he leads, the more is he actually helping them to increase their capacity as well; and, ultimately, to deal with their pain in better ways. One of the basic lessons I learned from Ed Friedman is that we generally grow more from challenge than from comfort. You will leave yourself open to the charge of not caring, of being cold and heartless, but true compassion can often require helping people to grow by managing their own pain rather than looking to someone else to fix it for them."

"That's a new thought for me, Jacob," Mike said. "I have always felt responsible for the morale of my folks, but you're saying that is not my job. My job is to help them deal with difficult and challenging situations by NOT intervening too quickly, rather than by stepping in to shield them from the worst of it."

"Right. My mentor Ed Friedman used to talk about what he called the 'fallacy of empathy.' He said that societal regression has perverted empathy into a disguise for anxiety. His insistence was on the importance of focusing on strength, not weakness, and his observation was that the weak often use their weakness and pain as a tool to manipulate leaders. He was insistent that good leadership requires a leader to promote greater responsibility for self, and that is best done by challenge, not comfort. It requires of a leader a higher threshold for the pain of others, and that will be judged negatively by many. But the alternative is the tyranny of those with the greatest sensitivities. In the end, we all wind up tiptoeing around the hypersensitivities of the lowest functioning members of society. That's the downside of 'political correctness' in its many forms."

Mike added, "Jacob, I have discovered over the months we have been working together that I combine two coping mechanisms to avoid my anxiety. First I try for a quick fix to relieve my immediate distress. If that fails, then I go into cutoff. Because I cannot tolerate the anxiety, I distance myself from it. I do this all the time."

"You are not alone, my friend. That combination is very typical. I see it going on all the time," Jacob said. He went on, "Staying connected in the right way is tricky business, a real balancing act. Leaders need to be close without getting too close, which means keeping a certain distance, but without being so separate that they're cut off. I should point out to you, however, that when I speak of the need to **stay connected**, I include the notion of a person's connection to self. To the extent that a person is in touch with self in a healthy way, his or her ability to be connected to others is promoted as well."

Mike registered a look of surprise. "**Stay connected** to self—I hadn't thought of it in that way, for sure."

"Most people don't spontaneously think of it in that way, but as far as I'm concerned, the idea of being connected to self is foundational to a person's ability to be in healthy relationships with others. In the same vein, leaders who are cut off from self often demonstrate that same behavior with regards to others."

"This is feeling a little too theoretical for me, Jacob. Can we get more concrete about what it looks like to stay connected?"

"Certainly, it's important for us to talk about this dimension of leadership in practical terms that make sense to you. It's impossible to describe every scenario, of course, but I like to sum up the behaviors by describing a leader's capacity for engaging in '*respectful dialogue without cutoffs*' as well as '*being connected without fusion.*' Let me explain what each of those looks like in more detail. But before I do, let's take a break for ten minutes," Jacob said.

After a brisk walk outside for Mike, and a bathroom break for Jacob, they were back at it again.

Jacob began, "Mike, I'd like to start by talking about what 'respectful dialogue without cutoffs' looks like in a well differentiated leader. But I suspect you already have a feel for what this implies. Can you describe to me what sort of behaviors you would expect to find in such a leader?"

Mike thought for a moment and then said, "I suppose he would be able to engage in disagreements without getting defensive, being dogmatic or going on the attack. I've learned from you that I need to be more open to mutual exchange, honest listening, and make a sincere attempt to understand the viewpoint of those who hold an alternative perspective."

"That's it exactly, Mike. Instead of shutting down and cutting off from those who appear to be adversarial, a resilient leader will continue to be in contact, even in those situations where agreement cannot be reached. It is also important that such a leader be willing to admit mistakes and to take criticism gracefully, with no interest in retaliating against those who have confronted him or proven him wrong. When things have gone wrong, when mistakes have been made, an effective leader will come together with others to understand what lessons can be gleaned from those mistakes and errors."

"You know, Jacob, all of this sounds pretty obvious and basic. But if I'm honest with myself, I recognize how often I have fallen short on these behaviors over the years. It's all easier said than done, I'm afraid!"

"It's something all of us need to keep working on over a lifetime, Mike. The point I want to make to you, however, is that the more you work on your own differentiation, the less you will engage in either/or thinking, the more you will appreciate that reality can embrace a variety of viewpoints and accommodate many degrees of nuance. I know you have it in you to be that kind of leader—someone who is open to explore with others the bigger picture or the more comprehensive solution, rather than holding fast to a single-minded approach or insisting on an exclusive claim on the truth. Staying connected is about inclusivity and building relationships, not scoring victories. Respectful dialogue without cutoffs often means seeking to find common ground, rather than taking stands that polarize."

"I appreciate your vote of confidence in me, Jacob, but we both know that there is still an awful lot of reactivity in me."

"Of course there is, Mike. It's in us all. That is another reason why I include staying connected to self in my understanding of what it means to focus on differentiation. Each and every one of us has a lifetime of work to do in this area, and we need to be in touch with our own reactivity in order to manage it more successfully.

"Let me layer a few more thoughts on this notion. The **Resilient Leadership** model understands that communication is primarily an emotional phenomenon, rather than a mere exchange of ideas. Because of this, effective communication with someone only happens when there is a connection, when they are moving toward you rather than moving away. The leader who wishes to communicate successfully understands this and is always attentive to the relationship dynamics that are part of any communication effort. That is why avoiding cutoffs—or at least minimizing their pull—is so important."

"Jacob, you're really laying a lot more on me than I can absorb. Would you mind if I take a pause here and make some notes? This is good stuff, and I don't want to lose any of it."

"Of course not, Mike. Go ahead and jot down whatever you feel is important to remember."

Mike was already furiously punching the keys on his cell phone. After a few minutes, he said, "Thanks, Jacob. You said there were two behaviors you wanted to discuss, and the first was about 'respectful dialogue without cutoffs.' But I've already forgotten what you said was the second aspect of staying connected."

"That's okay, Mike. I said that my second category for describing the desirable behaviors of a well-differentiated leader is what I call 'being connected without fusion.'

"In any relationship network, there is a continuum that ranges from cutoffs at one extreme to fusion at the other. This is just another way of approaching those **self-other forces** we talked about months ago. We also spoke some time ago about societal regression and how one of the symptoms of reactivity in our society today is a tendency to herding and group-think—two more ways of describing relationship fusion."

Mike interrupted, "Jacob, I'm sorry to be so dense, but can you translate what you're talking about for a layman's level?"

Jacob laughed softly. "Mike, it's the professor in me, I know. Let me try to be more practical. One sure sign that someone tends toward the extreme of fusion in his relationships is an excessive preoccupation with what others think. Or sometimes relationship fusion is manifested in the opposite direction—as a complete disregard for the opinion of others. So, a person can act out this pattern of fusion by always seeking approval or permission from others before taking a personal stand, or by being rebellious and never seeking approval when it is appropriate to do so. Another sign of relationship fusion is when someone is particularly needy for encouragement, to the point where their interest or motivation falls apart unless they receive constant affirmation. Are these examples helpful, Mike?"

"Yes, thank you. I think I'm getting a handle on what you're saying now. If I'm hearing you correctly, the more differentiated self a person has, the less he is likely to exhibit behaviors that are symptomatic of relationship fusion. The more of a 'self' there is in someone, the less you expect to see of these patterns."

"You've got it, Mike. I trust you're recognizing more and more now what I'm getting at in the **Resilient Leadership** model when I say that 'A New Way of LEADING' is to **focus on differentiation of self**.

"Remember, we said earlier that we get our *basic* level of differentiation in the context of how our family and especially how our parents function. As with so many other aspects of our life, we learn early on in our family setting to judge as 'normal' a certain style of relating that is more or less close, more or less distant. In general, the higher the levels of reactivity in any system, the more fusion there is. So when someone grows up in that kind of environment, they often lean in the direction of relationship fusion."

Mike was nodding, "You have just described Steve Parker in marketing to a tee. He is in my office five times a week to check on every single issue, big or small, to be sure I am aware of and supportive of his views. And if I am not in agreement, he conveniently finds a way to adjust his views. When he has to broker a disagreement between two or more people, especially when they are at senior levels, he almost goes into convulsions."

"That's exactly what I'm talking about, Mike. A resilient leader, on the other hand, is interested but does not worry excessively about what others think. He has a sufficiently strong sense of self and a clear vision of what he is about, and so he is able to function without constantly seeking reinforcement from others.

"We've talked before about the ways that a system seeks to maintain its equilibrium with various reciprocal processes; for example, when one person in a relationship over-functions, the other person will almost always be inclined to under-function. This kind of dynamic is another expression of a fused emotional pattern. Once it's in place, it's a very slippery pattern to change. It appears that one person's functioning is determined by how another is functioning, but it's a bit like the chicken and the egg, in that you're never sure who is influencing whom. The point is that both parties to a reciprocal functioning pattern are examples of relationship fusion."

Somewhat sheepishly, Mike said, "I'm afraid I know what you're talking about—all too well. I've been getting along better with my father lately, and I was chalking it up to how much *he* has changed. But on deeper reflection, I've come to realize that I've played an equal role in the conflict we've had over the years. We were locked into a back-and-forth that never seemed to go anywhere. It was like we both had scripts that we were reading, and the script never changed."

"Murray Bowen called this reciprocal functioning, Mike, and I'm glad it is getting clearer to you how often we get caught up in it. By the way, the progress you've made with your father I'm sure has helped you in your work setting as well. Emotional fusion is in the air we breathe, and none of us escapes its effects.

"If you want proof that this issue of staying connected without being fused is a difficult skill to master, just think about how many people find healthy conflict management an elusive goal. People get so tied up in the emotions that swirl around when there is a disagreement that they just want to avoid facing the conflict. Ironically, conflict avoidance is a sign of fusion just as much as an argumentative spirit. You've certainly seen how disastrous it is when a boss is a peace-monger, always seeking to appease everyone in order to avoid facing any conflicts. It's a doomed proposition, but some leaders are so keenly attuned to potential conflict that a large portion of their functioning is aimed at trying to keep everyone happy. It's an impossible goal, of course, and the results are inevitably the very thing that the leader was seeking to avoid."

Mike jumped in, saying, "I know exactly what you mean, Jacob. Early in my career at CHI I had a regional manager who was absolutely paralyzed whenever there was a disagreement that surfaced within his team. We couldn't even have a healthy discussion of the pros and cons of an issue without him breaking into a sweat. Folks learned quickly to just avoid hot-button topics, and the overall effect was disastrous on the team. Everyone just shut down, and the whole region suffered from his poor leadership."

"It's good you recognize how important an issue this is, Mike. The processes around fusion operate in a subtle way that requires a leader to be very alert. It's one of those places where you need to trust your gut, since often you will first realize the pull towards fusion as a vague sense of uneasiness. That's your **automatic functioning** alerting you to danger, in this case the danger of losing some degree of 'self' by being swallowed up in a morass of relational binds. You have been working, I know, at recognizing triangles and learning how to reposition yourself in them.

"Being alert to relationship fusion provides fertile ground for you to practice those skills at repositioning. When you feel you are being drawn into a level of intensity that is disproportionate to the situation, you can be sure that there is fusion operating within the system. You won't always be able to name exactly where or how it's happening, but you will know it's going on. The key thing for you to do at that point is to work on self definition."

Mike smiled at Jacob and said, "So, when it comes to differentiation of self, the bottom line is this: 'Stay connected,' but avoid the fusion!"

"Not exactly, Mike. You can never avoid fusion—it's inevitable. Relationship fusion is what we humans do—all of us. Managing it or navigating through it in better ways is what we should aim for, not avoiding it."

Jacob paused and collected his thoughts. After a moment he

said, "Mike, I am about finished here. By that I mean finished not only for this session but also finished introducing you to the basic concepts in the **Resilient Leadership** model."

Pointing to the **Resilient Leadership** graphic posted on one corner of his white board, Jacob said, "We have gone completely around the wheel here, so to speak."

Mike responded, "I could go around this wheel with you a half dozen more times and learn something new each time."

"There is a lifetime of learning to be had, but the best way to really grasp it is to get out there and practice. Murray Bowen used to speak of the lifelong attachments we all have in our relationship with our parents, and how we replicate those all over the place. Working on differentiation of self is a process we are never finished with, Mike."

"Jacob, I am not at all ready to end our coaching work, but I know things need to change. I am about to move full-time into the COO role in the next month, and I have several big challenges ahead of me as I make the transition. I want to be able to visit with you and call you as I head down this new path."

"That is great with me. What I've learned over the years is that **Resilient Leadership** is not something you can learn just by reading a book and immediately putting it into practice. Lots of self-help books promise that kind of quick relief. In order to become a resilient leader, I'm convinced that the best way forward is to work closely with a coach. Not everyone can afford the luxury of time and money that requires, but I know it's the best way to make steady progress. How do you want to set things up going forward?" Jacob asked.

"Well, I am not exactly sure what will work best for me. I will figure it out and give you a call," Mike said.

"That's fine, give me a call when you want to get together," Jacob said.

The two men stood up, shook hands, and Mike left for CHI.

CHI Revitalization

The CHI National Conference took place in Washington, DC, over a three-day period in late September. At the meeting James McMaster made the formal announcements to publicly confirm what everyone already knew from internal communications and rumor about Mike's and Kelly's new positions.

Vanessa Jackson was leaving the company after 22 years to run the bakery business that her grandfather began in 1911. Her older brother had been the day-to-day operations manager up until the previous year when he had a stroke. She was returning home to take over his responsibilities.

The unexpected and exciting announcement that was made at the conference was the formation of a joint venture with Universal Holdings out of Stockholm, Sweden. Seventeen locations around the country were to be either renovated or converted into top-end mixed use office buildings, retail space and a new upscale boutique hotel called A-G-E-N-D-A. James McMaster, Ian Brier with Universal Holdings and architect E. X. Yee unveiled the boutique concept, which was based on new hotel concepts being created in Europe and the Middle East.

A recognition dinner was held for Vanessa on the first evening of the conference. James McMaster gave a warm and heartfelt speech celebrating Vanessa's career and wishing her well. It was a great evening.

Overall, the conference was a huge success. On the final day, Mike's first public address as COO built confidence and enthusiasm in him as a leader. During his speech, he announced the creation of a national strategy planning team with representatives from each geographical area and organizational segment of the company. Over the next six months, the planning team was tasked with developing the CHI Revitalization Plan. He announced that Craig Hernandez, the district vice president from Monroeville, would assume a coordinating role for the revitalization effort, reporting to him.

The day after the national conference, Mike held his first Senior Management Team meeting as COO. The energy was high. The agenda had only four topics:

1. What do we need to know and do to be successful in the next six months?
2. What are the top issues, problems, challenges or opportunities we need to take on as a team?
3. What will success look like for our team over the next six months?
4. How will we work together?

Each discussion topic created a lot of dialogue, and Mike worked hard at effectively playing his COO role. He used many of the tools that he had picked up during his coaching. He worked at remaining open and really listening to his team. He set expectations and boundaries for the discussions but remained patient with "old school" dialogue. He engaged and challenged people and ideas that sapped energy.

Mike also watched for **emotional process** and saw it everywhere as he took an observer role in the meeting. He was now much more aware of how **emotional process** was at work in the team. He heard ideas that were presented for the thousandth time and saw how new voices and ideas were discounted or simply ignored. He was seeing and thinking in new ways as he observed the culture he had inherited and was determined to change. The "cash is king" mentality drove much of the dialogue related to his second topic about top issues. The road ahead was a long one.

Irwin Briggs, the senior vice president for the Southeast Division, was of particular concern. He continued to sound off about limitations and constraints and how change efforts in the past had little or no success. Mike made a cell phone note about specific points he wanted to discuss with Irwin privately. Irwin was going to have to change his tune and his mental model of leadership if he was going to stay on the team that Mike intended to lead. To close the meeting, Mike made a few final comments.

"Thank you all very much for your time today. Coming off a three-day national conference, it is difficult to stay here in DC for a fourth day, especially when so much is happening back home.

"I think we have made a good start in our dialogue, and we all have a number of things to follow up on. I want to leave you with a few thoughts as we begin our new fiscal year in about three weeks.

"As leaders we have an extraordinary opportunity and immense responsibility in front of us right now. We are about to change the direction and focus of CHI and revitalize our quality of service and profitability. Or we could fall short of the challenge by failing in our responsibilities. We are at a crossroads with a choice to make.

"For the first three days of this week, I witnessed the enthusiasm that is in the bones of our company. It was exciting for us all. In the last eight hours here with you, I have seen glimmers of that enthusiasm sometimes almost smothered within a blanket of frustration, concern and downright disillusionment.

"I did not hear a single problem or challenge or issue that we as a leadership team can't either fix or work to neutralize. But, frankly, I heard a lot of 'we can't' and not enough of 'we will.' Each of us has a choice to make about which attitude we will operate out of in the days ahead. The people I want on my team are those who are willing to change the way we think about and execute our responsibilities as senior leaders. My job is to be sure that as individuals—you and I—and as a team, we are ready to take the active steps that will lead to success.

"So here is what I am going to do. I will visit with each of you individually within the next 30 days. I want to understand what each of you will need from me to be successful, and I want to let you know my expectations of you. From our discussion we will create a written 'win-win agreement.' I will ask for your assessment of my effectiveness in meeting these agreements in March-April and September-October. I will also give you feedback two times a year.

"As preparation for the one-on-one sessions, I want to let you know that I will be asking you how the glimmer of enthusiasm I mentioned a moment ago can grow into a raging fire of enthusiasm in you and me and the entire team."

The team was silent. Among them were an equal number of optimists and pessimists and three or four cynics. The cynics were very uneasy as they walked out of the meeting room.

TRANSITIONS

On Monday morning Mike met with Craig Hernandez at 8:00 and Kelly O'Reilly at 10:30. Mike had given Craig the job of identifying an outside consultant to help with the revitalization process. Craig laid out the plan and identified the resources he would need to get the initiative off the ground and moving. Mike was thankful that Craig was on point for this work. His drive and operational savvy were already kicking in. Mike knew he had the right guy for the job.

Kelly arrived promptly and was ready with a number of questions from the national conference and from the Senior Management Team. She had been quiet for much of the four days. Mike knew that she was not only learning a lot but making some deeper observations about her new employer. During the conversation Mike began to see what a strong personality she had and how much guidance he would need to provide her as she entered the CHI culture.

He was glad that they were going to spend a few days traveling together. Mike also made the mental note that he needed to introduce Karla to Kelly before he went on a trip with Kelly. He had already made too much of Kelly's appearance and ability, and Karla needed to get a sense of Kelly for herself. He invited Kelly to dinner Saturday night to meet his better half. She accepted.

Mike had his first one-on-one meeting that afternoon with Irwin Briggs, who had stayed in the DC area for the weekend.

"Hello, Mike," Irwin said. "I guess I am the first up."

"Indeed, you are Irwin, thanks for meeting with me today."

"Well, I had the chance to stay over the weekend and play golf with the old man and a few of his other buddies. We had a great time. He sure is glad you are in the job of COO."

Irwin was trying to gain an edge on Mike by creating the impression that he had special access to James. Mike wasn't fooled by Irwin's ploy.

"Great. It's good that James stays connected with you and others to get a sense of things in the business," Mike said.

"Let's take a look at this idea of a 'win-win agreement,'" Mike said.

"Sure, I've done a lot of these in the past. They work pretty well as long as they are written so that the unpredictable nature of the business can be accommodated."

The agreement that Mike had prepared had five evaluation categories: one each for sales growth, profits, employee engagement, customer satisfaction and leadership effectiveness.

The discussion began with setting targets for sales growth, profits and customer satisfaction, using the upcoming fiscal year's projections that had just been submitted to headquarters for review. As of yet, CHI had not established a standardized measurement system for employee engagement. The category of leadership effectiveness was new and wide open at this point.

Irwin had submitted very modest improvement targets. His sales, profits and customer satisfaction performance targets were about three to five percent above last year's year-end performance.

"Irwin, what would it take to triple and meet your performance targets for customer satisfaction?"

"Fifty million dollars," Irwin said with a laugh.

Mike smiled, "No, really, what would it take to achieve a 30 percent increase in customer satisfaction in the Southeast Division?"

"You're serious?" Irwin said.

"Yes, I am," Mike said.

"Customers of our hotels have expectations we cannot meet, given the demands for margin and the financial constraints we face. My cost of operations is going to be up 25 to 30 percent next year, and I cannot pass all of that on to the customer and still be competitive in the market. You know that. Come on, Mike. We are not running the Marriott Corporation here."

"Irwin, I know you can answer my question. I need someone with your experience to help me get the answer to the question I asked," Mike said.

"I just told you the answer," Irwin said.

"You gave me the answer to a different question; you answered the question, 'Could it be done?' I asked you what it would take to get it done."

Mike went on, "Irwin, if you can't or don't want to get the factual answer to the question, then let's discuss who in the organization or outside the organization can get the answer."

Irwin was now getting very irritated and a little worried.

"Okay, I will get the answer, but I can't just call up someone and tell them to go look up the information. I will have to touch base with each hotel and get others involved. Are you telling me that the budgets we submitted from the Southeast Division need to be changed, need to be increased by 30 percent?"

"That depends on the answer to the question I asked you," Mike said.

"Are you going to be doing this with all of the divisions?" Irwin asked.

"Well, not all of them, but many. I am asking you to do the

research on the biggest increase because of the capabilities of the team and the comparatively low projections you submitted for next year."

"So you are punishing us for being low man on the pole?" Irwin complained.

"I am asking you to gather factual information that will let us know what it would take for your division to have 30 percent higher customer satisfaction next year," Mike repeated.

Finally Irwin blew up. "Look, Mike, you have been in the job of COO for a matter of days, and it's like you made the transition to corporate from division management in the blink of an eye. I know you're trying hard to impress the boss quickly, but you need to be careful how hard you push, or you will end up with no team rather than a good team."

Mike held his ground and his cool. "Irwin, I can see that you are irritated. Believe me, I am not trying to get you upset, nor am I trying to impress James McMaster. Frankly, I am just trying to see what it will take to substantially increase customer satisfaction in your division and everywhere else where we have lower performance. And I am asking you to get answers to that question."

Mike paused. "Here is the bottom line for you and me and this discussion. I want the answer to the question within 30 days so I can report back to you and your colleagues and to James what CHI will need to do to get much better customer satisfaction. I will get this information with or without your help. That part is up to you."

Irwin began to see the inevitability of the situation and tried to end the conversation by saying, "So what are we going to do with this 'win-win agreement'?"

"We are going to get the facts, and then we can have a fact-based conversation and reach agreements that will make the exercise have real value and the promise of real results," Mike said.

"It feels pretty win-lose to me, Mike," Irwin said.

"Let's collect some information and then see where we are at that point."

During the next three weeks, Irwin's division team contacted each hotel to collect information from general managers about how a 30 percent increase in customer satisfaction could be accomplished. Because Irwin characterized the request as a mandate from headquarters and an activity that he was only complying with, the ideas generated lacked much creativity or in-depth thinking. It was becoming another paper exercise. Irwin did not openly criticize the effort. He was too smart for that level of sabotage, but he obviously was just going through the motions of meeting another request from headquarters.

Word got back to Mike from several sources about the half-hearted manner in which Irwin was going about completing the project, and it made him really hot. He decided to ignore the situation for a while and let Irwin just dig his own grave, but then it occurred to him that he might profit from talking the situation over with Jacob. In a 20-minute telephone call, Jacob helped him see the following points:

- His strategy of letting Irwin "dig his own grave" was another instance of Mike's default setting kicking in as a response to heightened anxiety. It was a form of cutoff behavior.
- If Mike continued to respond to Irwin's reactivity with his own, the cycle would only escalate. Mike needed to focus on his own functioning, **stay connected** and work on being less anxious.
- There was an anxious triangle at work here: Mike (A)—Irwin (B)—the question Irwin was supposed to answer (C). As long as Mike tried to get involved in the B-C axis, the resistance would only increase and Mike would be the one carrying the stress. Mike needed to focus on A-B, being non-anxious while holding firm on his expectations of Irwin; and on A-C, being clear about what he wanted and determined to get the answer either from Irwin or elsewhere.
- Irwin's reactive sabotage was a predictable systemic response to Mike's efforts to introduce change into CHI. Mike must not take Irwin's resistance as a personal attack, since it was almost certainly an unconscious example of reactive functioning. Staying connected to Irwin in a well-differentiated manner, rather than withdrawing, was the key to bringing him around.

Mike was disappointed to have missed so much of what seemed obvious after discussing the situation with Jacob. At Jacob's recommendation, he decided to ask Irwin to provide an interim update of his progress and encourage him to get more personally involved in supporting the assignment. He decided not to tell Irwin about the subtle sabotage tactics that had been reported to him, but instead to let him know how much he appreciated the extra effort he was putting into Mike's request.

When Mike got the draft report—nearly a week late—he was pleasantly surprised that it actually had some very good ideas, and he took the time to acknowledge these while encouraging the whole Southeastern Division leadership team to continue their promising first efforts.

Mike stayed in touch with Irwin regularly and the effort, while time consuming, gradually began to increase Irwin's level of interest and commitment. Over time, Mike could see two things happening: first, the reports were getting better; and, second, the more he worked with Irwin, the more relaxed and cooperative he became, at least to a point. Irwin was never going to change dramatically, but when Mike began to acknowledge and respect the effective attributes of Irwin's leadership capabilities, rather than criticize his limitations, his performance got better.

In subsequent discussions with Jacob, Mike was reminded that his decision to **stay connected** rather than engage in a cutoff as a response to Irwin's resistance was the catalyst that turned him in a different direction.

MIKE, RICHARD AND *A NEW EARTH*

Mike had listened to the book *A New Earth* on the ride home from Delaware; he found it too dense to comprehend from just listening. However, along the ride home, there were a number of points in the audiotape that made a lot of sense, and several seemed very similar to his **Resilient Leadership** coaching. The tape grabbed his interest, so one weekend he picked the book up and finished it during several mornings of early reading. Mike thought it was quite a remarkable book. Even more remarkable was the level of interest that Richard had in the book.

A key insight for Mike was the link between his coping strategy of jogging and the deeper insight about life found in the work of Tolle. Mike was aware that he would cope with the stressful issues he faced by jogging. Frequently Mike actually visualized that he was running away from his problems when he ran. An added benefit was that his exercise program was beneficial to his physical health.

But, due to his knee condition, he was no longer going to be able run like he had in the past. He now had to face and manage his stress and deal with life in a different way. As he grew in his self-awareness, he realized he would need to reduce anxiety at its root by learning how to "be in the now." He was just beginning to understand how to do that through increased presence and self-awareness.

One morning Mike e-mailed Richard to exchange some thoughts about the material in Tolle's book, and Richard shot back a very thoughtful response within an hour. That began their correspondence, which subsequently grew in frequency and depth as they explored the material together. Over the course of several months, they had a few conversations about the book but found that writing to each about their thoughts and insights gave them the freedom to communicate at any time from almost anywhere and with considerably more insight.

Mike gathered a great deal from his study of the material and his Internet dialogue with Richard. He also found common ground that linked the Tolle material with Jacob's **Resilient Leadership** model and recorded many thoughts in his cell phone. One day about six months after his promotion to COO, he wrote:

> *Being fully present in the moments of your life enables you to have deep self-awareness and interconnectedness with others. The degree to which you will be self differentiated in any moment depends on the degree of your presence in that moment.*

He sent the note to Richard who sat down for a moment and savored the few words his dad had written. Richard had taken each memo his father had sent him over the last several months, numbered each one, and put them in a notebook that he read through from time to time. He finally had developed the kind of connection he had always wanted to have with his father.

KELLY – A NEW WAY OF SEEING

Mike and Kelly took off on their tour of the Northeastern Division on a Monday morning. They met at Reagan Airport to catch the 7:30 a.m. shuttle. Their first stop was Boston, where Mike had asked Sally Harrison to assemble the general managers for a breakfast meeting that was mostly an introduction but included a presentation of the new fiscal year budget numbers as well. Mike was eager to see Kelly in action for the first time and, as expected, she was quick and charming and direct.

At the first meeting in Boston, things went very well. The team seemed to warm up to her right away. The second visit was to New York, then Rochester, Pittsburg, Philadelphia and finally Baltimore on the way home. It was a full week. As the days went by, Mike got to know Kelly better and better as they spent morning, afternoon and evening together. She was a quick study and so self-assured that she often began to draw conclusions before she had a full understanding of issues.

Mike was a little concerned about the point, but it seemed such a minor issue that he brought it up only in passing a few times.

When they returned to DC on Friday and were saying goodbye at the gate, Kelly suggested that she prepare a trip report for Mike to review before she sent it off to the hotels. To Mike's surprise the report was finished and on his cell phone by Saturday at 4:00 p.m. The report was 43 pages long and filled with details that he could not even recall. It was the most thorough summary of a field visit he had ever seen. The report was not only thorough, but very authoritative in tone and downright offensive in a few spots. If Kelly had sent this out without his review, she would have been DOA before even getting started. Mike sent a quick note back to her, asking that she hold the memo until they could talk about it on Monday.

On Monday they met to discuss the report. It was factual, but it reached too far in drawing conclusions, making assumptions and assigning follow-up actions. Rather than telling everyone what needed to be done, the report needed to identify issues, pose questions and ask for responses. Kelly was receptive and appreciative of Mike's input. Mike was happy with her openness about his feedback, but he felt some uneasiness with her level of awareness about how her communications would be received. Kelly was so smart and so quick on her feet that she could leave others behind quickly during an analysis of business challenges. She could critique an operational plan faster than even the brightest CHI general managers. Within a very short time, Mike began to worry about her "fit" in the culture of CHI.

Also during the first few months, Kelly began to undertake the work needed to finalize the partnership agreement with Universal Holdings. This responsibility took her back to London frequently, which helped her with the transition she was making. Her skills and knowledge of the partnership process was of irreplaceable value to CHI. She did a great job in this aspect of her job. But she was not as successful in her operational role. In her return visits to the northeast, she quickly began to formulate views about who was doing the job and who was not. Once her mind was made up, she moved with lighting speed to make changes in leadership assignments or in strategic priorities.

Because Mike had been in the role before her, a number of his old teammates would call him from time to time to see how he was doing. They were always circumspect in their comments about Kelly, but her overbearing nature was coming through in all the calls. Mike was alert to the fact that these calls were subtle invitations to be triangled into situations that he should at all costs avoid.

One late afternoon he got a call from Sally Harrison. Sally had not gotten off to a good start with Kelly. Now Sally was dealing with several challenging issues related to strategy and a few general managers who were not solving problems as quickly as Kelly wanted. Kelly had a way of targeting people she felt were not keeping up with the pace she wanted to see.

The sum of the problem was that Kelly was beginning to direct Sally to take actions that she felt were not reasonable. The pressure was building, and now Sally was beginning to worry about her career. Mike listened to Sally's concerns, took notes and asked if she had expressed these concerns to Kelly directly. She indicated that she had, and when she did Kelly seemed to be even more intent on moving quickly, suggesting that Sally herself may be part of the problem.

Mike thanked Sally for the call. He was keenly aware of the triangle he was being involved in, but he remembered that Jacob had also taught him that he could leverage his position in a triangle to move forward his own agenda. Mike asked Sally to be patient while he considered steps that she and Kelly should take. He told her he would call her back as quickly as possible and that he would hold their conversation in confidence.

The next morning James, Kelly, Mike and Mercedes the CFO met to prepare for an upcoming decision-making meeting with Universal Holdings about three large hotels involved in the partnership agreement. The financial analysis developed for the last meeting was simply inaccurate for both demolition and new construction costs. Math and calculation errors had produced several cost estimate spreadsheets that were almost 40 percent off.

Mercedes presented this problem to start off the meeting.

"How did we get all the way to a decision-making meeting with our partners with information that was so inaccurate?" James asked.

Mercedes explained that the mistakes on the spread sheets were mistakes that her own department should have caught before the information was presented at the last partnership meeting, and she took responsibility for not catching the errors.

"Well, how do we recover from this problem now?" Mike asked. "Should we arrange for a conference call with their financial people before we meet as a full transition team again?"

As Mercedes was about to answer, Kelly jumped into the discussion. "This is a problem we should not be having at this point of the negotiations. It is one thing for a mistake to be made by an outside consultant that the partnership retained. We can take steps to be absolutely sure they never make that mistake again or get another firm. But sloppy, inaccurate data developed by our own staff is a whole different problem. This sort of thing makes us look inept. Our partners deserve better than that, and they will not stand for this kind of error at this stage of the game. I know I wouldn't."

Kelly's intervention was made with a deep level of disgust in her voice. Mike was observing the scene quietly, thinking that nothing Kelly had just said added anything helpful to the discussion.

Kelly went on with her criticism of the work done by Mercedes and her team. Kelly was absolutely right, deeply insightful and fast on her feet, but her remarks were much too caustic and accusatory. As she was speaking, Mike and James' eyes met across the table, and Mike could see by the expression on James' face that he was deeply disturbed by what was taking place in the room.

By the time Kelly finished, there were tears in Mercedes' eyes from the vitriol in Kelly's commentary. James stepped to Mercedes' defense, but even so Kelly continued in the same tone.

Finally it became clear that the beating needed to stop.

"Let's take a break and we can get started again in 15 minutes," Mike said. As he stood up, Kelly took out her cell phone, checked her messages and called one of her team members back to discuss an issue. For the next five minutes she engaged in a fairly complex and contested discussion about a personnel matter as James and Mike walked in and out of the meeting room during the break. Mike noticed how direct, almost harsh, she could become in contentious discussions. He reflected on the fact that contentious conversations always escalated with Kelly. She hated to lose, and she never did—at anything.

After the break, Mike moved the discussion forward quickly and a resolution was reached within a half hour. James reasserted his commitment to the process and his confidence in Mercedes. It was clear that he was trying to protect her now, and Kelly finally picked up on the point.

As the meeting ended, Kelly said, "I'm sorry if I came on too strong. We are in a very sensitive stage in the partnership process, and I want to be sure we do everything to build our relationship with Universal on solid footing. At the very least, we need good data to do that."

Even Kelly's attempt at an apology for being too direct was laced with a restatement of Mercedes' failure and a veiled justification for her initial remarks. Still, Mike thought, all in all she is a remarkable talent.

After the meeting ended, Mike asked Kelly to lunch.

Over lunch, Mike listened to Kelly talk about her progress with the Northeast Division and some significant challenges she was still encountering. At the end of her summary, he asked, "Kelly, how do you think you are being received by the people in CHI so far?"

"Well, I think they are still trying to get used to me. I can be pretty intense; this morning's meeting is a good example. I see what needs to be done, and I sometimes get too impatient. Plus, I hate making mistakes—especially ones that can be avoided. But, all in all, I think I'm being well received here at CHI. How do you see it, Mike?"

Mike paused before he spoke. He had not intended to make this conversation so significant, but he sensed that he had an opening he did not want to miss. He really wanted Kelly to succeed, and he was increasingly concerned over her lack of self-awareness and how her style was alienating people around her.

"Kelly, I am going to be very direct with you, and I hope you will believe me when I say that I am speaking out of a sincere desire to see you succeed here at CHI." Mike paused, deliberately, to emphasize the importance of his next statement. "But, if you continue on your present course, I believe you will fail and no longer be at CHI in a year's time."

Mike stopped and tried to gauge her reaction from the expression on her face. His statement had struck home, and the articulate Ms. Kelly O'Reilly was speechless. Before she could gather her thoughts for a response, Mike continued, "In my view, you did as much harm as good at today's meeting. You made your points, but you offended Mercedes and annoyed James. You saw the way he came to her defense right after we returned at the break."

"Yes, but I apologized," Kelly said.

"That you did," Mike answered. "But you did so almost as an afterthought, and you could have made your points without offending Mercedes in the first place.

"Another point I need to make with you, Kelly, is that I have been getting feedback from the Northeast Division that you are needlessly harsh on them, too, and morale is suffering. Instead of motivating them to higher performance you are demoralizing and browbeating them. The memo we talked about the other day—the one you were going to send after our visit up there—was really a disaster. I tried to be gentle in encouraging you to soften it, but you obviously had no awareness of how badly you were coming across with such a strident tone throughout. I could give you some other examples, but I am not trying to beat up on you. You have so much to offer here, it just makes me sad to see you throwing it away."

Mike went silent fearing that he had gotten carried away and said more than Kelly was able—or willing—to hear. He waited for her response.

Kelly thought for a long moment and then speaking softly, to herself as much as to Mike, said, "This is the same problem I had at All British Airline. It's why I was passed over there for the promotion. I've got to do something to fix this."

Her vulnerability disarmed Mike. This was the other side of the self-assured, bright, beautiful rising star that was so highly visible at CHI.

Finally, Mike said, "Kelly you are a remarkable talent, one of the smartest and quickest business professionals I have ever met. You have everything it will take to be a huge success here at CHI, except for one thing."

Kelly looked at Mike and said, "And that is...?"

Mike waited a moment and then reached into his pocket and took out his wallet. He pulled out a business card that read:

Jacob Wolfe, PhD. Executive Coach.

"Kelly, give this guy a call in the next day or two and pay him a visit. He will help you find out the answer to that question."

Kelly looked at the business card and flipped open her cell phone to record Jacob's number in her speed dial list.

Chapter 9: Stay Connected

<u>Review of Key Points</u>

- A leader is only able to influence a system to which he or she is connected.
    - o The *position* a leader occupies gives great leverage to affect the functioning of the organization, for better or for worse.

- One of a leader's most significant responsibilities is to function as a "step-down transformer" of the anxiety within the system.
    - o By being connected as a *less anxious presence*, the leader calms the system and helps others to be less anxious.
    - o No one can be completely "non-anxious"; it is sufficient to be less anxious than those around you.

- Staying connected in the right way is a balancing act between the extremes of fusion and cutoffs. The functioning of a leader who has learned to **stay connected** in a more differentiated way is characterized by two patterns of behavior:
    - o **Respectful dialogue without cutoffs**: This is reflected in the leader's ability to engage in disagreements without becoming defensive, respecting the viewpoints and boundaries of others, while maintaining one's own as well. Such a leader seeks common ground rather than either/or thinking and polarization. Respectful dialogue includes managing one's thoughts as well as one's words.
    - o **Staying connected without fusion**: This is reflected in one who does not seek approval or worry about what others think, but rather sets his or her course according to his or her own vision and principles. Neither does such a leader get caught up in reciprocal patterns that stem from relationship fusion (e.g., over- and under-functioning).

Questions for Reflection and Discussion

1. What evidence did you see of Mike's growing ability to **stay connected** as a less anxious presence in relationships, rather than responding to anxiety with cutoffs?

2. Can you name three people in your work environment who are "step-down transformers" whenever there is rising anxiety in the system? How do they do that? What do they do?

3. When you were growing up, what behavior patterns do you now recognize in retrospect were examples of relationship fusion/cutoffs on the part of family members? Do you see any evidence that these patterns still continue in some form among family members?

The Practice

There are four basic methods one can practice to help manage one's reactivity in order to remain connected as a less anxious (better differentiated) presence:

- **Watch the process.** By adopting the stance of a neutral observer of the **emotional process** unfolding in any situation, a person automatically is less driven by the anxious process of the situation. Leaders do well to remember that the content of an issue is not always "the issue" and that by developing the habit of "going up in the tree" in order to watch the process, they are less likely to get hooked by the content.

- **Expand your repertoire.** One can manage reactivity better if there is a range of responses that are available to use in anxious situations. Using humor, playfulness and irony can help one remain a neutral observer rather than being drawn into the anxious dynamics of a situation. Other calming and relaxing techniques such as breathing, visualization, and so forth are also useful.

- **Recognize your triggers.** Developing more self-awareness helps a person recognize and defend against the things that make one more reactive.

- **Avoid quick fixes.** The tendency to seek quick relief from painful or anxious situations is natural, but not always the best option for a leader who is seeking to build health and resilience in the system. The "fallacy of empathy" suggests we should relieve pain as quickly as possible, but experience has shown that people (and organizations) generally grow more from challenge than comfort. The more a leader increases his or her capacity to handle the pain of those he or she leads, the more will they increase their capacity as well.

1. Identify a situation in an important relationship in which you want to become a more self-differentiated presence by staying connected as a less anxious presence.

2. Using the four methods suggested above, first describe where/how you currently fall short.

3. Next, describe a better way of functioning by using each of the methods above.

Stay Connected

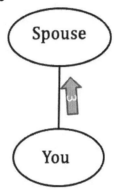

1. Identify situation: My husband and I always wind up in a fight over how best to deal with our son when he misbehaves. I am always forced to be the disciplinarian.		
Basic Methods	**2. Describe how you are functioning now**	**3. Describe how you might function in a better, less anxious manner.**
Watch the Process (Specific Actions)	**Now**: Our arguments end in both of us walking away and avoiding each other for hours. I am so angry at him I can hardly think of anything except his failure to support me.	**Better**: When I write in my journal I always seem to calm down and get a better perspective on the struggle between us. Do this immediately whenever I find myself avoiding him.

Expand Your Repertoire (Specific Actions)	**Now**: Whenever he tells me I am "being too hard on the boy" I accuse him of being a wimp and always wanting to appear the "good guy" in our son's eyes.	**Better**: I need to ask my husband how he would handle it, and then let him try his way, even if I think it's the wrong approach.
Recognize Your Triggers (Specific Actions)	**Now**: He can always get me going by saying I'm too much like my mother. I'm too domineering and interfering in our son's life.	**Better**: Anticipate this accusation, and remember it's not true, only a tactic he uses to win arguments with me. Don't let it set me off so easily.
Avoid Quick Fixes (Specific Actions)	**Now**: We usually try to resolve things by ignoring the issue, and as a result our son is not held accountable for his misbehavior.	**Better**: Don't drop it, no matter how much work it is to come to a common solution. Our son needs us to have a firm, united front.

To learn more, go to www.resilient-leadership.biz.

Appendix

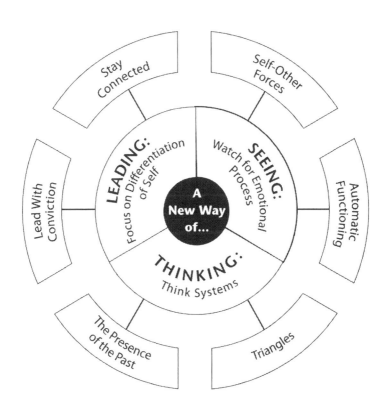

Bowen Family Systems Theory & the Resilient Leadership Model

All too often, new ideas are described as representing a "paradigm shift" when in fact they fall far short of representing such a watershed moment.

The lifelong work of Dr. Murray Bowen[4] (1913-1990), however, is a body of thought that truly merits that designation. Bowen Family Systems Theory has taken the study of human behavior to a new level of inquiry, and his disciples are still in the early stages of unpacking the many implications of his work and applying it across a broad spectrum of scientific research. Some have even said that Bowen Theory is sufficiently robust to replace Freudian thinking as the dominant therapeutic framework of the twenty-first century.

Dr. Bowen, a psychiatrist, developed his theory over forty years by combining his research into the functioning of families from a systems perspective with his knowledge of the human species as the product of evolutionary processes. Central to his theory is the assumption that an emotional system has evolved over billions of years and is an unseen force regulating the relationship networks of human beings, in units as small as the family and as large as work organizations or even entire societies. Despite the significant differences that arise as a result of our human capacity for thought, language and culture, we share more in common than we recognize with the life forms that preceded us on the evolutionary ladder. Bowen insisted that his was a "natural systems theory," based on careful study of how all living systems function and built on universal laws that can be observed in every living species.

Bowen revolutionized the world of individual therapy by recognizing the family as a basic unit of study. The complex interactions of individual family members can be understood best when seen as part of a system of reciprocal dynamics within the family emotional network. Family members so profoundly influence one another's functioning that it is evident that they share a common emotional field, reacting to one another's approval or disapproval, needs and expectations, supportive or distancing moves. When the functioning of one member of the family changes, there are predictable changes on the part of other family members.

Appendix

The intensity of the emotional process varies from family to family and can rise and fall as anxiety fluctuates due to internal and external factors, but all families—regardless of where they are on a continuum of functioning—are subject to the laws of emotional process. Bowen theorized that these processes evolved to promote cohesiveness and cooperation, qualities that are essential for survival in order to provide necessities such as food and shelter, protection against hostile forces and so forth.

Problems can arise, however, when tensions escalate, anxiety increases and reactivity spreads throughout the family unit. Under such circumstances, the connectedness of family members within the emotional system can become more burden than benefit, and members—particularly the most vulnerable—can feel overwhelmed and out of control. These are the individuals who develop clinical problems such as schizophrenia, addiction or even physical illnesses. They are the ones Bowen described as the "symptom bearers" for the intensities of the family's emotional process, and therapeutic interventions are most effective when those symptoms are seen as manifestations of forces much larger than the individual's psychodynamics.

Although Bowen recognized that the fundamental processes of emotional systems were identical regardless of the size of the relationship network in question, his research was focused primarily on family units. A number of his disciples have explored the application of his thinking to other organizations, but none with the depth and breadth of Edwin Friedman (1932-1996). Dr. Friedman was an ordained rabbi, a family therapist, internationally known lecturer, author, teacher and consultant who studied his own family, his congregational family and a variety of other organizations with whom he consulted over many decades. He took Bowen's ideas about leadership and began to explore and deepen and apply them within an array of organizational contexts in new and exciting ways.

Friedman had the courage to present the complexities of Bowen Theory in "popular" formats. In addition to his scholarly writing,[5] he produced a book of fables[6] and lectured and taught extensively to groups ranging from U.S. Army generals to community activists prior to an untimely death that left a major book on leadership[7] in unfinished manuscript form. While Bowen's work provides the theoretical foundation for the

Resilient Leadership model, Friedman's insights also find a prominent place in the authors' application of Bowen Theory to leadership.

There is a saying in Italian, "*traduttore, traditore*," which can be translated loosely as "every translator is a traitor." Anyone who has attempted to translate someone else's ideas into another idiom, let alone another language, can identify with the profound truth contained in this bit of Italian folk wisdom. It is, quite simply, impossible to capture the full scope of another person's work in a context that would have been foreign to the original author. The project of this book—to take a highly nuanced, sophisticated theory from the world of the human sciences and "translate" it into a popular tale about leadership in the world of business—might well suggest another bit of folk wisdom: "Fools rush in..."

From the outset, the authors have recognized and readily admit the impossibility of doing full justice to source material that has been developed in a scholarly context of clinical research and theoretical reflection over more than half a century. They are convinced, however, that the importance of making more widely available to a new audience thinking that is truly groundbreaking merits the risks inherent in a project of "popularizing." The authors have taken great pains to remain faithful to the core ideas of Bowen Theory while rendering them accessible to an audience that is unlikely to wade through the dense primary research of Bowen and his disciples.

Friedman's willingness to translate Bowen Systems Theory and its ideas about leadership into anecdotal and parabolic form has given the authors encouragement to convey this same material in narrative fashion, as a contemporary tale about leadership that resonates with the real-life challenges, joys and sorrows of leaders who struggle to make a difference in their organizations, their communities and even their own families. We have written a simple story about a man who aspires to become COO and his attempt to grow into a better leader at work and at home. Our challenge in doing so has been to write about a very complex subject in plain language, without being simplistic. We believe we have accomplished that task.

The pages that follow offer a brief summary of the key ideas of Bowen Theory as they have been incorporated into the

Appendix

framework of the **Resilient Leadership** model. These pages repeat material found in the story of Mike Sampson, but we hope that its arrangement in summary form will help the reader to identify and remember more easily the key insights of this material. If any inadequate, misleading or erroneous portrayals of Bowen Theory have resulted, the authors take full responsibility for those failures. For whatever genius they have been able to convey, the authors are indebted to Murray Bowen and Ed Friedman.

A New Way of SEEING

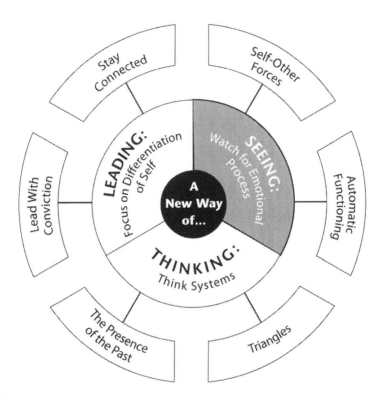

1. Watch for Emotional Process

The **Resilient Leadership** model borrows the phrase **"emotional process,"** from Bowen Systems Theory to refer to a level of functioning that is much deeper than we generally associate with the word "emotions," or feelings. Popular use understands the word "emotions" to refer to feelings such as fear, anger, erotic desire, and so forth. Although we are not always conscious of those feelings, in general they are accessible to our conscious awareness if we focus and get in touch with them in a deliberate manner. Bowen Theory's use of the phrase "emotional process," while including the realm of feelings, refers primarily to instinctual dimensions of our makeup that are often too deep for conscious awareness.

Appendix

Roger Schwarz[8] uses the term "diagnostic frame" to describe how a person selectively chooses certain behaviors and ignores others when observing group functioning. The data generated by people functioning in relationship networks is so vast that no observer can possibly attend to more than a fraction of what is available. Given this fact, Schwarz rightly underscores the importance of making a very deliberate choice about what to watch for in order to understand group process. The **Resilient Leadership** model makes much the same point, suggesting that watching for emotional process yields extremely useful data that allows a leader to make critical inferences and take highly effective action in light of those inferences. The **Resilient Leadership** model is a uniquely valuable diagnostic frame that reveals an organization's "hidden chemistry" to a leader who embraces this "New Way of SEEING."

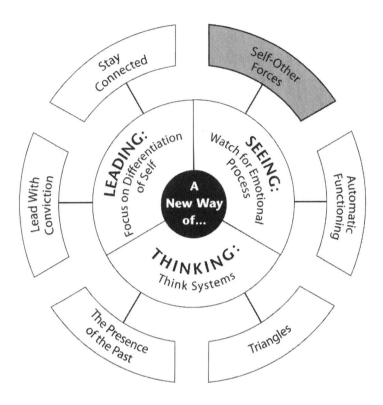

2. Self-Other Forces

Among the telltale behaviors that a leader must pay attention to when watching for emotional process are two primal, instinctual forces: the drive to be a separate, independent self, and the drive to be in relationship with others. It is a universal law in nature that living beings are constantly balancing their need to be separate and their need for togetherness. Loss of a proper balance between those two forces is a root cause of the various diseases and dysfunctions that threaten healthy life. This is true at all levels of life, from the cellular level to the complexities of human communities. Both too much separateness and too much togetherness are destructive. Similarly, not enough space for self to flourish, or not enough closeness with others, results in damage to the organism.

Appendix

Achieving the right balance between these two primal forces—**self-other**, individuality and togetherness, autonomy and intimacy—is one of the fundamental challenges in the "dance of life" at every level of complexity.

The **Resilient Leadership** model teaches a leader to recognize emotional process by learning to watch how the **self-other** balance is being managed, both by individuals as well as by organizations. This requires A New Way of SEEING on the part of the leader. Not only is each individual engaged in an ongoing process of managing that balance, the organization itself is a large-scale relationship system that works to maintain a relative balance—a dynamic equilibrium that represents its own unique comfort zone and that is manifest in its typical style of functioning. Watching how an organization strikes a balance between **self-other forces** can reveal significant information; for example, the degree of anxiety that is present, and this awareness can help a leader determine appropriate intervention strategies to correct imbalances or maintain a healthy equilibrium.

Developing one's skill at recognizing how an organization is managing this balance will be more successful if a leader is attentive to his or her own functioning. Becoming aware of one's own tendencies in this regard develops a first-hand sensitivity to the subtleties of emotional process. While they are not the only places where one can learn about oneself in this regard, it is nonetheless true that the relationships in our nuclear family and in our family of origin are the best places to observe how we manage those **self-other forces**. We would often like to think that we operate in a professional setting quite differently than how we do in our sometimes "messy" personal lives. But on the level of these primal forces that are rooted in emotional process, our functioning cannot escape the pervasive influence of certain fundamental, deeply ingrained patterns.

Developing our skills at "SEEING" in this new way takes time and patient perseverance. We humans are so easily caught up in our own subjectivity that the discipline of being an objective observer is cultivated only gradually. A leader learns to see in this way by paying attention to the facts of what is actually transpiring. The more we can expand the range of our observations to include as much information as possible, the better. Thoughts, feelings and behaviors all need to be monitored, both in ourselves and in others who are part of the relationship system in question. Over time, such careful observation will improve a leader's ability to recognize recurring patterns and to interpret them correctly so as to be better positioned to take appropriate action that will keep the system in healthy balance.

Appendix

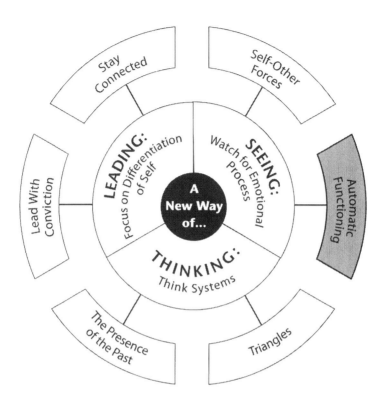

3. **Automatic Functioning**

In addition to the balance of **self-other forces**, there is another set of observable behaviors that will tip off a leader to the way that emotional process is present in a relationship network. These behaviors can be lumped together under the term "**automatic functioning**," a phrase meant to imply the instinctual dimension that humans share in common with our evolutionary ancestors.

Bowen Theory focuses on *reactivity* as one of the primary expressions of **automatic functioning**. In order to talk about reactivity, however, one must first consider how Bowen Theory understands the notion of *chronic anxiety*. The word "anxiety" refers to any response to a threat, real or imagined. *Acute* anxiety is a response to an immediate threat, such as being in a burning building. *Chronic* anxiety, on the other hand, is a pervasive uneasiness that operates at the level of emotional process—prior to our conscious awareness—and is a more generalized, free-floating phenomenon that does not present itself in such compelling, immediate fashion as acute anxiety.

In order to understand how deeply chronic anxiety is rooted in us all, it is helpful to reflect on what it is that gives life to it in the first place. A respected British psychotherapist by the name of John Bowlby wrote a book called *Attachment and Loss* in which he developed the notion that anxiety is rooted in our infancy, when we first become aware of the possibility of abandonment by our primary caregiver (usually, our mother). When an infant experiences the threat of physical separation from his or her mother, even momentarily, the seeds of anxiety are planted deep within his or her psyche. Successive experiences of abandonment (e.g., the hungry infant whose mother is nowhere in sight to relieve his or her desperate cries for food) reinforce our awareness of contingency and teach us early on that little is guaranteed in life and that the possibility of loss/abandonment is all too real.

For the infant, these experiences are intensely physiological as well as psychological. Bowlby observed meticulously how a young child tracks the presence of the parent to ward off the threat of abandonment, even as the child's growing curiosity to explore his or her surroundings naturally leads the child to stray farther and farther from the protective parent. As adults, the inner child within us continues to track the presence of significant relationships, anxious at some deep level over the possibility of abandonment and loss. An anxious response to the perception of possible abandonment makes it more difficult for us even as adults to maintain a healthy self-other balance in our key relationships.

The principal sources of chronic anxiety for most people, then, are disruptions that occur in their relationship networks. Within families, the kind of predictable events that upset the equilibrium of a family system are births, deaths, marriages, and divorces. In larger organizational families, the predictable events that disrupt relationship networks are often more complex, but analogous: new hires or reassignments, retirements or layoffs, major reorganizations and relocations that require new working relationships, and so forth. These are some of the hidden anxiety-generators that are routinely at work in any organization.

Existential philosophers have taken up these psychological insights and written about the *angst* that is embedded in us as finite creatures who must face our own limitations and, ultimately, our own mortality. The business of life is full of threats, and this means that each of us carries around an impressive amount of baggage that is anxiety-laden. The circumstances of our early environment as well as sibling position and idiosyncratic factors related to our individual personality result in more or less chronic anxiety being part of the package. But family systems research has shown that one of the most determinative factors in how much anxiety we carry on a day-to-day basis is the family in which we grow up. Like the DNA code that gives us blue eyes or a tendency to cancer, it seems that the level of chronic anxiety in the family system in which we are raised sticks with us pretty much for a lifetime, all things being equal.

A child is born into the global reality of the emotional system of its caregivers, and so a mother whose chronic anxiety is elevated automatically incorporates her child into a world where threats abound. That child grows into adulthood with a heightened level of chronic anxiety that seems perfectly "normal" (i.e., familiar) to the child. There is no way for parents to protect their children from this process of transmission, since the parents' chronic anxiety is, in a sense, "hard wired" into the way they function as a result of their own upbringing.

The level of anxiety that characterizes the parental relationship is the baseline within which the children of a family are raised. And although each child will "inherit" different degrees of anxiety (depending on birth order and many other factors), all of the children grow up within a given range that is more or less chronically anxious. Each individual within a family—as well as the family itself—develops a basic way of being in the world that is reflective of a certain range of chronic anxiety. Some families are characterized by a high sense of threat, elevated anxiety and considerable reactivity. The chronic anxiety levels of individual children within that family will vary, but only within a given range. Similarly, some families are characterized by very calm parents, and the entire family system is more secure, feels less sense of threat, and functions in a less reactive manner. The children in that family will vary in their individual levels of reactivity, but within a much lower range than children growing up in a highly anxious/reactive atmosphere.

Organizations function in this regard in much the same way as families. The degree of chronic anxiety carried by an organization's past leaders as well as the current leader—analogous to the role of one's ancestors and parents in a family—is enormously influential in setting the overall level of anxiety within the organization. It is important to keep in mind that chronic anxiety is a phenomenon that is part of emotional process—it operates at a level generally too deep for direct observation or measurement.

Our response to chronic anxiety is instinctual, rooted in what is sometimes called our reptilian brain. That is the part of our brain where the fight-flight-freeze response is spontaneously triggered, bypassing the neocortex where we tend to deliberate and evaluate before acting. Scientists recognize that the automatic fight-flight-freeze response has been necessary for the progress of evolution. If our animal ancestors had to stop and think over whether to stay put or run for shelter every time a predator appeared on the horizon, survival rates would have been significantly diminished. We are heirs to this same instinct. Most of us can easily search our memories and recount a time when we reacted spontaneously and immediately, without deliberation or evaluation, because our flight-response was triggered by an imminent threat. **Automatic functioning** can operate at its lifesaving best in such situations.

But not all **automatic functioning** is desirable, and the art of **Resilient Leadership** involves learning to recognize the presence of **automatic functioning** in a way that permits our neocortex to evaluate and deliberate whether a more thoughtful response is appropriate in a particular circumstance. It is in the nature of our **automatic functioning** to bypass logical thought, and when physical survival is at stake, this is usually (but not always) in the service of life. Threat triggers strong feelings that move us to immediate action. But in an organization, threat is usually best dealt with when our thinking functions are not overridden. Leaders need to watch for the presence of

APPENDIX

automatic functioning (in themselves and in their organizations) so that they are better able to bring to bear a thoughtful rather than a reactive response. Just as a healthy balance of **self-other forces** is a component of **Resilient Leadership**, so too a healthy balance of thinking-feeling responses is a sign of a well differentiated, resilient leader.

Reactivity is the name we give to feeling-driven responses to anxiety that come from a more primitive part of our brain. Reactivity is the public face of anxiety, which is why a resilient leader is one who learns how to "read" the level of anxiety by observing reactive behaviors. This is a very subtle skill, since reactivity can surface in so many different guises—for example, in physical symptoms and even in an "excessive" reasonableness! The notions of anxiety and reactivity are intertwined, and they are sometimes spoken of as if they were the same thing. But it is important to recognize that they are in fact different realities. Reactivity is about being feelings-driven. But not all strong feelings are related to anxiety. Someone who is sexually aroused, for example, may be highly reactive and demonstrate behaviors consistent with those strong feelings, without any hint that the reactivity is symptomatic of anxiety. An important aspect of the **Resilient Leadership** model is learning to watch for reactive behavior patterns that signal the presence of anxiety-driven **automatic functioning**. Leaders who "see" in this new way are better equipped to lead more effectively because they possess tools that surpass those of others who fail to recognize the crucial organizational dynamics that are in play.

A New Way of THINKING

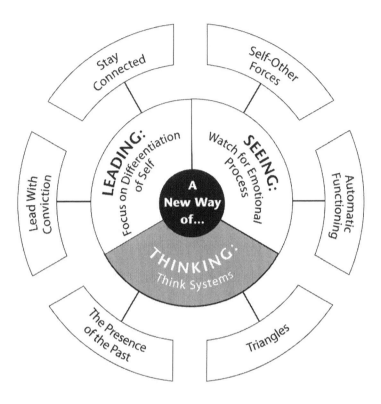

4. Think Systems

In addition to offering A New Way of SEEING, the **Resilient Leadership** model encourages A New Way of THINKING that enables deeper understanding and more effective action. Insistence on the importance of systems thinking is a staple of leadership training in the business world and elsewhere, and one might well inquire what is "new" about **Resilient Leadership's** encouragement to **"think systems."** While it shares much in common with General Systems Theory, the uniqueness of the **Resilient Leadership** model lies in the fact that it is rooted in the life sciences rather than the physical sciences. Traditional systems thinking in the business world is based on a more mechanistic understanding of how parts interrelate in a whole, while the **Resilient Leadership** model is more organic and is based in evolutionary biology. The fundamental structures of life arc similar in form, and this allows for a particular, distinctive application of systems thinking to the way that emotional process functions in every living species.

The breakthrough research of Murray Bowen that focused on the functioning of entire family systems rather than individual family members has made possible a much more sophisticated understanding of the emotional process that operates at the deepest level in every relationship network, whether it be a nuclear family, a multi-national corporation, or the global family of nations. Bowen called his theory a "natural systems theory" because it was developed on the basis of careful, empirical research into how nature itself governs life processes. Colonies of living beings cluster and function in remarkably similar ways, and the **Resilient Leadership** model shows leaders A New Way of THINKING about the systems dynamics that drive the organizations for which they have responsibility. Understanding the "natural laws" that we follow in our relationship networks provides a new and unique leverage for leadership initiatives such as driving change efforts, seeking greater efficiencies, reengineering critical work processes, and so forth.

Systems thinking reveals how reciprocal functioning operates, striving to maintain a dynamic equilibrium (homeostasis) within any relationship network. The primal life forces (self-other, for example) are always being balanced in an organization through the reciprocal interactions of its members who are constantly seeking to maintain the *status quo* to which they are accustomed. These dynamics generally operate below the level of conscious awareness and remain invisible to the naked eye; but when leaders "**think systems**," they can understand the reality of what is happening within the organization at an extremely deep level.

The "emotional field" of an organization powerfully influences the functioning of those who are part of its sphere of influence. Like the gravitational field that we can neither see nor feel—yet dramatically shapes every aspect of our existence—the emotional field of a relationship network is a powerful determinant of individual and collective human behavior. The **Resilient Leadership** model provides a framework for understanding how seemingly disparate phenomena are connected and subject to the influence of forces such as chronic anxiety, reactivity, and so forth.

A leader who is thinking systems will respond to symptoms in a more skillful fashion. Rather than rushing to "fix" a problem, the resilient leader will recognize that problems are generally symptoms that provide an invaluable window to learn about the larger system of which they are a part. When he or she is curious about a problem and recognizes it as an opportunity to learn more about the **automatic functioning** of the system, a leader is positioned quite differently than when he or she is anxiously threatened by it and feels an urgency to come up with a quick fix.

Systems thinking avoids the error of focusing on any single person, issue or factor when trying to understand the source of a problem. By thinking of problems as symptoms of system-wide phenomena, a leader's horizons are automatically broadened, and the chance of spotting relevant data is significantly enhanced. Such a leader understands the power of an emotional field over its parts and will focus attention on information that is truly relevant, i.e., the emotional processes at work in the relationship system. That leader is also better equipped to resist being regulated by those same forces, and hence can lead the system in a less reactive, more effective manner. A systems perspective increases the likelihood that a leader's response will be thought-driven rather than feeling-driven, especially in critical, high-pressure situations.

Particularly in view of today's "knowledge explosion," leaders who recognize what information is most important for them to gather possess an invaluable edge over competitors and other "hostile forces" that threaten the integrity (and success) of the organization for which they are responsible. With information today expanding exponentially in every domain, organizations and their leaders can easily fall prey to "paralysis by analysis." Knowing what data to follow, and when to stop seeking more information, are important qualities of successful leaders. **Resilient Leadership** does not dismiss the value of gathering and tracking the kind of metrics that organizations have traditionally relied on for important decisions. But it makes such data relative and contextualizes its importance by insisting that leaders need a new way to "**think systems**" at least as often as they are thinking metrics, measures, trends or other important data that have been gathered from a social-scientific perspective based in General Systems Theory.

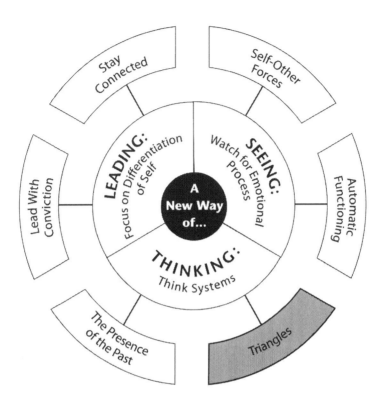

5. Triangles

The **Resilient Leadership** model has incorporated the notion of a relationship triangle from Bowen Theory and sees it as key to helping leaders "**think systems**" as they seek to understand the functioning of their organizations. Every two-person relationship system is inherently unstable because of the anxiety that is generated as each person works to manage the self-other balance, both within self and with his or her partner. When anxiety increases in a relationship, the "natural" reaction is to seek relief from the intensity of the relationship by focusing on a third person. Thus is born the triangle, the basic molecule of an emotional system. This process of triangle formation is a universal phenomenon and should not be regarded as a sign of pathology or dysfunction. **Triangles** exist as nature's way to

Appendix

manage anxiety by sharing or dispersing it more widely.

Each point of a triangle, it should be noted, can be occupied either by an individual or by a group of persons. By analogy the notion of the triangle can also be usefully employed when one point of the triangle is something non-human (e.g., a cause, an entity, or an idea) that is the focus of emotional process by the other two (living) points.

By way of example, typical triangular configurations can include any of the following:

- spouse/spouse/child
- child/parent/grandparent
- CEO/COO/CFO
- CEO/Board/stockholders
- CEO/VP/manager
- worker/union/management
- US citizens/illegal immigrants/government agency
- peace activists/"hawks"/the war
- spouse/addicted spouse/addictive substance

Once formed, triangles are remarkably sturdy and persistent over time. They are also extremely dynamic, constantly shifting the balance of **self-other forces** among the three parties, with two parties coming together as "insiders" and the third party feeling the effects of being an "outsider." It is worth noting that in highly conflictual situations, the "outsider" position in a triangle may be the preferred position. At other times, however, the "outsider" is usually striving to gain more comfort by moving closer to one of the others in order to become an "insider." This is the "dance of life" that keeps relationship systems energized. It is a "dance" that generally operates beneath conscious awareness, yet leaders can learn how to observe its subtle movements to great advantage. By virtue of their position, leaders are constantly being "triangled," and recognizing the complexities and subtleties of that process enables them to reposition themselves in various triangles in ways that result in significant leverage over the functioning of the organization.

Here is an example of what this dance may look like: Two co-workers are competing for the favor of the boss in view of an impending promotional opportunity. One of them perceives (or imagines) herself more distant than the other in terms of the boss's trust and confidence, and becomes sullen and withdrawn. Picking up on that worker's distress—perhaps only at a subliminal level—the boss tries to be a bit more attentive by asking her to take on a "special" project. The other co-worker, sensing that he is suddenly on the "outside" position of the triangle, begins to interact more intensely with the boss. The first worker, sensing that she is being edged out, over-functions in her relationship to the boss by taking on more and more responsibilities as a way of demonstrating her capacity and capability. And so it continues —unless the boss is sufficiently savvy about triangles and knows how to reposition in a less stressful manner.

The **Resilient Leadership** model highlights certain "laws" of how triangles operate in systems in order to help leaders capitalize on that knowledge. For example, it is important to know that the tendency of triangles to become interlocking increases as anxiety rises within an organization. As anxiety continues to rise, those triangles also become more locked in, less flexible. One positive dimension of the phenomenon of interlocking triangles is that it allows a leader to influence an entire organization very quickly—as long as he or she knows how to manage those triangles to his or her benefit. The down side is that triangles are also nature's way of helping a system remain stable. Nature designs systems to defend against change in order to remain in existence, and the phenomenon of interlocking triangles is one important source of the considerable resistance that leaders typically encounter when pushing for organizational change. Understanding the laws according to which those interlocking triangles operate can help leaders spot alliances and understand forces that are interfering with their attempts to motivate or impart new lessons.

Edwin Friedman warned of what he called the "togetherness position" in which a leader feels responsible for keeping a system together. He described this as one of the most subtle—and most subversive—effects of emotional triangles. The issue has to do with the fact that whenever one side of a triangle tries to change what is happening between the other two sides, the "responsible" member who is attempting to bring about that change will absorb the anxiety that more properly belongs in the relationship between the other two. This is the classic "burnout" position of an overly responsible leader.

Systems thinking understands that a leader's stress is not the result of the *amount* of work that he or she is doing. Rather, stress is an emotional phenomenon that comes from being responsible for more than one's fair share of the action. The boss who is feeling responsible for the relationship between two of his or her direct reports (e.g., Steve and Craig) will absorb the stress that rightly belongs to the direct reports. Paradoxically, such efforts will usually reinforce the very pattern the leader is attempting to change. Triangles resist change, and every effort of the boss to engage in a test of will with two direct reports will meet with resistance and in most cases with failure.

The **Resilient Leadership** model suggests that the way out of the trap of the "togetherness position" is for the leader to take responsibility for self, thus making the other two persons responsible for their own relationship *while still remaining part of the triangle with them*. This last phrase—*while still remaining part of the triangle*—is crucial, since it is relatively easy to avoid stress by withdrawing from a triangle. The problem with that strategy, however, is that it lessens the leader's influence over the system. The ideal situation is when a leader remains in a triangle but keeps focused on his or her own functioning, careful not to become responsible for the others while simultaneously holding them responsible for their functioning.

Since all three sides of a triangle are in constant movement, a leader needs to be "thinking systems" all of the time in order to avoid getting hooked into the wrong position in key triangles. Even so, no one gets it right all of the time. In fact, getting it right even half of the time is like batting .500! For this reason leaders also need to know how to "reposition" themselves when they find that they are being "triangled" in unhealthy ways. Ultimately, the art of repositioning is an expression of one's ability to be a better differentiated self. This requires focusing on taking a neutral stance towards the emotional process of the triangle. In order to achieve such a perspective, however, leaders have to manage their own anxiety level so that they can be more thoughtful and observant. Then they must define their position vis-à-vis each of the other two points of the triangle and avoid taking responsibility for the interaction between those other two.

A leader who attempts to reposition himself or herself in a triangle of some intensity will want to observe how **self-other forces** are at work, and how anxiety is impacting that interplay. The leader will also want to watch how his or her own reactivity within the system is influencing the ability to manage the thinking-feeling balance so as to observe better the process dynamics from a more or less neutral stance.

As a leader learns how to focus on the relationship process between two others, he or she becomes less judgmental and is less inclined to get caught up in his or her own sense of what "ought to be." This does not mean such a leader abandons personal goals, principles or values. Rather, he or she feels less need to judge and change the others, and that frees him or her to be a better observer as well as more emotionally neutral within a particular triangle. Furthermore, once some measure of these gains has been realized, one who is practicing **Resilient Leadership** must also be able to communicate his or her neutrality effectively to the others involved in the triangle.

However, it is not enough to have achieved a measure of interior detachment. In order to reposition successfully, both words and body language have to communicate to the others involved that the leader is in the process of repositioning self within the triangle. Communicating to the other two points of the triangle that one's relationship with each of them continues to matter, but that one is neutral to what goes on between them can be tricky, but it is an essential dimension of the process of repositioning.

APPENDIX

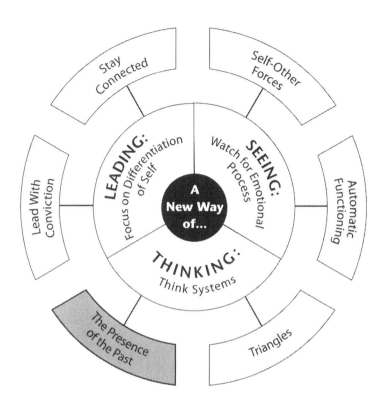

6. The Presence of the Past

Because linear thinking comes so naturally, we tend to understand the world around us in terms of simple cause-effect interactions. I bump into the table, it shakes a bit, and the bowl sitting on the table jiggles just enough to spill some of its contents over the edge. My bumping into the table caused the spill. Fairly simple, and it seems that the physical world around us works that way most everywhere. When it comes to our interactions with other people, we tend to think of their functioning in the same cause and effect way, perhaps filtered through a few notions from popular psychology. The boss chewed me out over something that seems very trivial. So I ask myself, "What caused her to be so angry? What did I do? What did someone else do, that caused her to dump on me like that?"

We look for the simple cause that explains her behavior. And if there appears to be no outside force sufficient to explain her behavior, there must be a psychological explanation. "Maybe I remind her of her ex-husband!" Cause and effect—it appears that simple.

In light of our innate tendency to look for simple, concrete and direct causal links, it is not difficult to understand why learning to "**think systems**" can be a challenging undertaking. Our understanding of relationships is "naturally" very linear and generally focused on an individual level, while to "**think systems**" is counterintuitive and requires a very deliberate effort to think at a more complex level. Using the notion of triangles is a useful tool in this regard, since it automatically organizes our thinking to look at relationships from a systems perspective. However, there is another level of insight that expands one's understanding of how relationships function as part of an even larger framework.

This level recognizes that the emotional process that generates triangles is the product of multi-generational systems dynamics. **The presence of the past** is evident in more aspects of our functioning than we realize! Here is how this happens: The classic, primary triangle that most of us know firsthand is the one that exists between us and our parents. No matter how healthy and good the relationship might be between any two parents, they each carry into their marriage a certain level of chronic anxiety. As they relate to one another in the ups and downs of married life, there are times when the anxiety in their relationship escalates and creates more than usual tension. Automatically, and generally beyond conscious awareness, they discover that by focusing on a third person—their child—their relationship becomes more calm and easy. The anxiety of a two-person system is instinctively "off-loaded" onto a third party, and a triangle is born.

Some parents, of course, do a relatively good job of keeping their anxiety mostly within the marriage relationship. But when that is not the case, the *amount* of anxiety that is transferred to each child varies. For a number of reasons, a particular child will receive a disproportionate share of the parents' concern and attention. The result is a greater degree of chronic anxiety being transmitted to that child. That is why one of the reasons not all of the children in a single family turn out the same. Each child is focused on by his or her parents in different measure. Other factors enter in, of course, but each child in the family grows up with his or her own degree of "baggage" from the amount of chronic anxiety off-loaded by the parental triangle. In general, the child who has less parental focus escapes to a greater degree the negative effects of this transfer of anxiety.

Of course, it is important to remember that each parent grew up in a family in which similar dynamics were at work. The result is that every person is the recipient of chronic anxiety handed down from parents, grandparents, great-grandparents, and so forth. Research has shown that over many generations, **emotional process** is passed on from one generation to the next in ways that establish certain patterns of **automatic functioning** that are characteristic of a given family system. The past is always present to us in our family systems. For example, one family might have a tendency to express its emotional fusion by cutoffs while another tends to become excessively close under stressful conditions. These patterns get deeply embedded in the **emotional process** of the family system and keep replicating in the behaviors of children, grandchildren, great-grandchildren, and so forth.

For many leaders who have wanted to explore more deeply the implications of the **Resilient Leadership** model, it has proven very fruitful to look into their families of origin to understand more about what has been passed down to them on the level of emotional process. One tool that is available to do that kind of work is the genogram, a graphic representation that allows a person to visualize multiple generations of a family and note key bits of information that can provide insight into recurring patterns of emotional process.

A person can become a more effective leader by working to understand more deeply how relationship dynamics work, whether in a family or in an organization. Each of us belongs to multiple relationship systems. For most adults, the greatest influence on how they function in their relationship networks comes from their family of origin, their current nuclear family, and their workplace "family." It is also possible that when a person's participation in another relationship system (e.g., a religious community or other voluntary association organization) is particularly intense, that system will exert a significant influence as well.

Bowen Theory has shown that of all the relationship networks that we belong to, it is our multi-generational family of origin that plays a primary role in shaping who we are and how we function in other systems. This truth has important implications for a leader who wishes to enhance his or her functioning in a work setting. The good news is that because we belong to interlocking systems, all of the personal gains a leader makes in one relationship network are also available in the others. Progress that a leader makes in the relationship network of family might seem on the surface to be unrelated to how he or she functions on the job. But the opposite is the case. It is also the case that growth that takes place in the workplace is available in ways that can enrich family relationships, especially if a leader is deliberate about applying the lessons in that world as well.

While it is true that to some extent various social environments can elicit and support the emergence of different *functional* levels of differentiation, it is also true that our brain is "wired" with certain templates (**the presence of the past**) governing a *basic* level of differentiation. We bring these templates to any relationship network, whether at home or at work. But the good news is that a growing body of research into the brain's ability to build new neural pathways throughout the adult lifespan indicates that a far greater measure of reprogramming of our brain is possible than was previously thought. This is referred to as the "neuroplasticity" of the brain. It is never too late to reap the benefits in every area of our lives when we learn how to "**think systems**" in ways that enhance our functioning. Of course, change at the fundamental level of how we manage emotional process is very gradual, and it requires persistent effort across a significant period of time. Bowen Theory emphasizes the importance of reconnecting with one's family of origin with an intentional effort to be less reactive and more differentiated. But progress is accelerated if we are working on a consistent growth agenda in all of our interlocking relationship systems, which is why effort both in one's family and in one's work setting is so relevant to strengthening the skills associated with the **Resilient Leadership** model. The role of a qualified coach in supporting and expediting this growth process can be considerable.

Another valuable aspect of thinking about the multi-generational transmission of emotional process is its relevance on an organizational level. Just as families pass on certain patterns of **automatic functioning** from generation to generation, so do organizations. The past is as present in organizations as it is in families. Leaders can develop a more sophisticated understanding of their organizations by looking back over a period of years and searching for themes, patterns and recurring issues that are indicative of how emotional process has operated in the organization over a number of generations. By recognizing how periods of heightened anxiety gave rise to typical patterns of reactive behavior in the organization, leaders can **think systems** at a more complex level. The more leaders can understand the history of the company with an eye to systems dynamics, the better they will understand the impact that emotional process is currently having on them and on their organization.

It is helpful to emphasize that simply because these processes have been passed down from generation to generation does not imply that relationship systems can never improve their functioning. Emotional systems—like individuals—are growing, living realities, and things can happen in the course of successive generations to change prevailing patterns. Some of those things can be damaging, but some of them can also make the system healthier. When these changes take place, the culture of an organization shifts for the better or for the worse. The challenge of leadership is to create opportunities—or make use of the ones that present themselves—to promote healthier organizational functioning that minimizes or overcomes previous destructive patterns. A leader is in a very powerful position, and by learning to **think systems**, a leader can leverage his or her presence in ways that influence the organization's emotional field for the better.

A New Way of LEADING

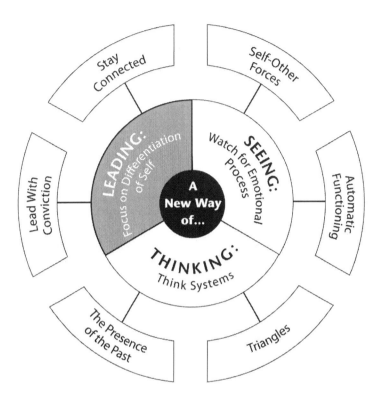

7. Focus on Differentiation of Self

It is the *position* of the leader in a system that explains why his or her influence is felt so strongly throughout the organization. In any system the leader has a natural leverage that results in his or her having a disproportionate impact on the organization, one that far outweighs the influence of any other individual. This greater influence of a leader is not the result of any inherent quality or personality trait. Rather, it is the *fact of being a leader* that gives one this power, for better or for worse.

Most of the literature on leadership assumes that a leader's effectiveness is the result of such things as personality factors, mastery of a particular set of competencies, charisma, better communication skills, role modeling certain behaviors, or implementing great strategies and techniques that promote organizational change. All of those factors can contribute to success, but they operate on a more superficial level. There is a much more significant contribution to exercising effective leadership. And that is for a leader to focus on his or her own differentiation of self, rather than on how others are behaving. A leader's main focus should be on *how he or she is being,* not on *what others may be doing.*

To grasp accurately what the notion of **differentiation of self** means can be challenging. We are tempted to think of it much like the concept of psychological maturity or self-actualization or individuation. But those categories are different, because they describe a certain developmental level or stage of growth that can be arrived at once and for all. Differentiation of self, on the other hand, is never a point of arrival or a goal that can be reached. Rather, it is a life-long process, continual and ongoing, a way of being in the world that is never "achieved."

Differentiation of self involves maintaining a healthy balance, and one of its primary dimensions is how well we are balancing the **self-other forces**; that is, how well we manage our attempts to be a separate self without cutting off from others, while, on the other hand, how well we **stay connected** to others without getting too close and becoming emotionally "fused" with them.

Murray Bowen suggested the value of a theoretical scale of differentiation, from 0 to 100, as a way of describing the range of variation that is possible in human functioning. There are many factors that go into where a person might be placed on that scale. Success in the balancing act between **self-other forces** puts one higher on the scale. However, our ability to maintain a healthy balance of closeness and separateness in our relationships is just one of many factors involved in assessing one's level of differentiation. Another important factor is how much a person sets his or her life course on the basis of fundamental values and principles; that is, how much he or she is goal-oriented and led by a consistent vision and set of priorities in making life choices.

Another balancing act that is indicative of a person's level of differentiation is the ability to integrate thinking and feeling responses. Someone who is consistently feeling-driven, with very little ability to think objectively, would be lower on the scale than someone who may be in touch with his or her feelings, but still remains able to think through charged situations in a more objective fashion. The ability to distinguish between what one is feeling and what one is thinking is key here. If every feeling response is immediately translated into a firm conviction or belief—without any testing—that suggests a person has difficulty distinguishing what he or she feels from what he or she thinks. Also significant is how often a person makes choices on the basis of what he or she is feeling or on the basis of what he or she is thinking. For example, does a person have such strong feelings of friendship for someone that he can't bring himself to do what he knows is best, (such as passing over that friend for a promotion when it is not deserved, or giving him a reprimand when he needs it)?

Determining where someone might be on Bowen's scale of differentiation is far more complex than calibrating any two or three factors. It is ultimately about how much of a self a person has, and how that self is manifested in a variety of ways that make up the whole of a person's life. Differentiation describes our ability to claim a unique identity in the world and to be responsible for and manage our functioning, both internally and in external relationships. Differentiation of self is manifested in every dimension of life, from health (both physical and emotional) to success or failure in relationships, from career success and social standing to one's ability to achieve life goals, and so forth.

A person's *basic* level of differentiation is, like so much else in life, mainly the result of the family he or she is born into. Most individuals have pretty much reached their *basic* level of differentiation by the time they leave home. This level is the cumulative result of what has been handed down from previous generations, inherited most immediately from one's parents and whatever level they in turn received from their families of origin. In addition, for a variety of reasons, each of the siblings in a family gets a bit more or less of their parents' emotional "baggage" than the other siblings, and this results in different levels of differentiation for each child.

Bowen Theory distinguishes what is called our *basic* level of differentiation, which is the default setting that we operate out of, "all things being equal." But there is also our *functional* level of differentiation, which is variable and susceptible to being influenced by our surroundings. If we are part of a high-functioning system, we find it easier to operate at a higher *functional* level of differentiation. In a sense, we "borrow" a bit more self from those around us in the system. If we are part of a lower functioning system, then we find it harder to act in more differentiated ways and our *functional* level may slip somewhat. The lower a person's *basic* level of differentiation, the more susceptible they are to having their *functional* level raised or lowered by the systems around them. The higher on the scale someone is, the less easily are they influenced by those around them.

Although it is a difficult and gradual process, there are four approaches one can take to work on increasing one's *basic* level of differentiation:

- **Learn Theory**. By studying Bowen Theory, one can gain understanding and insight that will help in the process of differentiation.
- **Manage Anxiety**. The more one is able to develop a calmer way of being, the more one is able to balance **self-other forces** and to integrate feeling and thinking responses, so that reactive feelings do not hijack thoughtfulness so easily.
- **Clarify Your Vision**. An essential task for anyone who wishes to raise his or her basic level of differentiation is to be clear about the "big picture" of his or her life—what his or her goals are, what core values really matter to him or her, what guiding principles shape his or her choices large and small. The more deeply a person probes to clarify these, the more will he or she be able to take actions that are consistent with his or her vision.
- **Gain More Self**. Gaining more self happens when one encounters reactive dynamics and learns how to remain neutral to those forces, rather than being drawn into familiar, reciprocal patterns of reactivity. Over time, this effort results in a stronger sense of self. The more difficult it is to remain neutral and non-reactive in any situation, the more valuable that situation is for the work of differentiation of self.

Whenever a person is in a relationship with someone who is emotionally significant to him or her to some degree, whether in a family setting, at work or otherwise, he or she has the opportunity to work on raising his or her basic level of differentiation. Each of us has some measure of unfinished business with members of our own families. Since that is the system where our basic level of differentiation was originally shaped, that is usually the more challenging (and more fruitful) place to go to continue to work on it. Any gains a person makes there will be immediately transferable into every other system he or she is part of. It is also true that successful efforts in one's workplace can benefit corresponding efforts being made within one's family system.

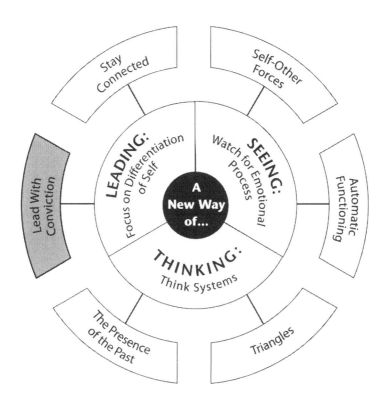

8. Lead with Conviction

One needs to be forewarned that when making an important move in the direction of becoming more of a "self," there is a predictable response from others that can be anticipated. This is not a deliberate or calculated attempt of others to block growth. It is just another manifestation of emotional process at work, as a relationship system tries to maintain its familiar equilibrium. The predictable reactions go something like this, in some form or another: (1) You are wrong! (2) Change back! (3) Here is the price you'll pay if you don't change back!

It is important not to take these reactions personally, but to be ready to deal with them for what they are—an automatic effort to preserve togetherness. It is only when a person is able to withstand the pressure to return to familiar patterns that one can claim to have made a real change in one's level of differentiation of self.

When a well-differentiated person chooses to "**lead with conviction**," others, especially those lower on the scale of differentiation, often misunderstand it. Firm resolve and single-minded tenacity can appear to be foolhardy, ruthless, and so forth to those who are less differentiated. Particularly in a risk-adverse society such as ours, the bold, adventurous spirit of highly differentiated leaders is often misunderstood. Such leaders are not afraid to expose their ideas to ridicule or critique by others. They know they are fallible, but they still have the courage of their convictions and are willing to take risks for what they believe is the right course of action. But in order to remain steadfast in the face of others' misunderstanding and resistance, such leaders must have the capacity to step outside of the reactive emotional climate that surrounds them and keep the big picture in view.

This capacity to stand apart from the crowd is easier if one has a strong sense of boundaries—knowing where one's "self" ends and the "self" of others begins. Leaders almost always have times when they must stand alone on an issue. The well-differentiated leader knows when that is necessary and does not flinch from the pain or solitude isolation involves. Another aspect of recognizing appropriate boundaries is having a deep respect for the "self" of others. A well-differentiated person does not intrude on the space or functioning of the other person and is able to handle disagreements without taking it personally or without ascribing motives to those on the other side of an issue. The ability to listen deeply to the other person—especially when that person is disagreeing with something you hold dear—is a good indicator of a higher level of differentiation.

One of the greatest challenges a leader faces is how to deal with reactive sabotage. It is axiomatic that the differentiated moves of a leader will meet initially with some measure of resistance and sabotage. When a leader encounters these behaviors, it is essential to recognize that they are a form of anxious reactivity. Otherwise, the leader is tempted to take it personally and judge it to be an act of disloyalty or a vendetta or some other label that ascribes motive when none is present. Misreading and misdiagnosing reactive sabotage will prevent a leader from dealing with it effectively.

APPENDIX

Sabotage is the natural way that a system tries to regain its balance after a leader has upset its equilibrium by introducing change. Even though members of an organization agree to and support the leader's change effort, on the deep level of emotional process every significant change is threatening. That threat provokes anxiety, which in turn surfaces as reactive sabotage. As a "natural" phenomenon in the face of self- differentiating moves initiated by the leader, sabotage is a force of nature, deeply ingrained in our being from our evolutionary past as a protective mechanism, a tool meant to help us survive the destabilizing threat that change always represents. A leader who engages directly in a test of will with those who are resisting his or her leadership is almost sure to fail. Nature inevitably wins a contest of will!

The forms that reactive sabotage take are almost always camouflaged, and since the resistance is generally beneath the level of conscious awareness, any attempt to name it as such and confront it head-on will usually meet with denials and disbelief. Reactive sabotage can be very subtle: forgetfulness, careless mistakes, accidents, new alliances being formed to produce alternative options, and so forth. Quite often these forms of resistance will appear on the surface unrelated to their true source, but they are reactivity at work all the same. Nonetheless, leaders trained to **watch for emotional process** can anticipate and be prepared for the inevitable pushback that their leadership generates.

By holding to a steady course in as calm a way as possible, a leader will eventually lead others beyond their reactivity, at least to some degree. By watching the process as suggested above, the leader is far less likely to get hooked by the *content* of the resistance. Keeping focused on the hidden chemistry—the emotional process—that is surfacing as reactive sabotage, a leader is less likely to fall into the trap of thinking that the "issue" being raised is really *"the"* issue. What matters most is how the leader manages his or her own functioning: by leading with conviction, with resolute persistence, calmness in the midst of the "crisis" meant to derail change efforts, clarity of vision, and so forth.

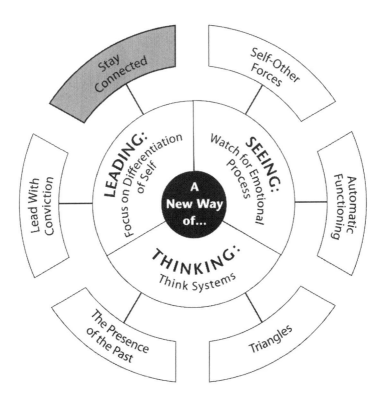

9. Stay Connected

The reminders of the **Resilient Leadership** model to **"lead with conviction"** and **"stay connected"** are practical applications of the self-other continuum discussed earlier. Leading with conviction places the emphasis on being a "self" who is able to take clear I-positions, while staying connected emphasizes the importance of relationships with significant others.

The fundamental insight underneath the reminder to **stay connected** is that we can only influence a system to which we are connected. We have already observed how powerful the leader's presence is for the system he or she leads. The emotional field that a leader projects is extremely contagious, which is another way of saying that the leader's functioning exerts an influence on others throughout the system that is hard to overstate. But it is not just the *fact* that a leader stays connected that matters; it is the *way* the leader connects that is most important. What is crucial is for the leader to be a calming, less anxious presence.

The image of an electrical transformer serves as a helpful metaphor for how a leader should be present to the organization he or she leads. A transformer can either step down the current of the electricity flowing through the power grid, so that it delivers 120 or 220 volts; or, it can step up the current as well. If one thinks of the chronic anxiety that pulses through every relationship system as a form of energy, then the metaphor speaks directly to the role of a leader as the one whose job it is to keep stepping down the "charged" anxiety within the "grid" that is the organization's emotional system.

Each of us is, in a sense, a "transformer" of the energy (anxiety) in the emotional field of which we are a part. We either step it up and make those around us more reactive, or we help to bring greater calm by stepping it down. But the position of the leader makes his or her functioning more significant than that of any other individual for the health of the entire organization. The leader's responsibility is to be the step-down transformer for the anxiety that threatens to impede the healthy functioning of the entire system.

How is this accomplished? Since the anxiety of the system flows, in a sense, through the leader, he or she must focus on managing his or her own anxiety in order to remain a step-down transformer. This does not mean the leader is expected to be totally non-anxious. Such an expectation is never going to be met. Rather, it is sufficient if the leader is *less* anxious than others in order to help lower the anxiety of those in the system.

There are several strategies a leader can adopt in order to work on lowering his or her own anxiety. (Another way to put this is to say these are strategies that help a leader to **focus on differentiation of self**.)

- The first is to "***watch the process***." One of the best ways to remain a less anxious presence is to adopt the stance of an observer, a researcher, who is interested in the dynamics of the emotional process within the organization. A person's anxiety is automatically lowered whenever he or she stands apart from a situation enough to become a neutral observer, suspending judgment and just watching the process unfold. In addition to helping lower his or her own anxiety, a leader who is dealing with a group that is caught up in an anxious, reactive cycle will help to calm others' anxiety if he or she is able to be genuinely curious about how they see their situation. Asking them what they think of it immediately puts them in the position of being observers; and, as soon as they are in that position, their anxiety also tends to lessen.

- A second strategy a leader can adopt to work on lowering his or her anxiety is to *"**expand the repertoire of responses**"* that are available when faced with situations that elevate anxiety. Most of us, when we are caught up in emotionally charged situations, tend to fall back on one or two default settings, often reactive in nature. Learning alternative responses is a gradual process but in the long run allows a leader to **stay connected** as a less anxious presence. One such response is to learn to be more playful when stressed. This not only helps to unhook a person from the grasp of his or her own reactivity; it also helps others to be less anxious as they catch on to the playful spirit. Whenever a leader encounters someone who is overly serious—deadly serious—it is fairly certain that the person is experiencing a high level of reactivity. Such seriousness comes from the reptilian brain, the part that is all about instinct and survival, not much more. It is our ability to be playful that sets us humans apart and makes it possible for a leader to bring a presence marked by a lightness of spirit that immediately encourages others to be more calm. A related response that is a helpful addition to one's repertoire is learning to be paradoxical. Paradox interrupts linear, one-dimensional thinking and requires others to step back and shift perspective in order to follow the leader's thinking. It also helps the leader to maintain a measure of distance from the situation that threatens to raise anxiety.
- A third strategy for lowering anxiety is to learn to *"**recognize your triggers**."* We will never recognize all of

our triggers, since those associations generally operate beneath conscious awareness. But with persistence and attention, we can come to recognize many of them. Body language, facial expressions, certain tones of voice or physical situations, how some people dress or carry themselves—all of these and many more can be triggers for our anxiety and catch us unaware. But greater self-knowledge can reveal to us how some of those triggers "hook" us, and that awareness is the first step to disarming them of their potency.

A common pitfall for leaders in anxious organizations is what Friedman called the "fallacy of empathy." He said that societal regression has perverted empathy into a disguise for anxiety. His insistence was on the importance of focusing on strength, not weakness, and his observation was that the weak often use their weakness and pain as a tool to manipulate leaders. He was insistent that good leadership requires a leader to promote greater responsibility for self, and that is best done by offering challenge rather than comfort.

This kind of leadership requires of a leader a higher threshold for the pain of others, and that will often be judged negatively by many who see it as a sign of insensitivity or a lack of compassion. But the alternative is the tyranny of those with the greatest sensitivities. When that happens, in the end we all wind up tiptoeing around the hypersensitivities of the lowest functioning members of society. A better alternative is when a leader increases his or her own capacity to tolerate the pain of others. In doing so the leader is actually helping others to increase their capacity to endure hardship and, ultimately, to deal with their pain in more responsible ways. True compassion, it seems, often requires helping those who are oversensitive to grow by learning how to manage their own pain, rather than looking for others to rescue them.

Staying connected in the right way involves a very subtle balancing act. Leaders need to be close without getting too close, which means keeping a certain distance, but without being so separate that they are cut off. One might describe this as engaging in respectful dialogue without cutoffs as well as being connected without fusion.

A well differentiated leader who knows how to **stay connected** in the right way is able to engage in disagreements without getting defensive, being dogmatic or going on the attack. There is mutual exchange, respectful listening, and a sincere attempt to understand the viewpoint of those who hold an alternative perspective. Instead of shutting down and cutting off from those who appear to be adversarial, a resilient leader continues to be in contact, even in those situations where agreement cannot be reached. It is also important that a leader be willing to admit mistakes and to take criticism gracefully, with no interest in retaliating against those who have confronted or proven him or her wrong. When things have gone wrong, when mistakes have been made, the wise leader will come together with others to understand what lessons can be gleaned from those mistakes and errors.

Respectful dialogue without cutoffs means always seeking to find common ground, rather than taking stands that polarize. The higher on the scale of differentiation a leader is, the less he or she engages in either/or thinking, the more he or she appreciates that reality can embrace a variety of viewpoints and accommodate many degrees of nuance. Such a leader is open to explore with others the bigger picture or the more comprehensive solution, rather than holding fast to a single-minded approach or insisting on an exclusive claim on the truth. Staying connected is about inclusivity and building relationships, not scoring victories.

The **Resilient Leadership** model understands that communication is primarily an emotional phenomenon, rather than a mere exchange of ideas. Because of this, effective communication only happens when there is a connection, when someone is moving closer rather than moving away. The leader who wishes to communicate successfully understands this and is always attentive to the relationship dynamics that are part of any communication effort. That is why avoiding cutoffs is so important.

In any relationship network, there is a continuum of behaviors that ranges from cutoffs at one extreme to fusion at the other. Another aspect of a well-differentiated leader's behavior is his or her ability to be connected without fusion. As with so many other aspects of our functioning, we learn early on in our family setting to judge as "normal" a certain style of relating that is more or less close, more or less distant. In general, the higher the levels of reactivity in any system, the more fusion we can witness. That is why a leader who is trying to **stay connected** in a healthy way needs to be particularly attentive to behaviors that represent an excessive degree of emotional fusion. A cutoff—which appears at the other end of the continuum of reactive behaviors—is simply another expression of relationship fusion.

One sure sign that someone tends toward the extreme of emotional fusion is an excessive preoccupation with what others think. This can take the form of always seeking approval or permission from others before taking a personal stand. Another example of the same behavior pattern is being particularly needy for encouragement, to the point where one's interest or motivation fails without ongoing external support. In addition, total disregard for the opinion of others, which appears to be the opposite of needy dependence, is in reality just another expression of reactive fusion. A resilient leader, on the other hand, does not engage in excessive worry about what others think; neither is he or she totally disinterested in others' opinions. Such a leader is appropriately mindful of others' views and opinions, but has a sufficiently strong sense of self and a clear vision of what he or she is about, and so is able to function without constantly seeking reinforcement or approval from others. This is what it looks like to **stay connected**, but avoid fusion.

Resilient Leadership - In a Nutshell

Resilient Leadership	
A New Way of...	A Resilient Leader...
SEEING: 1. Watch for Emotional Process 2. Self-Other Forces 3. Automatic Functioning	• Can readily identify the presence of emotional process and how it is influencing situations • Recognizes when/how relationship dynamics are impacting his/her/others' functioning • Is aware of the way that self-other forces are having an effect on the performance of work teams and other collaborative efforts • Sees how reactivity is compromising performance, ability to learn, motivation, etc.
THINKING: 4. Think Systems 5. Triangles 6. The Presence of the Past	• Is able to think his or her way through complex situations • Grasps the underlying dynamics of resistance/sabotage and knows how to deal with it effectively • Recognizes the presence of relationship triangles and understands how to position self in them to achieve maximum leverage with minimum stress • Understands how previous generational patterns influence current organizational functioning and can use this insight to improve the present situation

APPENDIX

LEADING: 7. Focus on Differentiation of Self 8. Lead with Conviction 9. Stay Connected	• Has a clear and compelling vision for self and the organization he or she leads • Acts as a calming presence when others are increasingly anxious • Can take a personal stand on principle while still respecting the position of others • When important relationships are strained, is able to remain engaged and work towards win-win solutions

SUGGESTED READINGS

For Starters:

Cox, David. "The Edwin Friedman Model of Family Systems Thinking: Lessons for Organizational Leaders." Academic Leadership The Online Journal.
This article is a quick introduction and overview of how Friedman has applied systems thinking to organizational leadership.

Friedman, Edwin H. A Failure of Nerve: Leadership in the Age of the Quick Fix. New York: Seabury Books, 2007.
Friedman was working on this still-unfinished manuscript of his major work on leadership at the time of his death. His disciples have recently re-edited the volume but left it in the unfinished state of the original manuscript. It contains more of his thoughts on leadership than any other single source.

Friedman, Edwin H. Generation to Generation: Family Process in Church and Synagogue. New York: The Guilford Press, 1985.
This is Friedman's major theoretical work that lays out the foundations of his thought in Bowen Theory and applies it to the "family system" of congregational life. Dense, but essential reading and applicable to leadership in any kind of organization.

Friedman, Edwin H. Reinventing Leadership. Video with Discussion Guide. New York: The Guilford Press, 1996.
The video offers a glimpse of Friedman in action, and the Discussion Guide (49 pp.) is one of the best, short summaries of Friedman's thoughts on leadership that is available. A fuller development of this material is available in A Failure of Nerve.

Galindo, Israel, et al. <u>A Family Genogram Workbook</u>. Educational Consultants, 2006.
This is a popular, user-friendly introduction to how to use the genogram to understand the functioning of your family system. See www.galindoconsultants.com.

Kerr, Michael E. <u>One Family's Story: A Primer on Bowen Theory</u>. Washington, DC: Georgetown Family Center, 2007.
This popular introduction to Bowen Theory is authored by Bowen's chosen successor, Michael Kerr. He gives a short but readable summary of key concepts, together with examples from clinical experience.

Miller, Jeffrey A. <u>The Anxious Organization: Why Smart Companies Do Dumb Things</u>. 2nd Edition. Facts on Demand Press, 2008.
This is an excellent introduction to Bowen Theory and its relevance for understanding the dynamics of organizations. Popular, yet true to solid theory, and with lots of practical illustrations of how to apply Bowen thinking in the workplace.

Richardson, Ronald W. <u>Creating a Healthier Church: Family Systems Theory, Leadership, and Congregational Life</u>. Minneapolis: Fortress Press, 1996.
This is a very clearly written introduction/application of Friedman's thought for the general public. Its setting is congregational life, but its application to leadership in any organizational context is immediate.

For Further Reading:

Bowen, Murray. <u>Family Therapy in Clinical Practice</u>. New York: Jason Aronson, 1978.
This is one of two primary sources for Bowen's thought. It contains key papers published over a period of nearly 20 years.

SUGGESTED READINGS

Comella, Patricia A. et al. eds. The Emotional Side of Organizations: Applications of Bowen Theory. Washington, D. C.: Georgetown Family Center, 1996.
A collection of papers presented at the Georgetown Family Center's Conference on Organizations, April 22-23, 1995, representing a major effort to apply Bowen Theory to organizational life. The materials are of uneven quality, but some of the papers are well worth reading.

Friedman, Edwin H. The Myth of the Shiksa and Other Essays. New York: Seabury Books, 2008.
A collection of papers by Friedman reflecting the development of his thought.

Friedman, Edwin H. Friedman's Fables. New York: The Guilford Press, 1990.
A delightful embodiment of Friedman's thinking in the form of provocative parables.

Gilbert, Roberta M. The Eight Concepts of Bowen Theory. Falls Church & Basye, Virginia: Leading Systems Press, 2006.
A short, popular introduction to the basic ideas that comprise Bowen Theory.

Gilbert, Roberta M. Extraordinary Relationships: A New Way of Thinking about Human Interactions. Minneapolis: Chronimed Publishing, 1992.
Very readable introduction to how Bowen Theory offers valuable insights to our family relationships.

Heifetz, Ronald A. and Marty Linsky. Leadership on the Line: Staying Alive through the Dangers of Leading. Boston: Harvard Business School Press, 2002.
*One of today's leading approaches to leadership, this book contains remarkable similarities and convergences with the **Resilient Leadership** model.*

Kerr, Michael E., and Bowen, Murray. Family Evaluation: The Role of Family as an Emotional Unit that Governs Individual Behavior and Development. New York: W.W. Norton & Company, 1988.
This is the major sourcebook for Bowen Theory. It is technical and aimed at specialists in the field.

O'Neill, Mary Beth. Executive Coaching with Backbone and Heart: A Systems Approach to Engaging Leaders with their Challenges. 2nd Edition. San Francisco: Jossey-Bass, 2007.
Although written for professional coaches, this volume of the Jossey-Bass Business & Management Series reflects a very substantive grasp of how Bowen Theory can be applied to the challenges facing organizational leaders. Any leader who understands his role to include coaching others will profit from studying O'Neill's work.

Richardson, Ronald W. Becoming a Healthier Pastor: Family Systems Theory and the Pastor's Own Family. Minneapolis: Fortress Press, 2005.
Although written for clergy, this is for any leader who is convinced of the value of Bowen Theory and wants to integrate its insights more deeply into their own personal leadership.

Sagar, Ruth Riley and Kathleen Klaus Weisman, eds. Understanding Organizations: Applications of Bowen Family Systems Theory. Washington, DC: Georgetown Family Center, 1982.
A collection of papers from two conferences on organizations and Bowen Theory. An early effort with papers of uneven value, but several are worth reading.

ENDNOTES

[1] The **Resilient Leadership** model was developed by Dr. Robert Duggan and is based on more than 20 years of work applying the insights of Bowen Systems Theory, first in his own leadership roles and then helping others in their respective personal and organizational settings. The model has been refined and deepened as a result of a highly successful collaboration between Dr. Duggan and James Moyer, an executive coach and organizational consultant who brings more than three decades of experience working with senior leaders in major for-profit and non-profit settings.

[2] For a brief overview of the core ideas that **Resilient Leadership** draws from Bowen Theory, see the Appendix; for a summary of the eight basic concepts of Bowen Theory, see Michael E. Kerr, <u>One Family's Story: A Primer on Bowen Theory</u> (Washington, DC: Bowen Center for the Study of the Family), 2008.

[3] This term refers to the instinctual processes we share in common with many other species, as well as the affective energies—generally beneath conscious awareness—that we call emotions or feelings. A distinctive feature of this approach, and one that sets it apart from other leadership development perspectives, is its suggestion that we can often come to a deeper understanding of human functioning by focusing on what we share in common with lower life forms that preceded us on the evolutionary ladder. Rather than focusing only on the intellectual

functioning that sets us apart from our ancestors, Bowen Theory shows how the forces of emotional process operate in all life forms on this planet, and this perspective from evolutionary biology greatly enhances understanding of how those same forces operate in us humans.

[4] Murray Bowen, Family Therapy in Clinical Practice (New York: Jason Aronson, 1978); Michael E. Kerr and Murray Bowen, Family Evaluation: An Approach Based on Bowen Theory (New York: W. W. Norton & Company, 1988).

[5] Edwin H. Friedman, Generation to Generation: Family Process in Church and Synagogue (New York: The Guilford Press, 1985); The Myth of the Shiksa and Other Essays (New York: Seabury Books, 2008).

[6] Edwin H. Friedman, Friedman's Fables (New York: The Guilford Press, 1990).

[7] Edwin H. Friedman, A Failure of Nerve: Leadership in the Age of the Quick Fix (New York: Seabury Books, 2007).

[8] Roger Schwarz, The Skilled Facilitator: A Comprehensive Resource for Consultants, Facilitators, Managers, Trainers and Coaches (San Francisco: Jossey-Bass, 2002).